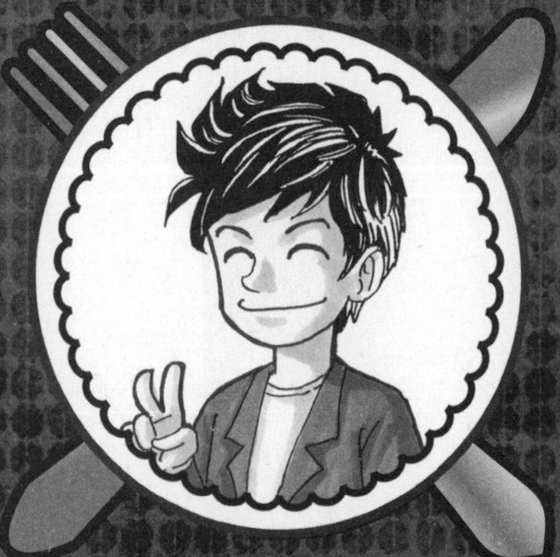

I feel like I've been getting a lot of gray hairs lately. I just realized I'll be 38 this year. Since that age undeniably labels me as middle-aged, I guess it's only natural that this should happen. Heh heh… Hitting this age feels good. I gotta start trading in my jerseys for suit jackets! After that, I'll start working on some lovely little wrinkles. Despite all this aging, I hope to keep my manga young and lively. (My current weight…68 kg!! Hmm…)

—Mitsutoshi Shimabukuro, 2013

Mitsutoshi Shimabukuro made his debut in **Weekly Shonen Jump** in 1996. He is best known for **Seikimatsu Leader Den Takeshi!** for which he won the 46th Shogakukan Manga Award for children's manga in 2001. His current series, **Toriko**, began serialization in Japan in 2008.

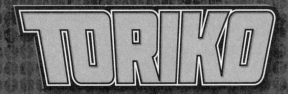

TORIKO VOL. 26
SHONEN JUMP Manga Edition

STORY AND ART BY **MITSUTOSHI SHIMABUKURO**

Translation/Christine Dashiell
Weekly Shonen Jump Lettering/Erika Terriquez
Graphic Novel Touch-Up Art & Lettering/Elena Diaz
Design/Matt Hinrichs
Editor/Hope Donovan

TORIKO © 2008 by Mitsutoshi Shimabukuro
All rights reserved. First published in Japan in 2008 by SHUEISHA Inc., Tokyo.
English translation rights arranged by SHUEISHA Inc.

Printed in the U.S.A.

Published by VIZ Media, LLC
P.O. Box 77010
San Francisco, CA 94107

10 9 8 7 6 5 4 3 2 1
First printing, February 2015

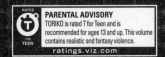

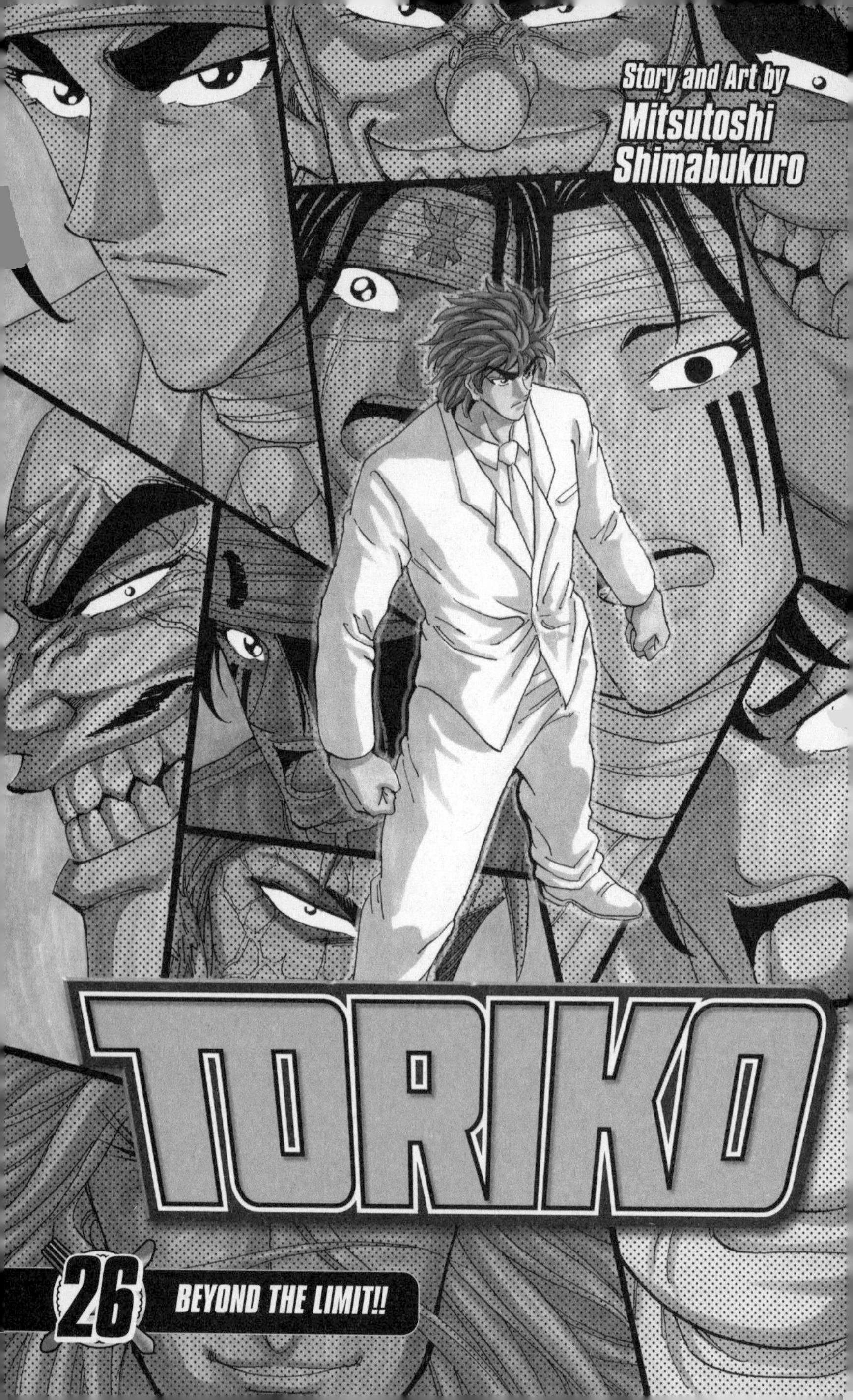
Story and Art by
Mitsutoshi
Shimabukuro
TORIKO
26
BEYOND THE LIMIT!!

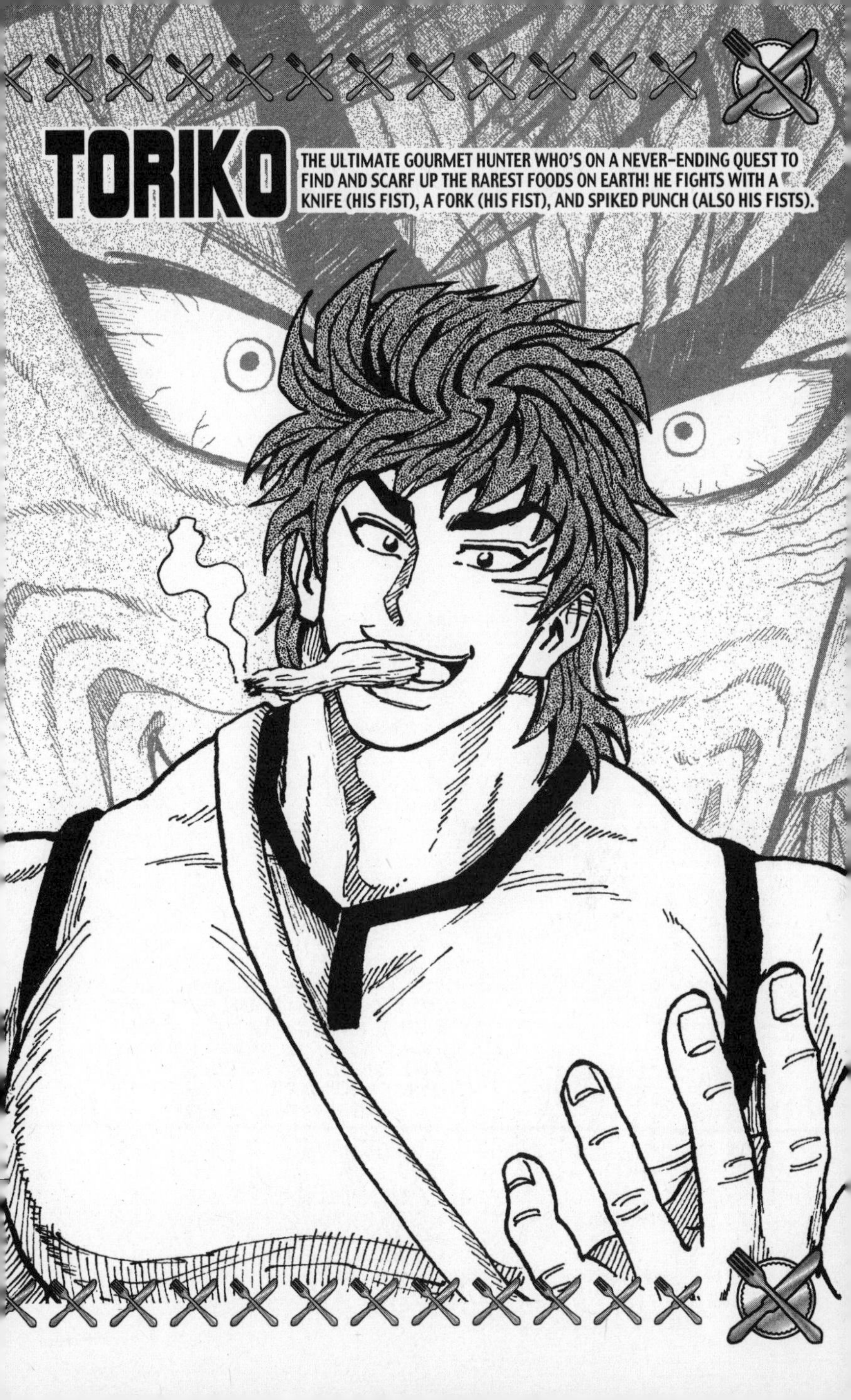
TORIKO
THE ULTIMATE GOURMET HUNTER WHO'S ON A NEVER-ENDING QUEST TO FIND AND SCARF UP THE RAREST FOODS ON EARTH! HE FIGHTS WITH A KNIFE (HIS FIST), A FORK (HIS FIST), AND SPIKED PUNCH (ALSO HIS FISTS).

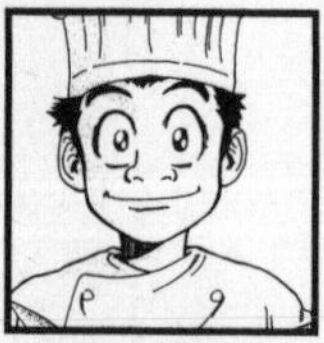

●KOMATSU
TALENTED IGO HOTEL CHEF AND TORIKO'S #1 FAN.

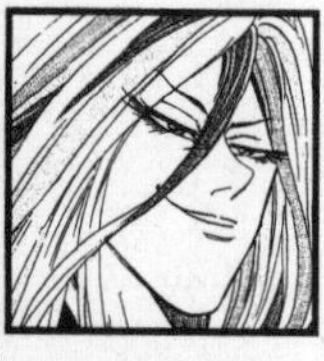

●SUNNY
A GOURMET HUNTER AND ONE OF THE FOUR KINGS. SENSORS IN HIS LONG HAIR ENABLE HIM TO "TASTE" THE WORLD. OBSESSED WITH ALL THAT IS BEAUTIFUL.

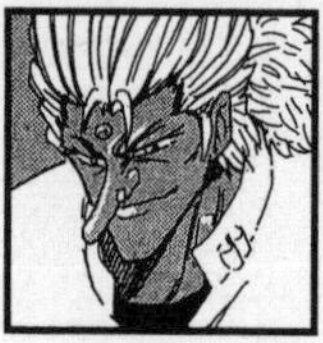

●BRUNCH
WORLD CHEF RANKING: #3. HEAD CHEF AT LEGENDARY "TENGU CASTLE."

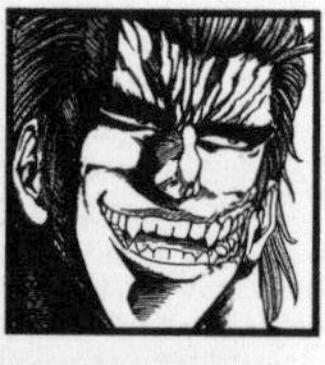

●ZEBRA
A GOURMET HUNTER AND ONE OF THE FOUR KINGS. A DANGEROUS INDIVIDUAL WITH SUPERHUMAN HEARING AND VOCAL POWERS.

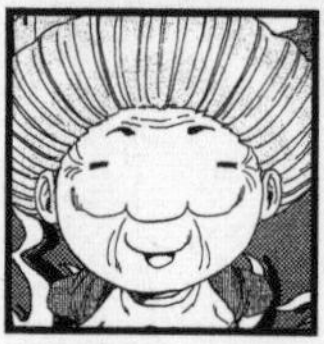

●SETSUNO
AKA GRANNY SETSU. FAMOUS CHEF AND GOURMET LIVING LEGEND.

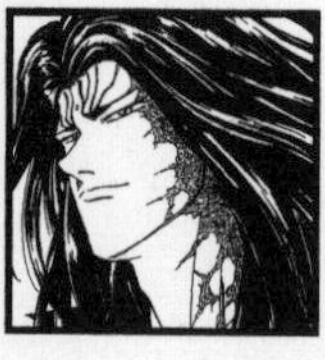

●STARJUN
ONE OF GOURMET CORP'S THREE VICE-CHEFS. WATCHFUL OF TORIKO'S GROWING POTENTIAL.

WHAT'S FOR DINNER

IT'S THE AGE OF GOURMET! KOMATSU, THE HEAD CHEF AT THE HOTEL OWNED BY THE IGO (INTERNATIONAL GOURMET ORGANIZATION), BECAME FAST FRIENDS WITH THE LEGENDARY GOURMET HUNTER TORIKO WHILE GATOR HUNTING. NOW KOMATSU ACCOMPANIES TORIKO ON HIS LIFELONG QUEST TO CREATE THE PERFECT FULL-COURSE MEAL. THROUGH THEIR ADVENTURES, THEY FIND THEMSELVES ENTANGLED IN THE IGO'S RIVALRY WITH THE NEFARIOUS GOURMET CORP. WITH TORIKO'S EVERY HUNT, THE INEVITABLE CLASH GROWS CLOSER! GOURMET CORP. ASIDE, NOW THAT TORIKO AND KOMATSU ARE PARTNERS, THEY HAVE BEGUN TRAINING TO ENTER THE GOURMET WORLD BY COLLECTING FOODS FROM A TRAINING LIST PROVIDED BY IGO PRESIDENT ICHIRYU.

THEN ONE DAY, THE FOUR-BEASTS AWAKENS! THE FOUR KINGS POOL THEIR APPETITE TO DEFEAT THE FOUR-BEASTS. BUT THE REAL SAVIOR OF THE DAY IS KOMATSU, WHO CURES MILLIONS OF PEOPLE WITH HIS LIFESAVING MEDICINAL MOCHI. HIS FEAT LIFTS HIM TO 88TH PLACE ON THE WORLD CHEF RANKING, WHICH QUALIFIES HIM FOR THE COOKING FESTIVAL.

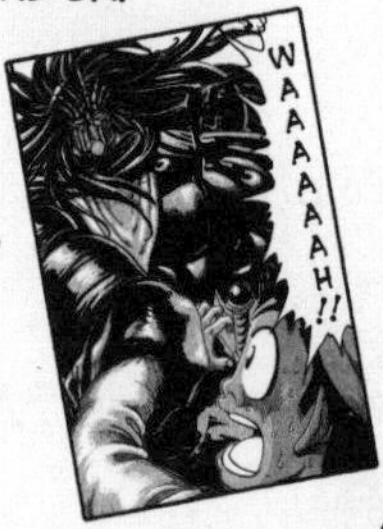
WAAAAAAH!!

DURING THE FESTIVAL, GOURMET CORP. ATTACKS! THEIR VILE ASSORTMENT OF SCUM BEASTS AND SUPER-SIZED ROBOTS CHALLENGE THE BEST GOURMET HUNTERS AND CHEFS OUT THERE, WITH THE CHEFS' FATES AT STAKE. TORIKO GOES INTO BATTLE MODE OVERDRIVE TO SAVE KOMATSU FROM STARJUN! MEANWHILE, COCO STANDS AGAINST GRINPATCH AND SUNNY CHALLENGES TOMMYROD! BUT WHO'S WATCHING THE BATTLE FROM THE SHADOWS?

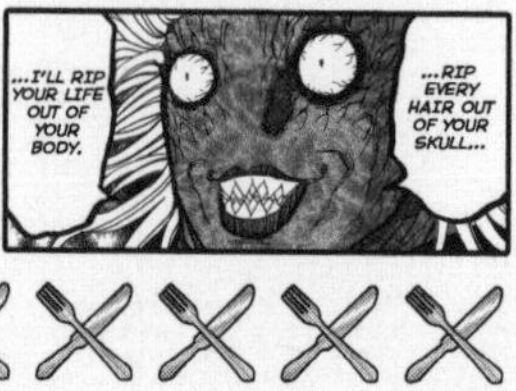
...RIP EVERY HAIR OUT OF YOUR SKULL...
...I'LL RIP YOUR LIFE OUT OF YOUR BODY.

Contents

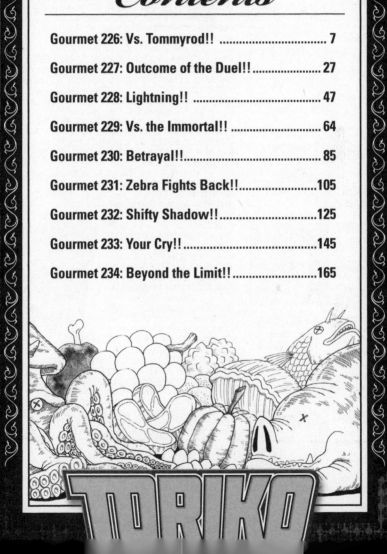

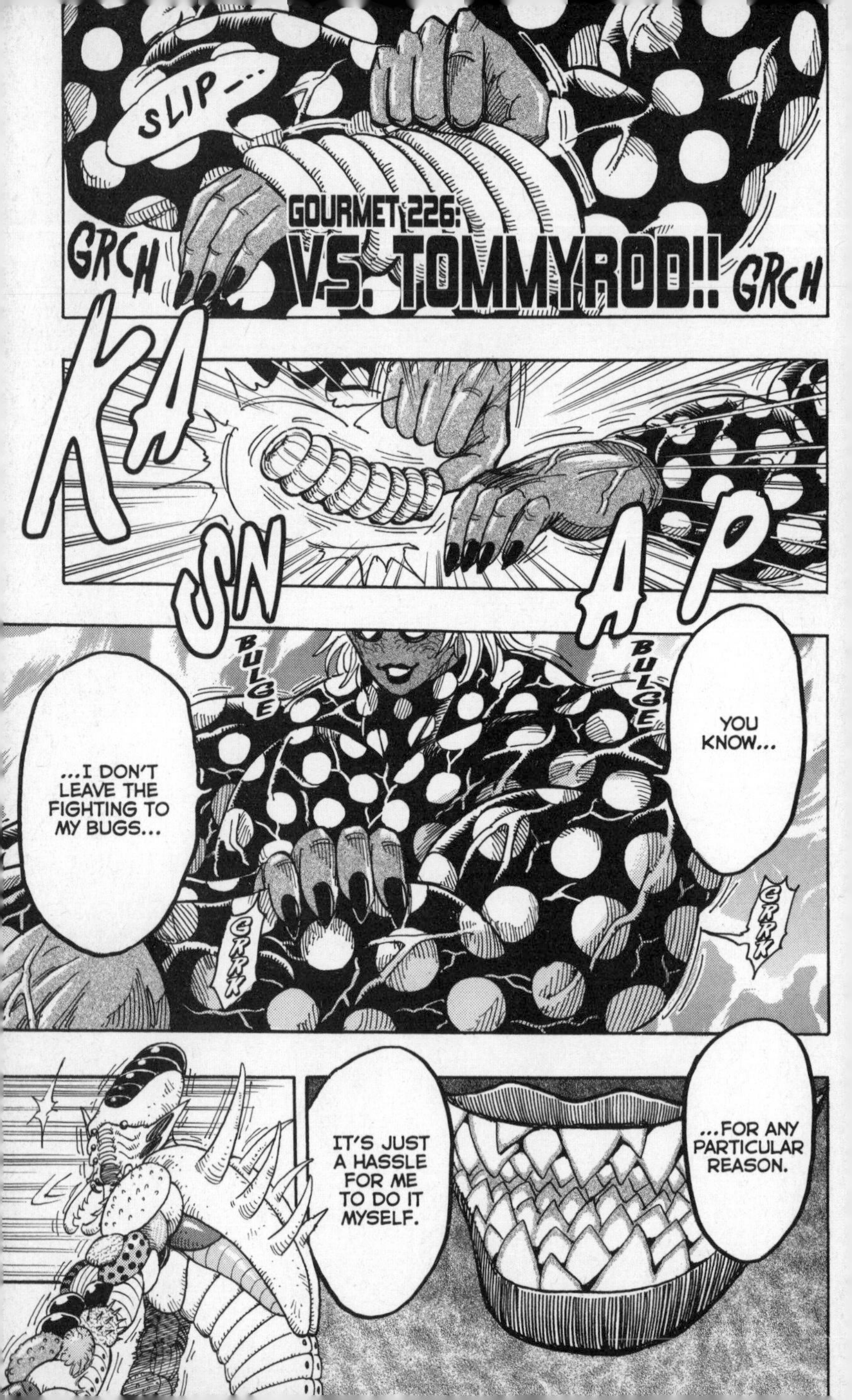
SLIP...
GOURMET 226:
V.S. TOMMYROD!!
GRCH
GRCH
KA
SNAP
BULGE
BULGE
YOU KNOW...
...I DON'T LEAVE THE FIGHTING TO MY BUGS...
GRRK
GRRK
...FOR ANY PARTICULAR REASON.
IT'S JUST A HASSLE FOR ME TO DO IT MYSELF.

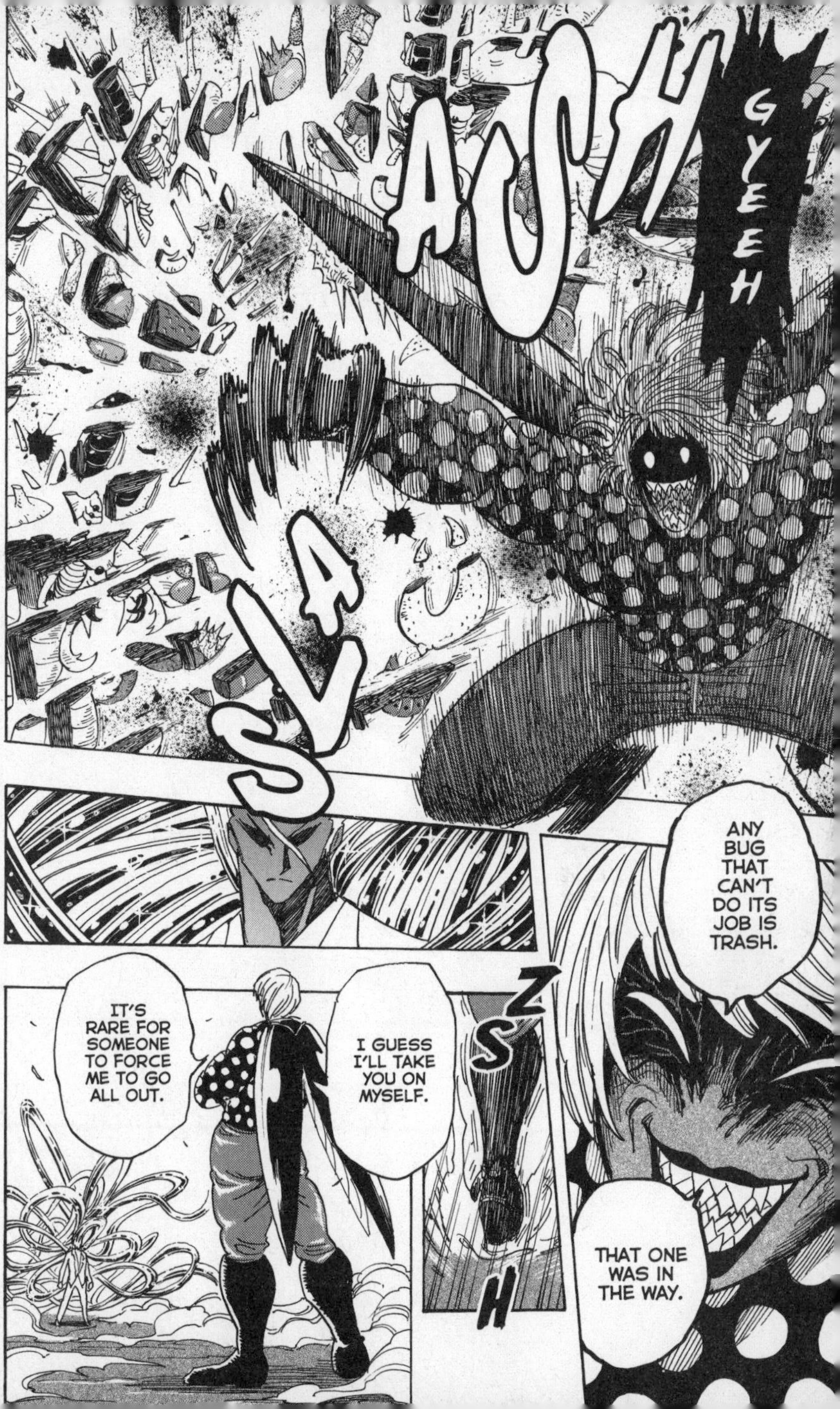
SLASH
GYEEH
ANY BUG THAT CAN'T DO ITS JOB IS TRASH.
THAT ONE WAS IN THE WAY.
ZSH
I GUESS I'LL TAKE YOU ON MYSELF.
IT'S RARE FOR SOMEONE TO FORCE ME TO GO ALL OUT.

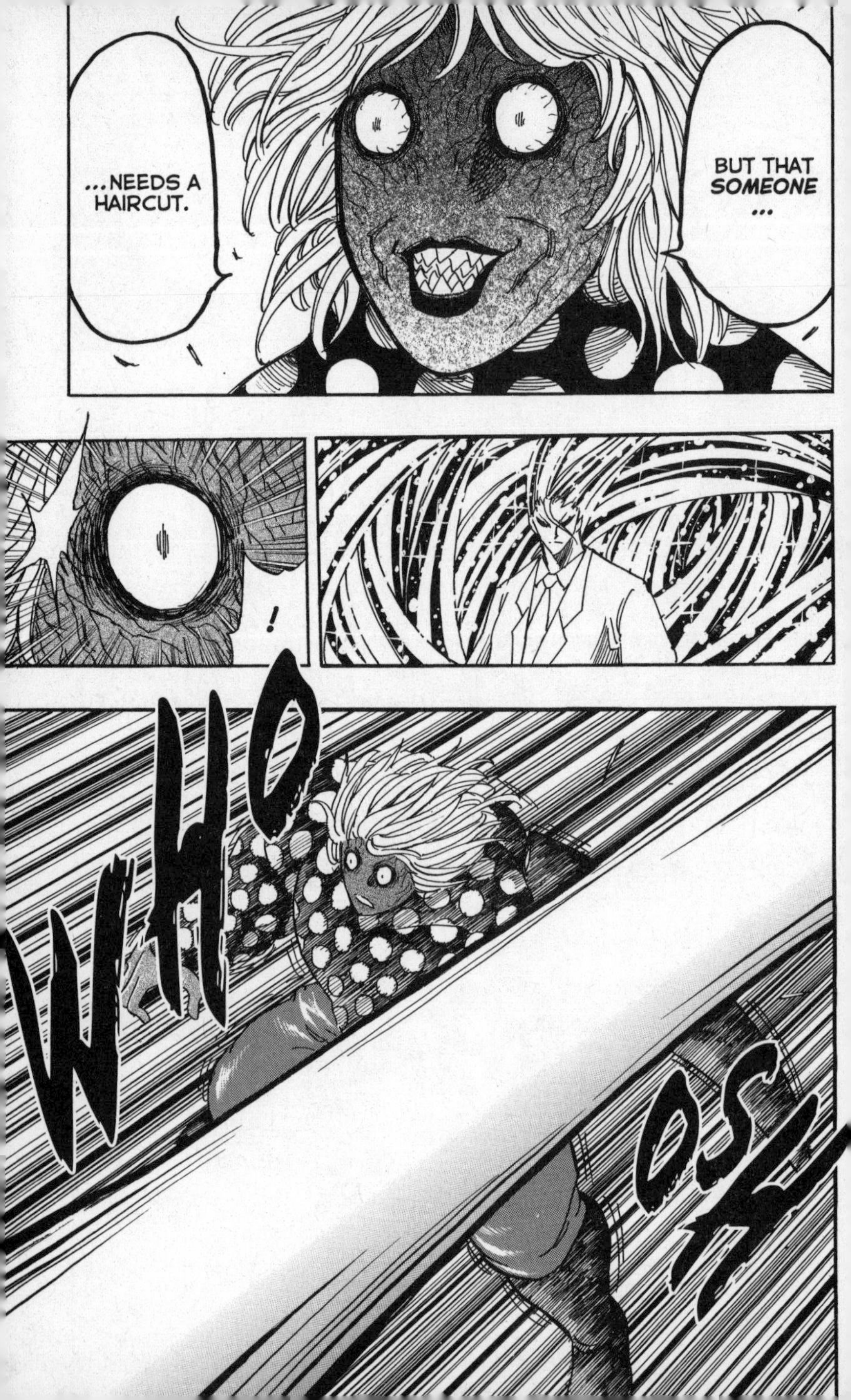
BUT THAT *SOMEONE* ...
...NEEDS A HAIRCUT.
!
WHO

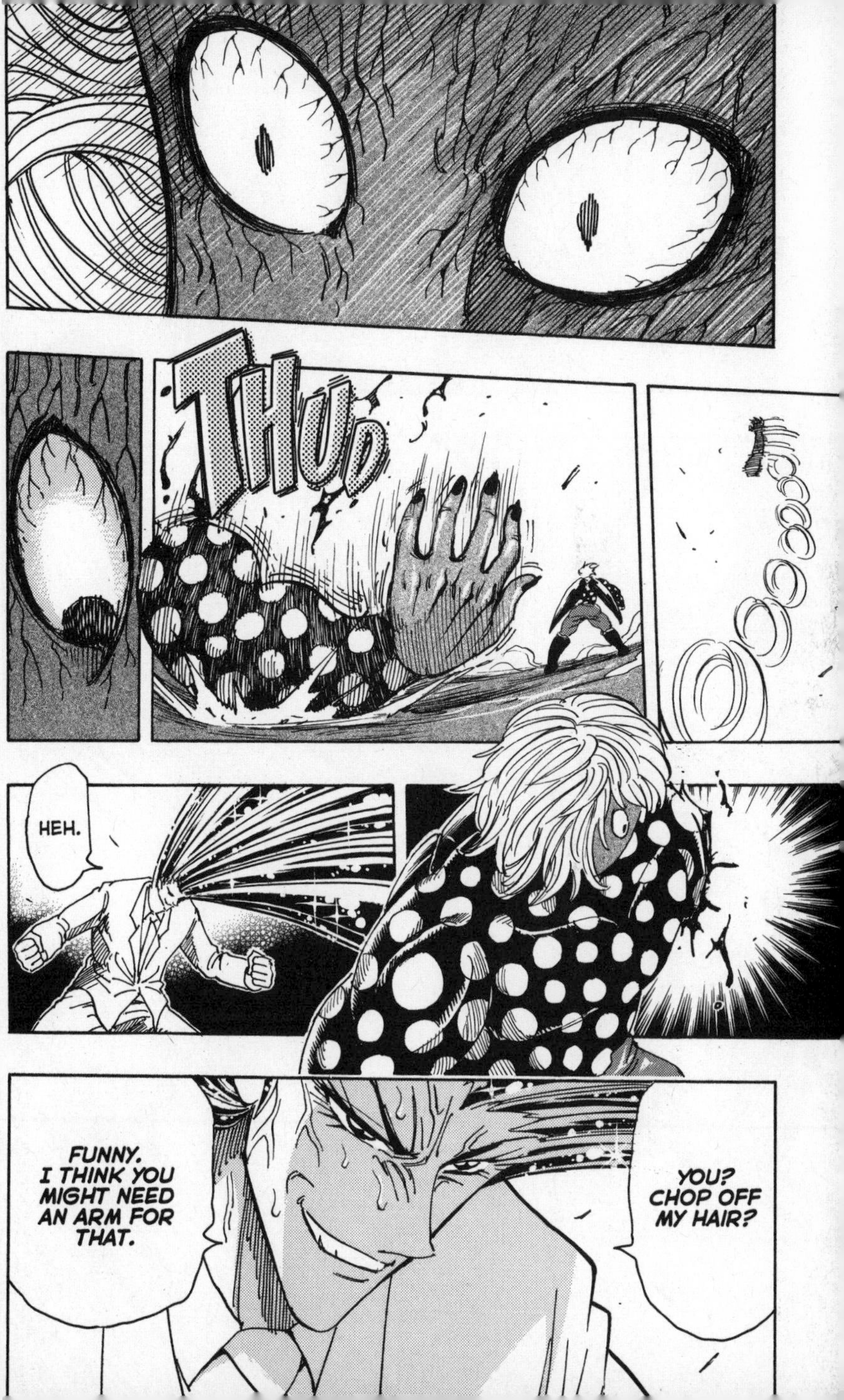
THUD
HEH.
YOU? CHOP OFF MY HAIR?
FUNNY. I THINK YOU MIGHT NEED AN ARM FOR THAT.

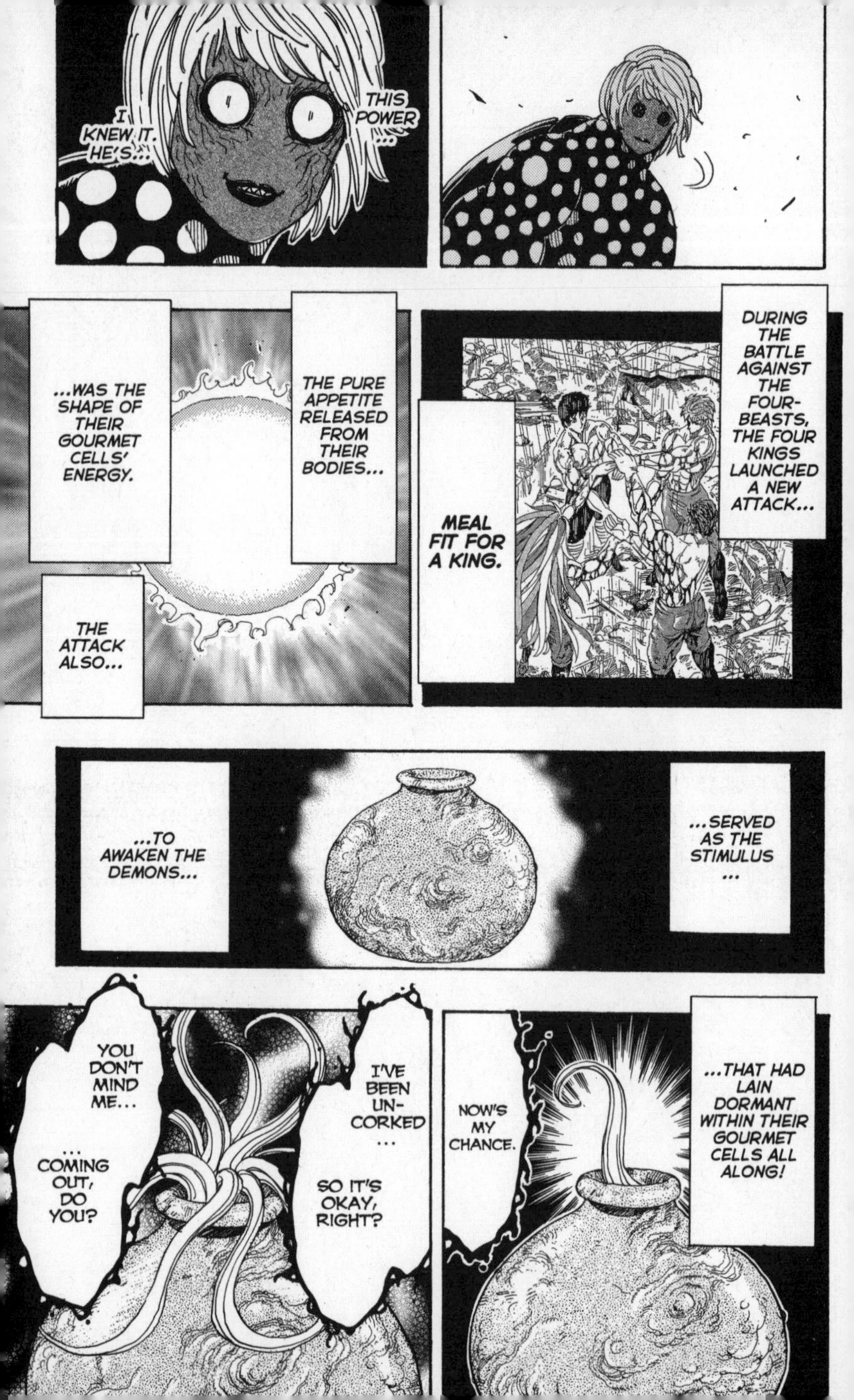
THIS POWER...
I KNEW IT. HE'S...
DURING THE BATTLE AGAINST THE FOUR-BEASTS, THE FOUR KINGS LAUNCHED A NEW ATTACK...
MEAL FIT FOR A KING.
THE PURE APPETITE RELEASED FROM THEIR BODIES...
...WAS THE SHAPE OF THEIR GOURMET CELLS' ENERGY.
THE ATTACK ALSO...
...SERVED AS THE STIMULUS...
...TO AWAKEN THE DEMONS...
...THAT HAD LAIN DORMANT WITHIN THEIR GOURMET CELLS ALL ALONG!
NOW'S MY CHANCE.
I'VE BEEN UN-CORKED...
SO IT'S OKAY, RIGHT?
YOU DON'T MIND ME...
...COMING OUT, DO YOU?

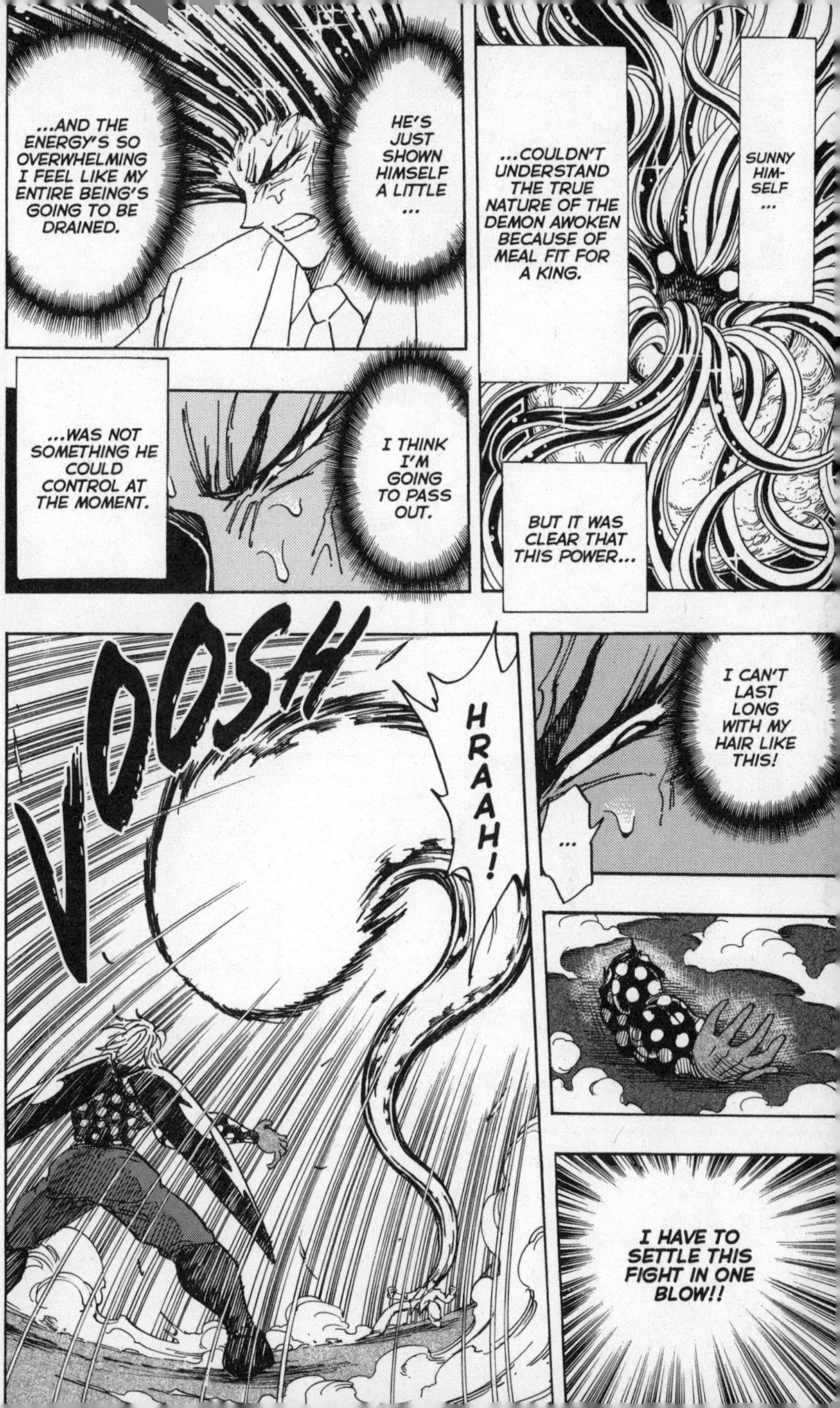
SUNNY HIMSELF...
...COULDN'T UNDERSTAND THE TRUE NATURE OF THE DEMON AWOKEN BECAUSE OF MEAL FIT FOR A KING.
HE'S JUST SHOWN HIMSELF A LITTLE...
...AND THE ENERGY'S SO OVERWHELMING I FEEL LIKE MY ENTIRE BEING'S GOING TO BE DRAINED.
BUT IT WAS CLEAR THAT THIS POWER...
I THINK I'M GOING TO PASS OUT.
...WAS NOT SOMETHING HE COULD CONTROL AT THE MOMENT.
I CAN'T LAST LONG WITH MY HAIR LIKE THIS!
...
I HAVE TO SETTLE THIS FIGHT IN ONE BLOW!!
HRAAAH!
VOOSH

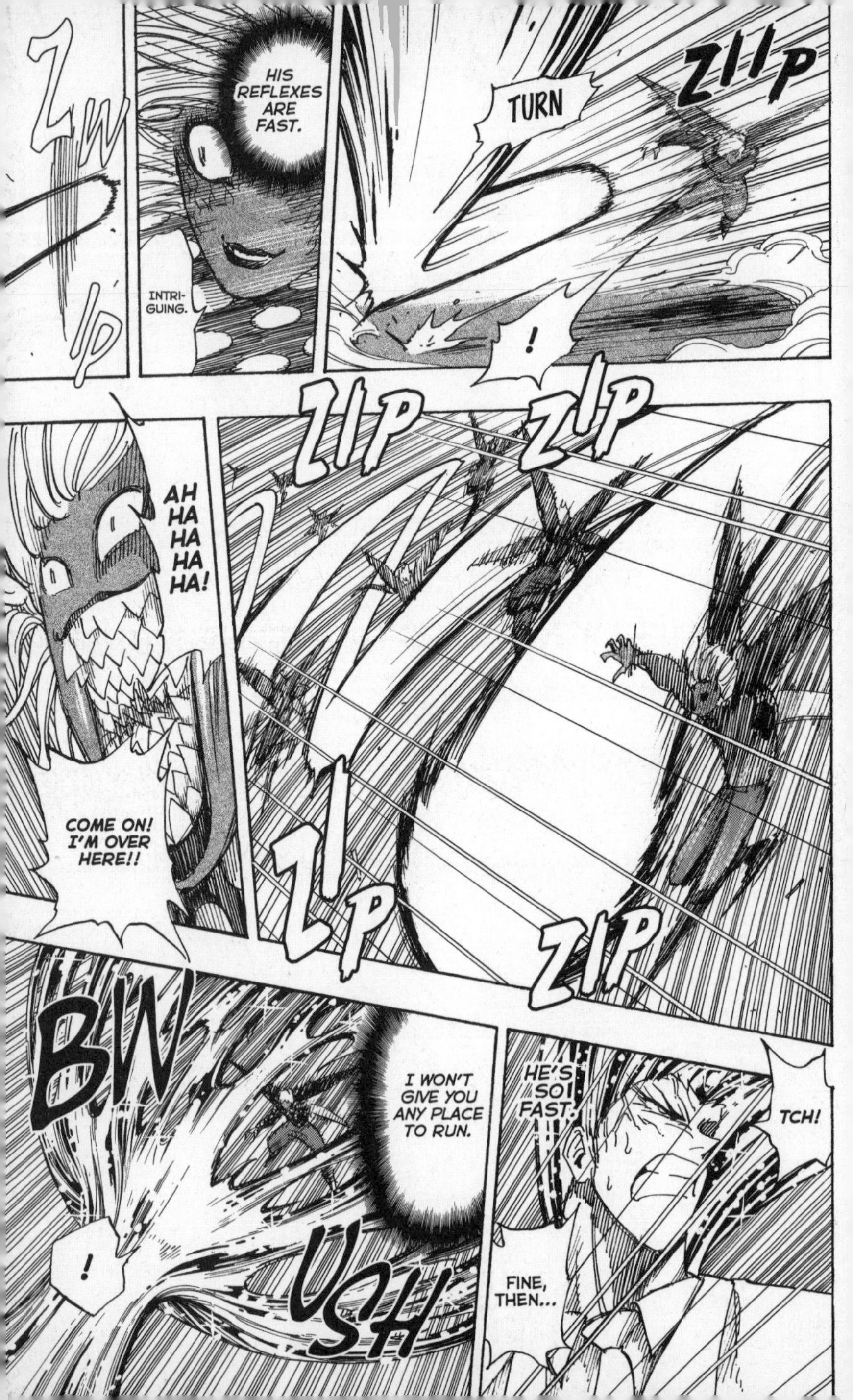
ZIIP
TURN
!
HIS REFLEXES ARE FAST.
INTRIGUING.
ZWIP
ZIP
ZIP
ZIP
ZIP
AH HA HA HA HA!
COME ON! I'M OVER HERE!!
TCH!
HE'S SO FAST.
FINE, THEN...
I WON'T GIVE YOU ANY PLACE TO RUN.
BWUSH
!

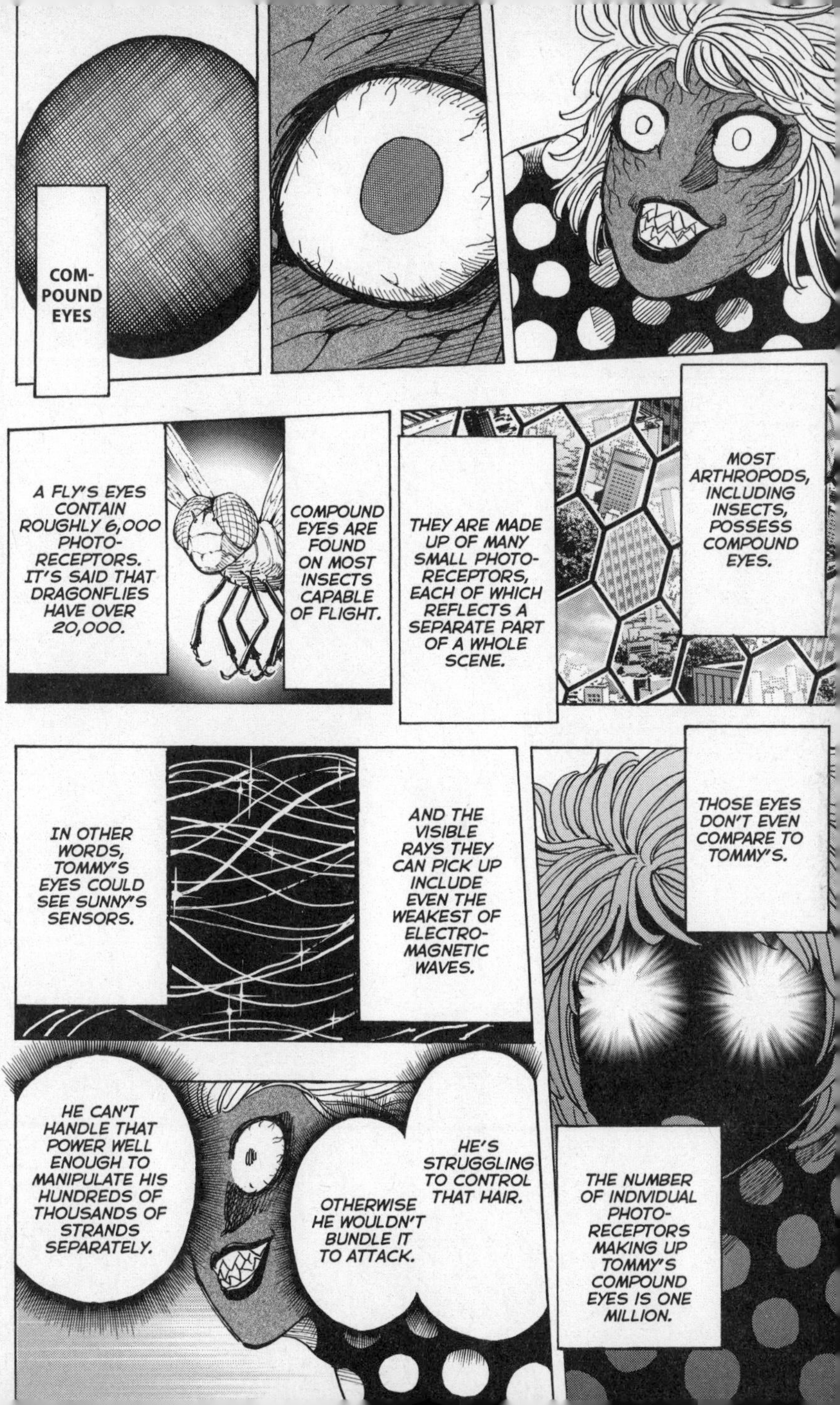
COM-POUND EYES
MOST ARTHROPODS, INCLUDING INSECTS, POSSESS COMPOUND EYES.
THEY ARE MADE UP OF MANY SMALL PHOTO-RECEPTORS, EACH OF WHICH REFLECTS A SEPARATE PART OF A WHOLE SCENE.
COMPOUND EYES ARE FOUND ON MOST INSECTS CAPABLE OF FLIGHT.
A FLY'S EYES CONTAIN ROUGHLY 6,000 PHOTO-RECEPTORS. IT'S SAID THAT DRAGONFLIES HAVE OVER 20,000.
THOSE EYES DON'T EVEN COMPARE TO TOMMY'S.
THE NUMBER OF INDIVIDUAL PHOTO-RECEPTORS MAKING UP TOMMY'S COMPOUND EYES IS ONE MILLION.
AND THE VISIBLE RAYS THEY CAN PICK UP INCLUDE EVEN THE WEAKEST OF ELECTRO-MAGNETIC WAVES.
IN OTHER WORDS, TOMMY'S EYES COULD SEE SUNNY'S SENSORS.
HE'S STRUGGLING TO CONTROL THAT HAIR.
OTHERWISE HE WOULDN'T BUNDLE IT TO ATTACK.
HE CAN'T HANDLE THAT POWER WELL ENOUGH TO MANIPULATE HIS HUNDREDS OF THOUSANDS OF STRANDS SEPARATELY.

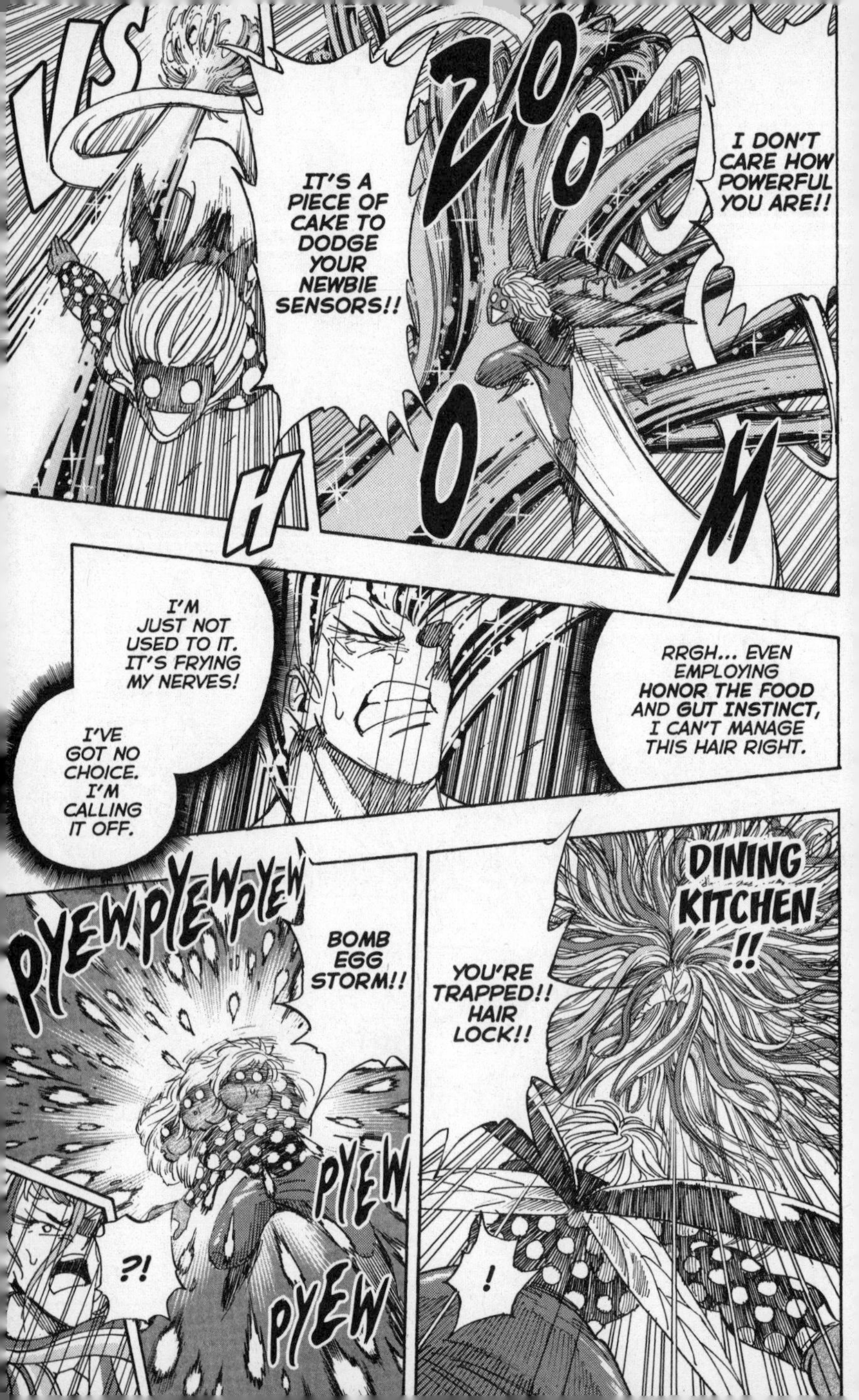
I DON'T CARE HOW POWERFUL YOU ARE!!
IT'S A PIECE OF CAKE TO DODGE YOUR NEWBIE SENSORS!!
RRGH... EVEN EMPLOYING HONOR THE FOOD AND GUT INSTINCT, I CAN'T MANAGE THIS HAIR RIGHT.
I'M JUST NOT USED TO IT. IT'S FRYING MY NERVES!
I'VE GOT NO CHOICE. I'M CALLING IT OFF.
DINING KITCHEN!!
YOU'RE TRAPPED!! HAIR LOCK!!
!
BOMB EGG STORM!!
PYEWPYEWPYEW
PYEW
PYEW
?!

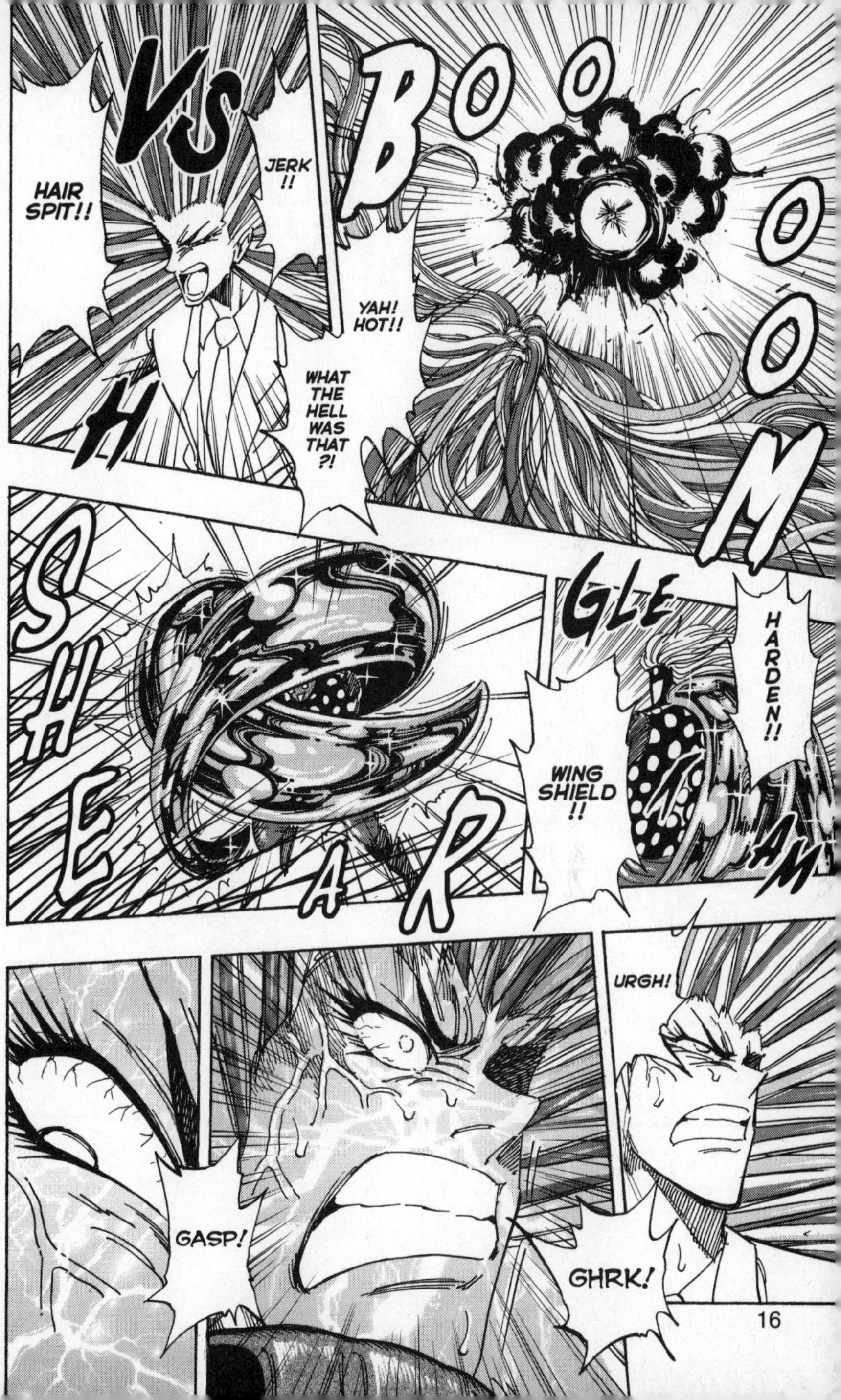
BOOOOM
YAH! HOT!!
WHAT THE HELL WAS THAT?!
JERK !!
HAIR SPIT!!
HARDEN!!
WING SHIELD !!
GLE
SHEAR
URGH!
GHRK!
GASP!

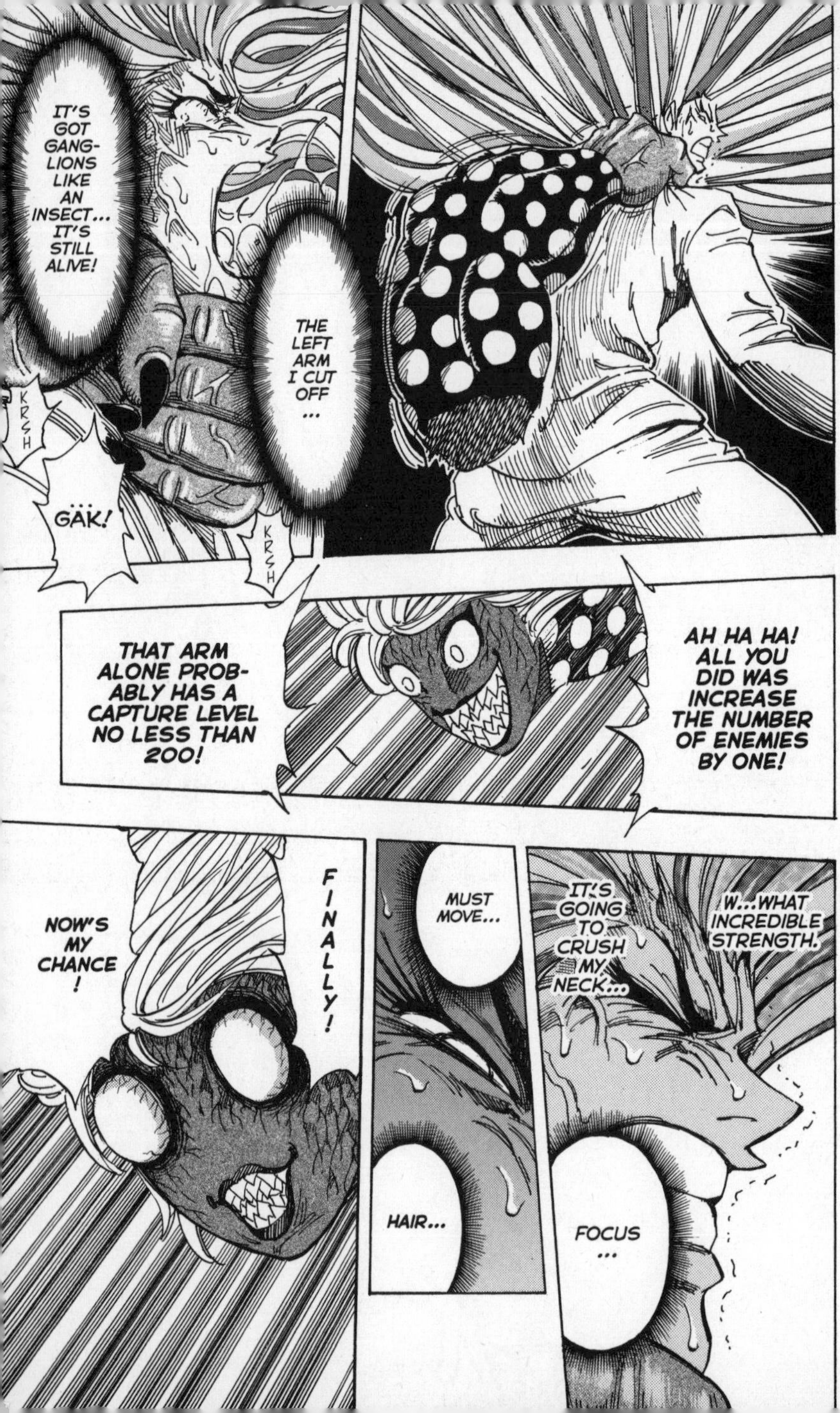
THE LEFT ARM I CUT OFF...
IT'S GOT GANGLIONS LIKE AN INSECT... IT'S STILL ALIVE!
KRSH
...GÄK!
KRSH
AH HA HA! ALL YOU DID WAS INCREASE THE NUMBER OF ENEMIES BY ONE!
THAT ARM ALONE PROBABLY HAS A CAPTURE LEVEL NO LESS THAN 200!
W...WHAT INCREDIBLE STRENGTH.
IT'S GOING TO CRUSH MY NECK...
FOCUS...
MUST MOVE...
HAIR...
FINALLY!
NOW'S MY CHANCE!

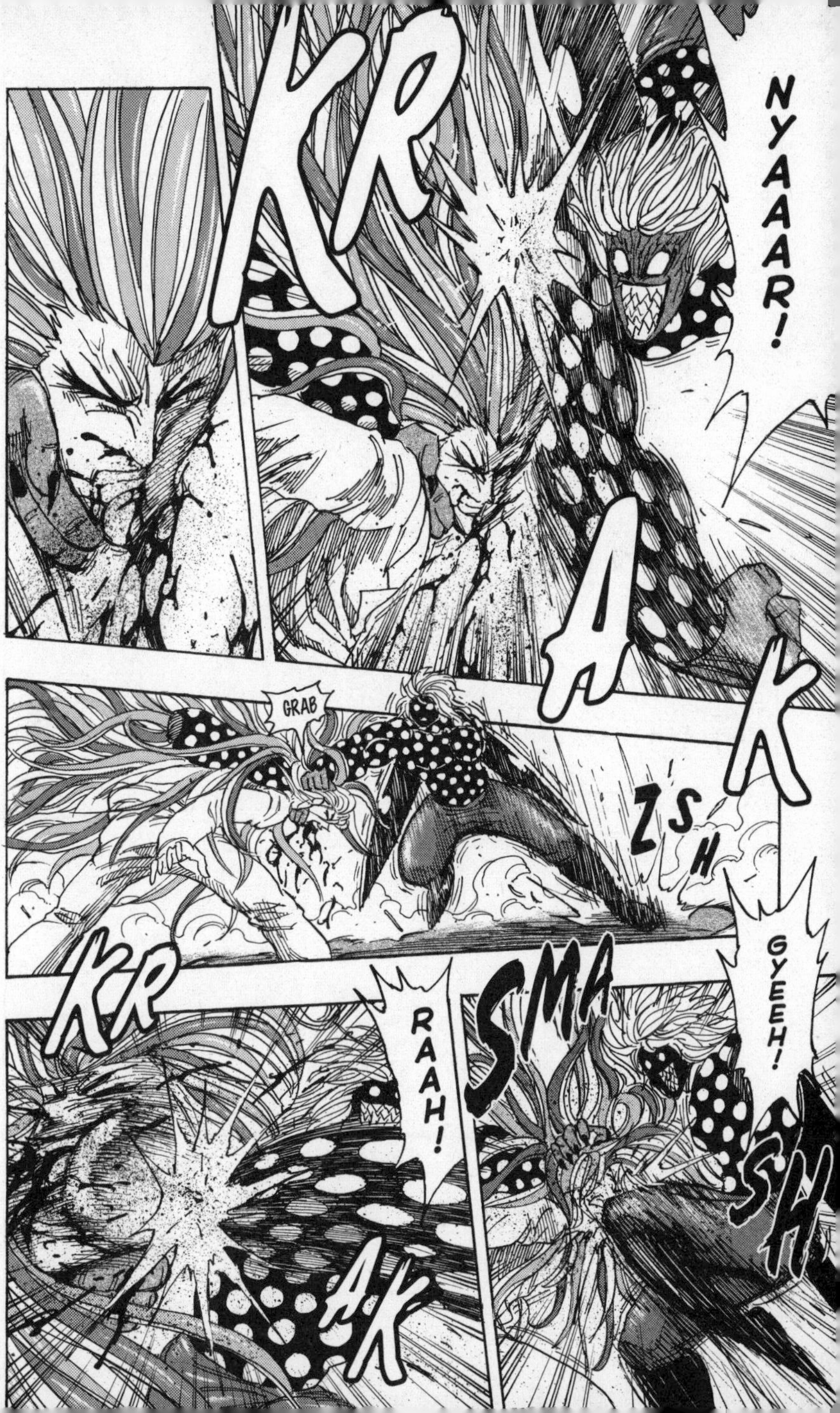
NYAAAR!
KRAK
ZSH
GRAB
GYEEH!
SMASH
RAAH!
KRAK

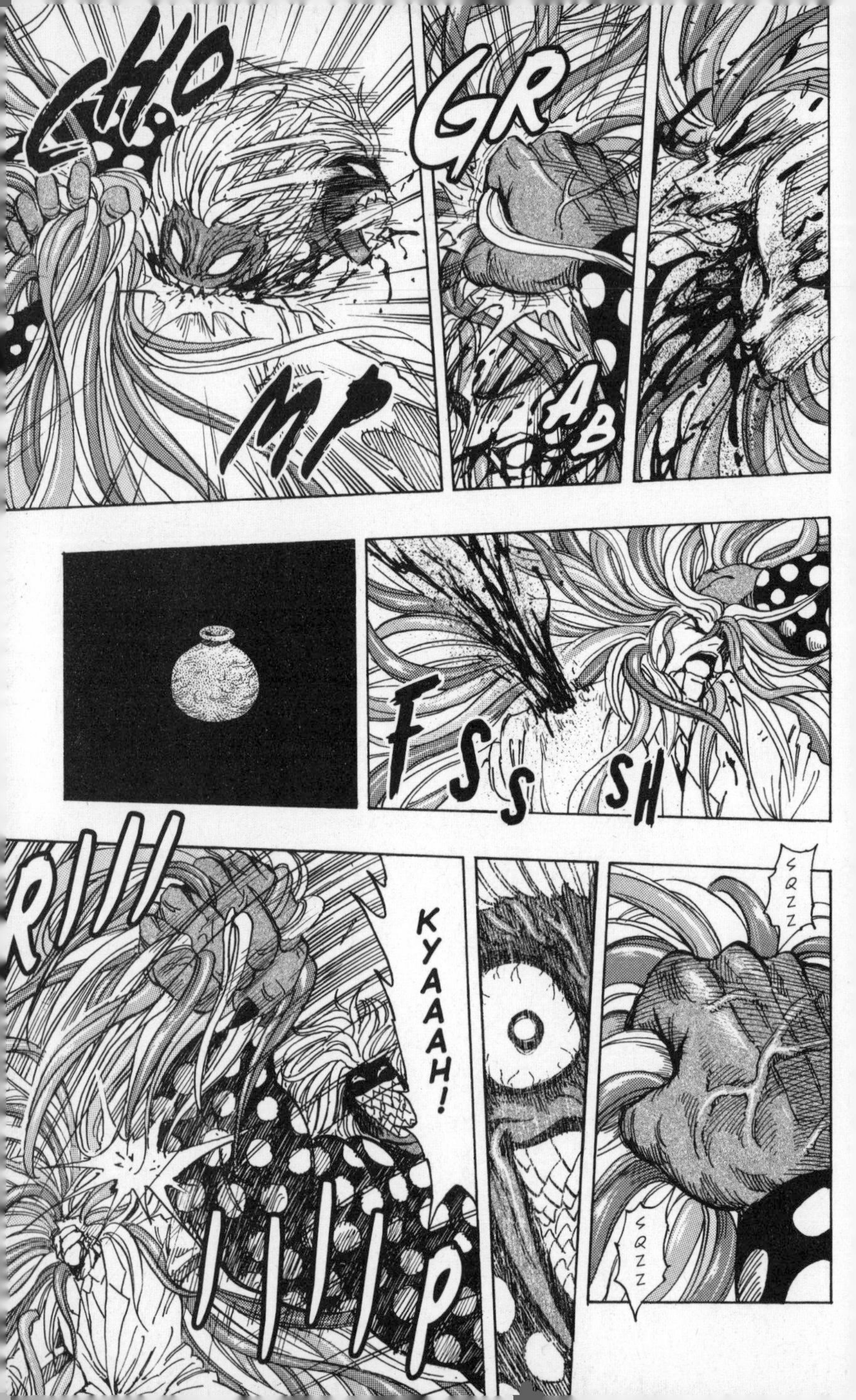
GR
AB
CHO
MP
FSSSH
SQZZ
SQZZ
KYAAAH!
RIII
IIIIP

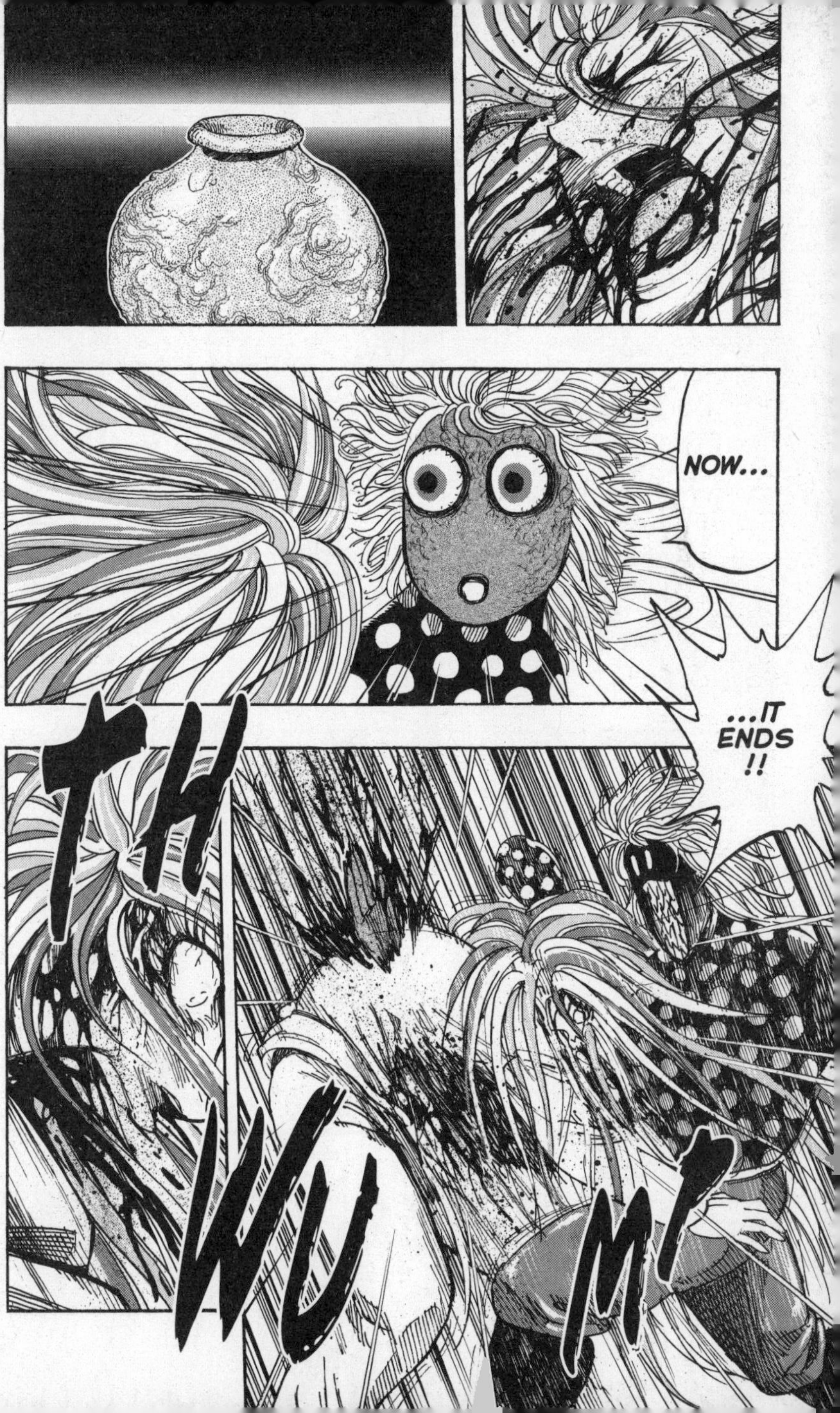
NOW...
...IT ENDS !!
THWUMP

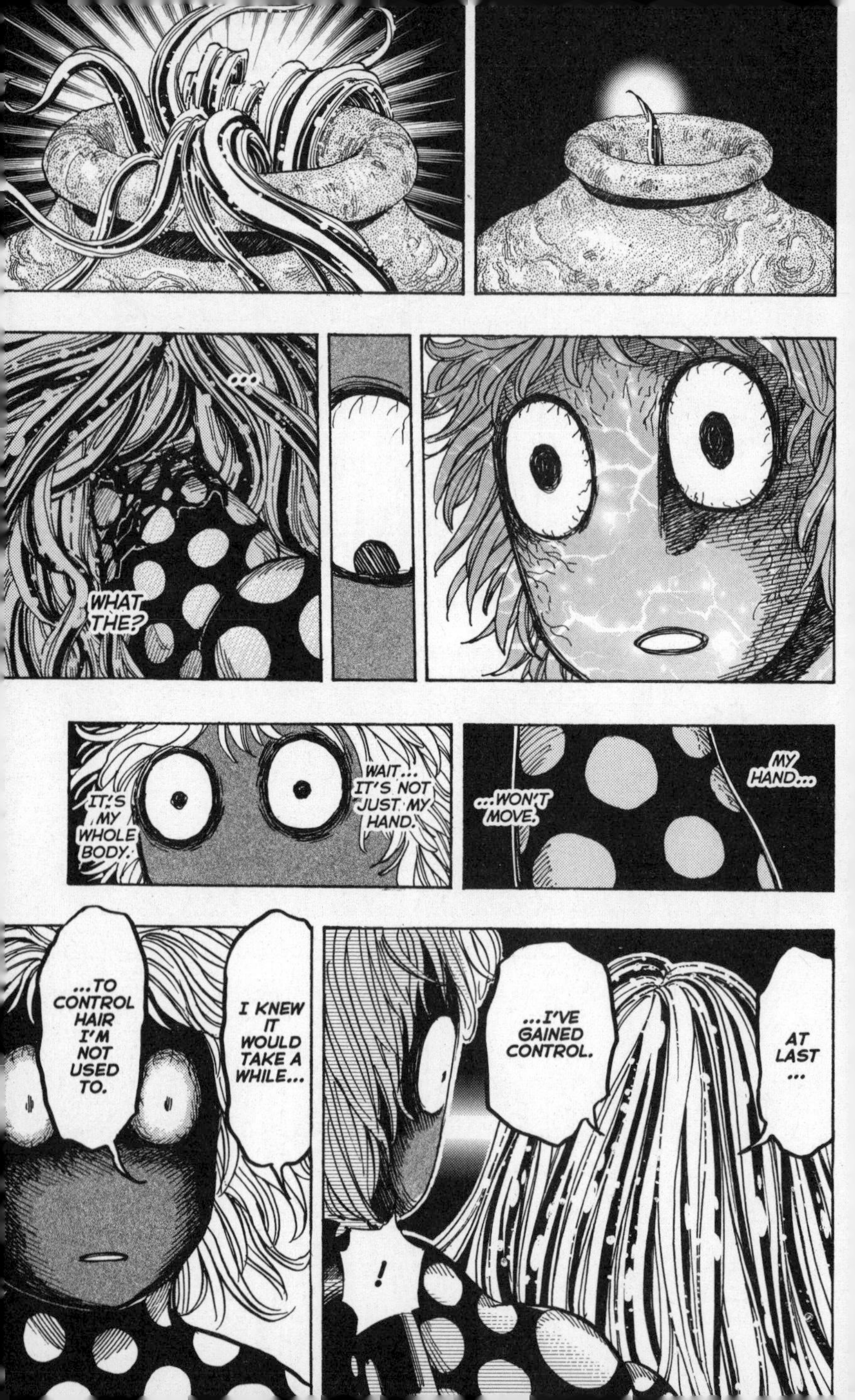
...
WHAT THE?
MY HAND...
...WON'T MOVE.
WAIT... IT'S NOT JUST MY HAND.
IT'S MY WHOLE BODY.
AT LAST...
...I'VE GAINED CONTROL.
!
I KNEW IT WOULD TAKE A WHILE...
...TO CONTROL HAIR I'M NOT USED TO.

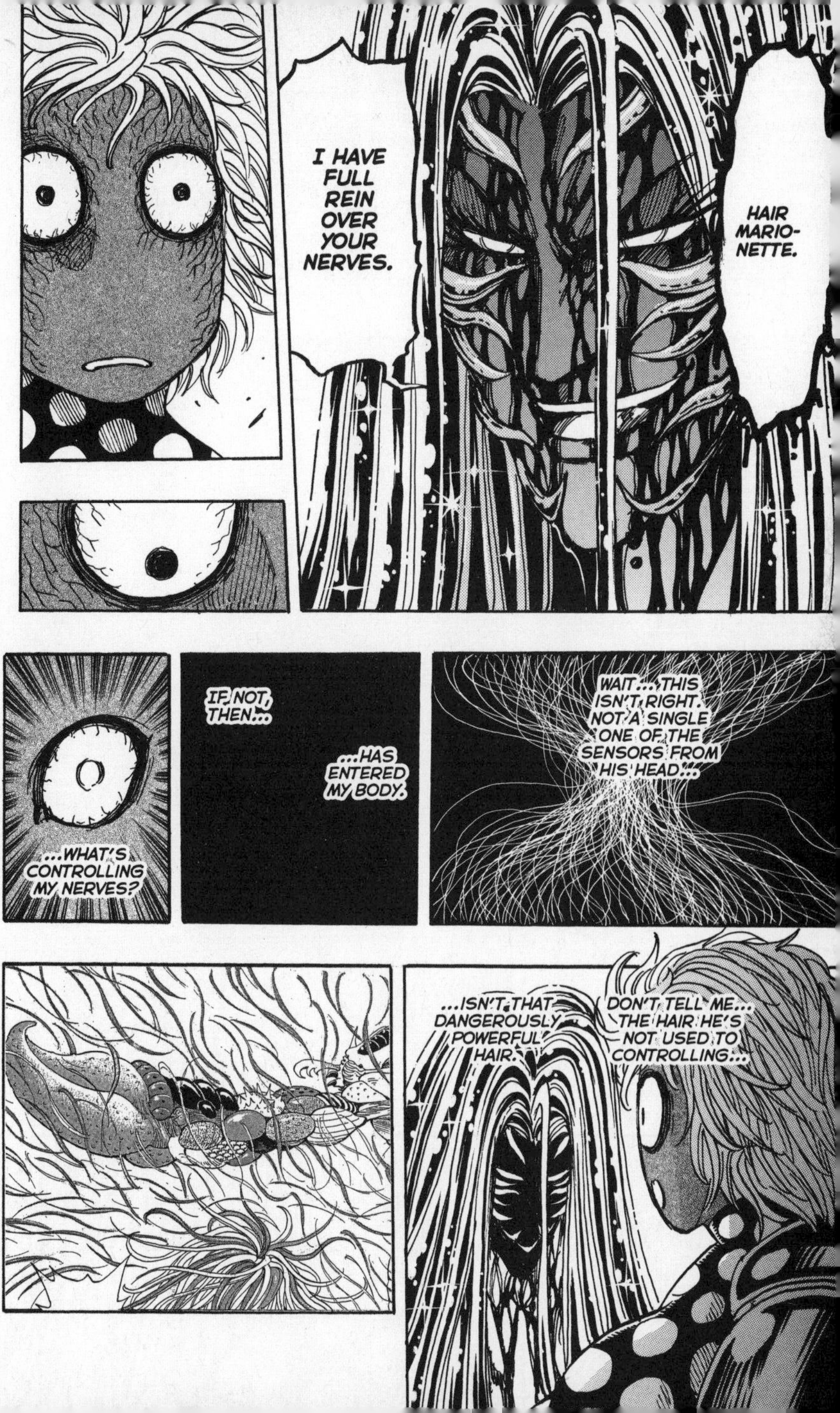
HAIR MARIO-NETTE.
I HAVE FULL REIN OVER YOUR NERVES.
WAIT... THIS ISN'T RIGHT. NOT A SINGLE ONE OF THE SENSORS FROM HIS HEAD...
IF NOT, THEN...
...HAS ENTERED MY BODY.
...WHAT'S CONTROLLING MY NERVES?
DON'T TELL ME... THE HAIR HE'S NOT USED TO CONTROLLING...
...ISN'T THAT DANGEROUSLY POWERFUL HAIR.

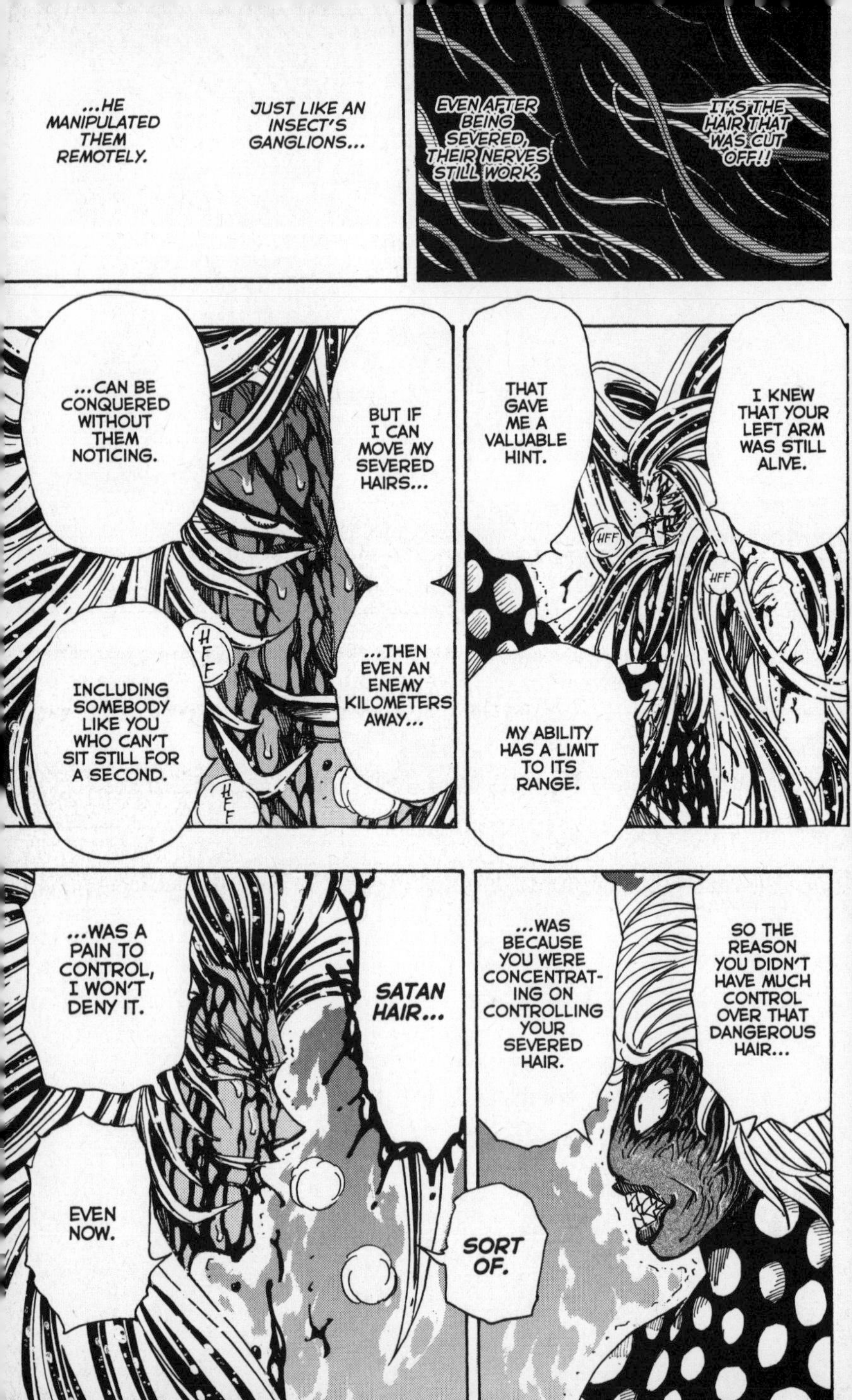
IT'S THE HAIR THAT WAS CUT OFF!!
EVEN AFTER BEING SEVERED, THEIR NERVES STILL WORK.
JUST LIKE AN INSECT'S GANGLIONS...
...HE MANIPULATED THEM REMOTELY.
I KNEW THAT YOUR LEFT ARM WAS STILL ALIVE.
HFF
HFF
THAT GAVE ME A VALUABLE HINT.
MY ABILITY HAS A LIMIT TO ITS RANGE.
BUT IF I CAN MOVE MY SEVERED HAIRS...
...THEN EVEN AN ENEMY KILOMETERS AWAY...
...CAN BE CONQUERED WITHOUT THEM NOTICING.
HFF
INCLUDING SOMEBODY LIKE YOU WHO CAN'T SIT STILL FOR A SECOND.
HFF
SO THE REASON YOU DIDN'T HAVE MUCH CONTROL OVER THAT DANGEROUS HAIR...
...WAS BECAUSE YOU WERE CONCENTRATING ON CONTROLLING YOUR SEVERED HAIR.
SORT OF.
SATAN HAIR...
...WAS A PAIN TO CONTROL, I WON'T DENY IT.
EVEN NOW.

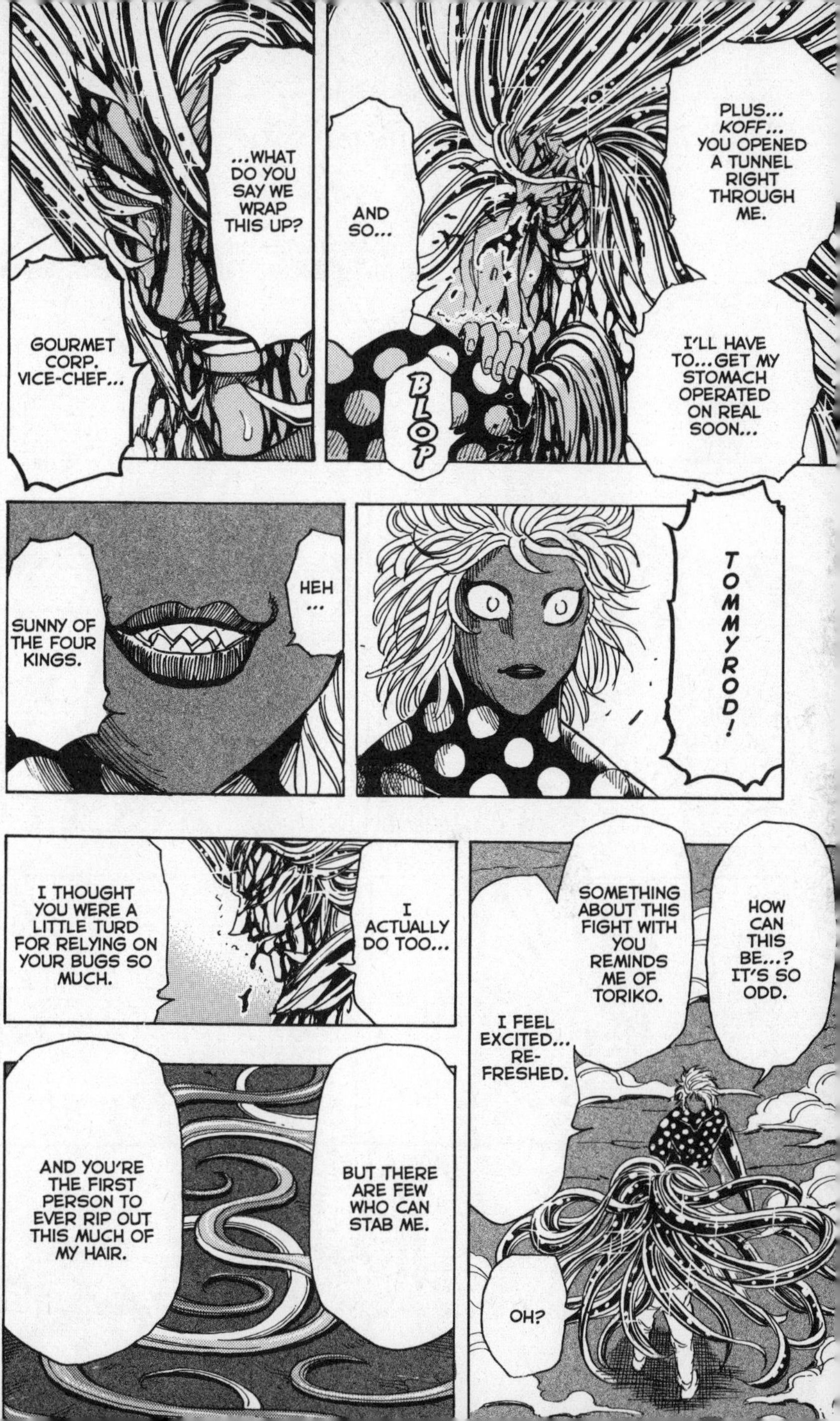
PLUS... KOFF... YOU OPENED A TUNNEL RIGHT THROUGH ME.
I'LL HAVE TO...GET MY STOMACH OPERATED ON REAL SOON...
AND SO...
BLOP
...WHAT DO YOU SAY WE WRAP THIS UP?
GOURMET CORP. VICE-CHEF...
TOMMYROD!
HEH ...
SUNNY OF THE FOUR KINGS.
HOW CAN THIS BE...? IT'S SO ODD.
SOMETHING ABOUT THIS FIGHT WITH YOU REMINDS ME OF TORIKO.
I FEEL EXCITED... RE-FRESHED.
OH?
I ACTUALLY DO TOO...
I THOUGHT YOU WERE A LITTLE TURD FOR RELYING ON YOUR BUGS SO MUCH.
BUT THERE ARE FEW WHO CAN STAB ME.
AND YOU'RE THE FIRST PERSON TO EVER RIP OUT THIS MUCH OF MY HAIR.

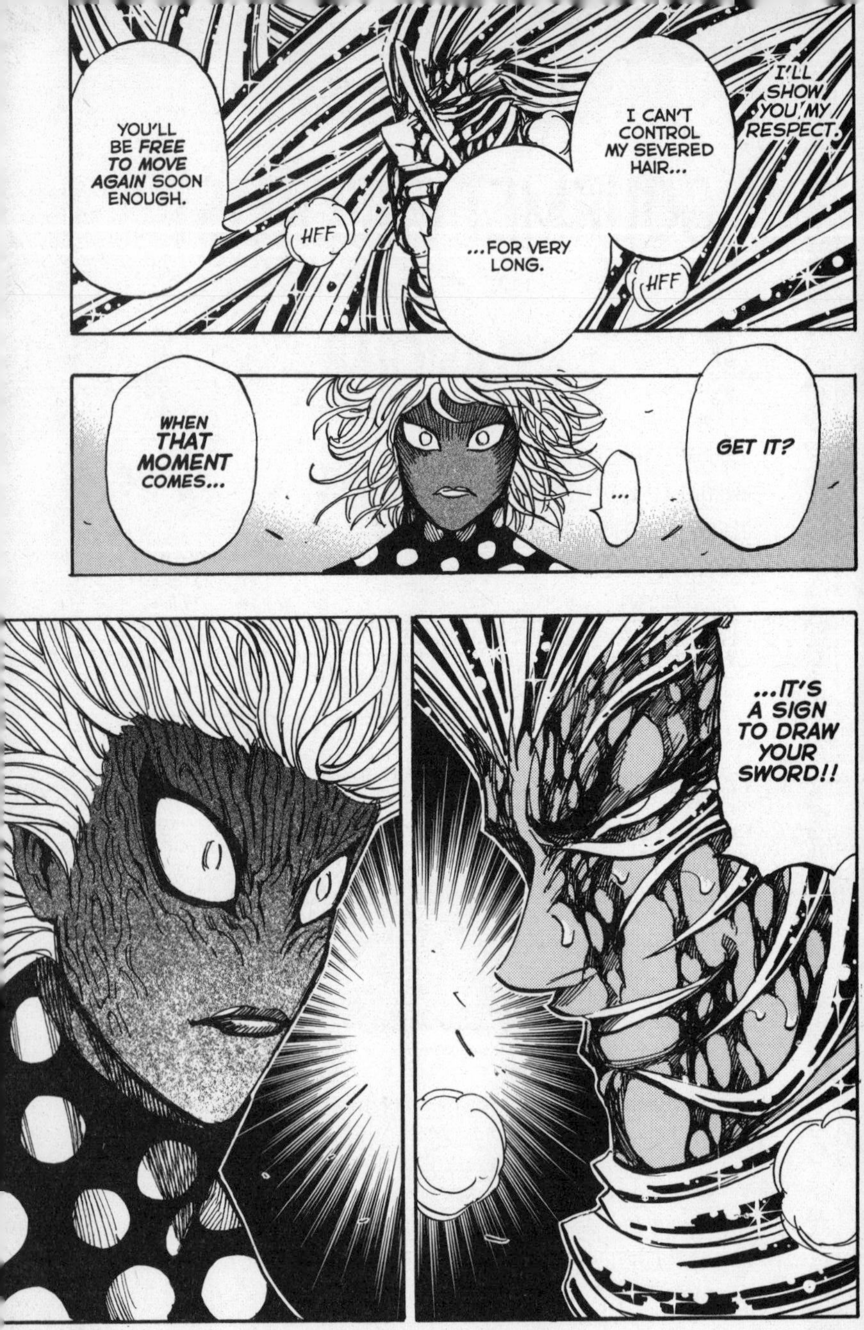
I'LL SHOW YOU MY RESPECT.
I CAN'T CONTROL MY SEVERED HAIR...
...FOR VERY LONG.
HFF
YOU'LL BE FREE TO MOVE AGAIN SOON ENOUGH.
HFF
GET IT?
...
WHEN THAT MOMENT COMES...
...IT'S A SIGN TO DRAW YOUR SWORD!!

TORIKO

GOURMET CHECKLIST
Vol. 251

ATLAS CRAB
(CRUSTACEAN)

CAPTURE LEVEL: 57
HABITAT: CLEAR SHALLOWS
LENGTH: 8 METERS
HEIGHT: 3.5 METERS
WEIGHT: 9 TONS
PRICE: 900,000 YEN (LEG);
    100 G / 400,000 YEN (INNARDS)

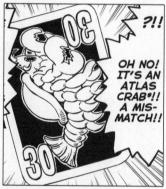

OH NO! IT'S AN ATLAS CRAB*!! A MISMATCH!!

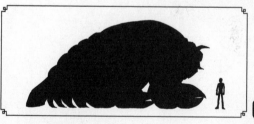

SCALE

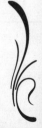

A LAND-DWELLING CRAB WITH THREE HORNS AND THREE SETS OF CLAWS. ITS SHELL IS AS TOUGH AS TITANIUM ALLOY AND ITS POWERFUL CLAWS CAN CUT THROUGH STEEL. IN ORDER TO MOVE ITS GIANT BODY ABOUT ON LAND, THE ATLAS CRAB HAS EVOLVED TO HAVE EXTREMELY STRONG LEGS. THAT SIZE AND STRENGTH IS WHAT EARNED IT THE NAME "ATLAS CRAB," FROM THE GREEK GOD ATLAS WHO HELD UP THE CELESTIAL SPHERE. IT'S DIFFICULT TO CAPTURE AND TO COOK, BUT ITS INNARDS ARE PRIZED AS A HIGH-END INGREDIENT.

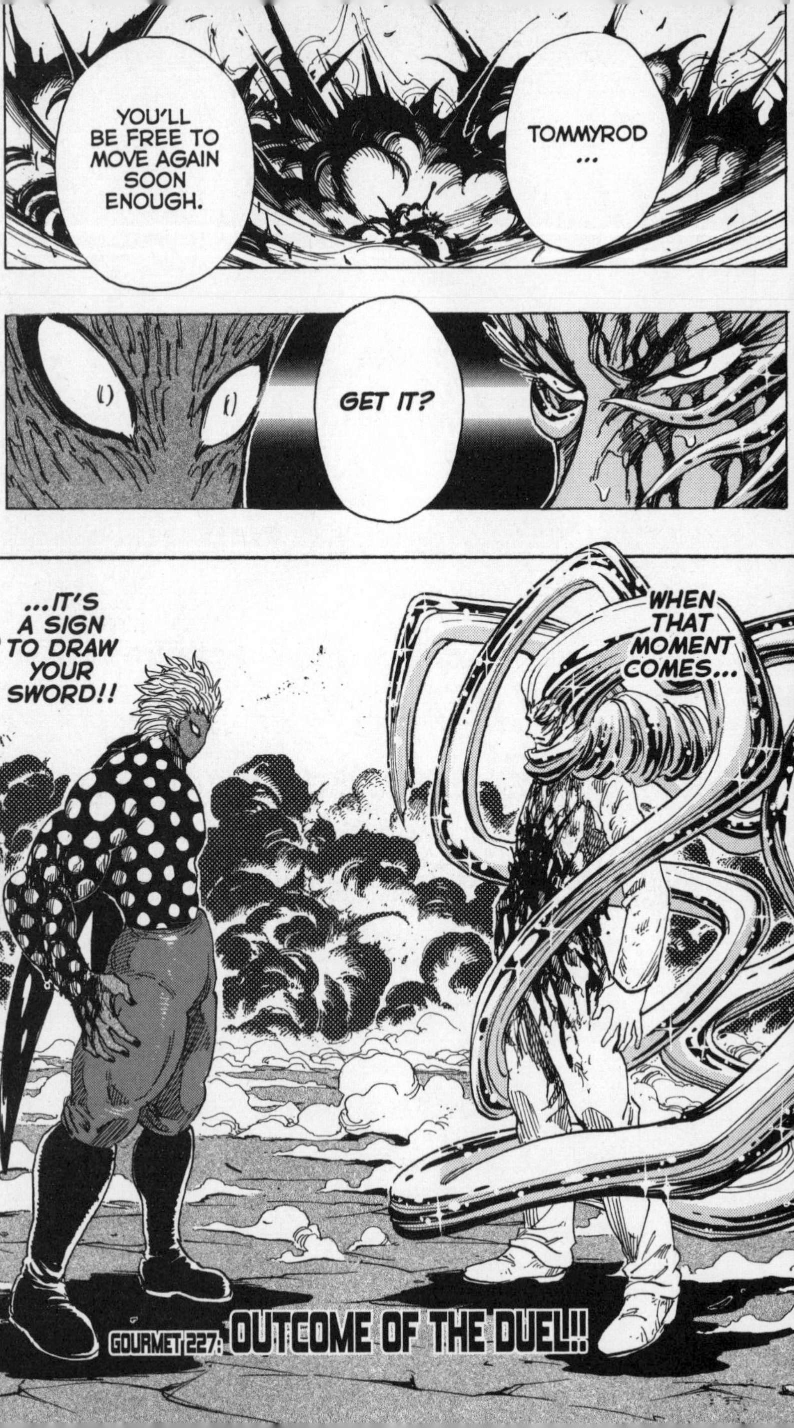
TOMMYROD ...
YOU'LL BE FREE TO MOVE AGAIN SOON ENOUGH.
GET IT?
WHEN THAT MOMENT COMES...
...IT'S A SIGN TO DRAW YOUR SWORD!!
GOURMET 227: OUTCOME OF THE DUEL!!

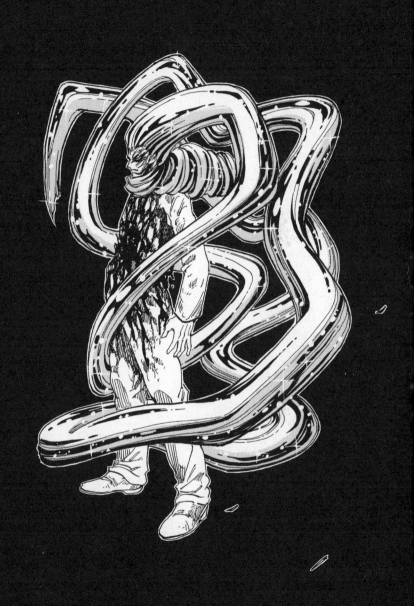

GOURMET 227:
OUTCOME OF THE DUEL!!

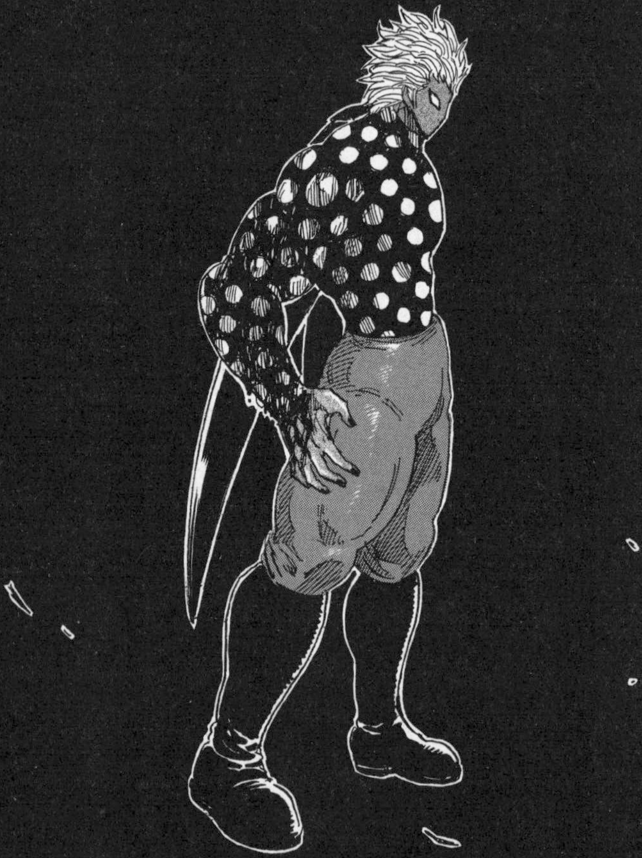

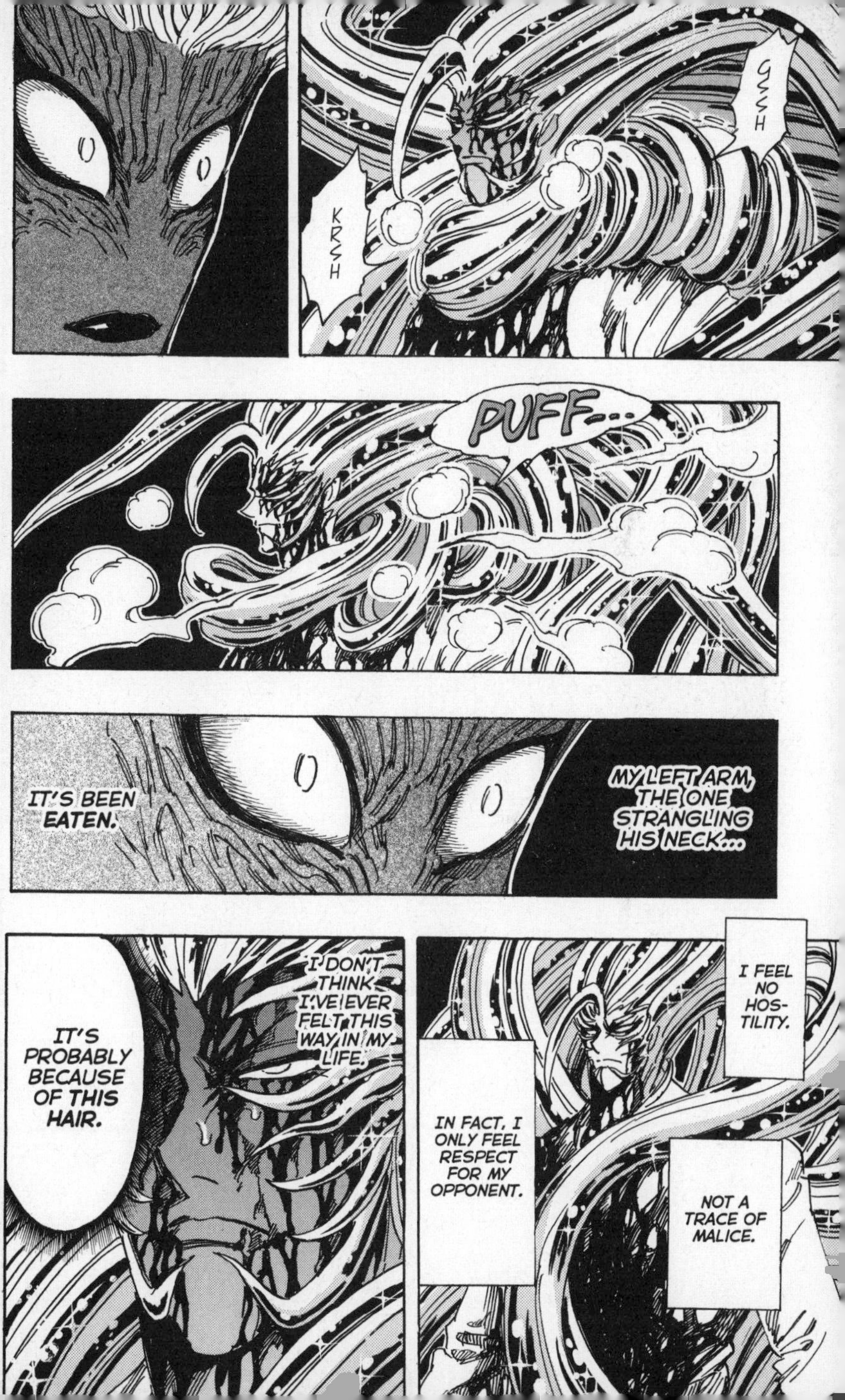
GSSH
KRSH
PUFF...
MY LEFT ARM, THE ONE STRANGLING HIS NECK...
IT'S BEEN EATEN.
I FEEL NO HOS-TILITY.
NOT A TRACE OF MALICE.
IN FACT, I ONLY FEEL RESPECT FOR MY OPPONENT.
I DON'T THINK I'VE EVER FELT THIS WAY IN MY LIFE.
IT'S PROBABLY BECAUSE OF THIS HAIR.

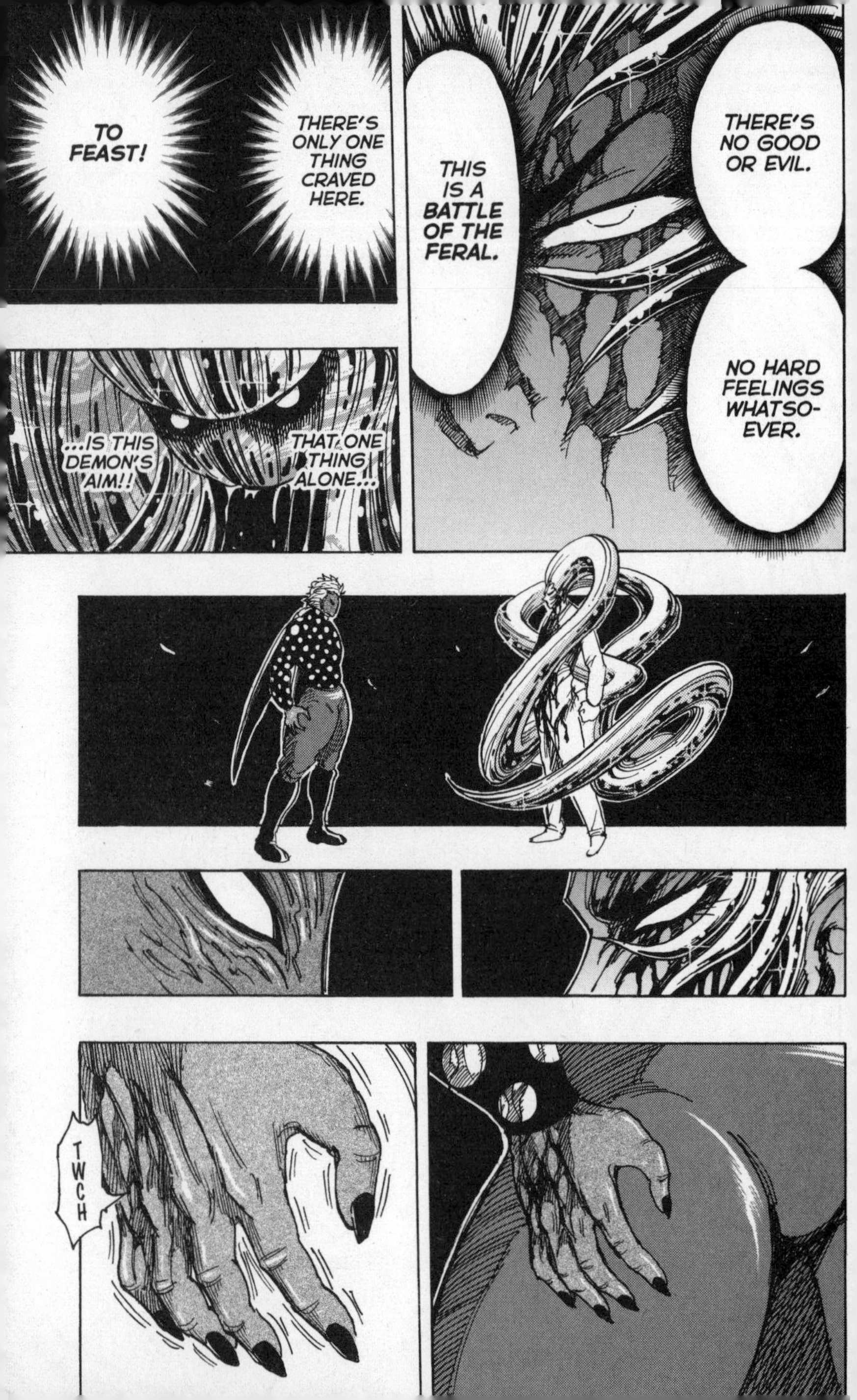
THERE'S NO GOOD OR EVIL.
NO HARD FEELINGS WHATSO-EVER.
THIS IS A BATTLE OF THE FERAL.
THERE'S ONLY ONE THING CRAVED HERE.
TO FEAST!
THAT ONE THING ALONE...
...IS THIS DEMON'S AIM!!
TWCH

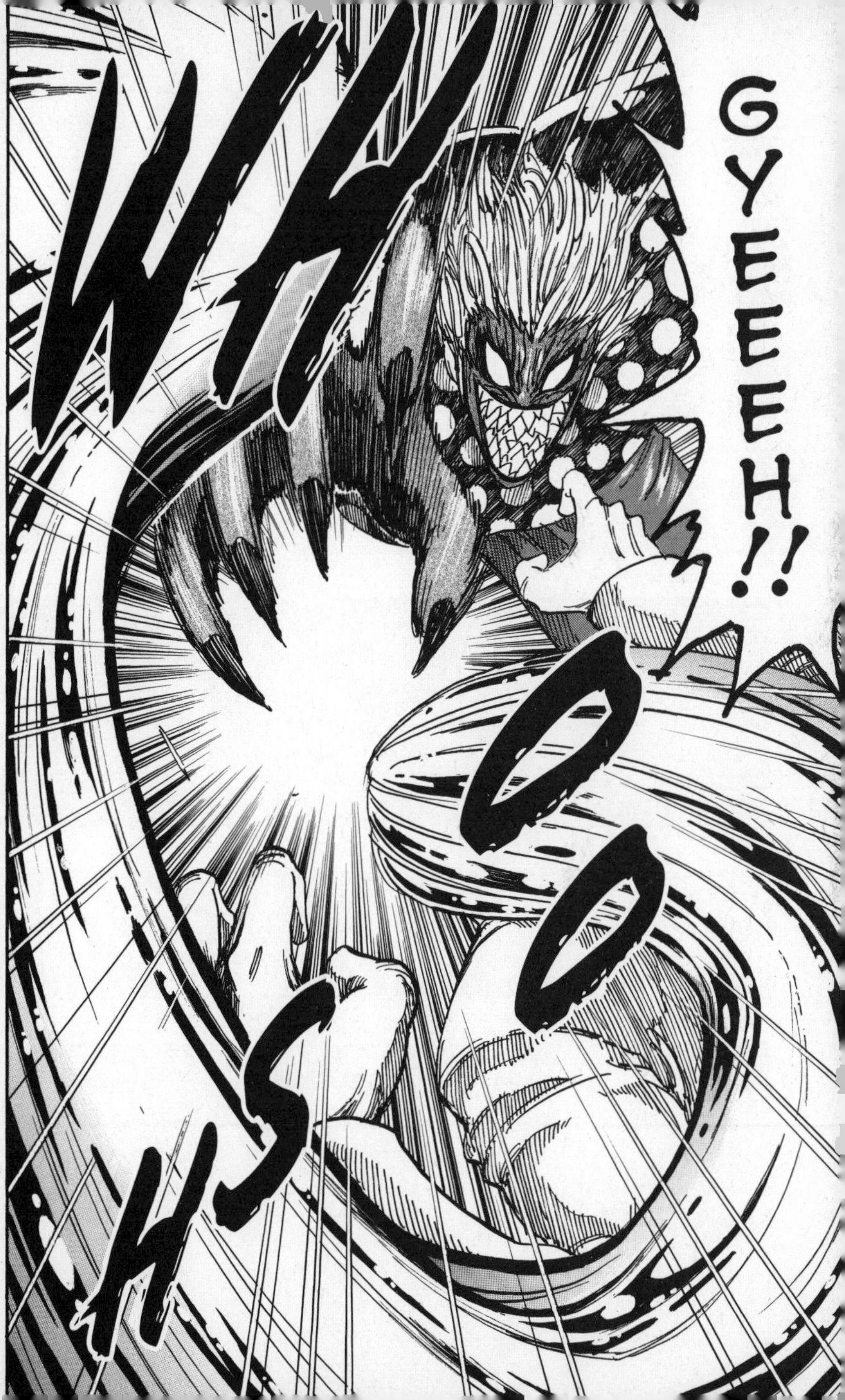
GYEEEH!!

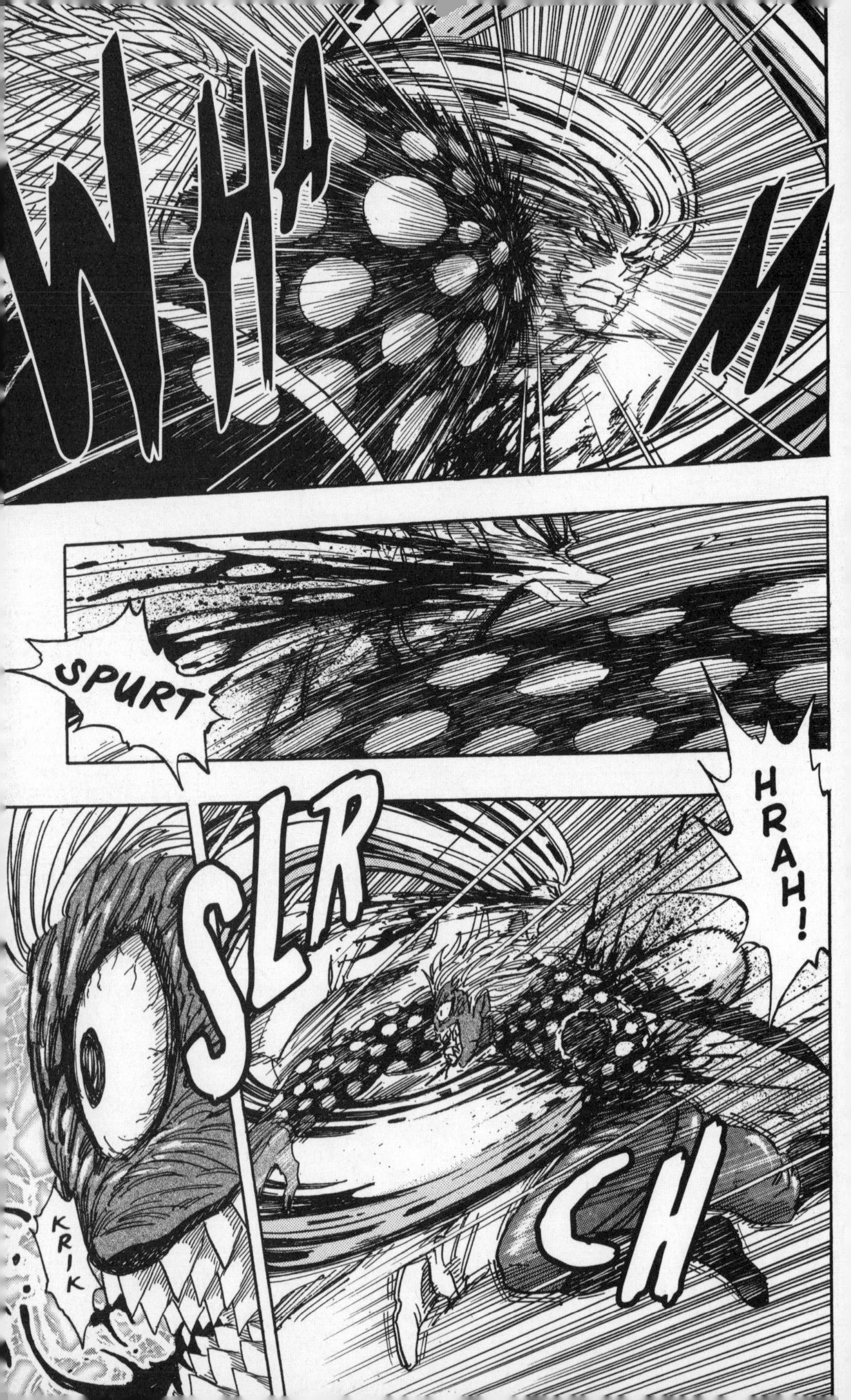
WHA
M
SPURT
HRAH!
SLR
CH
KRIK

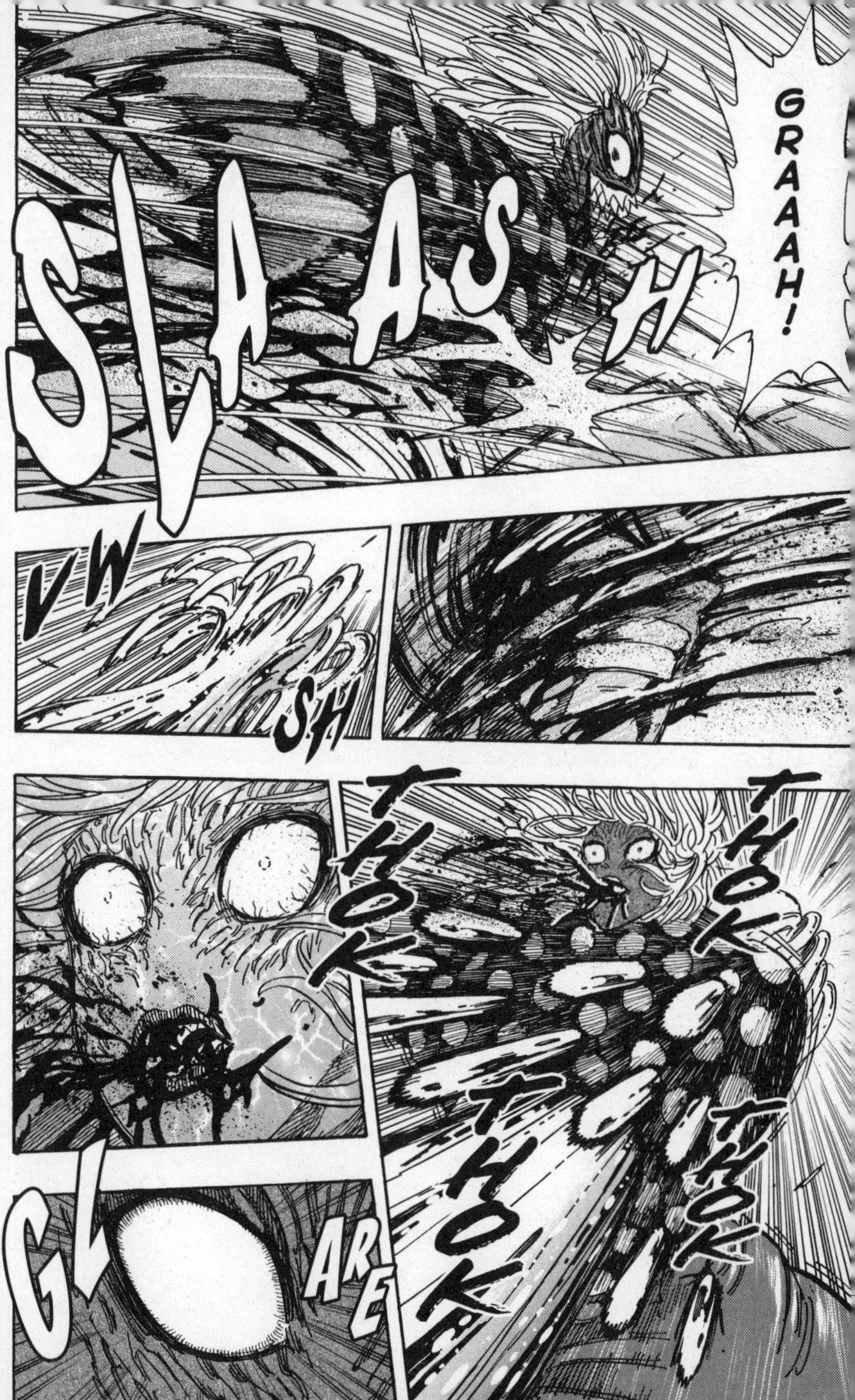
GRAAAAH!
SLASH
VWSH
THOK
THOK
THOK
THOK!
GLARE

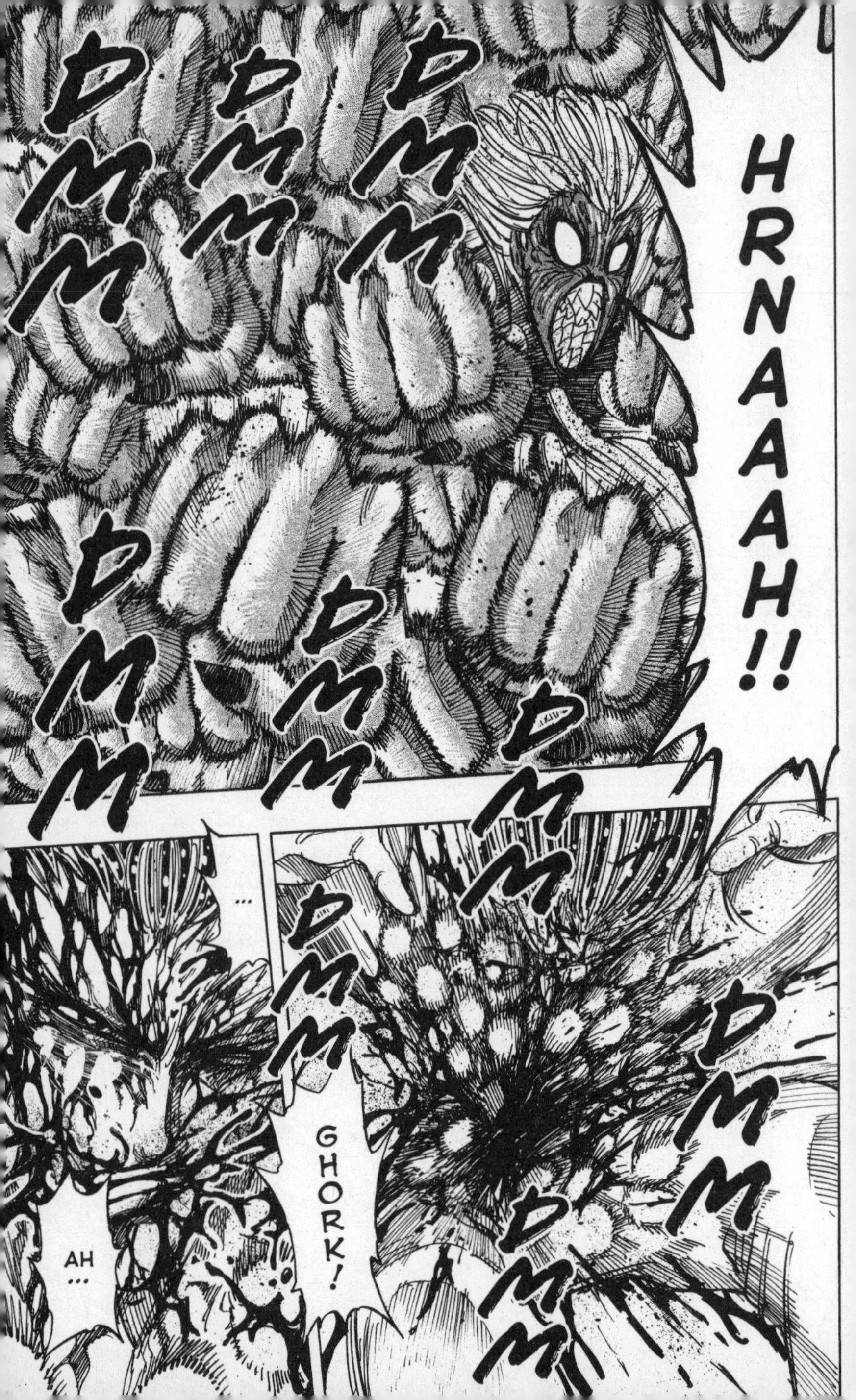
HRNAAAAH!!
DMMM
DMMM
DMMM
DMMM
DMMM
DMMM
DMMM
DMMM
GHORK!
DMMM
DMMM
...
AH ...

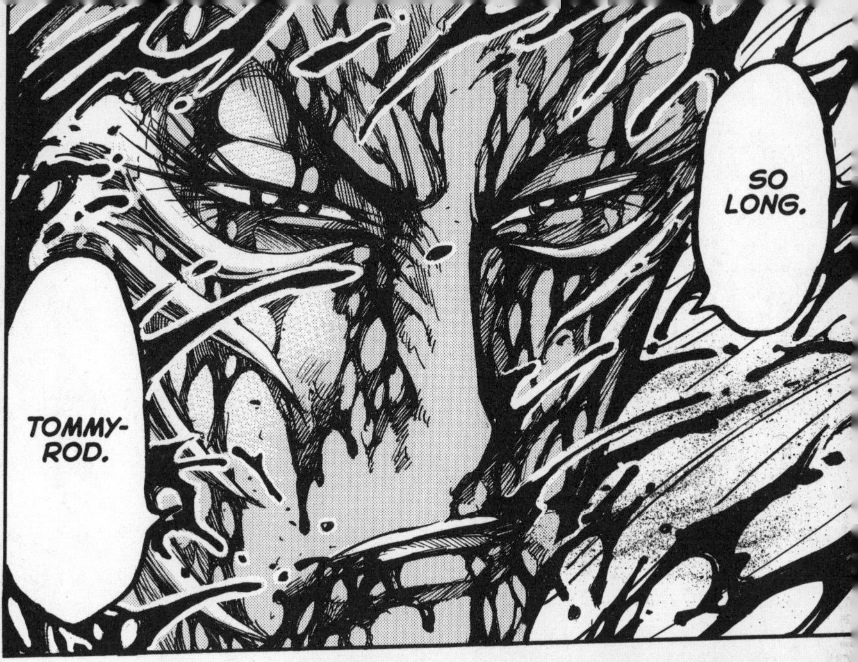
SO LONG.
TOMMY-ROD.

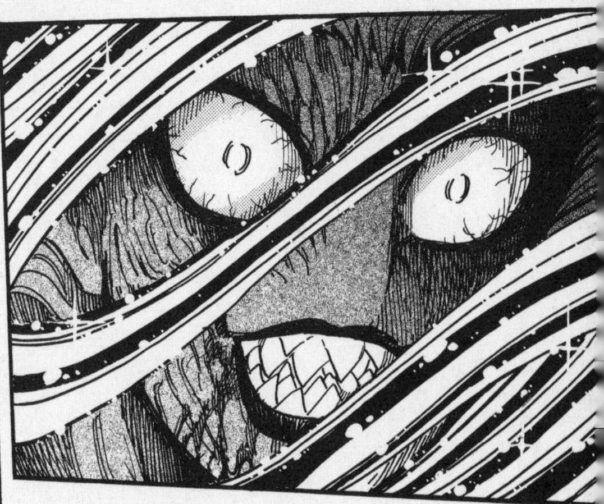

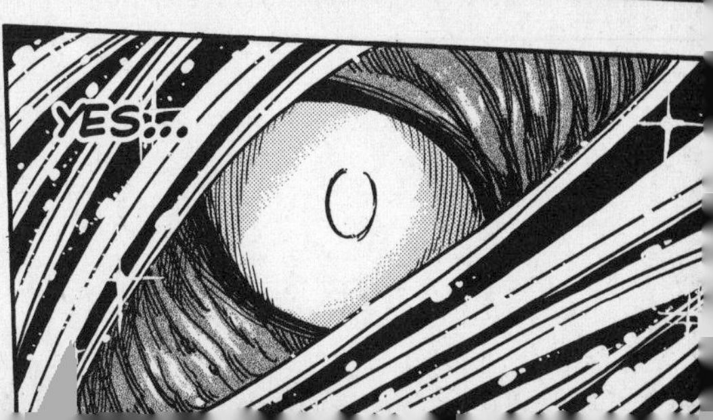
YES...

I ENJOYED THAT SO MUCH.

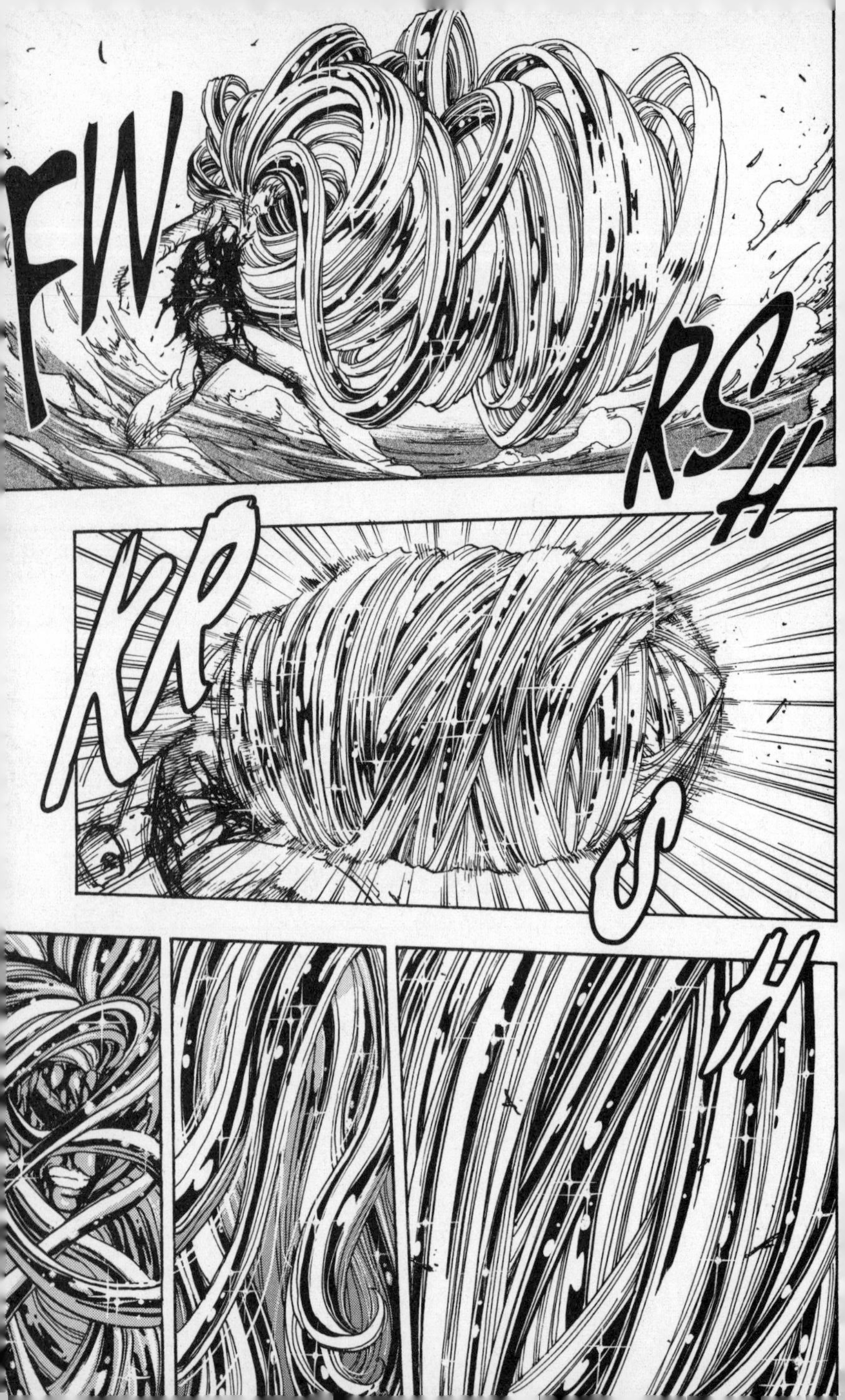
FW
RSH
S
SH

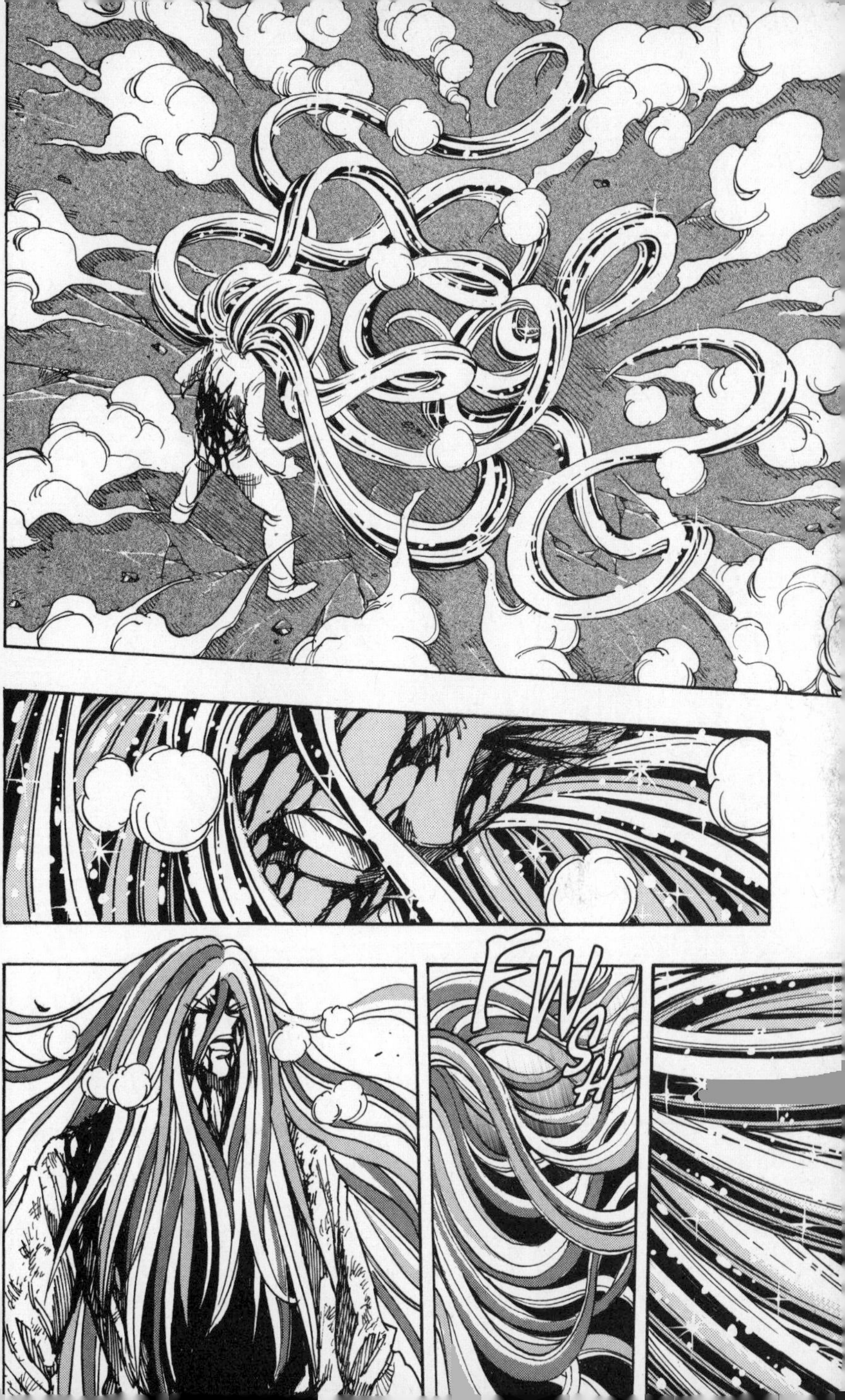
FWOSH

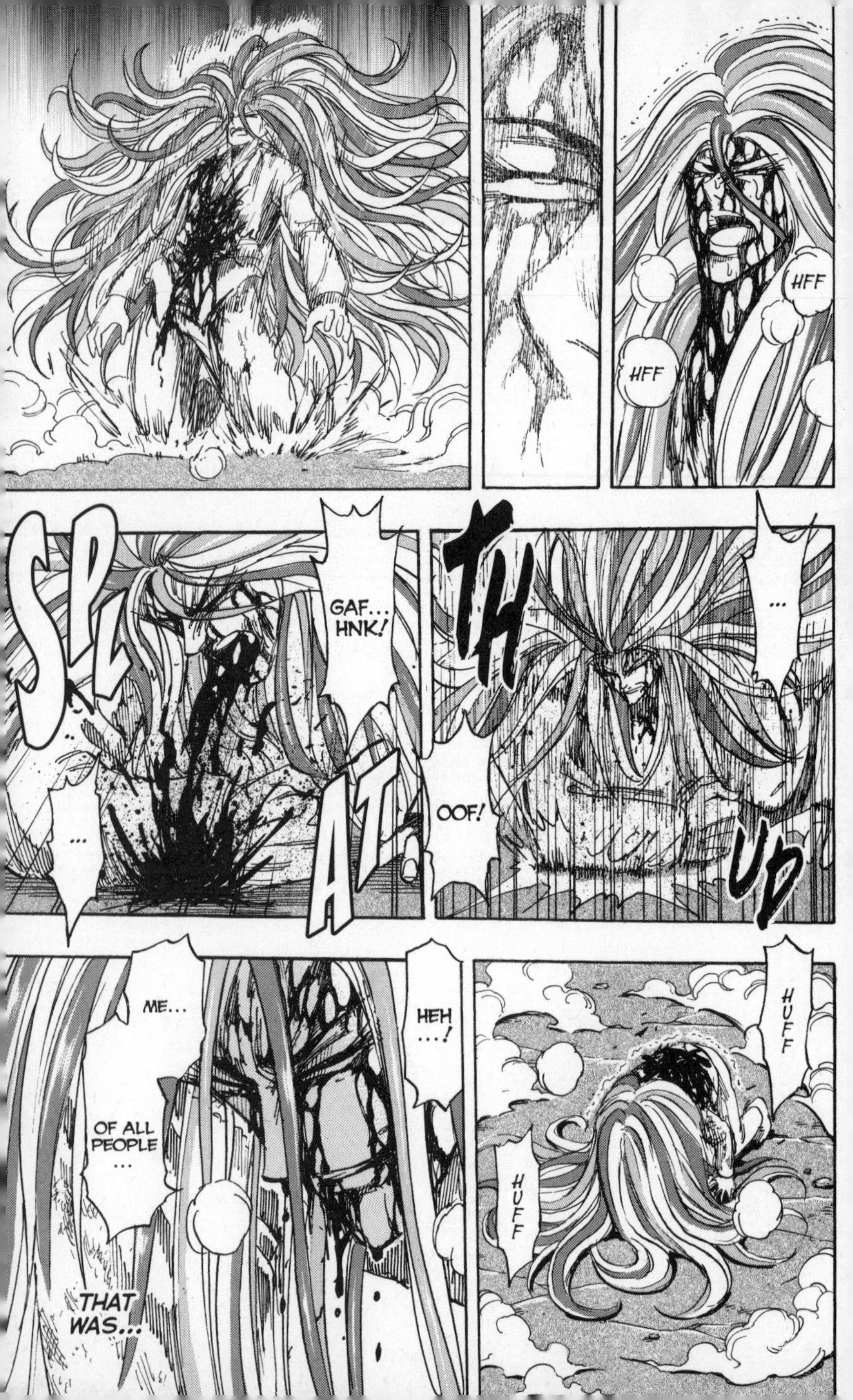
HFF
HFF
...
TH
UD
GAF... HNK!
SPL
AT
OOF!
...
HUFF
HUFF
HEH...!
ME...
OF ALL PEOPLE...
THAT WAS...

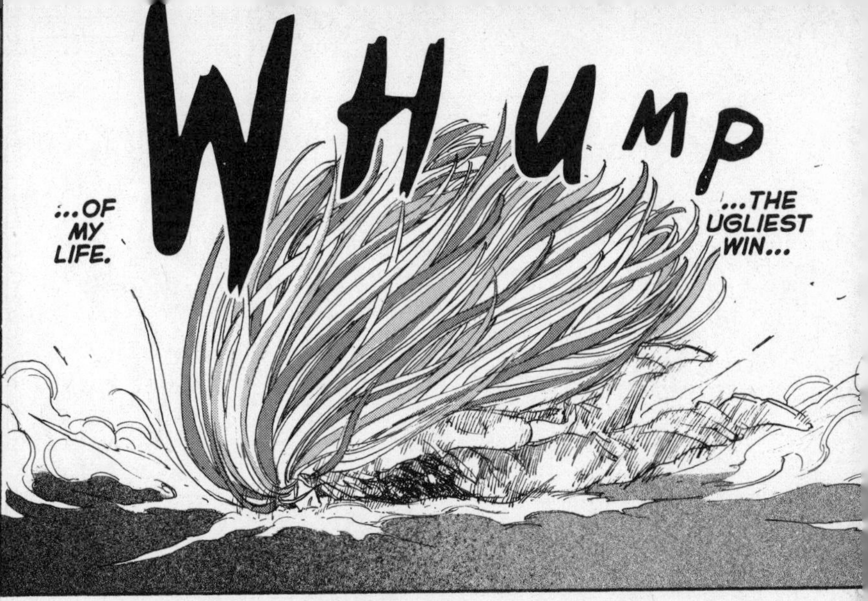
WHUMP
...THE UGLIEST WIN...
...OF MY LIFE.

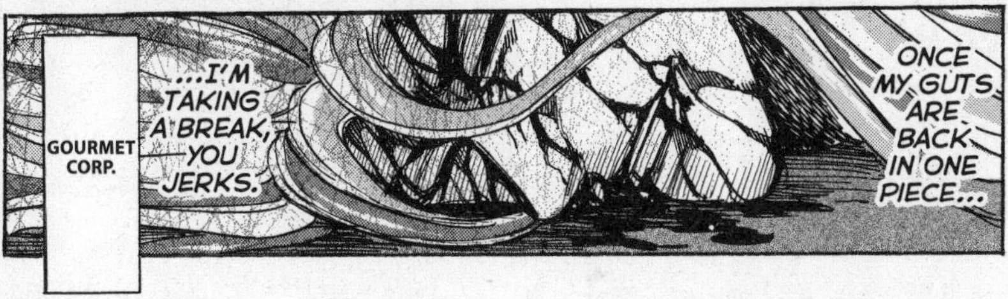
ONCE MY GUTS ARE BACK IN ONE PIECE...
...I'M TAKING A BREAK, YOU JERKS.
GOURMET CORP.

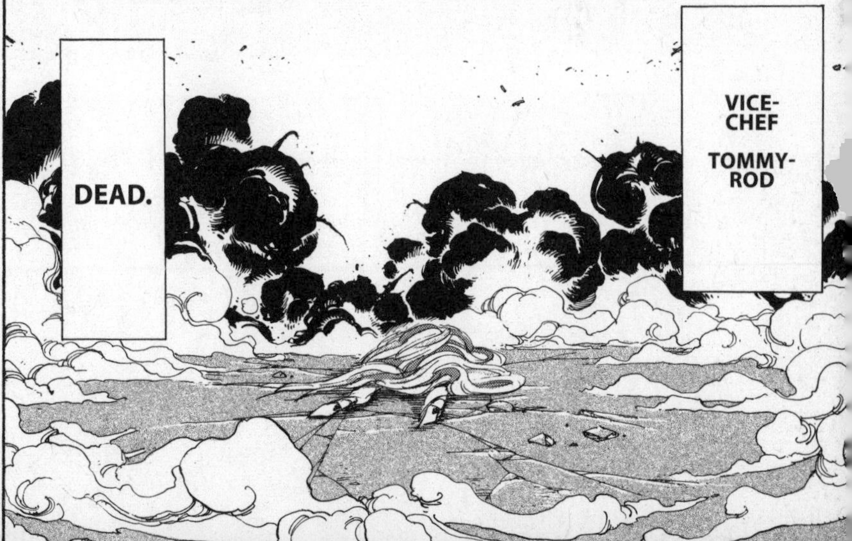
VICE-CHEF
TOMMY-ROD
DEAD.

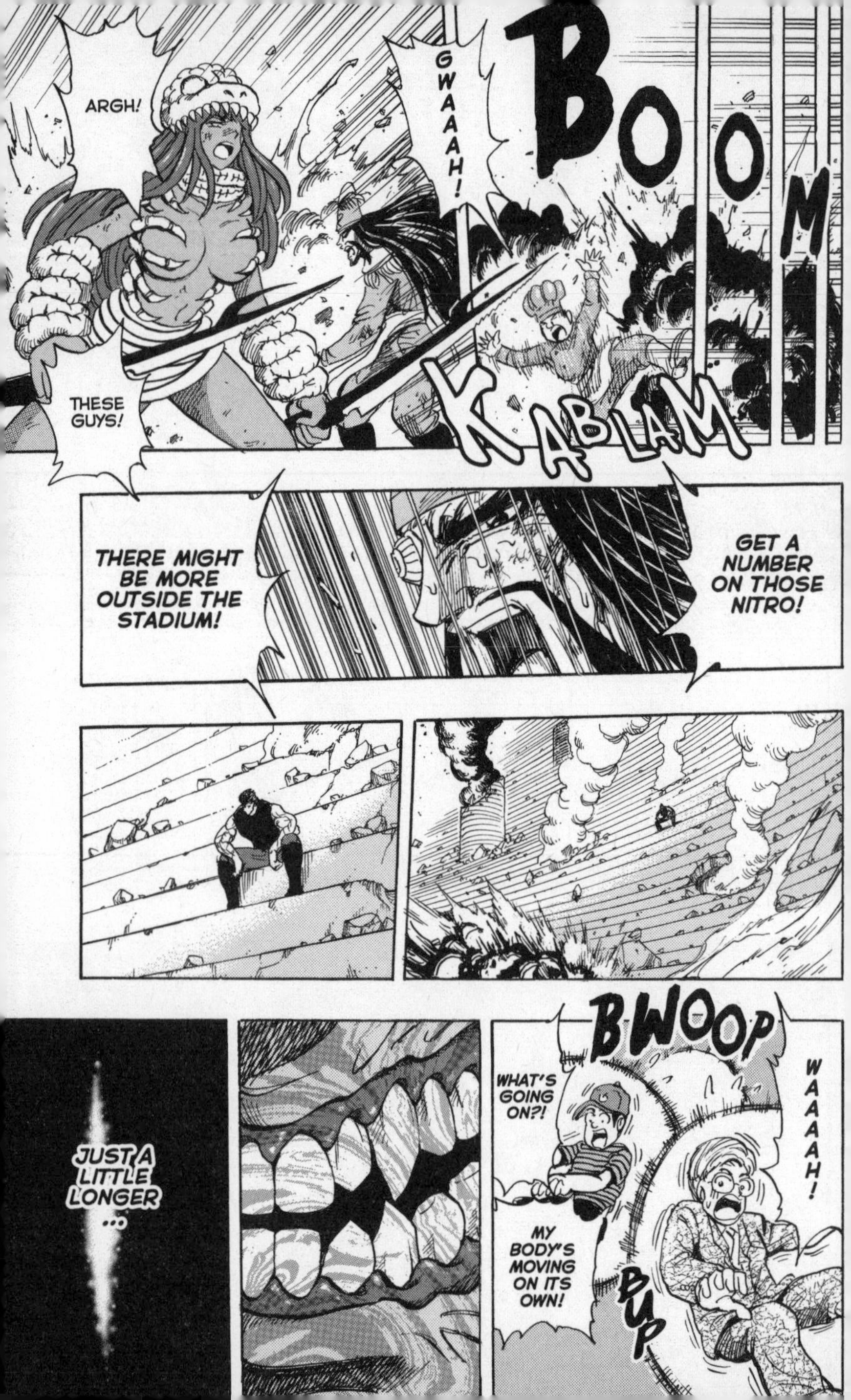
BOOM
GWAAAAH!
ARGH!
THESE GUYS!
KABLAM
GET A NUMBER ON THOSE NITRO!
THERE MIGHT BE MORE OUTSIDE THE STADIUM!
BWOOP
WAAAAAH!
WHAT'S GOING ON?!
MY BODY'S MOVING ON ITS OWN!
BUP
JUST A LITTLE LONGER...

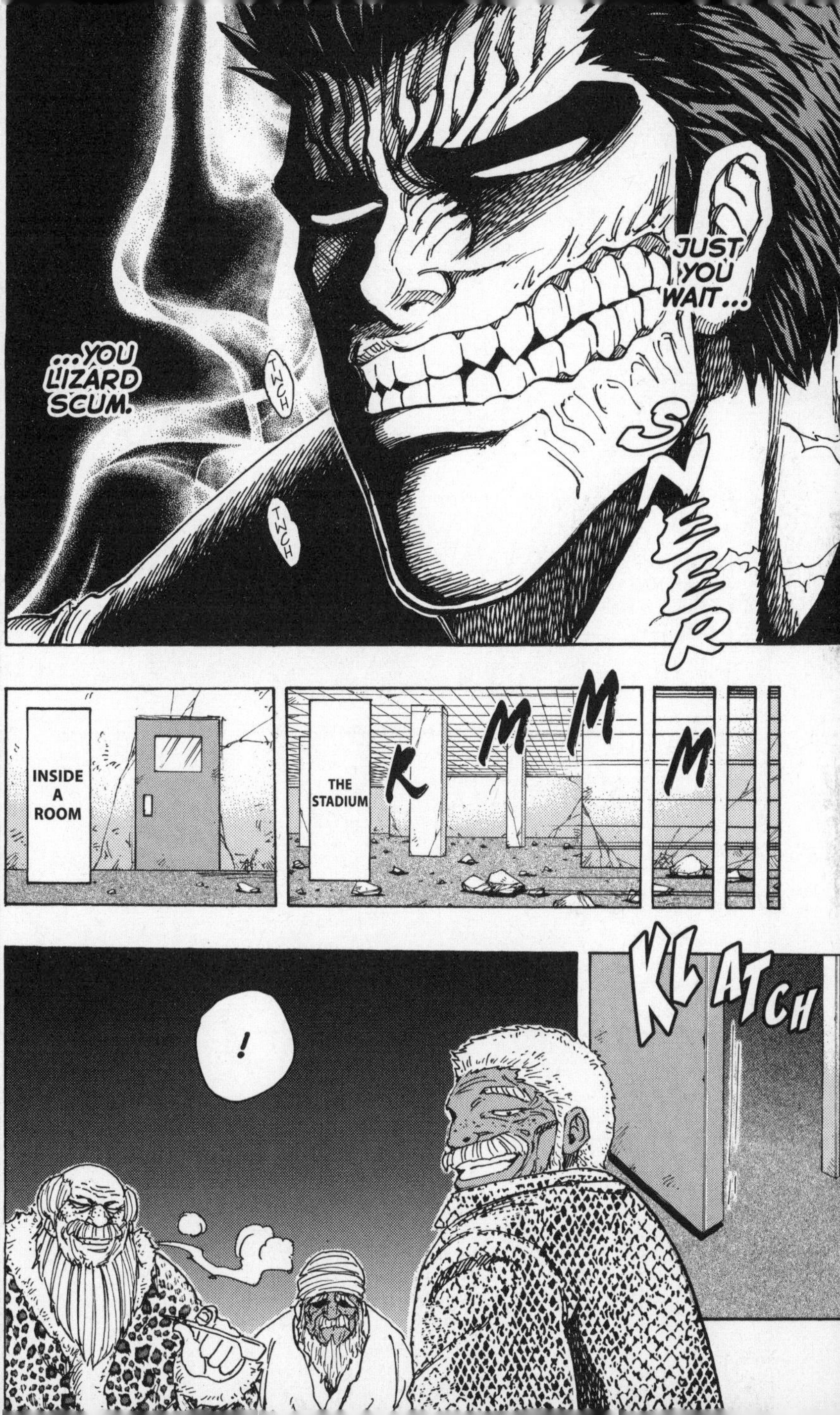
JUST YOU WAIT...
TWCH
...YOU LIZARD SCUM.
TWCH
SNEER
KRMMMM
THE STADIUM
INSIDE A ROOM
KLATCH
!

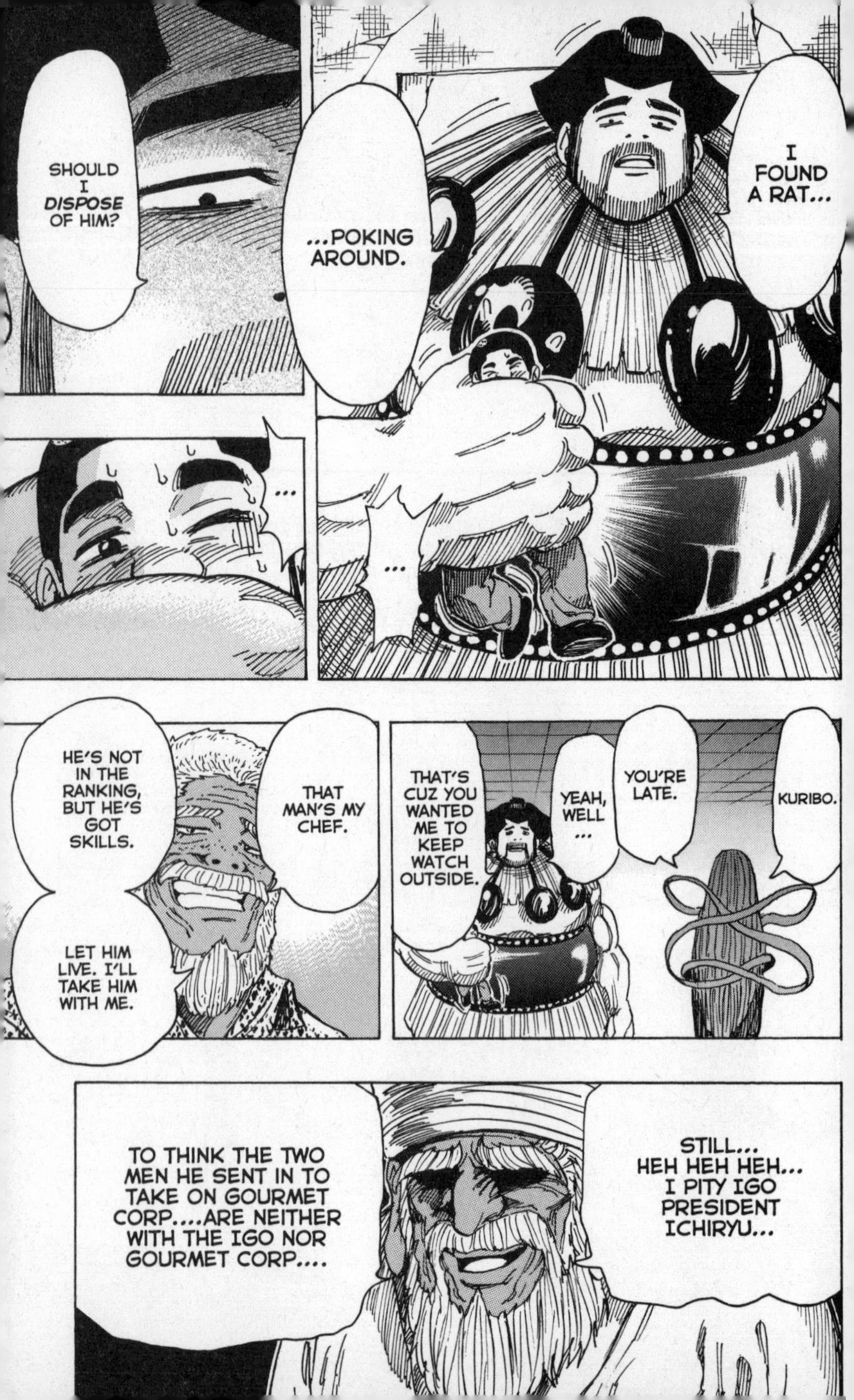
I FOUND A RAT...
...POKING AROUND.
...
SHOULD I *DISPOSE* OF HIM?
...
KURIBO.
YOU'RE LATE.
YEAH, WELL...
THAT'S CUZ YOU WANTED ME TO KEEP WATCH OUTSIDE.
THAT MAN'S MY CHEF.
HE'S NOT IN THE RANKING, BUT HE'S GOT SKILLS.
LET HIM LIVE. I'LL TAKE HIM WITH ME.
STILL... HEH HEH HEH... I PITY IGO PRESIDENT ICHIRYU...
TO THINK THE TWO MEN HE SENT IN TO TAKE ON GOURMET CORP....ARE NEITHER WITH THE IGO NOR GOURMET CORP....

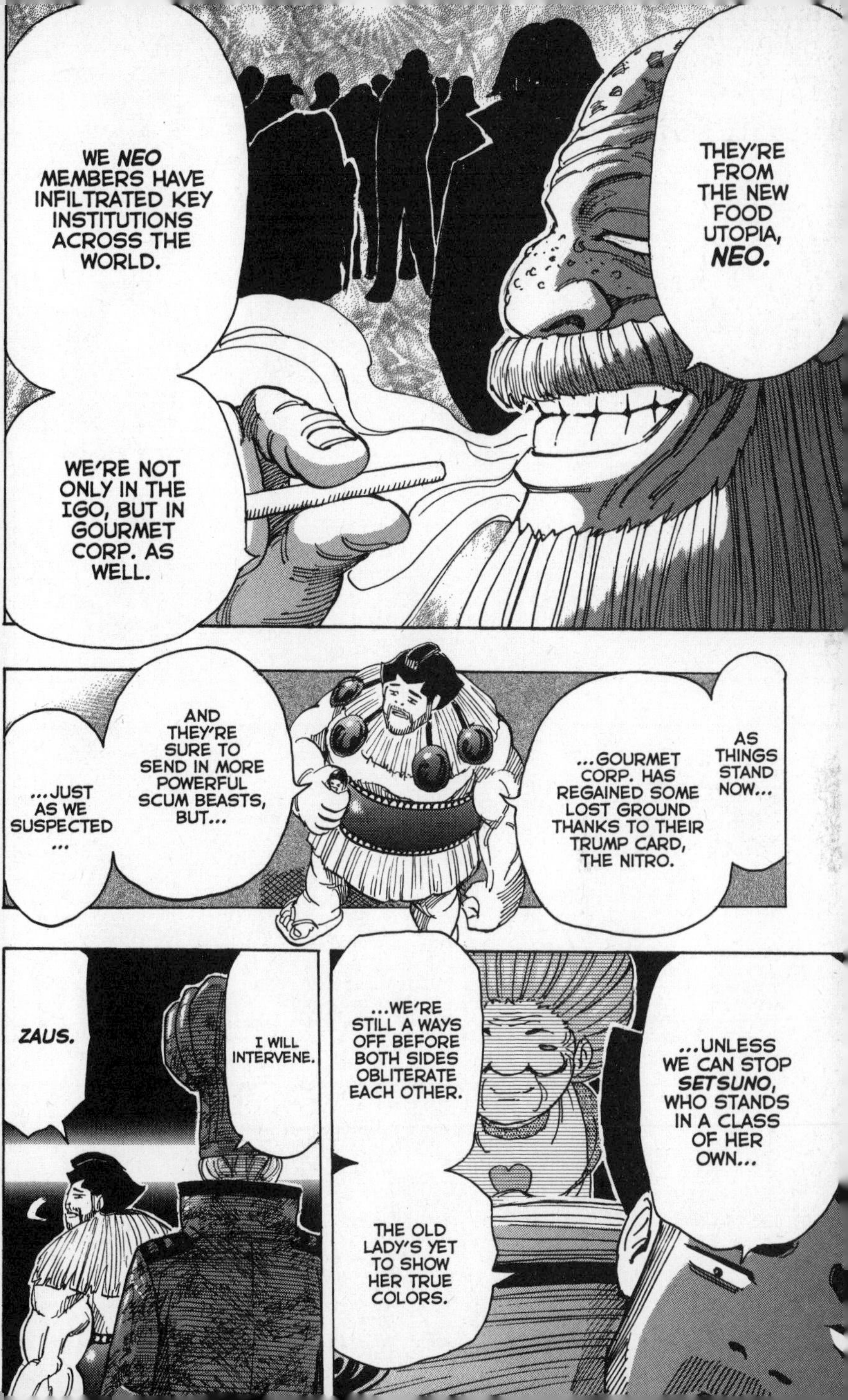
THEY'RE FROM THE NEW FOOD UTOPIA, *NEO.*
WE *NEO* MEMBERS HAVE INFILTRATED KEY INSTITUTIONS ACROSS THE WORLD.
WE'RE NOT ONLY IN THE IGO, BUT IN GOURMET CORP. AS WELL.
AS THINGS STAND NOW...
...GOURMET CORP. HAS REGAINED SOME LOST GROUND THANKS TO THEIR TRUMP CARD, THE NITRO.
AND THEY'RE SURE TO SEND IN MORE POWERFUL SCUM BEASTS, BUT...
...JUST AS WE SUSPECTED...
...UNLESS WE CAN STOP *SETSUNO,* WHO STANDS IN A CLASS OF HER OWN...
...WE'RE STILL A WAYS OFF BEFORE BOTH SIDES OBLITERATE EACH OTHER.
THE OLD LADY'S YET TO SHOW HER TRUE COLORS.
I WILL INTERVENE.
ZAUS.

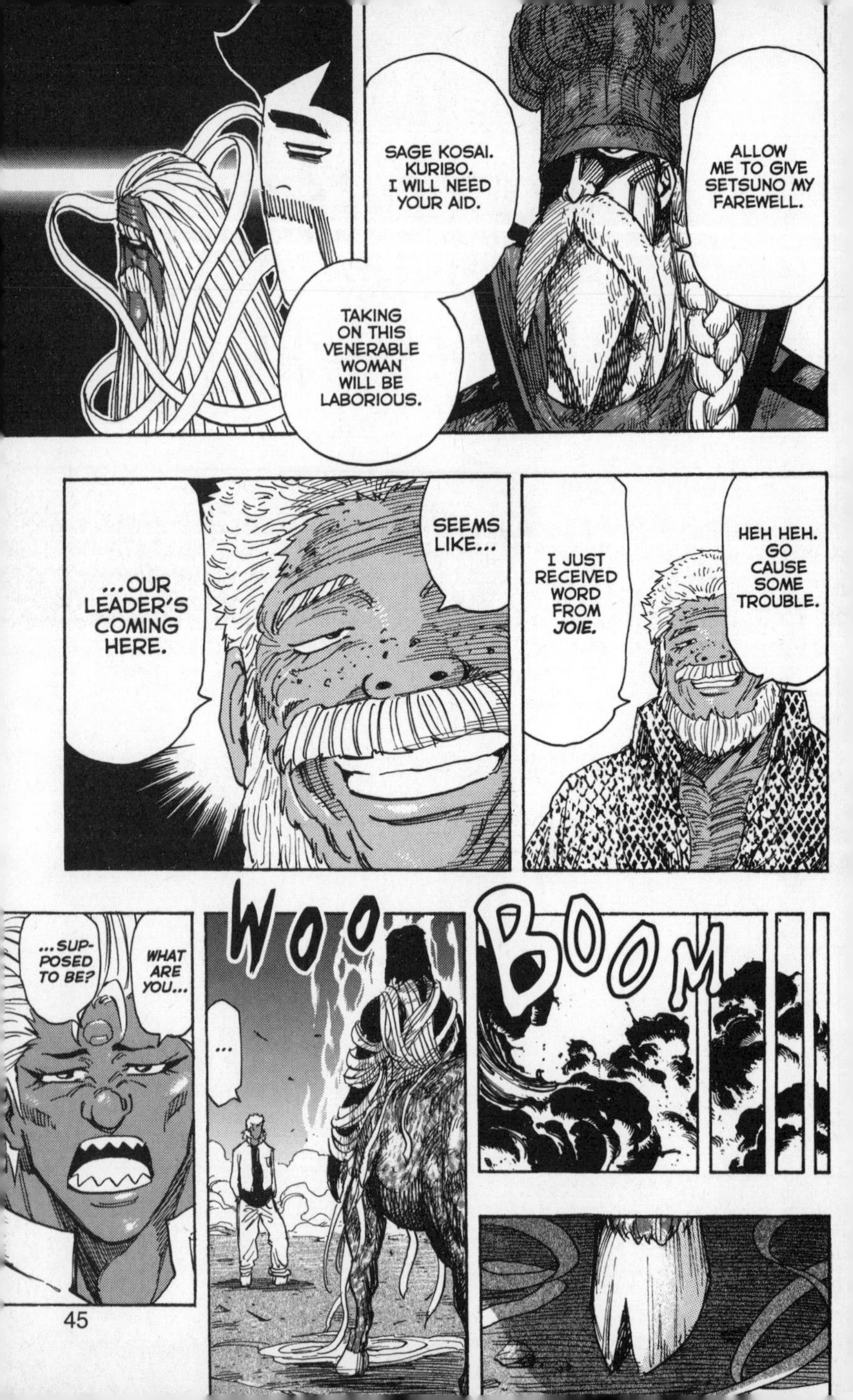
ALLOW ME TO GIVE SETSUNO MY FAREWELL.
SAGE KOSAI. KURIBO. I WILL NEED YOUR AID.
TAKING ON THIS VENERABLE WOMAN WILL BE LABORIOUS.
HEH HEH. GO CAUSE SOME TROUBLE.
I JUST RECEIVED WORD FROM *JOIE.*
SEEMS LIKE...
...OUR LEADER'S COMING HERE.
WOO
BOOM
...
WHAT ARE YOU...
...SUP-POSED TO BE?

TORIKO

GOURMET CHECKLIST

Vol. 252

ELECTRIC BANANA
(FRUIT)

CAPTURE LEVEL: 10
HABITAT: RAIN FORESTS
LENGTH: 40 CM
HEIGHT: ---
WEIGHT: 1.5 KG
PRICE: 500 YEN PER BANANA

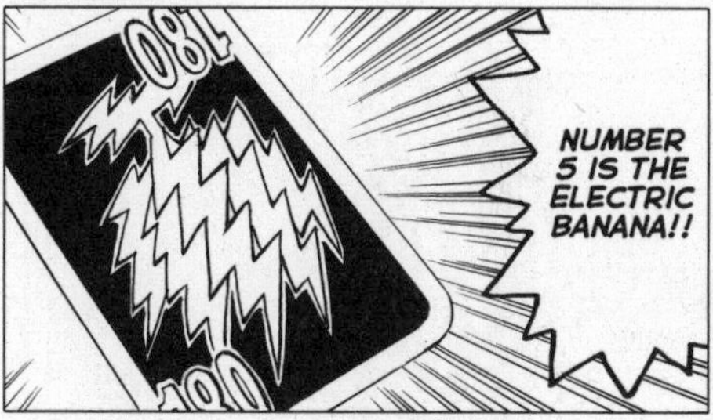
NUMBER 5 IS THE ELECTRIC BANANA!!

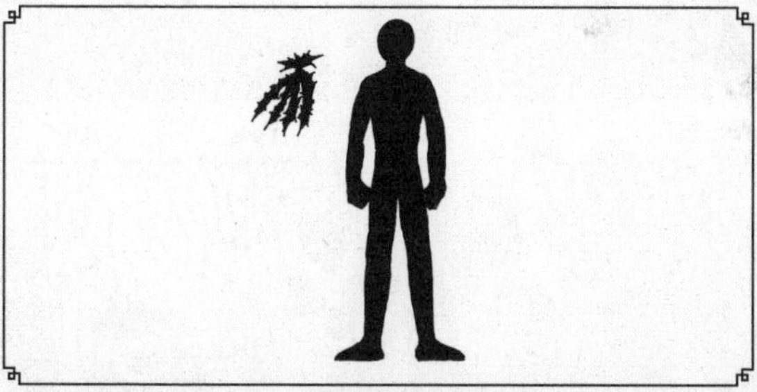

SCALE

A NARCOTIC FOOD FROM A BANANA TREE NATIVE TO THE TROPICS. ONE BITE AND A NUMBING ELECTRIC SHOCK WILL COURSE THROUGH YOUR BODY. IT ALSO SENDS A DIRECT SHOCK TO THE CENTRAL NERVOUS SYSTEM, PRODUCING A EUPHORIC FEELING OF BLISS. HOWEVER, THE DEPENDENCY IT CULTIVATES IN A PERSON IS ON A LEVEL FAR ABOVE NICOTINE AND ALCOHOL. IF A USER FAILS TO EAT A BANANA AT LEAST ONCE A DAY, THEY'LL BE HIT WITH WITHDRAWAL SYMPTOMS THAT WILL KILL THEM IF UNTREATED LONG ENOUGH. NATURALLY, SUCH A TERRIBLE NARCOTIC FOOD IS BANNED FROM THE MARKET AND CONSIDERED ILLEGAL.

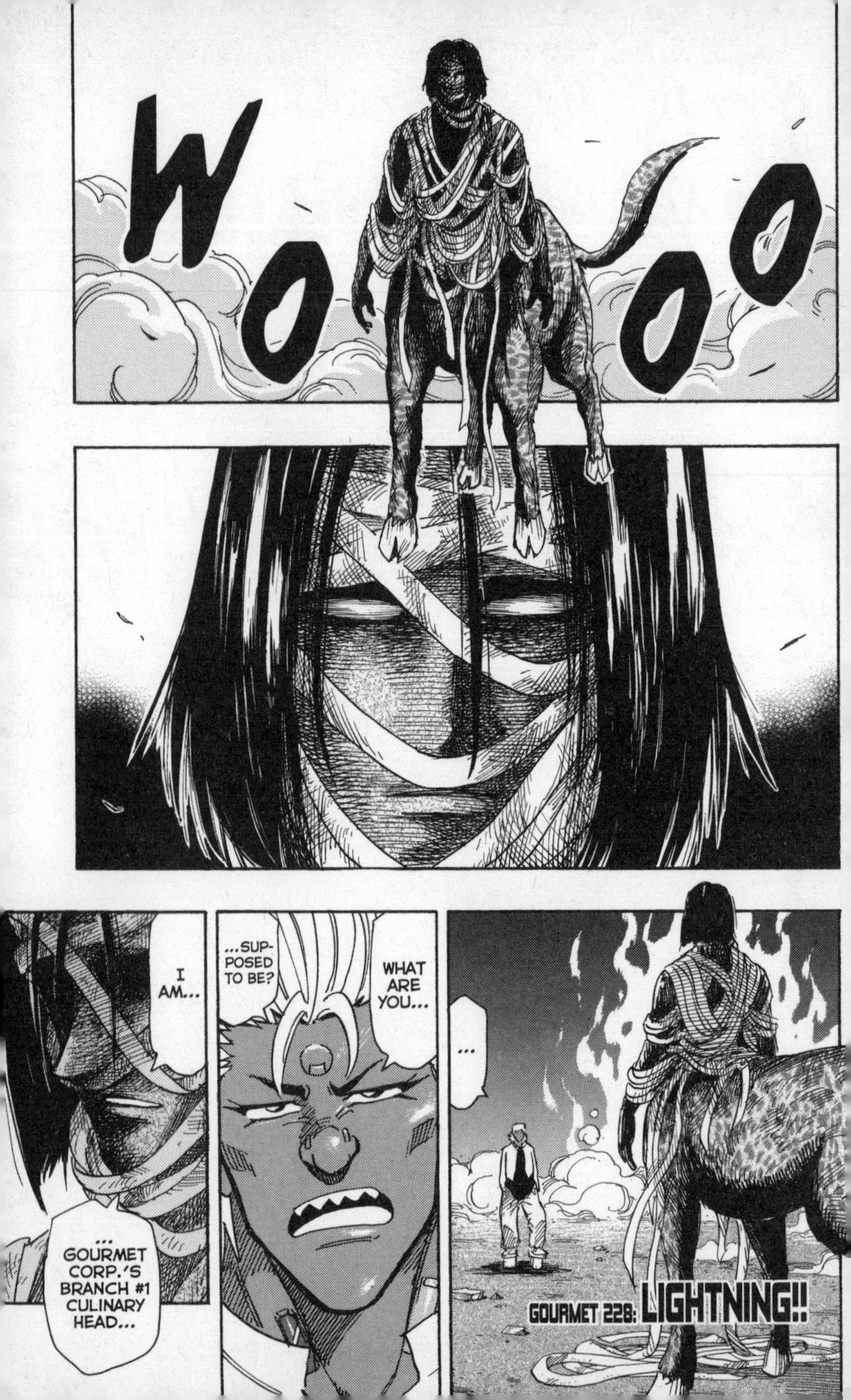
WOOOOO
...
GOURMET 228: LIGHTNING!!
WHAT ARE YOU...
...SUPPOSED TO BE?
I AM...
...GOURMET CORP.'S BRANCH #1 CULINARY HEAD...

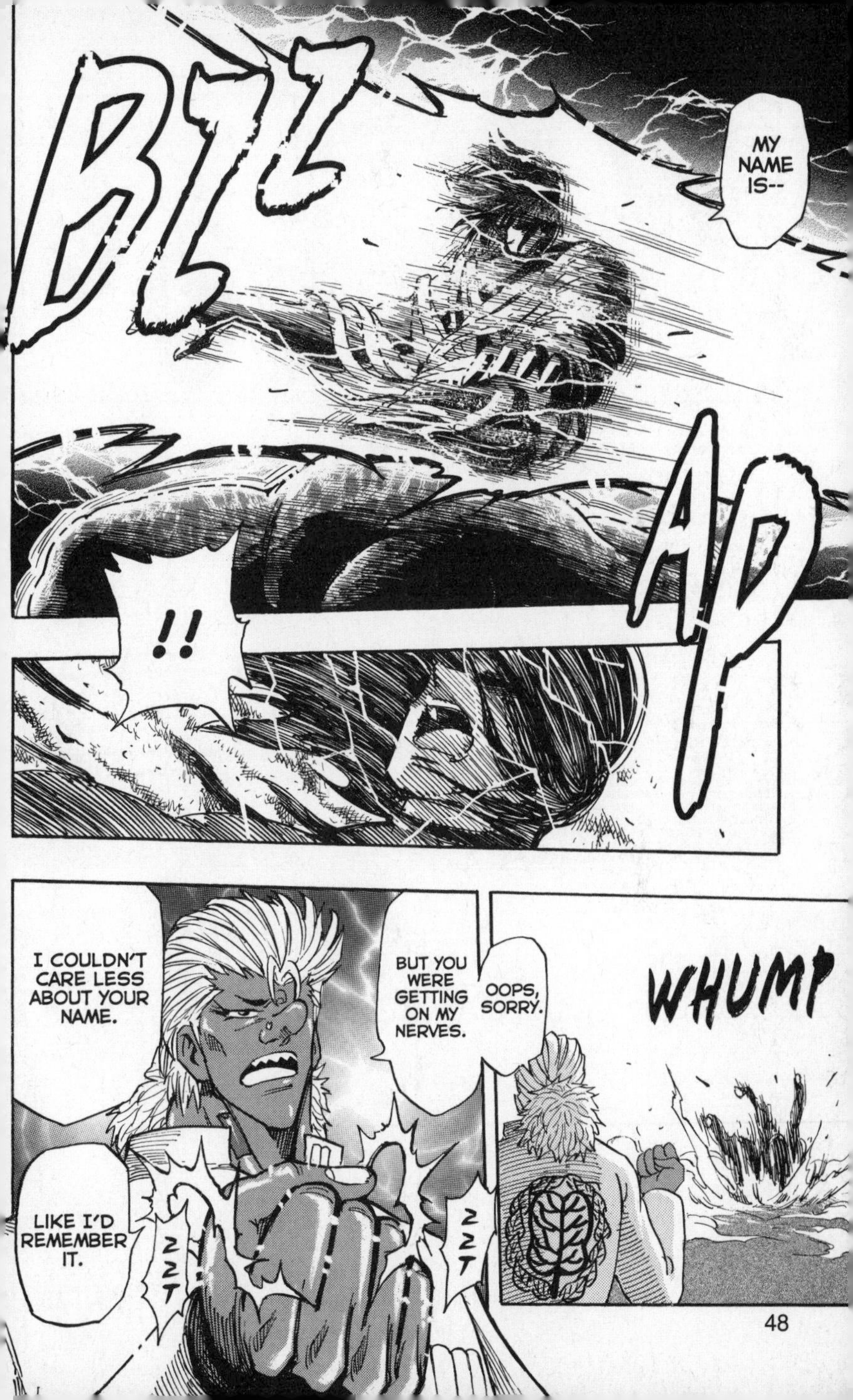
MY NAME IS--
BZZAP
!!
WHUMP
OOPS, SORRY.
BUT YOU WERE GETTING ON MY NERVES.
I COULDN'T CARE LESS ABOUT YOUR NAME.
ZZT
ZZT
LIKE I'D REMEMBER IT.

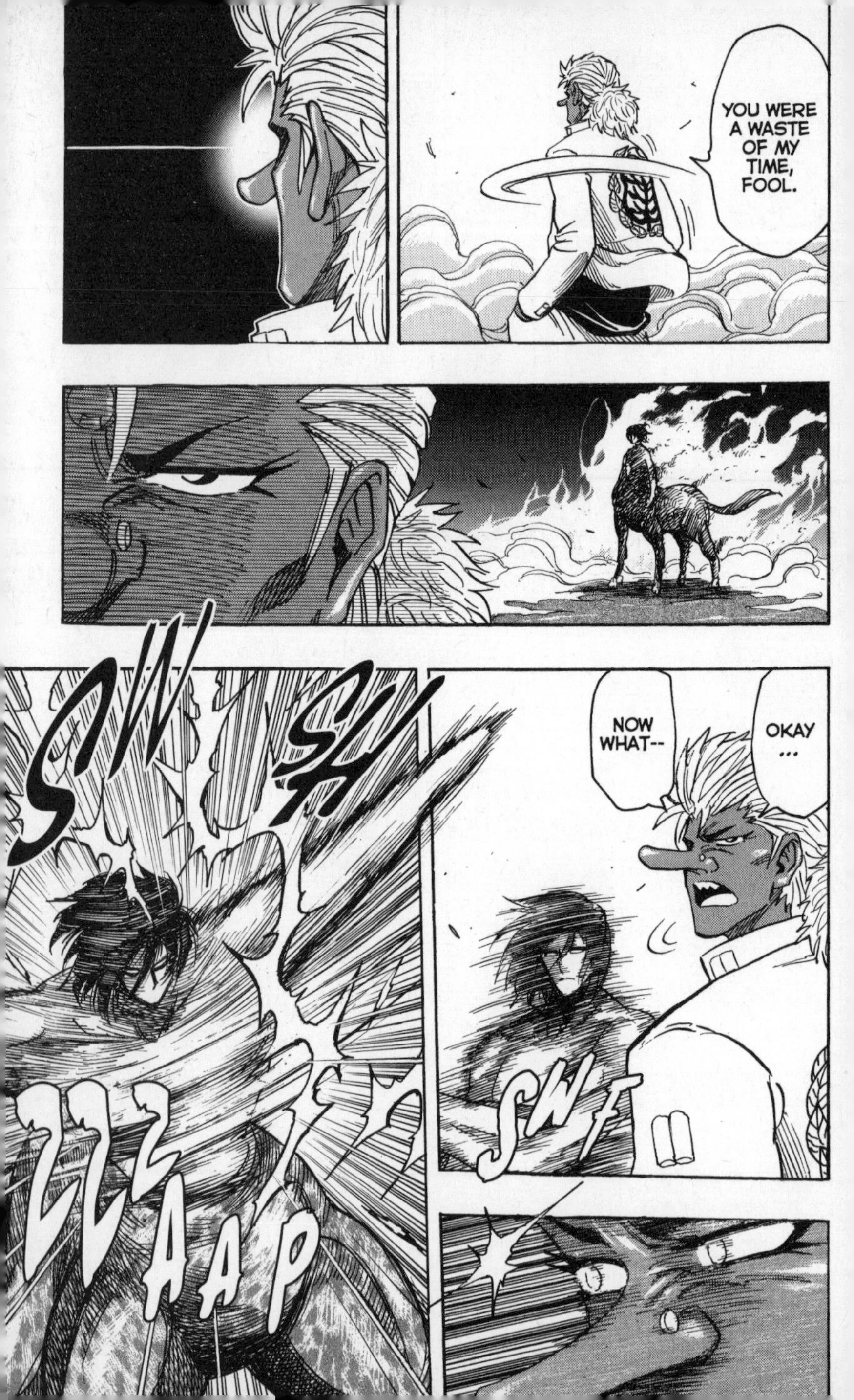
YOU WERE A WASTE OF MY TIME, FOOL.
OKAY ...
NOW WHAT--
SWF
SWISH

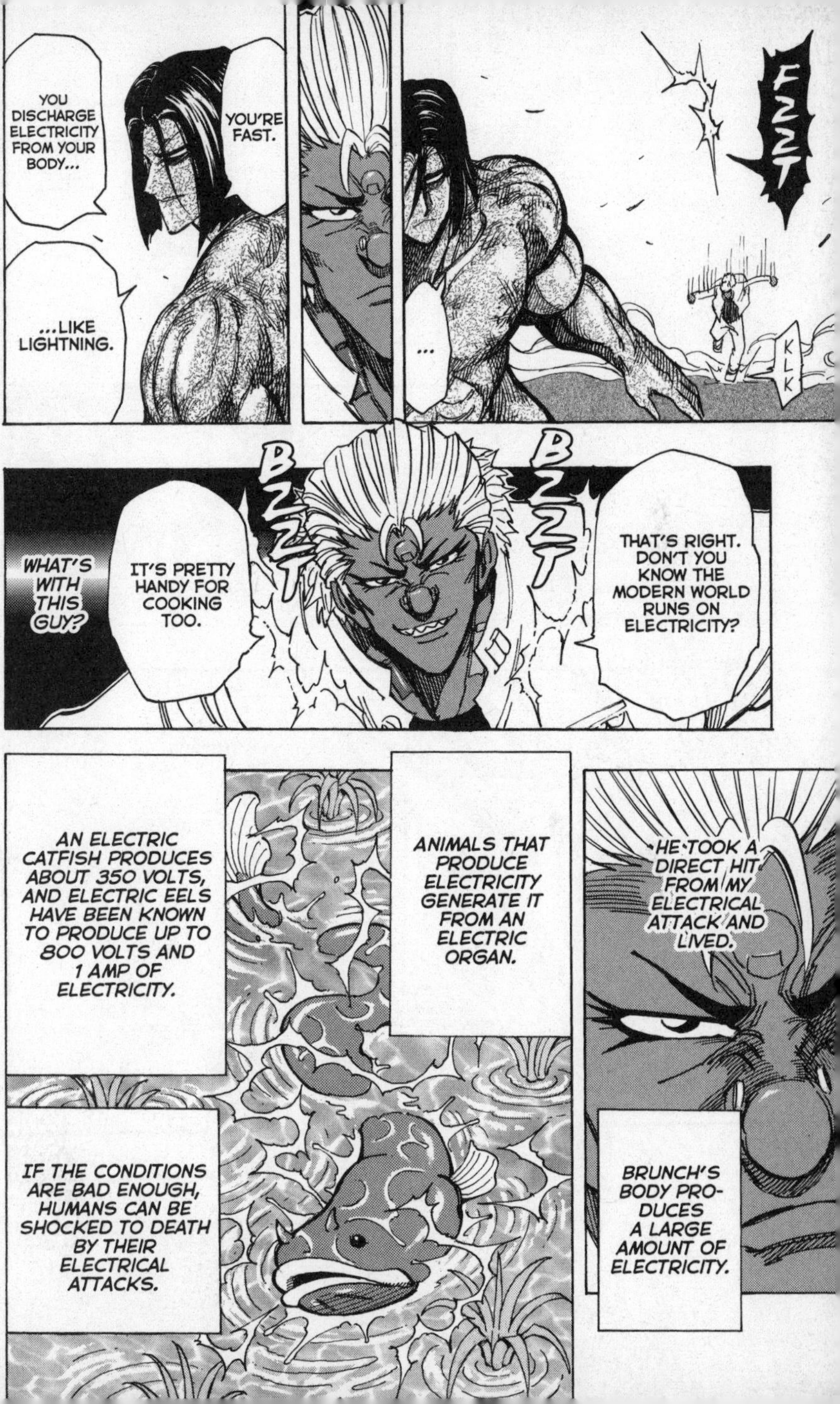
FZZT
KLK
...
YOU'RE FAST.
YOU DISCHARGE ELECTRICITY FROM YOUR BODY...
...LIKE LIGHTNING.
BZZT
THAT'S RIGHT. DON'T YOU KNOW THE MODERN WORLD RUNS ON ELECTRICITY?
BZZT
IT'S PRETTY HANDY FOR COOKING TOO.
WHAT'S WITH THIS GUY?
HE TOOK A DIRECT HIT FROM MY ELECTRICAL ATTACK AND LIVED.
BRUNCH'S BODY PRO-DUCES A LARGE AMOUNT OF ELECTRICITY.
ANIMALS THAT PRODUCE ELECTRICITY GENERATE IT FROM AN ELECTRIC ORGAN.
AN ELECTRIC CATFISH PRODUCES ABOUT 350 VOLTS, AND ELECTRIC EELS HAVE BEEN KNOWN TO PRODUCE UP TO 800 VOLTS AND 1 AMP OF ELECTRICITY.
IF THE CONDITIONS ARE BAD ENOUGH, HUMANS CAN BE SHOCKED TO DEATH BY THEIR ELECTRICAL ATTACKS.

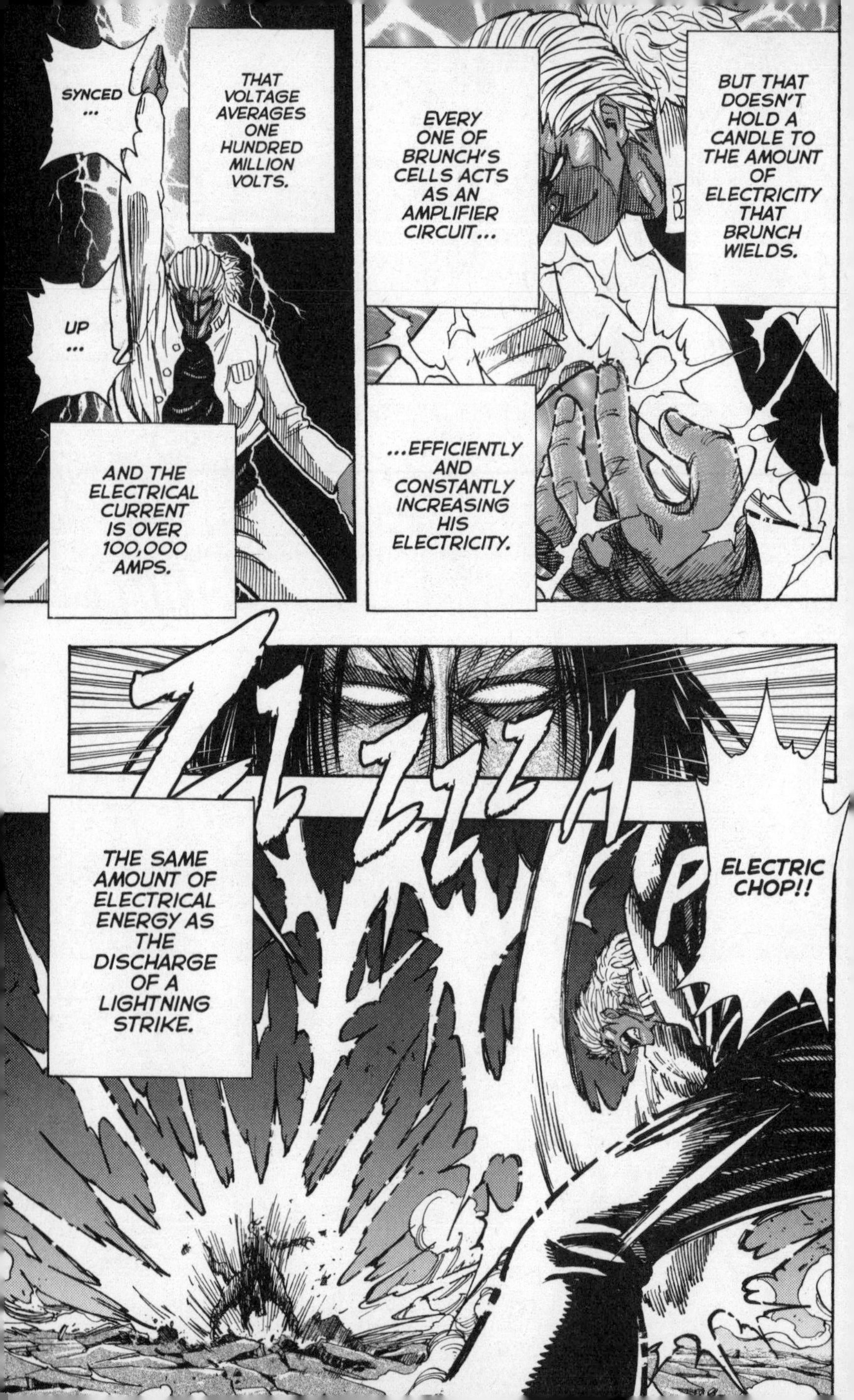
BUT THAT DOESN'T HOLD A CANDLE TO THE AMOUNT OF ELECTRICITY THAT BRUNCH WIELDS.
EVERY ONE OF BRUNCH'S CELLS ACTS AS AN AMPLIFIER CIRCUIT...
...EFFICIENTLY AND CONSTANTLY INCREASING HIS ELECTRICITY.
SYNCED...
THAT VOLTAGE AVERAGES ONE HUNDRED MILLION VOLTS.
UP...
AND THE ELECTRICAL CURRENT IS OVER 100,000 AMPS.
ZZZZAP
ELECTRIC CHOP!!
THE SAME AMOUNT OF ELECTRICAL ENERGY AS THE DISCHARGE OF A LIGHTNING STRIKE.

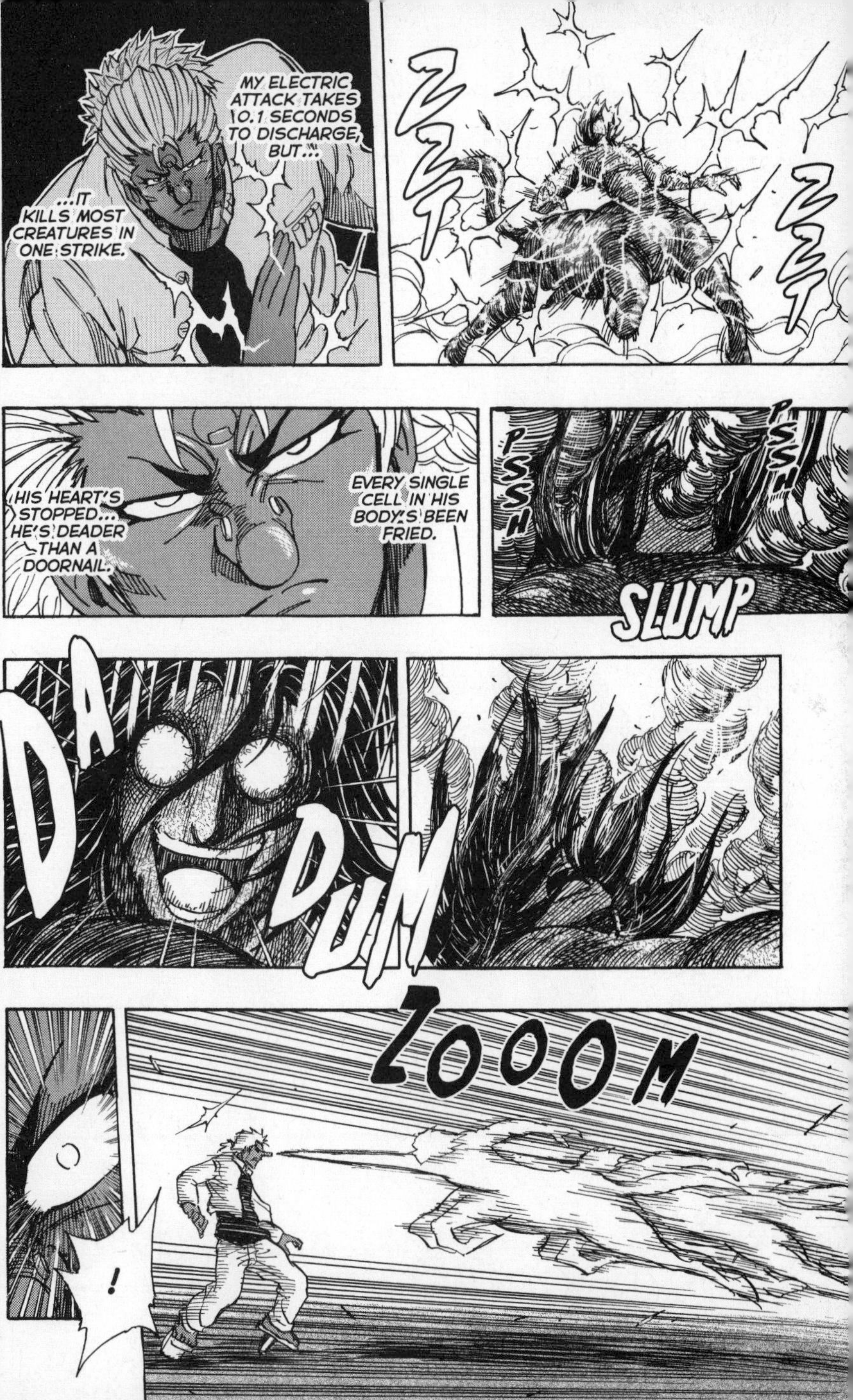
ZZZT
ZZZT
MY ELECTRIC ATTACK TAKES 0.1 SECONDS TO DISCHARGE, BUT...
...IT KILLS MOST CREATURES IN ONE STRIKE.
PSSH
PSSH
SLUMP
EVERY SINGLE CELL IN HIS BODY'S BEEN FRIED.
HIS HEART'S STOPPED... HE'S DEADER THAN A DOORNAIL.
DA DUM
ZOOOM
!

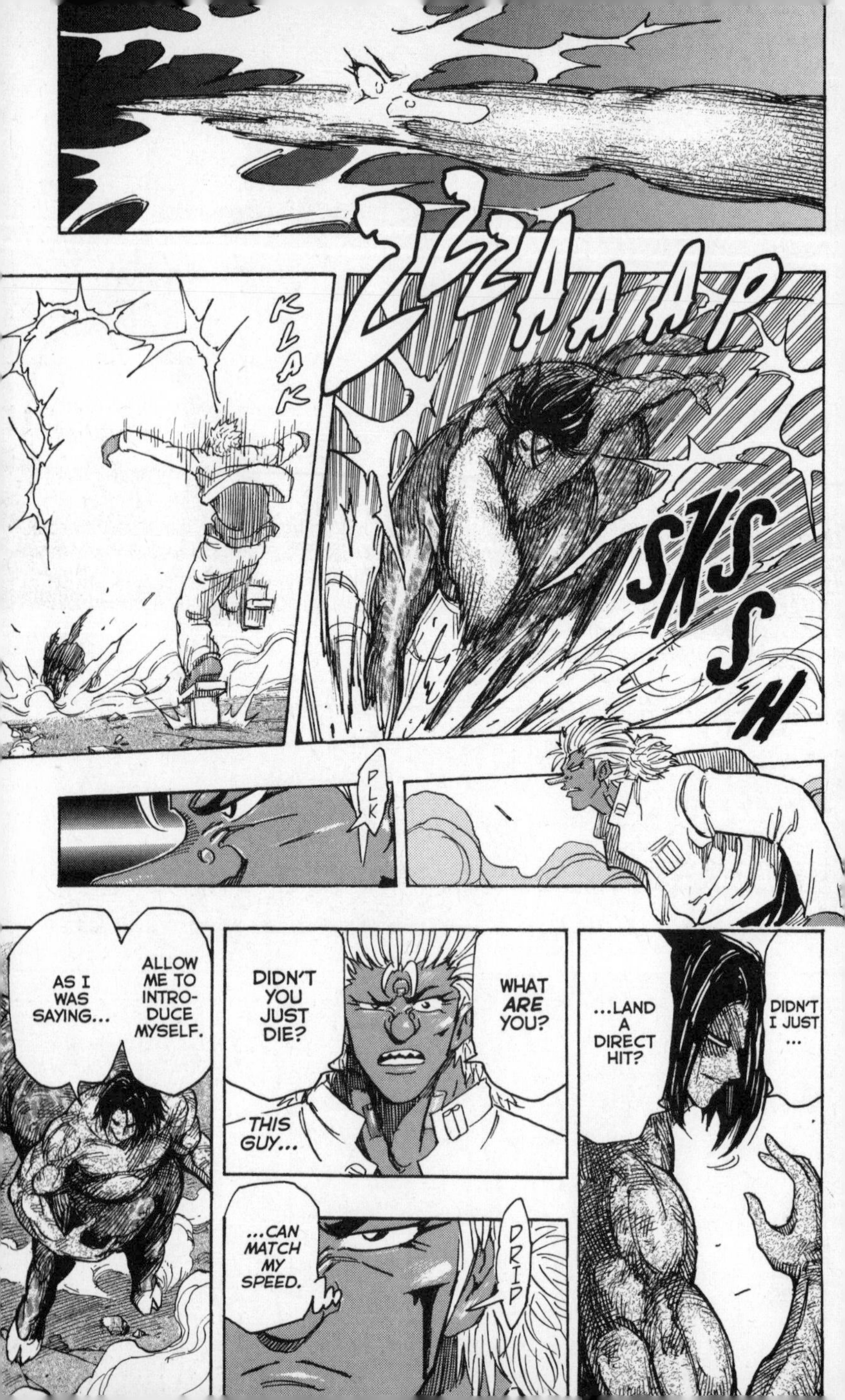
ZZZAAAP
SSSH
KLAK
PLK
DIDN'T I JUST ...
...LAND A DIRECT HIT?
WHAT ARE YOU?
DIDN'T YOU JUST DIE?
THIS GUY...
DRIP
...CAN MATCH MY SPEED.
ALLOW ME TO INTRO-DUCE MYSELF.
AS I WAS SAYING...

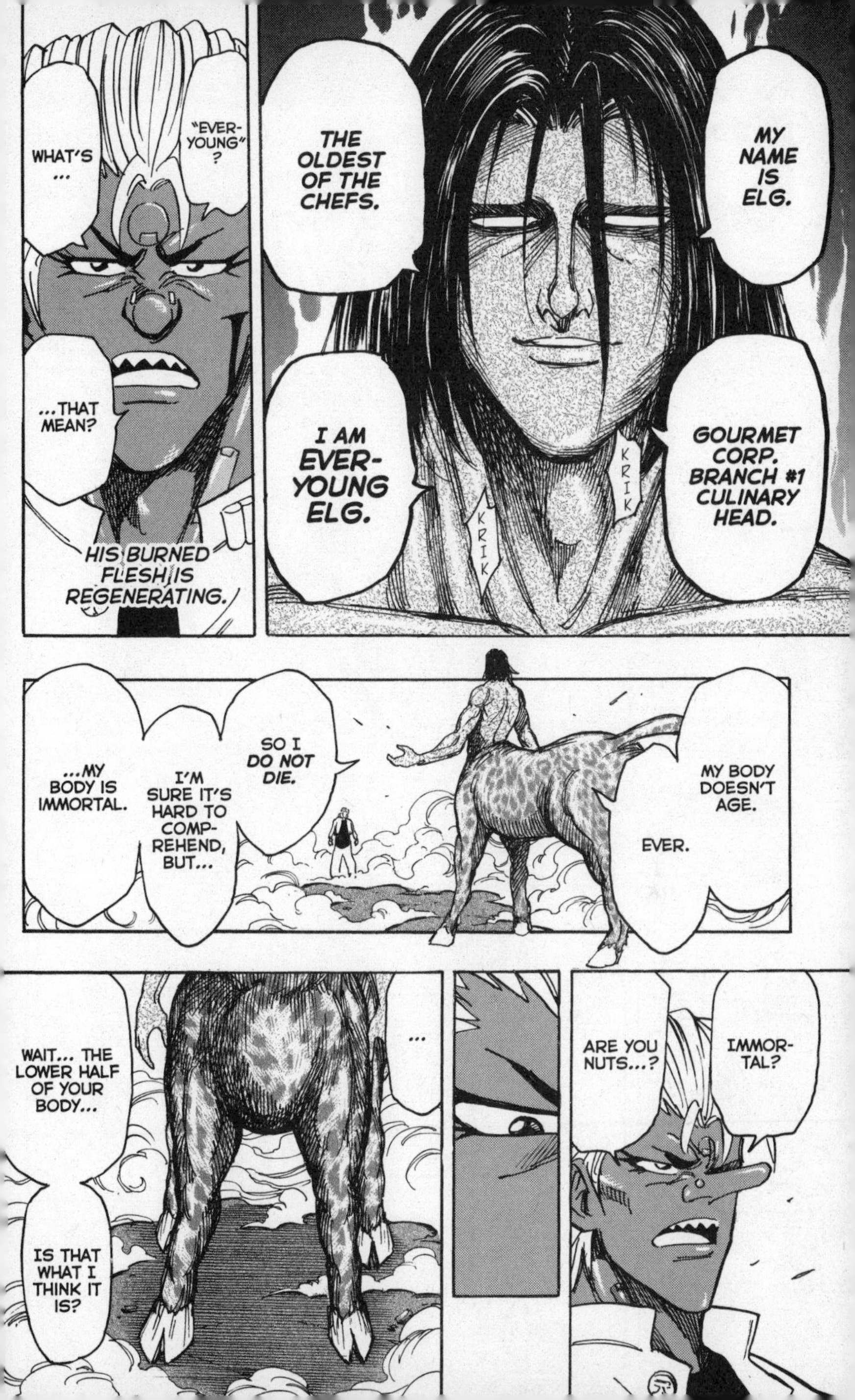
MY NAME IS ELG.
GOURMET CORP. BRANCH #1 CULINARY HEAD.
THE OLDEST OF THE CHEFS.
I AM EVER-YOUNG ELG.
KRIK
KRIK
"EVER-YOUNG"?
WHAT'S ...
...THAT MEAN?
HIS BURNED FLESH IS REGENERATING.
MY BODY DOESN'T AGE.
EVER.
SO I DO NOT DIE.
I'M SURE IT'S HARD TO COMPREHEND, BUT...
...MY BODY IS IMMORTAL.
IMMORTAL?
ARE YOU NUTS...?
...
WAIT... THE LOWER HALF OF YOUR BODY...
IS THAT WHAT I THINK IT IS?

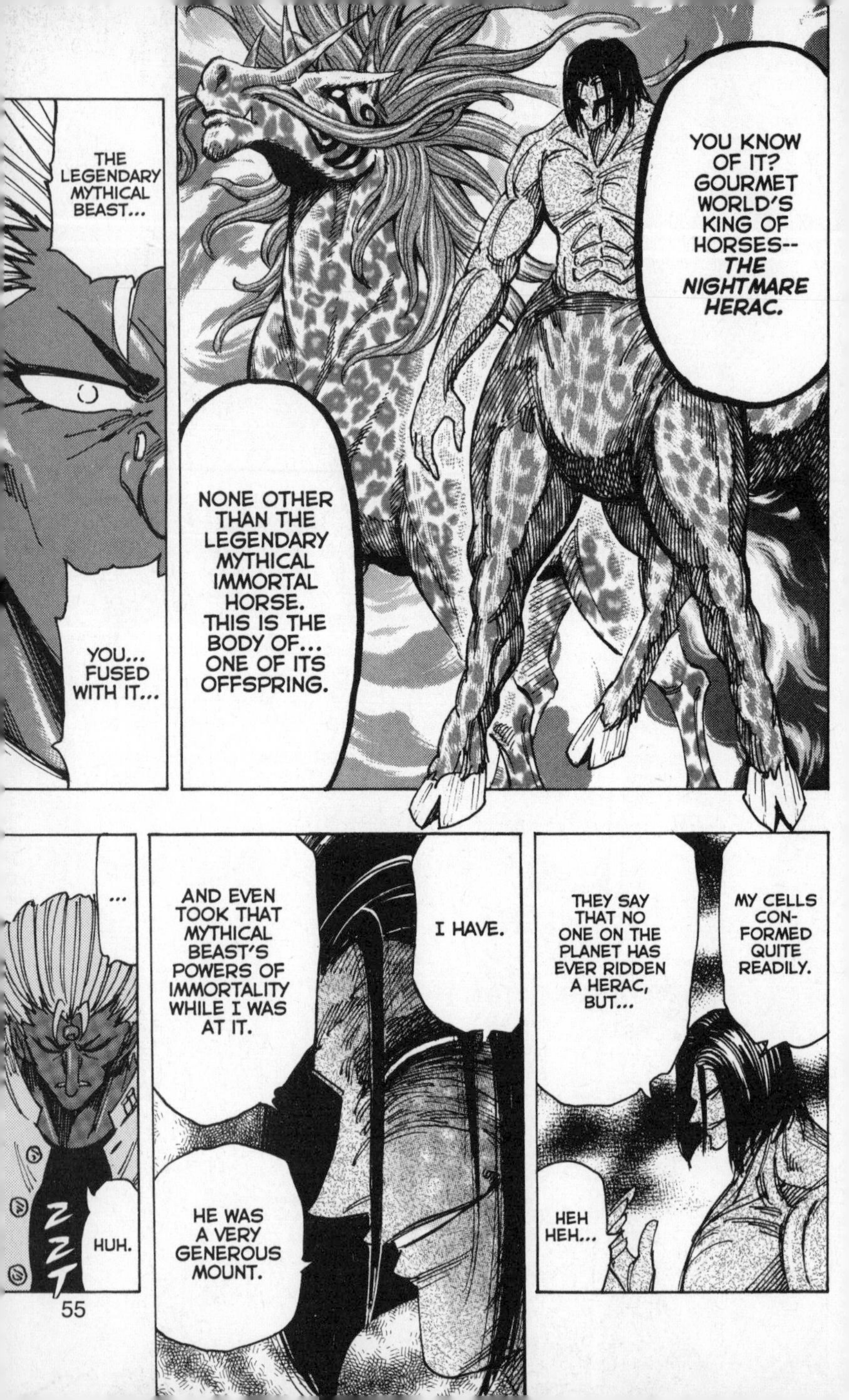
YOU KNOW OF IT? GOURMET WORLD'S KING OF HORSES-- *THE NIGHTMARE HERAC.*
NONE OTHER THAN THE LEGENDARY MYTHICAL IMMORTAL HORSE. THIS IS THE BODY OF... ONE OF ITS OFFSPRING.
THE LEGENDARY MYTHICAL BEAST...
YOU... FUSED WITH IT...
MY CELLS CON-FORMED QUITE READILY.
THEY SAY THAT NO ONE ON THE PLANET HAS EVER RIDDEN A HERAC, BUT...
HEH HEH...
I HAVE.
AND EVEN TOOK THAT MYTHICAL BEAST'S POWERS OF IMMORTALITY WHILE I WAS AT IT.
HE WAS A VERY GENEROUS MOUNT.
...
ZZT
HUH.

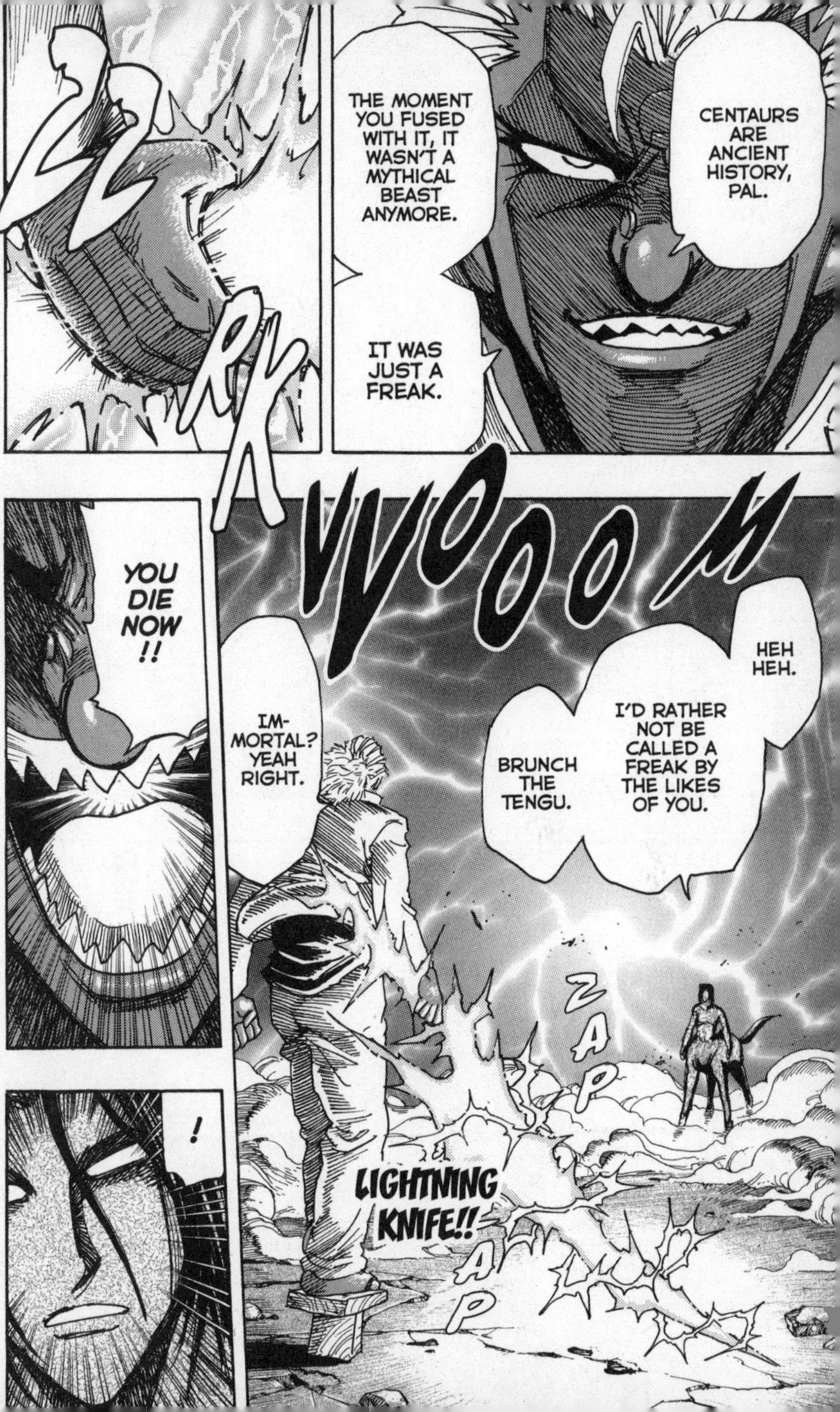
CENTAURS ARE ANCIENT HISTORY, PAL.
THE MOMENT YOU FUSED WITH IT, IT WASN'T A MYTHICAL BEAST ANYMORE.
IT WAS JUST A FREAK.
ZZRK
VVOOOM
HEH HEH.
I'D RATHER NOT BE CALLED A FREAK BY THE LIKES OF YOU.
BRUNCH THE TENGU.
IM-MORTAL? YEAH RIGHT.
YOU DIE NOW!!
ZAP
LIGHTNING KNIFE!!
AP
!

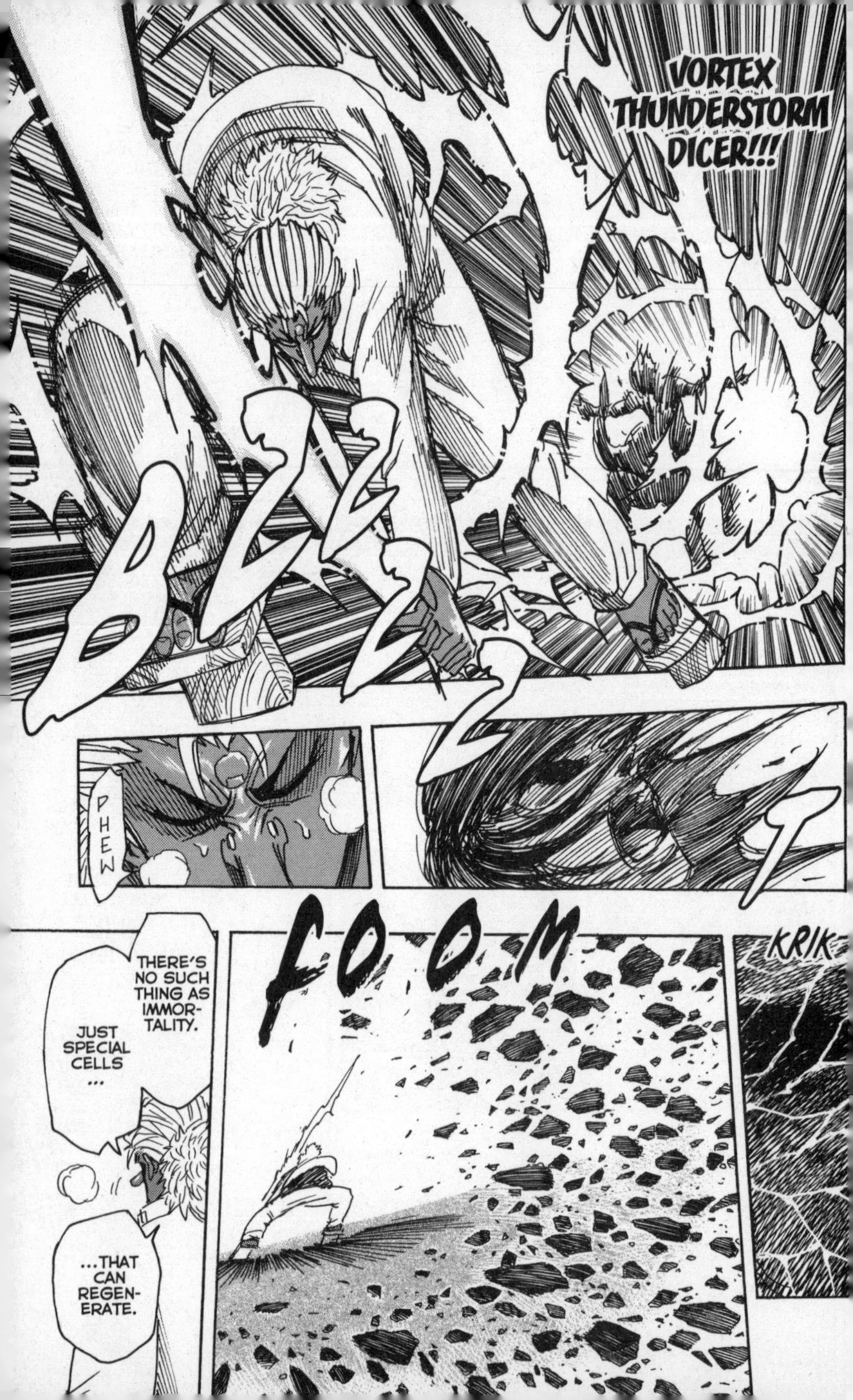
VORTEX THUNDERSTORM DICER!!!
BZZZZT
PHEW
KRIK
FOOM
THERE'S NO SUCH THING AS IMMORTALITY.
JUST SPECIAL CELLS...
...THAT CAN REGENERATE.

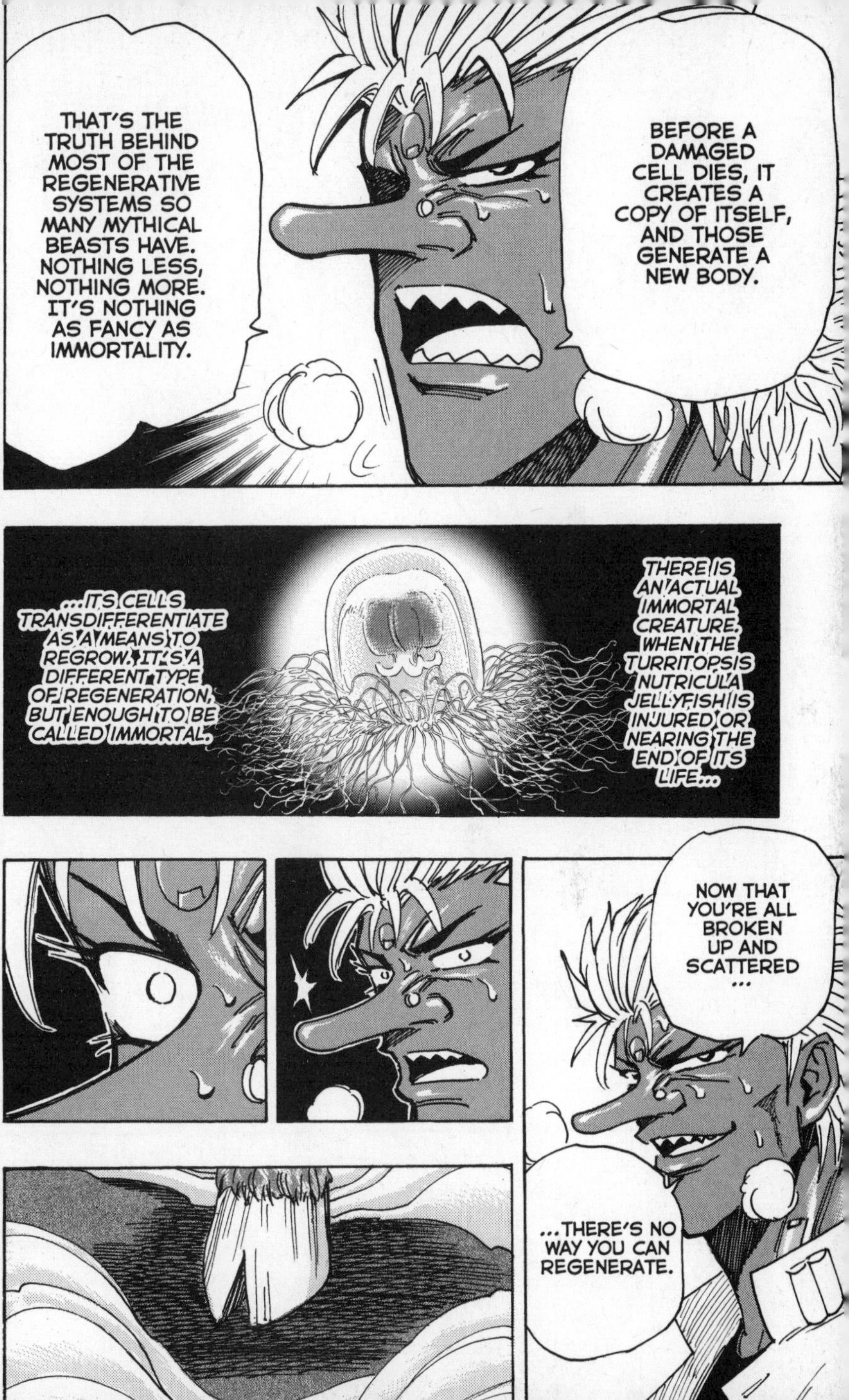
BEFORE A DAMAGED CELL DIES, IT CREATES A COPY OF ITSELF, AND THOSE GENERATE A NEW BODY.
THAT'S THE TRUTH BEHIND MOST OF THE REGENERATIVE SYSTEMS SO MANY MYTHICAL BEASTS HAVE. NOTHING LESS, NOTHING MORE. IT'S NOTHING AS FANCY AS IMMORTALITY.
THERE IS AN ACTUAL IMMORTAL CREATURE. WHEN THE TURRITOPSIS NUTRICULA JELLYFISH IS INJURED OR NEARING THE END OF ITS LIFE...
...ITS CELLS TRANSDIFFERENTIATE AS A MEANS TO REGROW. IT'S A DIFFERENT TYPE OF REGENERATION, BUT ENOUGH TO BE CALLED IMMORTAL.
NOW THAT YOU'RE ALL BROKEN UP AND SCATTERED...
...THERE'S NO WAY YOU CAN REGENERATE.

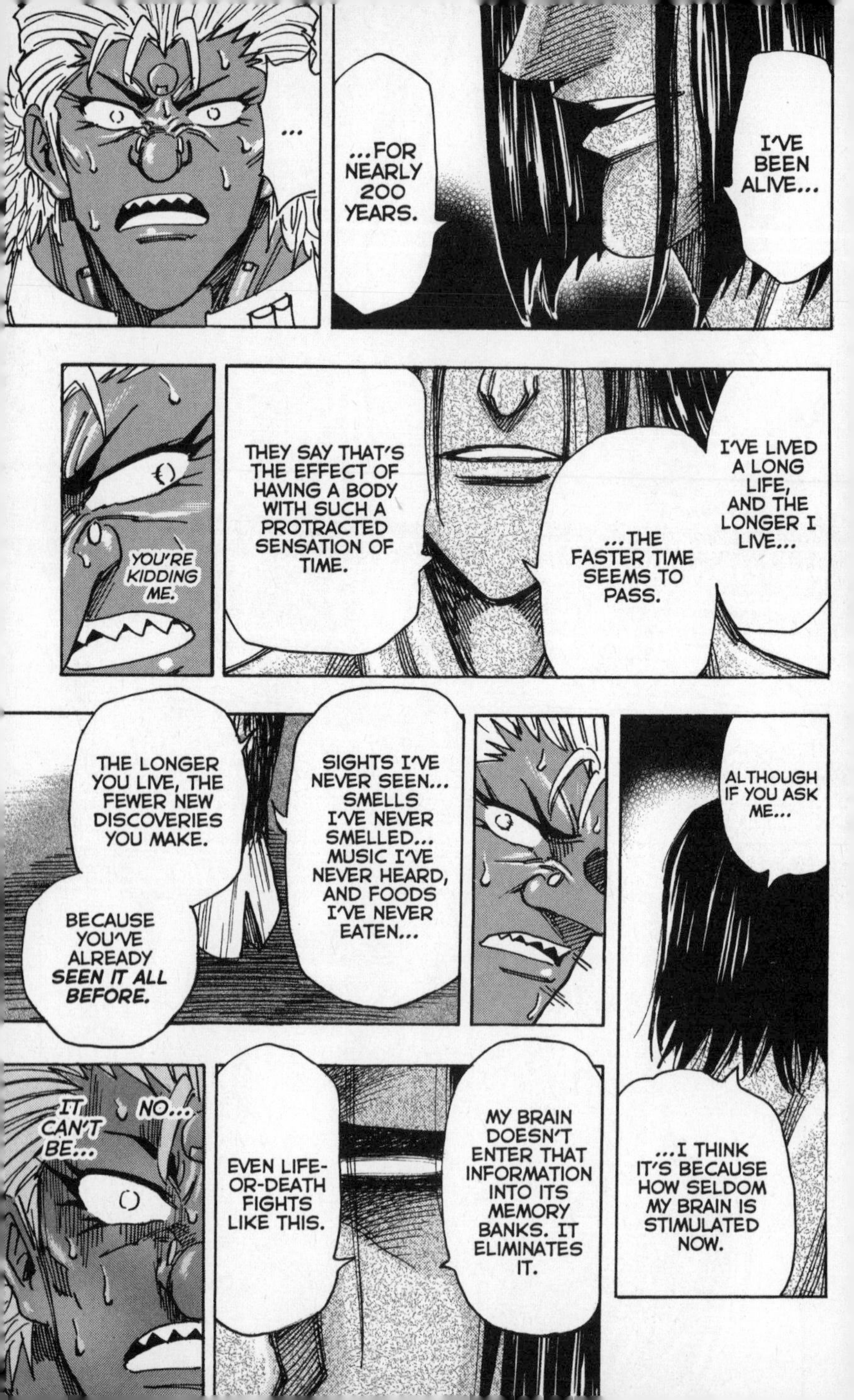
I'VE BEEN ALIVE...
...FOR NEARLY 200 YEARS.
...
I'VE LIVED A LONG LIFE, AND THE LONGER I LIVE...
...THE FASTER TIME SEEMS TO PASS.
THEY SAY THAT'S THE EFFECT OF HAVING A BODY WITH SUCH A PROTRACTED SENSATION OF TIME.
YOU'RE KIDDING ME.
ALTHOUGH IF YOU ASK ME...
...I THINK IT'S BECAUSE HOW SELDOM MY BRAIN IS STIMULATED NOW.
SIGHTS I'VE NEVER SEEN... SMELLS I'VE NEVER SMELLED... MUSIC I'VE NEVER HEARD, AND FOODS I'VE NEVER EATEN...
THE LONGER YOU LIVE, THE FEWER NEW DISCOVERIES YOU MAKE.
BECAUSE YOU'VE ALREADY *SEEN IT ALL BEFORE.*
MY BRAIN DOESN'T ENTER THAT INFORMATION INTO ITS MEMORY BANKS. IT ELIMINATES IT.
EVEN LIFE-OR-DEATH FIGHTS LIKE THIS.
NO...
IT CAN'T BE...

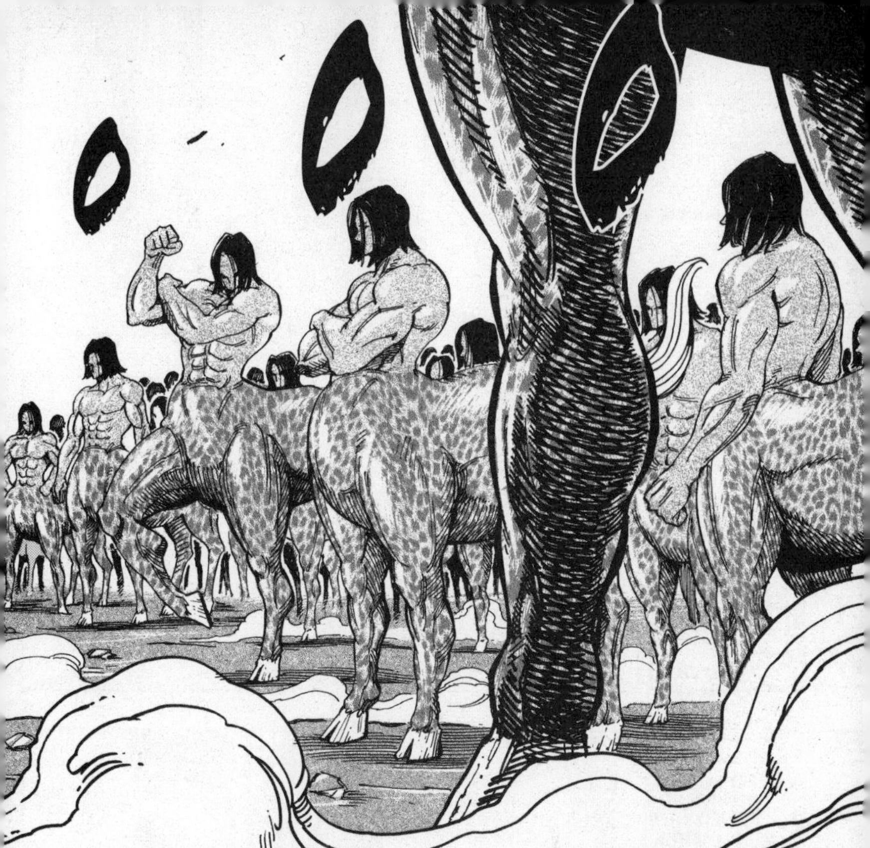

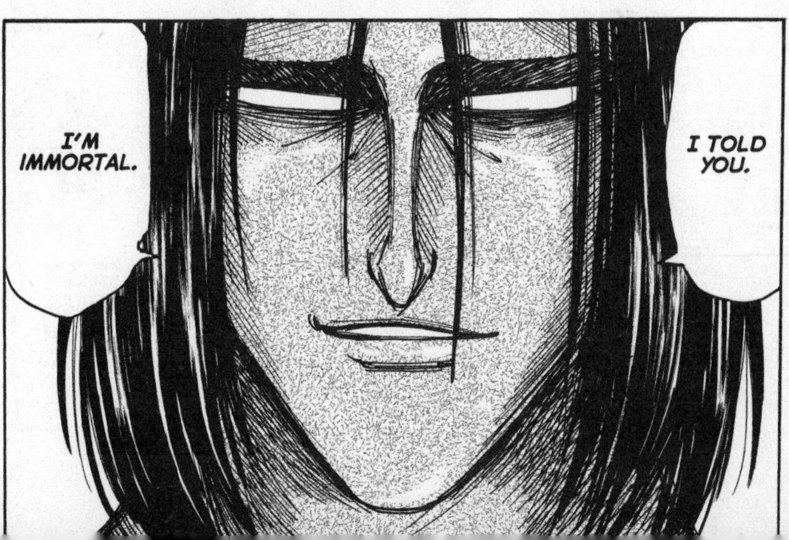
I TOLD YOU.
I'M IMMORTAL.

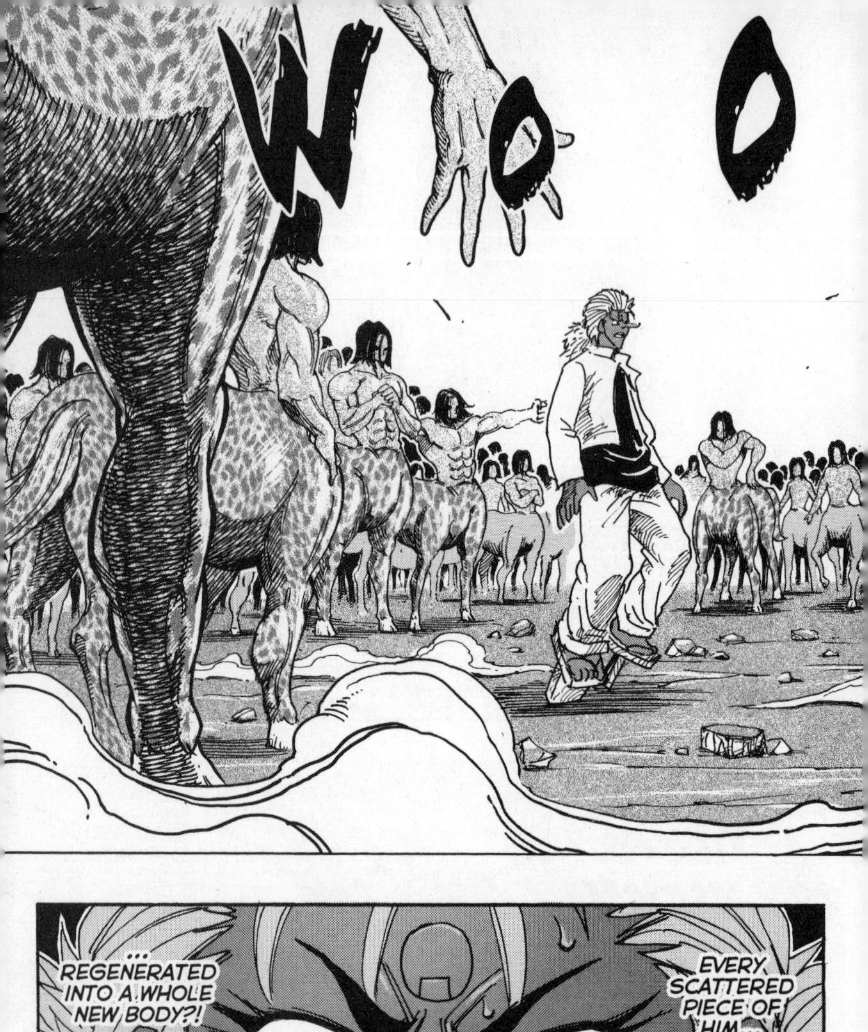
WOO
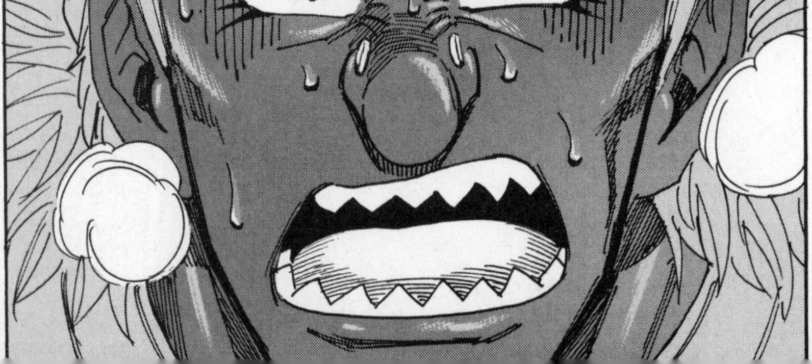
EVERY SCATTERED PIECE OF HIM...
...REGENERATED INTO A WHOLE NEW BODY?!

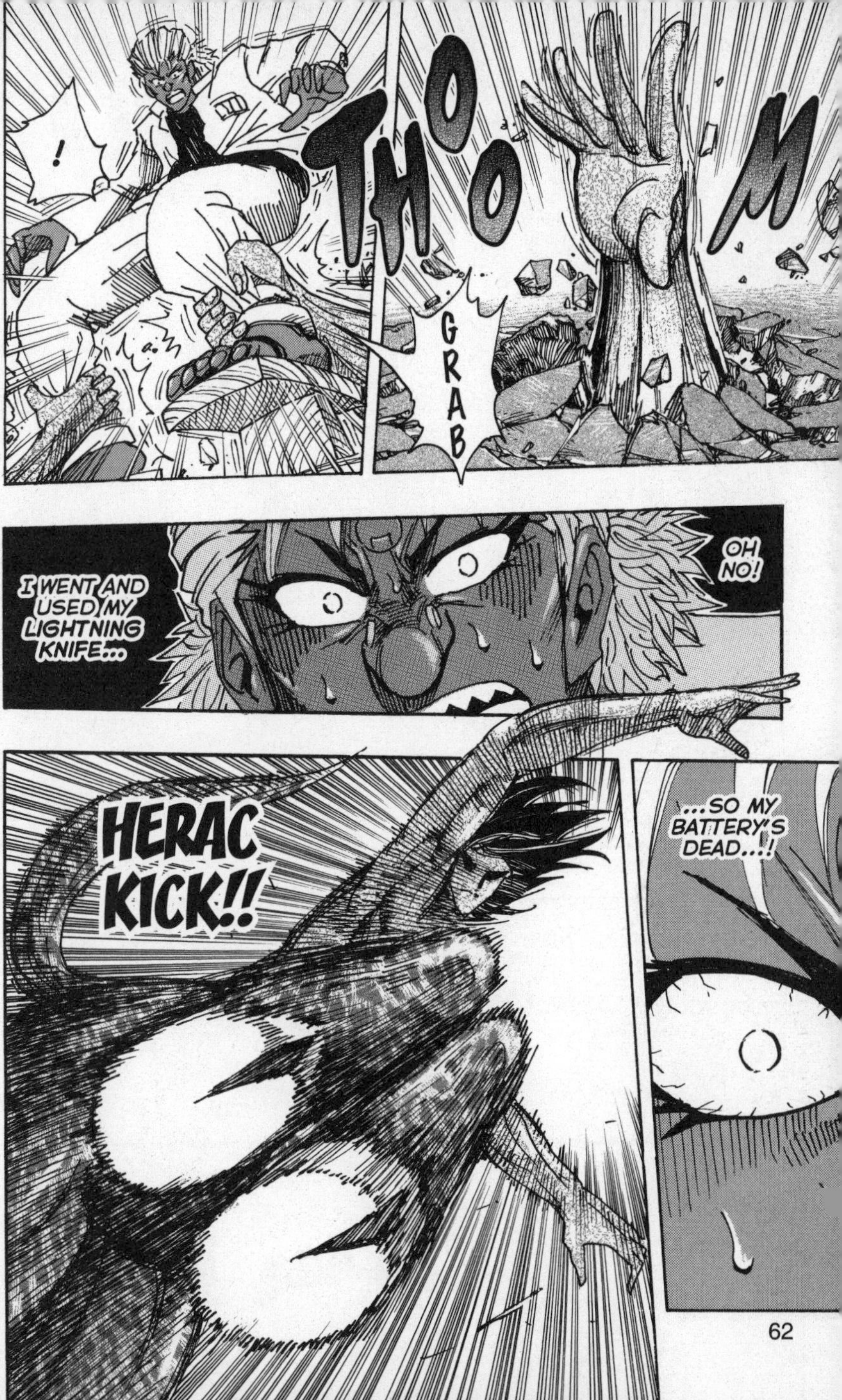
THOOM
GRAB
!
OH NO!
I WENT AND USED MY LIGHTNING KNIFE...
...SO MY BATTERY'S DEAD...!
HERAC KICK!!

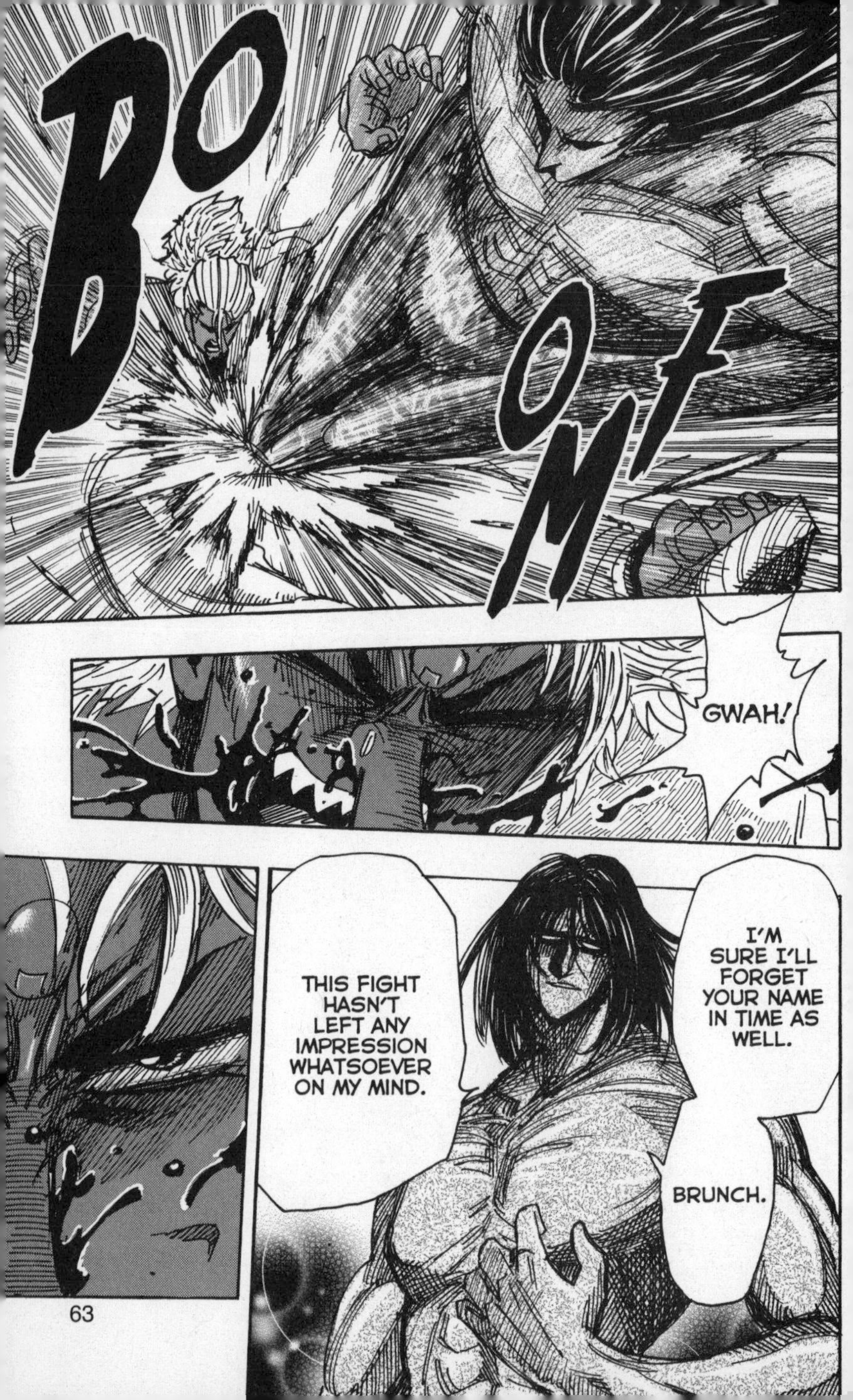
BOOM
GWAH!
THIS FIGHT HASN'T LEFT ANY IMPRESSION WHATSOEVER ON MY MIND.
I'M SURE I'LL FORGET YOUR NAME IN TIME AS WELL.
BRUNCH.

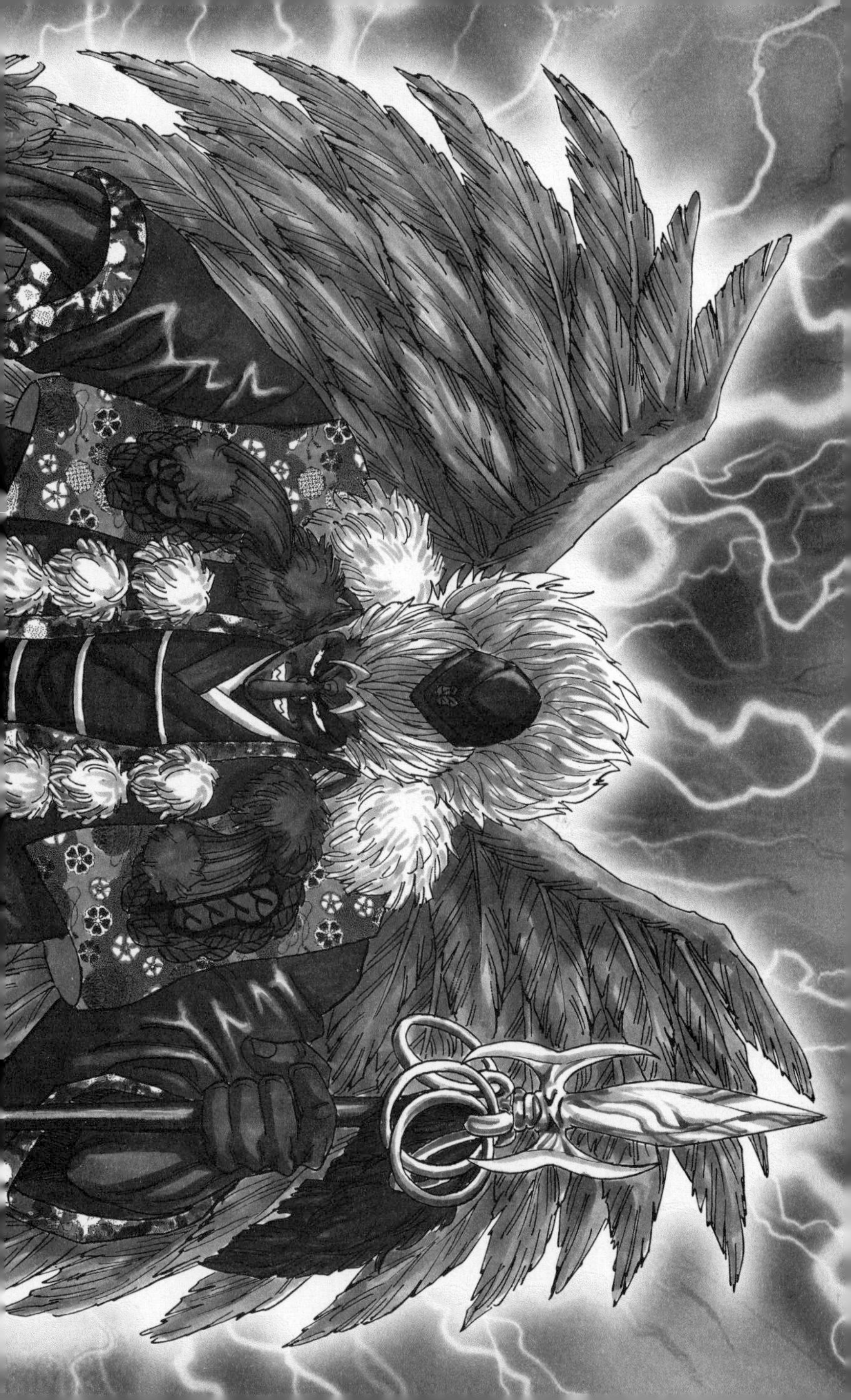

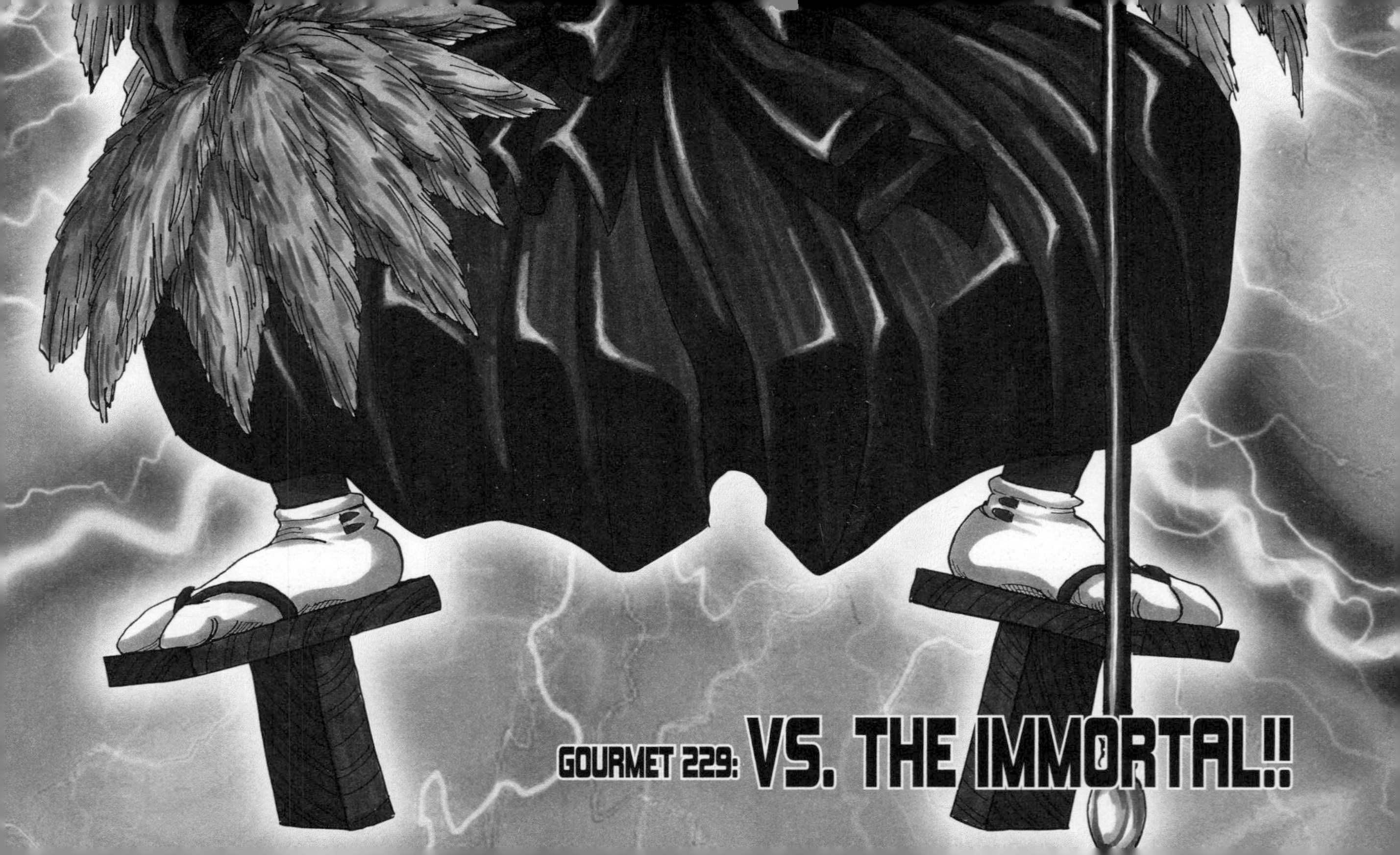
GOURMET 229: VS. THE IMMORTAL!!

TORIKO

GOURMET CHECKLIST

Vol. 253

ROCK POTATO
(CRUSTACEAN)

CAPTURE LEVEL: 10

HABITAT: VOLCANIC REGIONS

LENGTH: 15 CM

HEIGHT: ---

WEIGHT: 23 KG

PRICE: 2,000 YEN PER POTATO

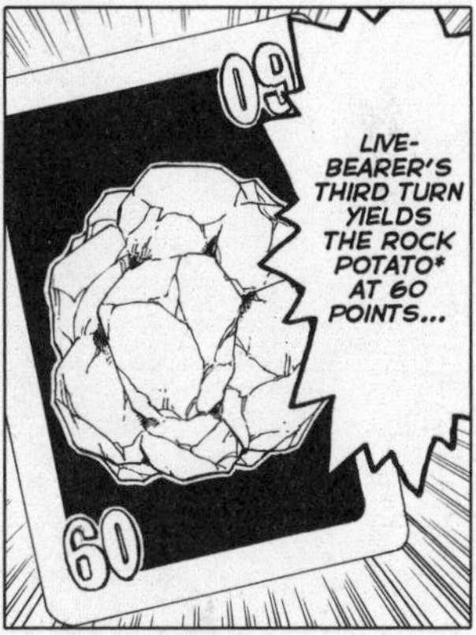
60
60
LIVE-BEARER'S THIRD TURN YIELDS THE ROCK POTATO* AT 60 POINTS...

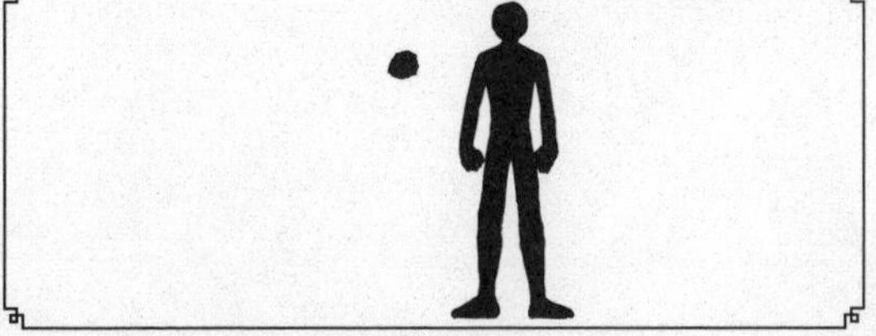

SCALE

A POTATO THAT GROWS DEEP INSIDE THE MAGMA OF ACTIVE VOLCANOES. IT CATAPULTS OUT WHEN THE VOLCANO ERUPTS, AND THE MAGMA ON ITS SURFACE SOLIDIFIES INTO TOUGH ROCK. WHEN SOAKED IN MAGMA AGAIN FOR TEN MINUTES, THE SHELL MELTS OFF. ROCK POTATO POSSESSES A UNIQUE STARCH THAT MATURES AT APPROXIMATELY 1,400 °C, YIELDING A FLAVOR THAT IS TOP QUALITY FOR THE CAPTURE LEVEL.

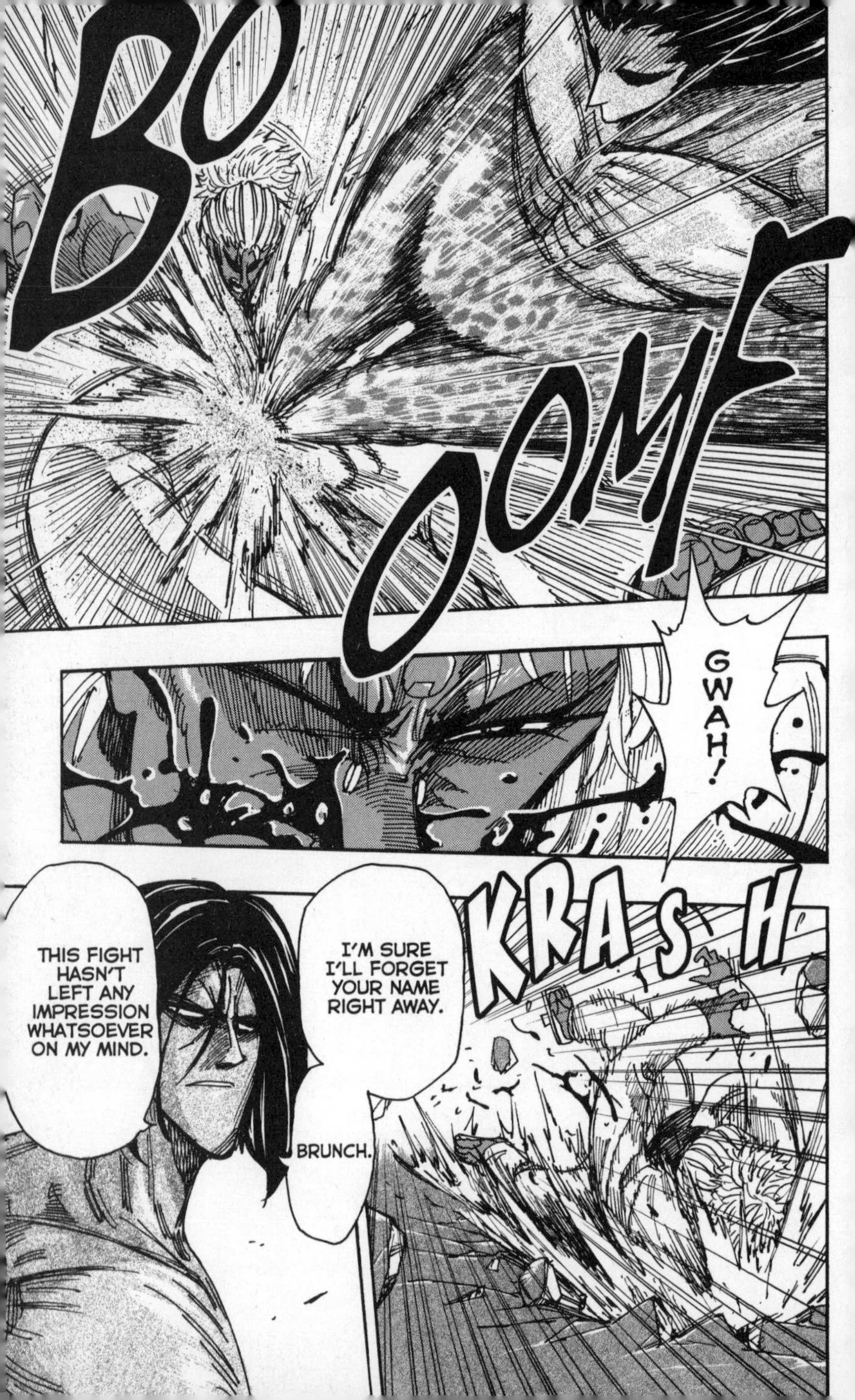
BOOOMF
GWAH!
KRASH
I'M SURE I'LL FORGET YOUR NAME RIGHT AWAY.
BRUNCH.
THIS FIGHT HASN'T LEFT ANY IMPRESSION WHATSOEVER ON MY MIND.

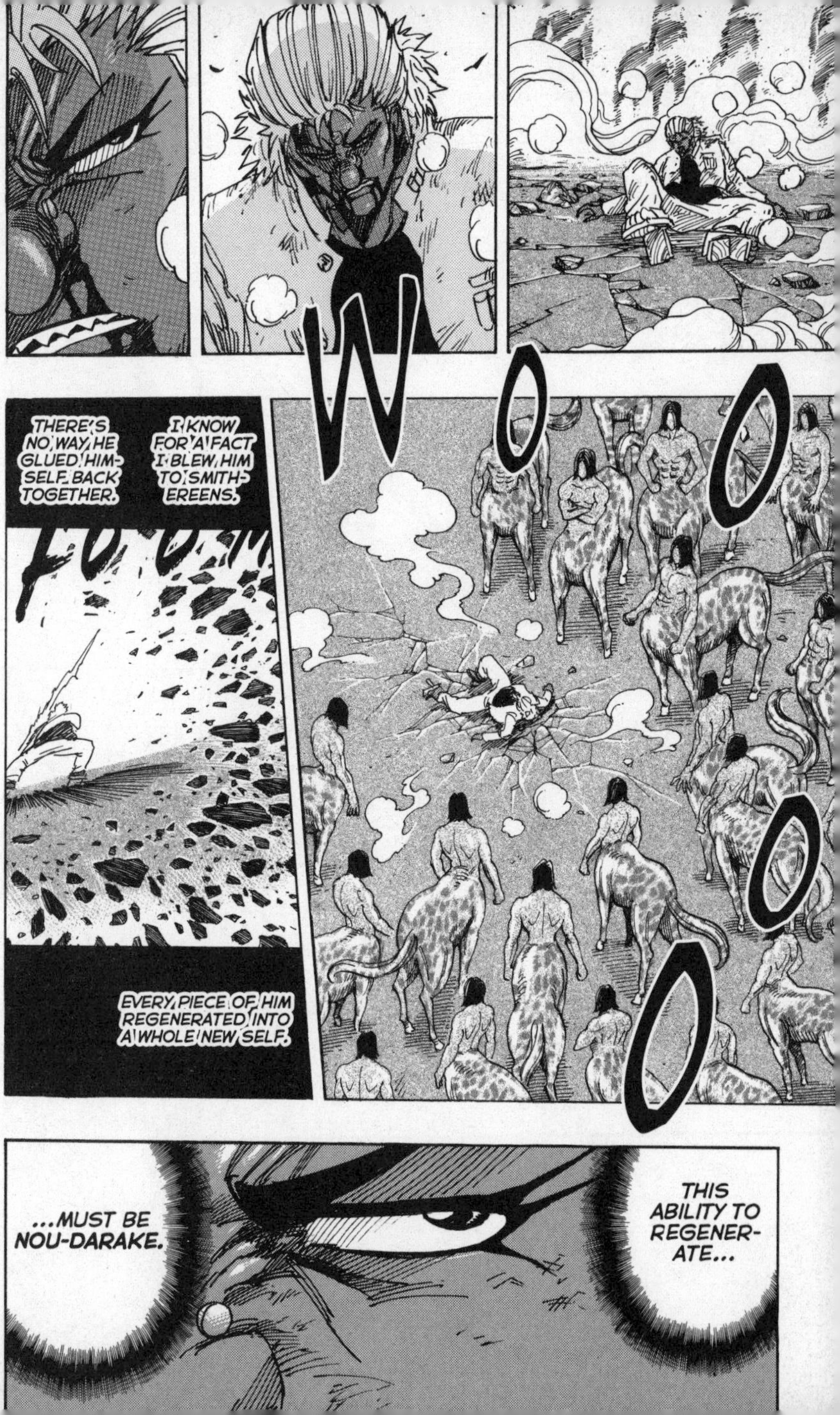
WOOOO
I KNOW FOR A FACT I BLEW HIM TO SMITH-EREENS.
THERE'S NO WAY HE GLUED HIM-SELF BACK TOGETHER.
EVERY PIECE OF HIM REGENERATED INTO A WHOLE NEW SELF.
THIS ABILITY TO REGENER-ATE...
...MUST BE NOU-DARAKE.

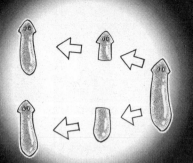

NOU-DARAKE GENE
A GENE PRESENT IN CELLS IN THE HEAD OF PLANARIAN FLATWORMS.
WHEN THE BODY OF THE PLANARIAN IS SPLIT INTO TWO, EACH PIECE CAN GENERATE THE MISSING HALF OF ITS BODY, RESULTING IN TWO PLANARIANS.
SPLIT IT INTO THREE, AND THREE ORGANISMS WILL ARISE. SPLIT IT INTO FOUR, AND FOUR WILL ARISE.
SCIENTISTS POSTULATE THAT THIS ABILITY CAN BE ACCREDITED TO THE NOU-DARAKE GENE.
GENES TYPICALLY PREVENT THE BRAIN FROM REFORMING OUTSIDE THE HEAD REGION, BUT...
...IF THAT FUNCTION IS SUPPRESSED, NERVES CAN GROW OUTSIDE OF THE HEAD AND CREATE A NEW BRAIN, FROM WHICH IT THEN GENERATES A NEW BODY.
WITH THIS REGEN-ERATIVE ABILITY, IT IS POSSIBLE THAT EVEN IF A BODY IS SPLIT INTO 100 PIECES, 100 NEW BODIES WILL RESULT.
I GET IT NOW...
SO THAT'S HOW MY CHEEK GOT CUT.
MY ELECTRIC ATTACKS FIRST CREATE ELECTRIC "PATHWAYS" THROUGH THE AIR.
THEN I DISCHARGE THE ELECTRICITY.

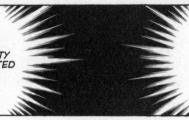

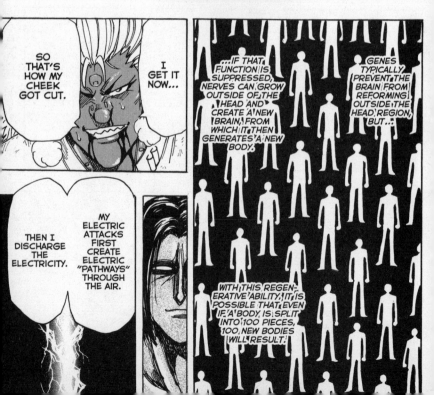

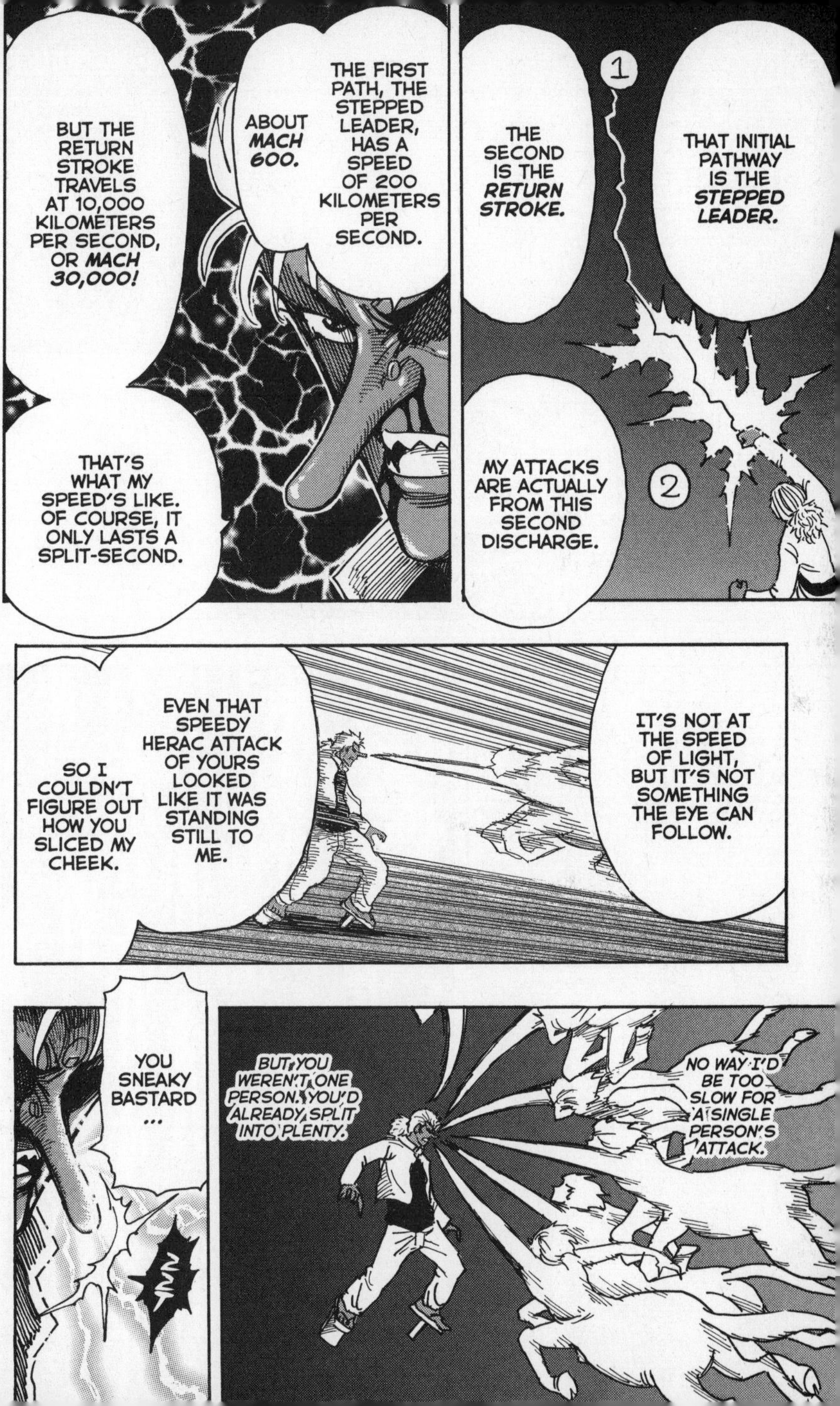
1
THAT INITIAL PATHWAY IS THE *STEPPED LEADER.*
THE SECOND IS THE *RETURN STROKE.*
2
MY ATTACKS ARE ACTUALLY FROM THIS SECOND DISCHARGE.
THE FIRST PATH, THE STEPPED LEADER, HAS A SPEED OF 200 KILOMETERS PER SECOND.
ABOUT *MACH 600.*
BUT THE RETURN STROKE TRAVELS AT 10,000 KILOMETERS PER SECOND, OR *MACH 30,000!*
THAT'S WHAT MY SPEED'S LIKE. OF COURSE, IT ONLY LASTS A SPLIT-SECOND.
IT'S NOT AT THE SPEED OF LIGHT, BUT IT'S NOT SOMETHING THE EYE CAN FOLLOW.
EVEN THAT SPEEDY HERAC ATTACK OF YOURS LOOKED LIKE IT WAS STANDING STILL TO ME.
SO I COULDN'T FIGURE OUT HOW YOU SLICED MY CHEEK.
NO WAY I'D BE TOO SLOW FOR A SINGLE PERSON'S ATTACK.
BUT YOU WEREN'T ONE PERSON. YOU'D ALREADY SPLIT INTO PLENTY.
YOU SNEAKY BASTARD ...

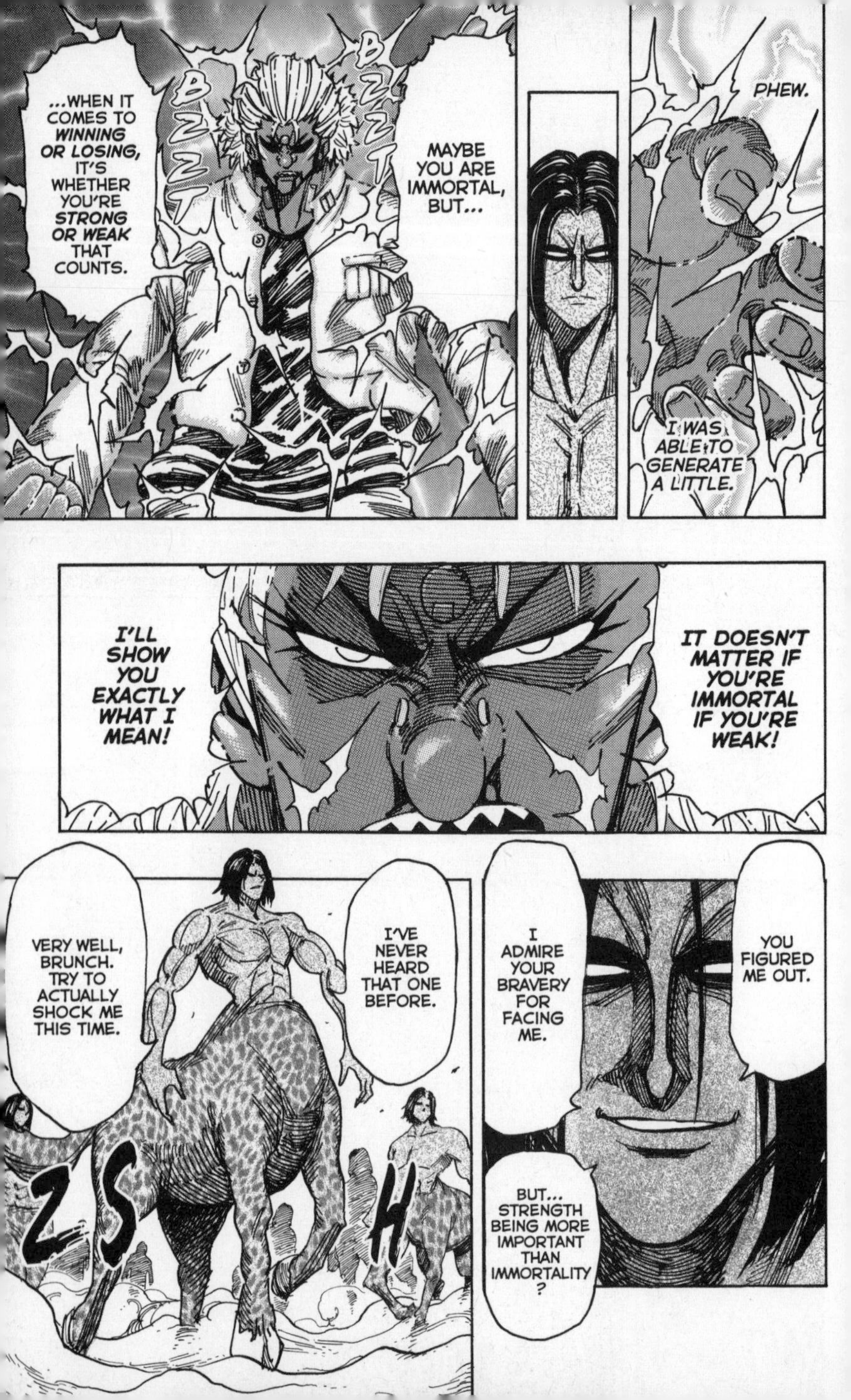
PHEW.
I WAS ABLE TO GENERATE A LITTLE.
B Z Z T
MAYBE YOU ARE IMMORTAL, BUT...
B Z Z T
...WHEN IT COMES TO WINNING OR LOSING, IT'S WHETHER YOU'RE STRONG OR WEAK THAT COUNTS.
IT DOESN'T MATTER IF YOU'RE IMMORTAL IF YOU'RE WEAK!
I'LL SHOW YOU EXACTLY WHAT I MEAN!
YOU FIGURED ME OUT.
I ADMIRE YOUR BRAVERY FOR FACING ME.
BUT... STRENGTH BEING MORE IMPORTANT THAN IMMORTALITY?
I'VE NEVER HEARD THAT ONE BEFORE.
VERY WELL, BRUNCH. TRY TO ACTUALLY SHOCK ME THIS TIME.
ZSH

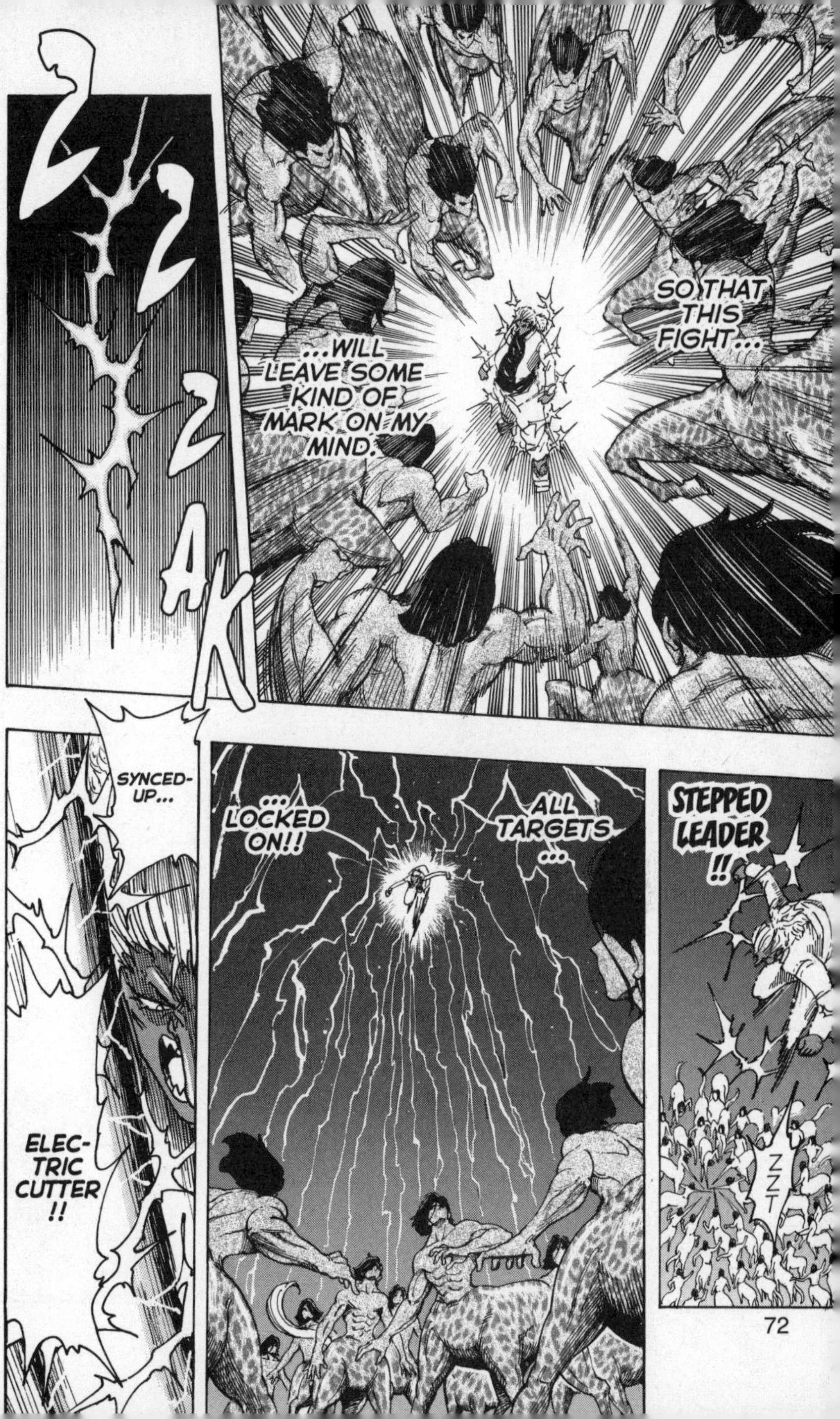
SO THAT THIS FIGHT...
...WILL LEAVE SOME KIND OF MARK ON MY MIND.
ZZZAK
STEPPED LEADER!!
ZZT
ALL TARGETS...
...LOCKED ON!!
SYNCED-UP...
ELECTRIC CUTTER!!

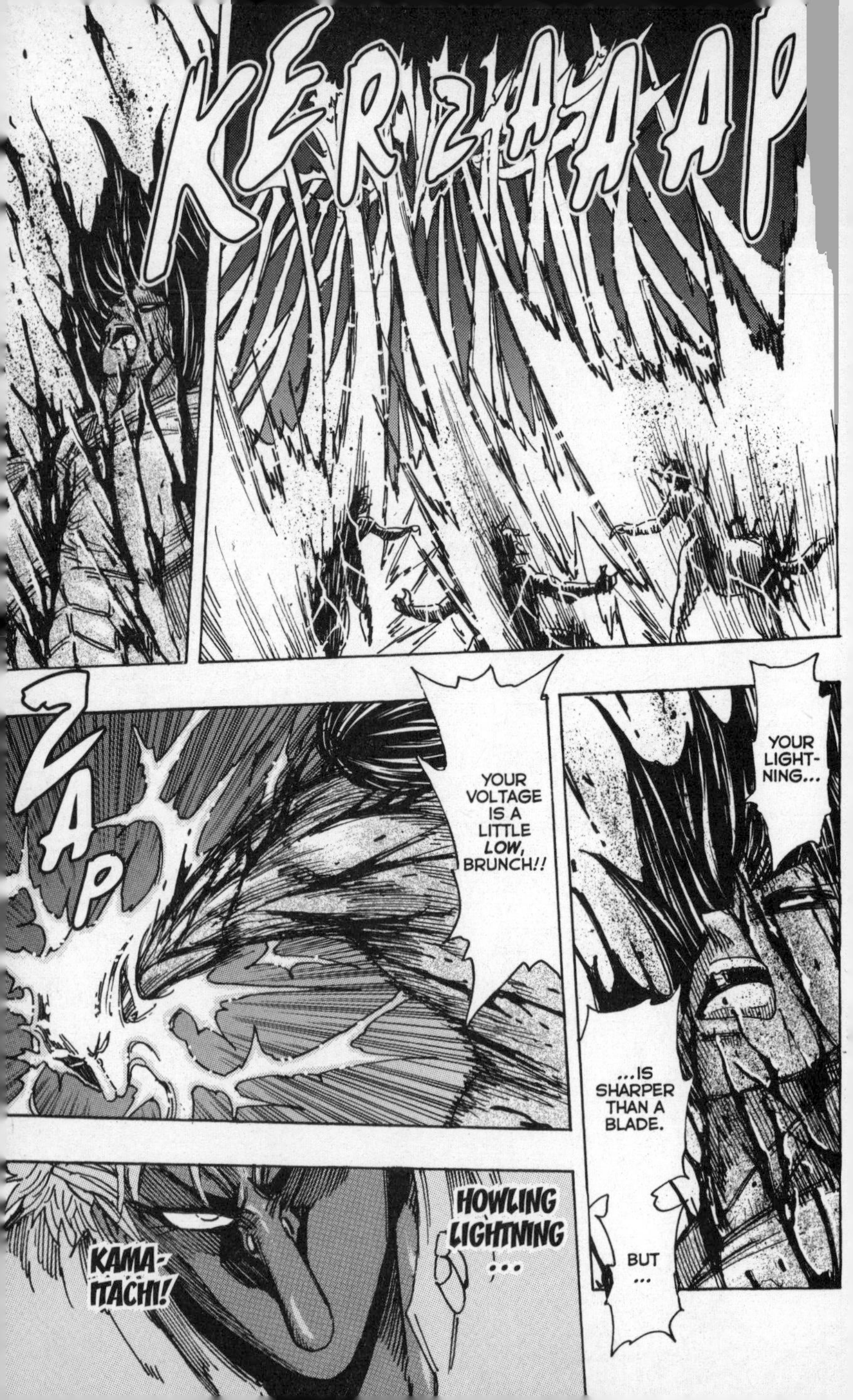
KERZAAAP
YOUR LIGHT-NING...
...IS SHARPER THAN A BLADE.
BUT ...
YOUR VOLTAGE IS A LITTLE *LOW*, BRUNCH!!
ZAP
HOWLING LIGHTNING ...
KAMA-ITACHI!

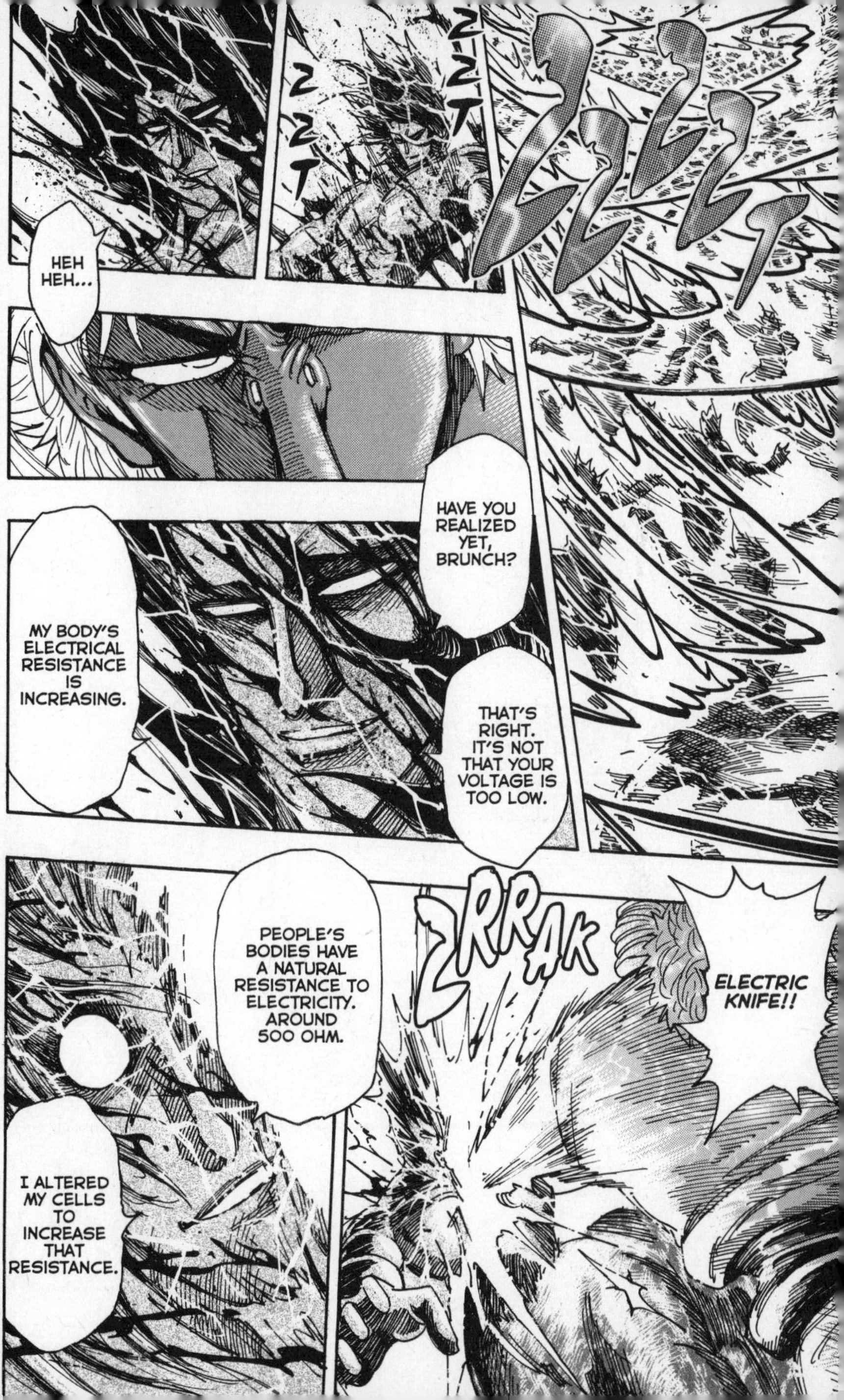
ZZZZT
ZZT
ZZT
HEH HEH...
HAVE YOU REALIZED YET, BRUNCH?
THAT'S RIGHT. IT'S NOT THAT YOUR VOLTAGE IS TOO LOW.
MY BODY'S ELECTRICAL RESISTANCE IS INCREASING.
ZRRAK
ELECTRIC KNIFE!!
PEOPLE'S BODIES HAVE A NATURAL RESISTANCE TO ELECTRICITY. AROUND 500 OHM.
I ALTERED MY CELLS TO INCREASE THAT RESISTANCE.

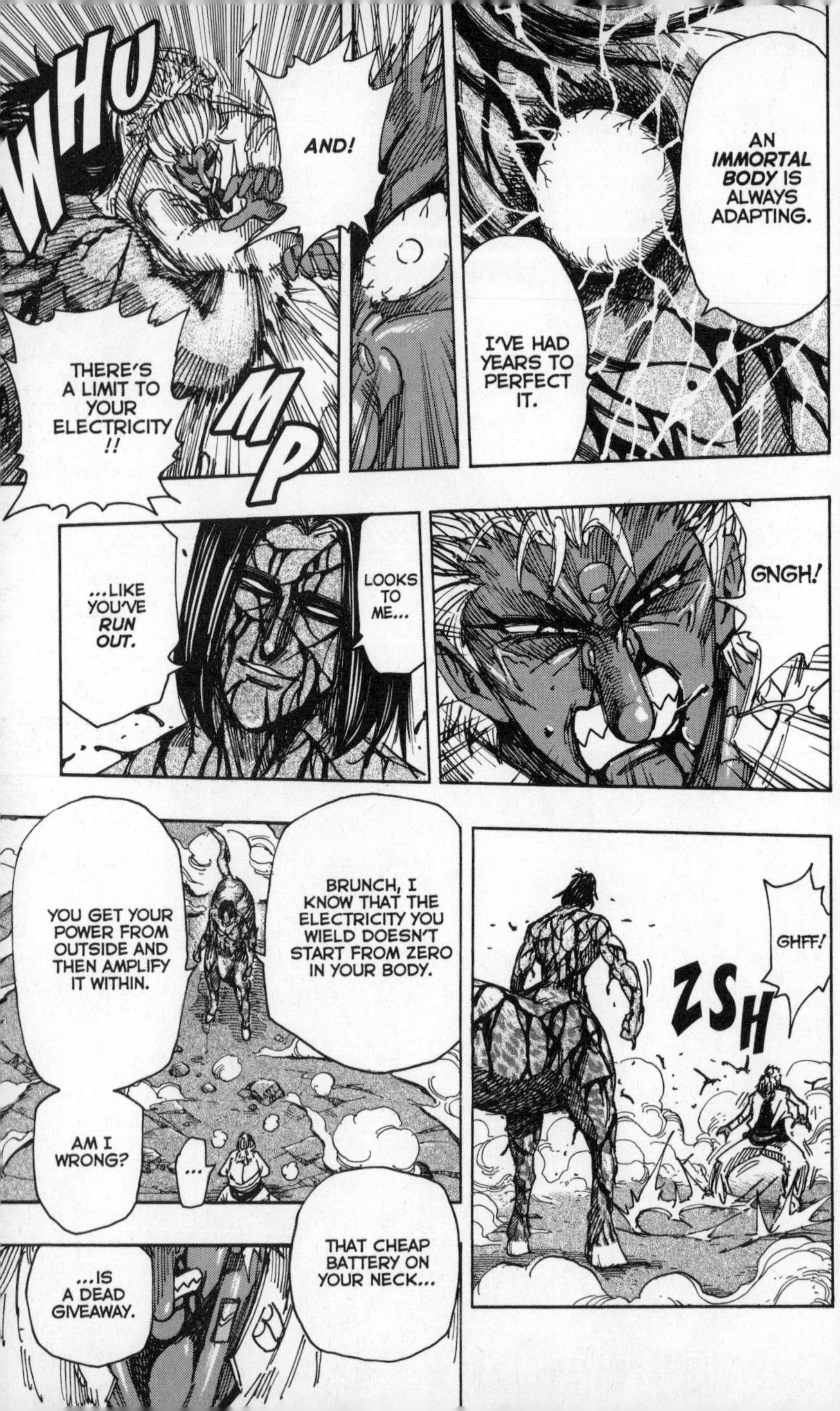
AN IMMORTAL BODY IS ALWAYS ADAPTING.
I'VE HAD YEARS TO PERFECT IT.
AND!
WHUMP
THERE'S A LIMIT TO YOUR ELECTRICITY!!
GNGH!
LOOKS TO ME...
...LIKE YOU'VE RUN OUT.
GHFF!
ZSH
BRUNCH, I KNOW THAT THE ELECTRICITY YOU WIELD DOESN'T START FROM ZERO IN YOUR BODY.
YOU GET YOUR POWER FROM OUTSIDE AND THEN AMPLIFY IT WITHIN.
AM I WRONG?
...
THAT CHEAP BATTERY ON YOUR NECK...
...IS A DEAD GIVEAWAY.

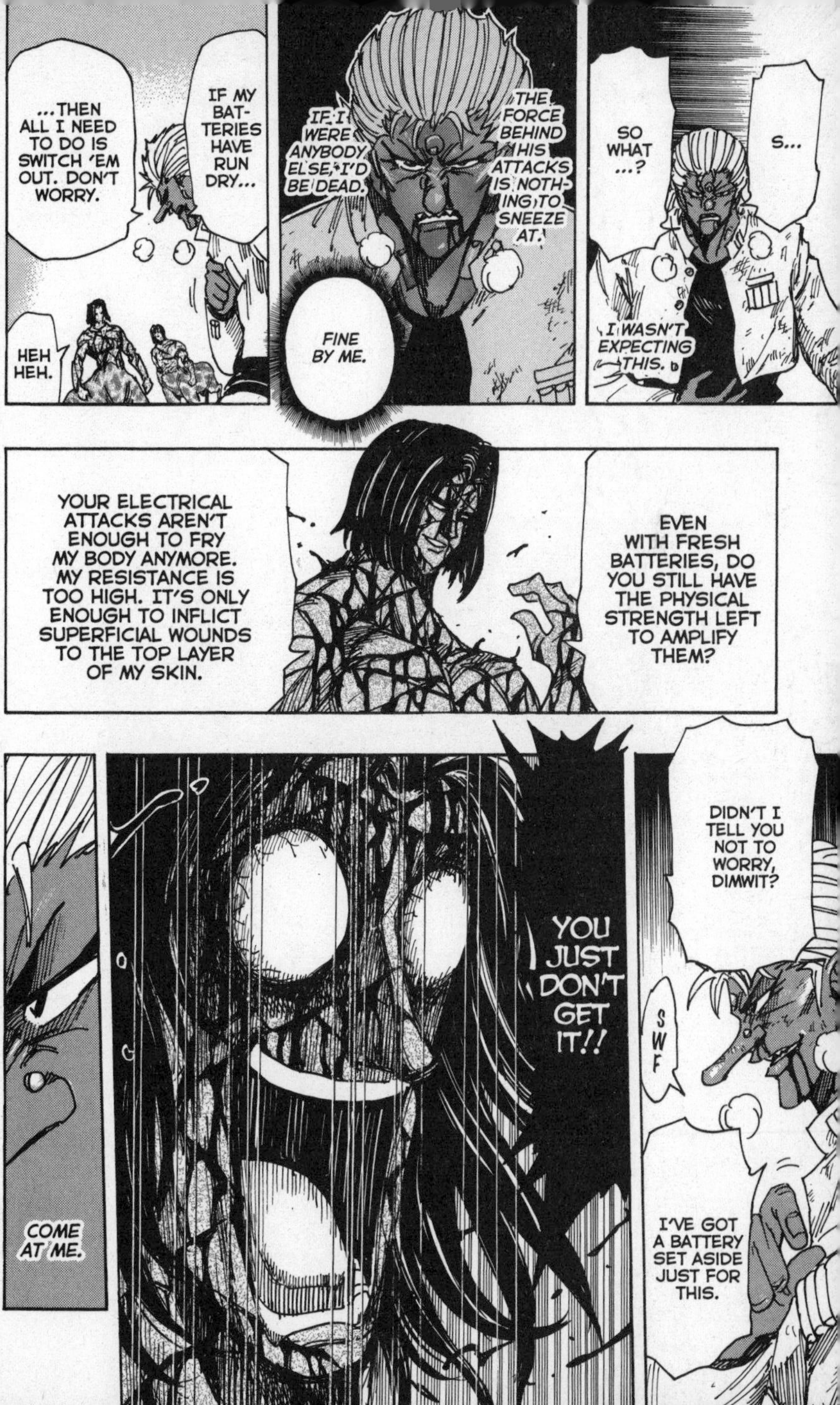
S...
SO WHAT ...?
I WASN'T EXPECTING THIS.
THE FORCE BEHIND HIS ATTACKS IS NOTHING TO SNEEZE AT.
IF I WERE ANYBODY ELSE, I'D BE DEAD.
FINE BY ME.
IF MY BATTERIES HAVE RUN DRY...
...THEN ALL I NEED TO DO IS SWITCH 'EM OUT. DON'T WORRY.
HEH HEH.
EVEN WITH FRESH BATTERIES, DO YOU STILL HAVE THE PHYSICAL STRENGTH LEFT TO AMPLIFY THEM?
YOUR ELECTRICAL ATTACKS AREN'T ENOUGH TO FRY MY BODY ANYMORE. MY RESISTANCE IS TOO HIGH. IT'S ONLY ENOUGH TO INFLICT SUPERFICIAL WOUNDS TO THE TOP LAYER OF MY SKIN.
DIDN'T I TELL YOU NOT TO WORRY, DIMWIT?
SWF
I'VE GOT A BATTERY SET ASIDE JUST FOR THIS.
YOU JUST DON'T GET IT!!
COME AT ME.

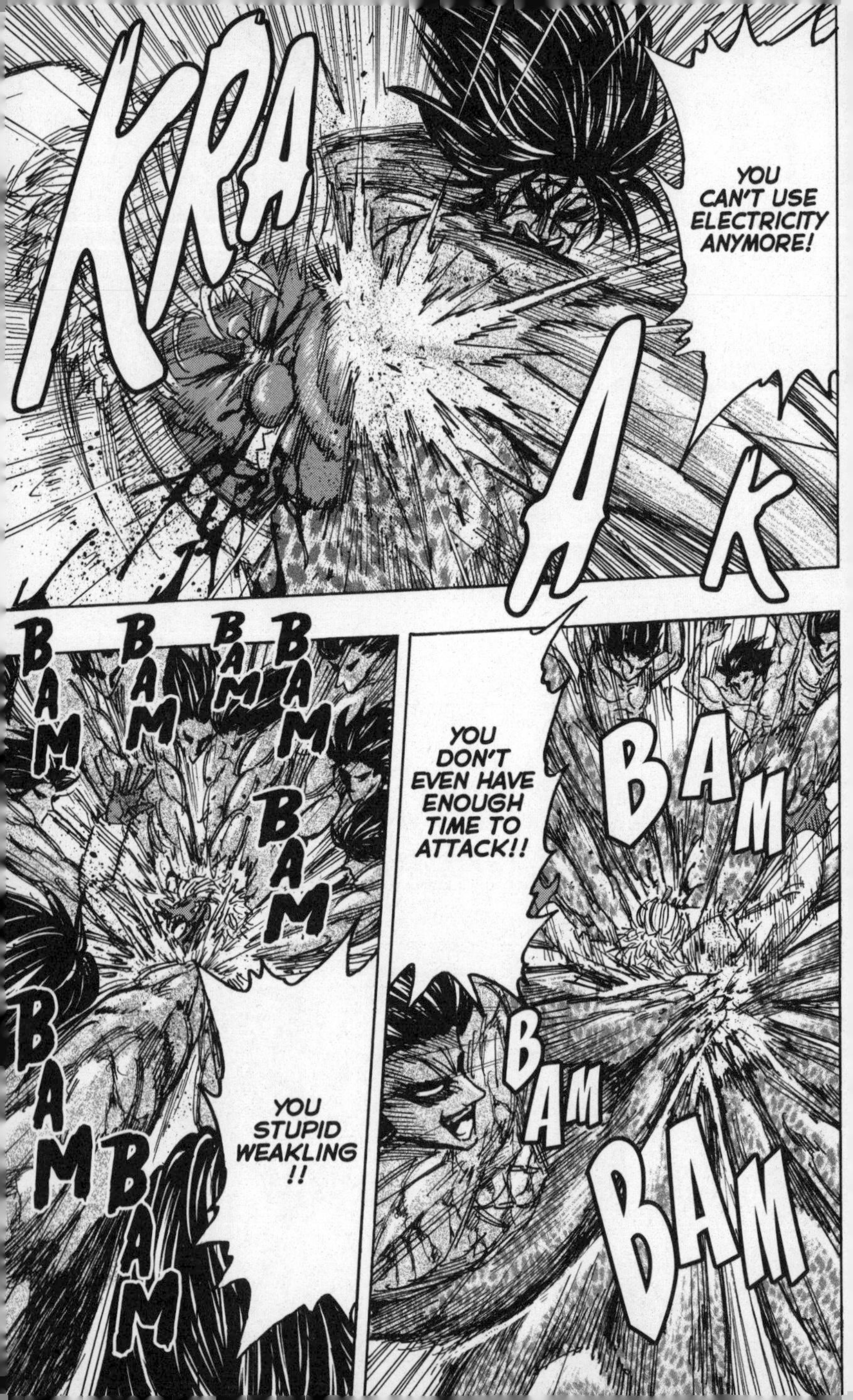
KRAAAK
YOU CAN'T USE ELECTRICITY ANYMORE!
YOU DON'T EVEN HAVE ENOUGH TIME TO ATTACK!!
BAM
BAM
BAM
BAM
BAM
BAM
BAM
BAM
BAM
BAM
BAM
YOU STUPID WEAKLING!!

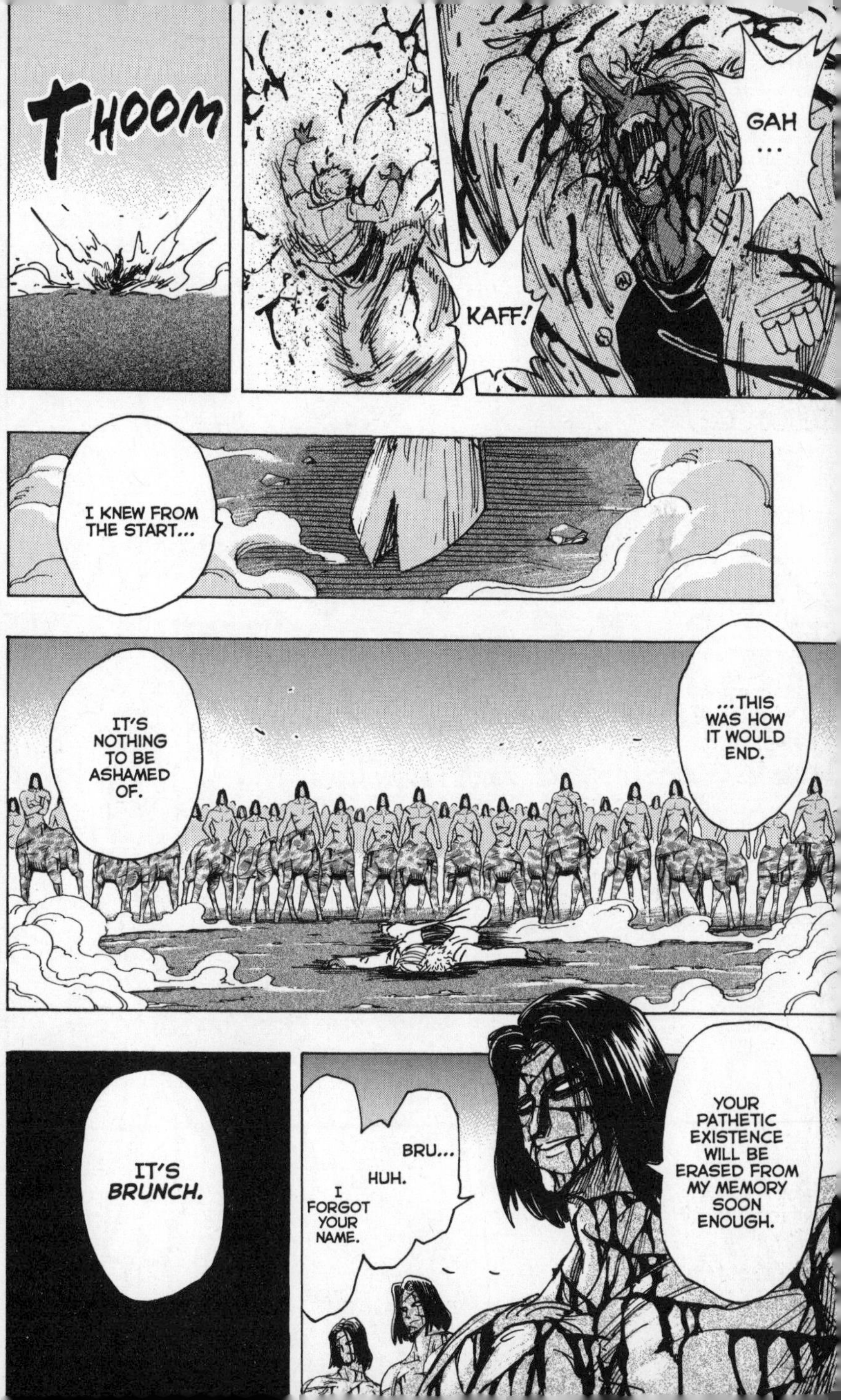
GAH ...
KAFF!
THOOM
I KNEW FROM THE START...
...THIS WAS HOW IT WOULD END.
IT'S NOTHING TO BE ASHAMED OF.
YOUR PATHETIC EXISTENCE WILL BE ERASED FROM MY MEMORY SOON ENOUGH.
BRU...
HUH.
I FORGOT YOUR NAME.
IT'S BRUNCH.

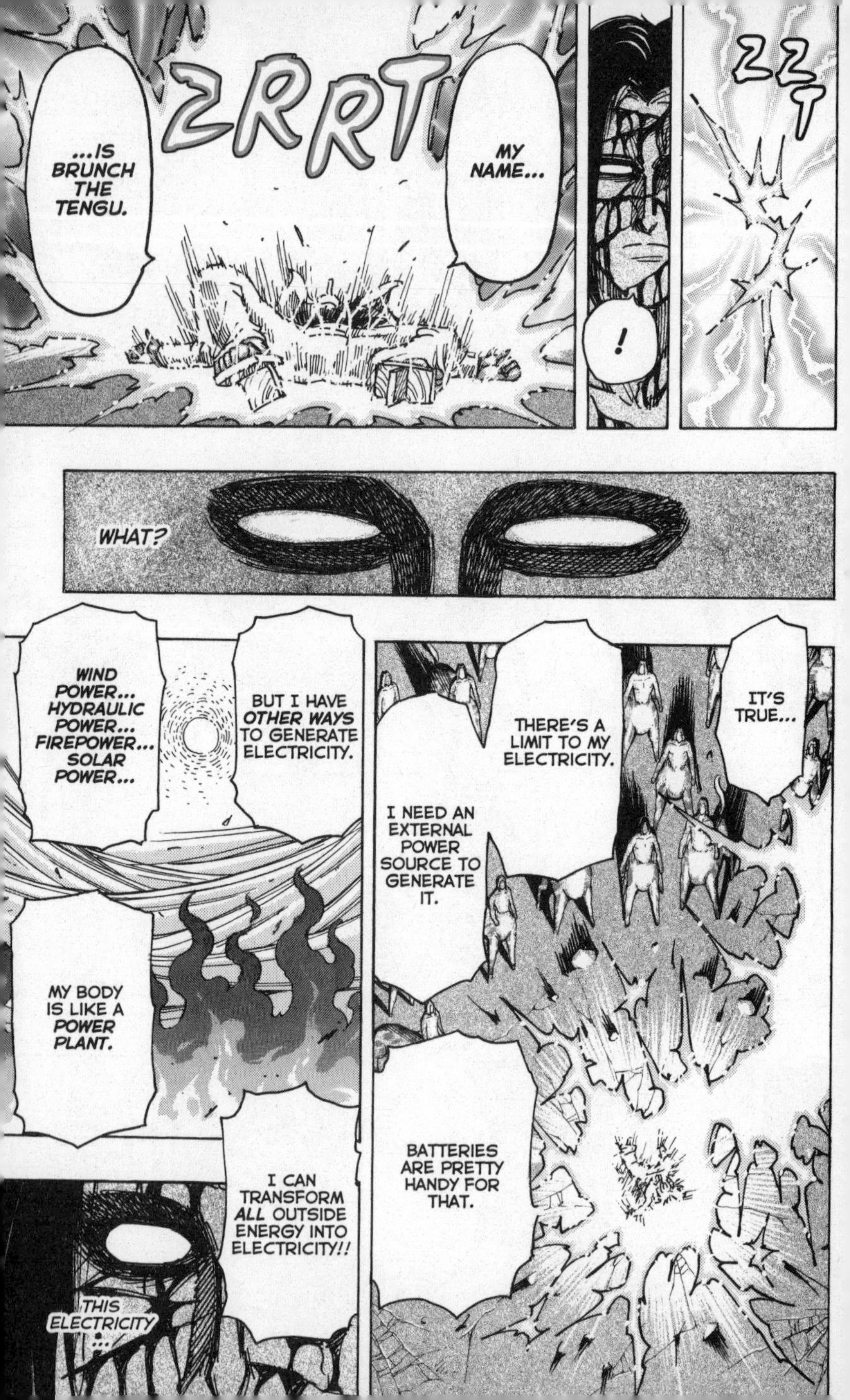

ZZT
!
MY NAME...
ZRRT
...IS BRUNCH THE TENGU.
WHAT?
IT'S TRUE...
THERE'S A LIMIT TO MY ELECTRICITY.
I NEED AN EXTERNAL POWER SOURCE TO GENERATE IT.
BATTERIES ARE PRETTY HANDY FOR THAT.
BUT I HAVE *OTHER WAYS* TO GENERATE ELECTRICITY.
WIND POWER... HYDRAULIC POWER... FIREPOWER... SOLAR POWER...
MY BODY IS LIKE A *POWER PLANT.*
I CAN TRANSFORM *ALL* OUTSIDE ENERGY INTO ELECTRICITY!!
THIS ELECTRICITY...

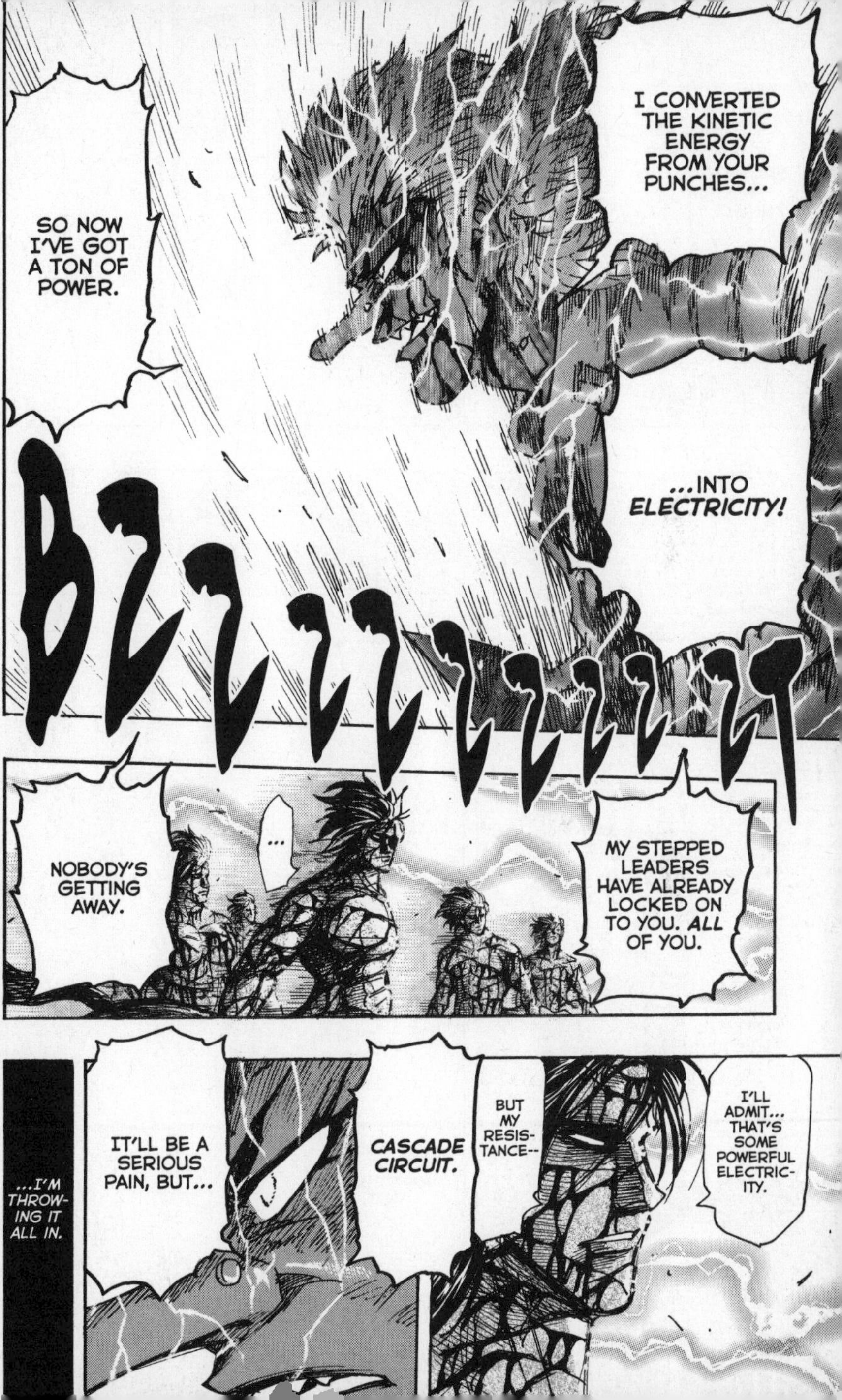
I CONVERTED THE KINETIC ENERGY FROM YOUR PUNCHES...
...INTO *ELECTRICITY!*
SO NOW I'VE GOT A TON OF POWER.
BZZZZZZZZZZZT
MY STEPPED LEADERS HAVE ALREADY LOCKED ON TO YOU. *ALL* OF YOU.
...
NOBODY'S GETTING AWAY.
I'LL ADMIT... THAT'S SOME POWERFUL ELECTRIC-ITY.
BUT *MY* RESIS-TANCE--
CASCADE CIRCUIT.
IT'LL BE A SERIOUS PAIN, BUT...
...I'M THROW-ING IT ALL IN.

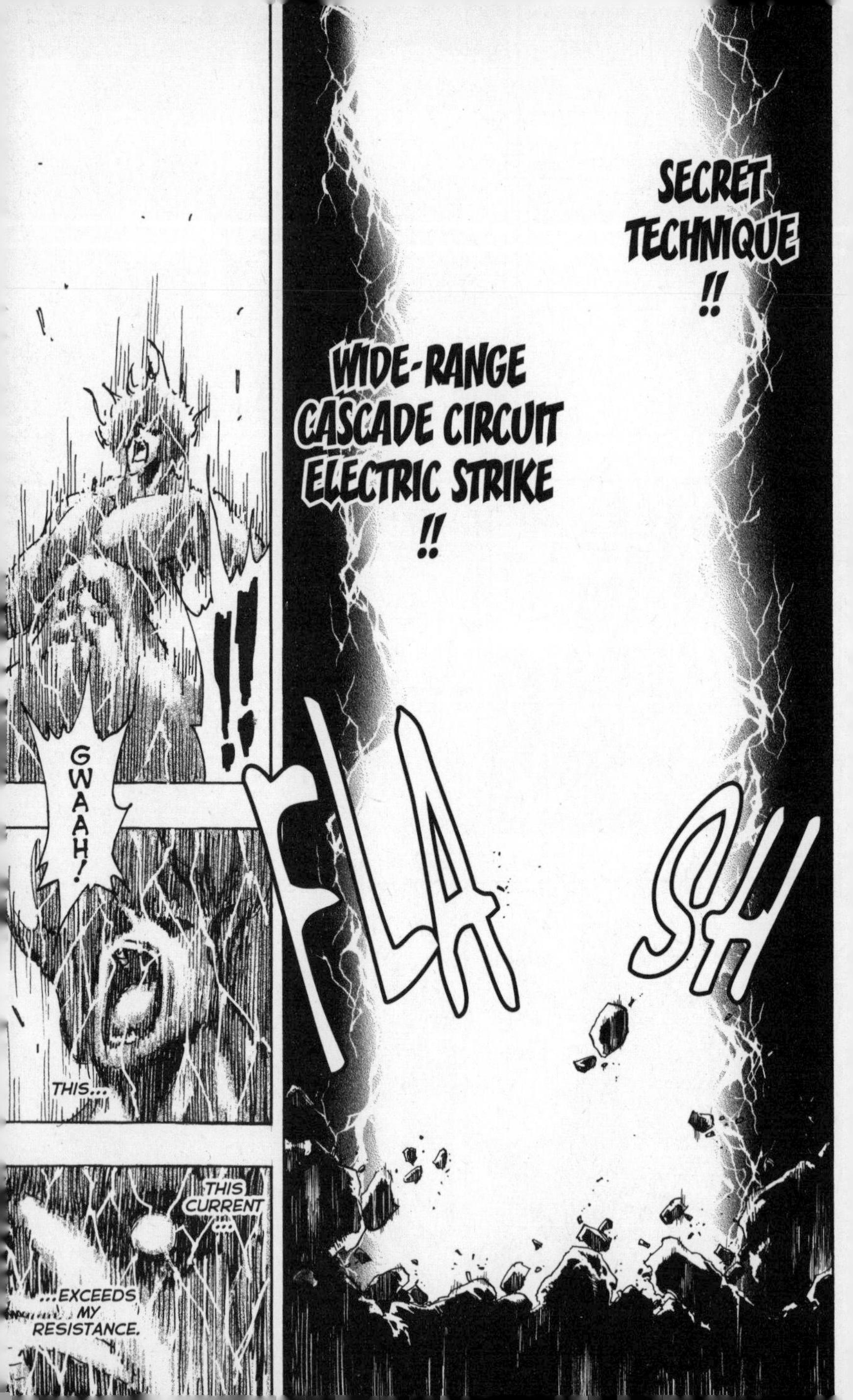
SECRET TECHNIQUE !!
WIDE-RANGE CASCADE CIRCUIT ELECTRIC STRIKE !!
FLASH
!!
GWAAH!
THIS...
THIS CURRENT ...
...EXCEEDS MY RESISTANCE.

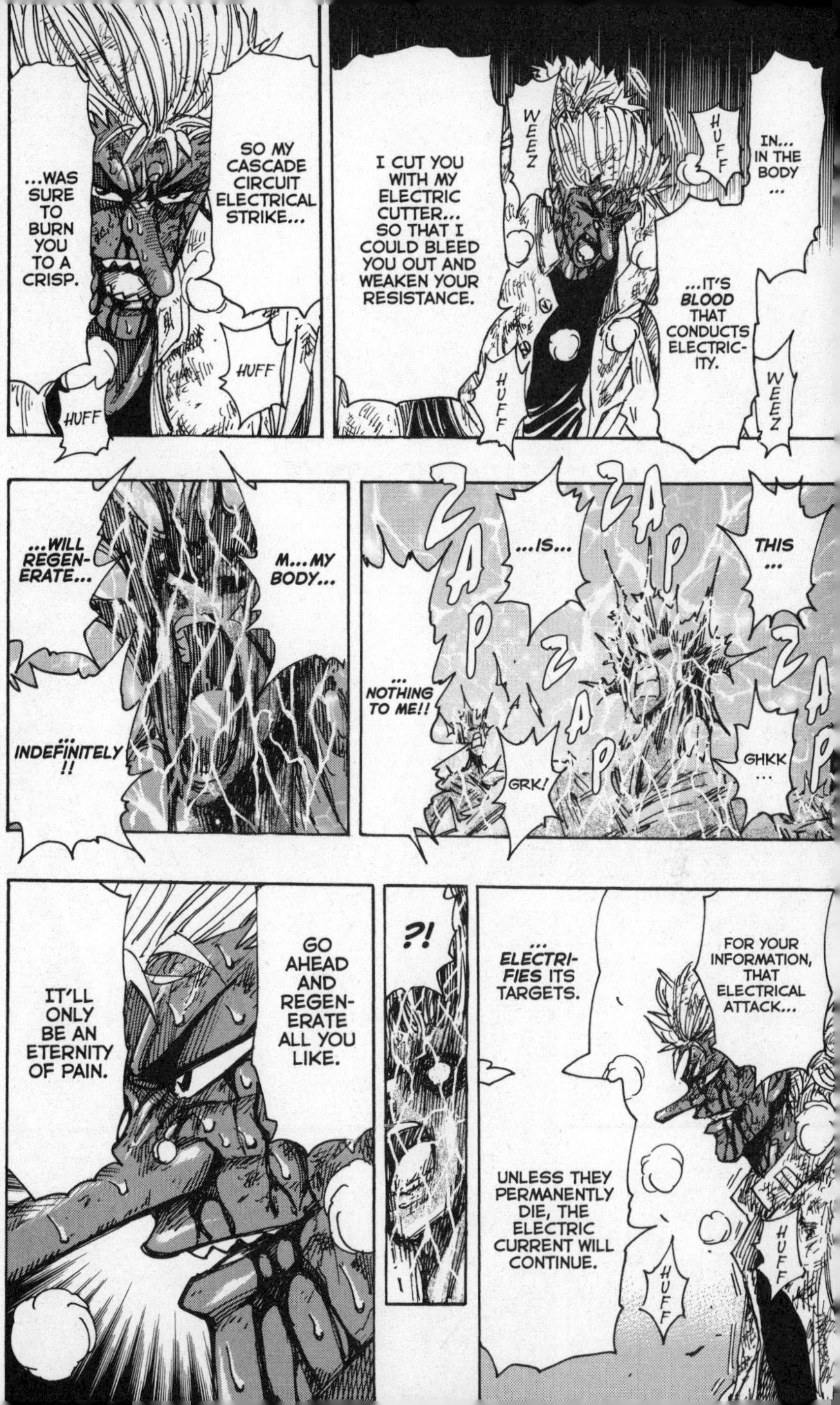
IN... IN THE BODY...
HUFF
WEEZ
...IT'S *BLOOD* THAT CONDUCTS ELECTRICITY.
WEEZ
I CUT YOU WITH MY ELECTRIC CUTTER... SO THAT I COULD BLEED YOU OUT AND WEAKEN YOUR RESISTANCE.
HUFF
SO MY CASCADE CIRCUIT ELECTRICAL STRIKE...
...WAS SURE TO BURN YOU TO A CRISP.
HUFF
HUFF
THIS...
ZAP
...IS...
ZAP
ZAP
ZAP
ZAP
GHKK...
...NOTHING TO ME!!
GRK!
M...MY BODY...
...WILL REGENERATE...
...INDEFINITELY!!
FOR YOUR INFORMATION, THAT ELECTRICAL ATTACK...
...*ELECTRIFIES* ITS TARGETS.
UNLESS THEY PERMANENTLY DIE, THE ELECTRIC CURRENT WILL CONTINUE.
HUFF
HUFF
?!
GO AHEAD AND REGENERATE ALL YOU LIKE.
IT'LL ONLY BE AN ETERNITY OF PAIN.

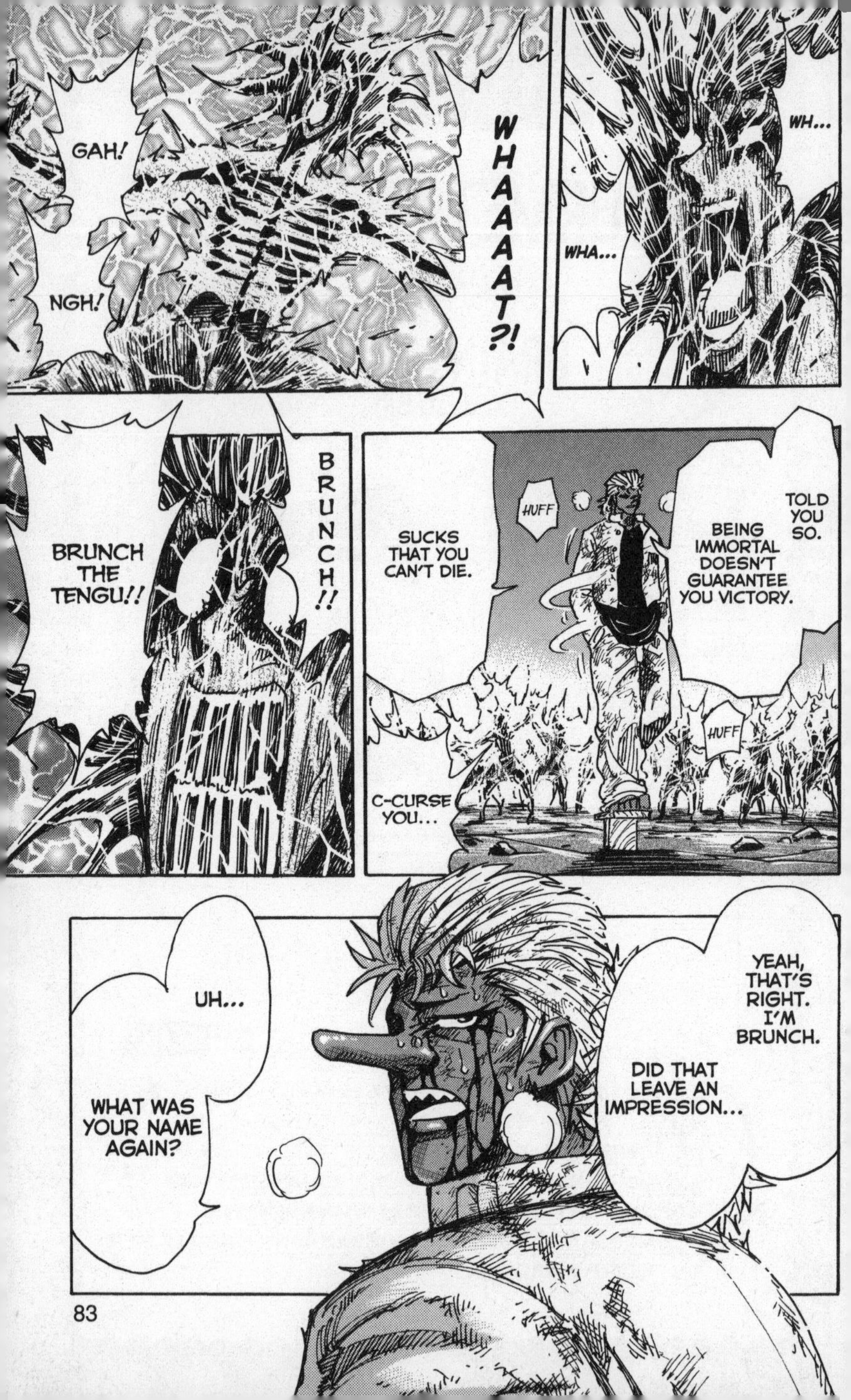
WH...
WHA...
WHAAAAAT?!
GAH!
NGH!
TOLD YOU SO.
BEING IMMORTAL DOESN'T GUARANTEE YOU VICTORY.
HUFF
HUFF
SUCKS THAT YOU CAN'T DIE.
C-CURSE YOU...
BRUNCH!!
BRUNCH THE TENGU!!
YEAH, THAT'S RIGHT. I'M BRUNCH.
DID THAT LEAVE AN IMPRESSION...
UH...
WHAT WAS YOUR NAME AGAIN?

TORIKO

GOURMET CHECKLIST

Vol. 254

BRAIN URCHIN
(SHELLFISH)

CAPTURE LEVEL: 5

HABITAT: CLEAR OCEAN WATERS

LENGTH: 15 CM

HEIGHT: ---

WEIGHT: 500 G

PRICE: 70,000 YEN PER URCHIN

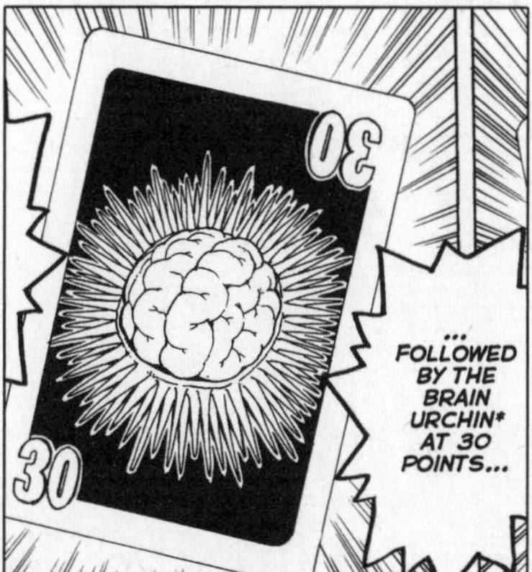
30
30
...FOLLOWED BY THE BRAIN URCHIN* AT 30 POINTS...

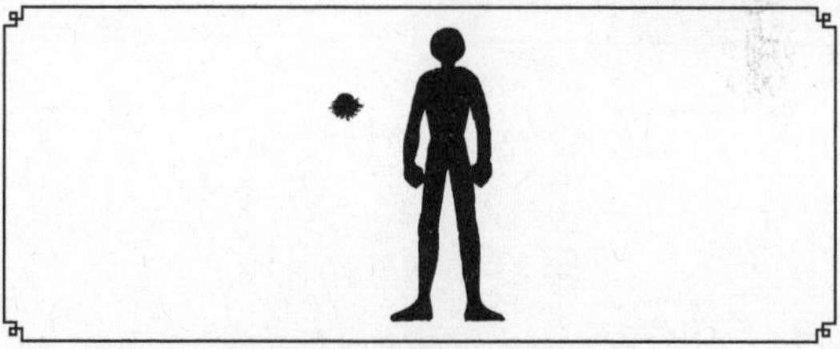

SCALE

REGARDED AS A LUXURY FOOD, THE BRAIN URCHIN CLASPS A BRAIN WITHIN ITS SPINES. IT HAS A REPUTATION FOR MAKING YOU SMARTER WHEN YOU EAT IT. IT'S ALSO SAID THAT THE MORE WRINKLES THE BRAIN HAS, THE MORE POTENT THE EFFECT AND RICH THE FLAVOR. OLDER BRAINS HAVE MORE WRINKLES, BUT THEY'RE ALSO SMARTER AND THEREFORE HARDER TO CAPTURE. ALSO, SINCE THE BRAIN CELLS DIE QUICKLY, IT IS ADVISABLE TO EAT BRAIN URCHIN IMMEDIATELY FOLLOWING ITS CAPTURE. IN CASES WHERE YOU WANT TO PRESERVE IT FOR A WHILE, IT CAN BE PICKLED IN ALCOHOL.

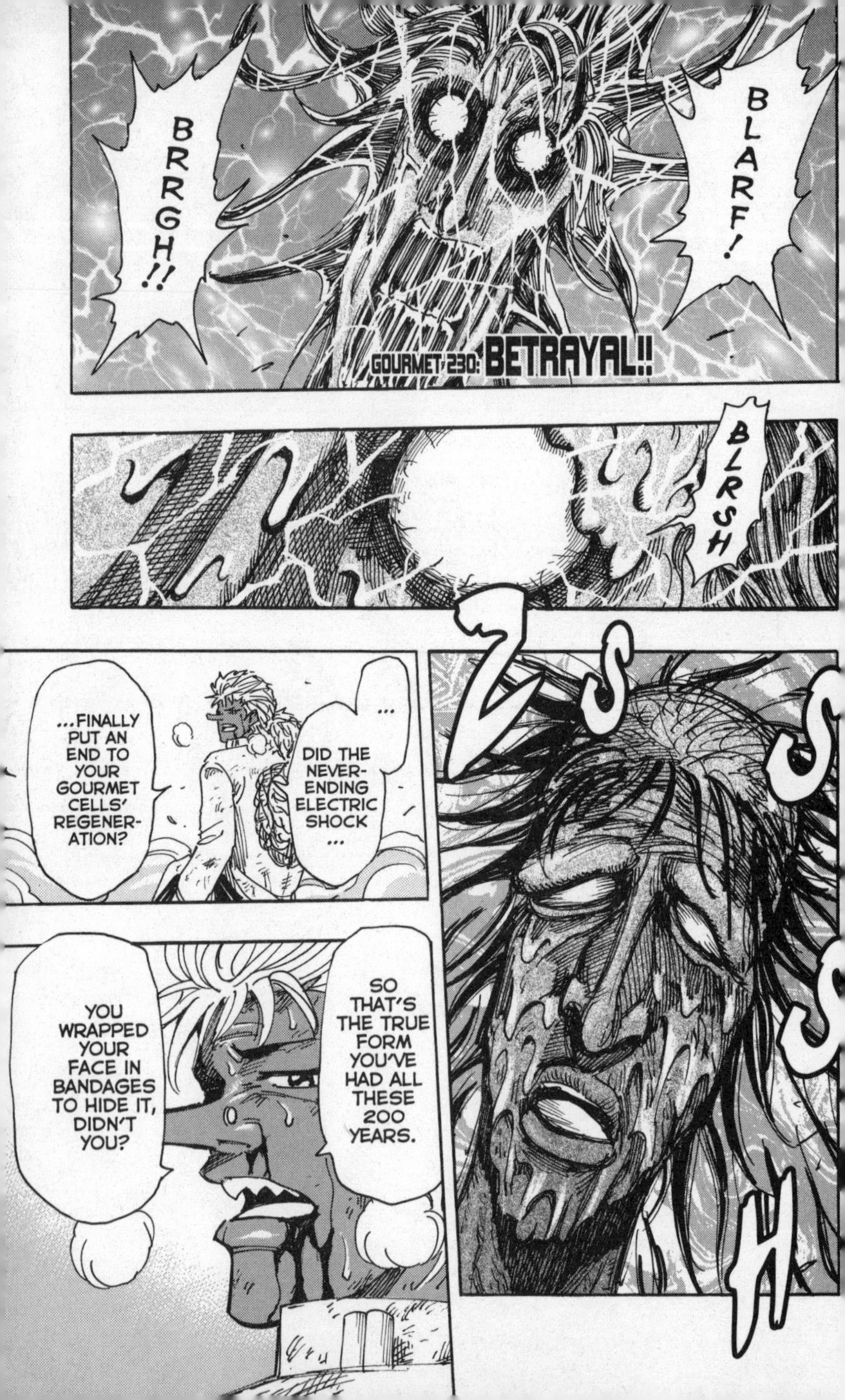
BLARF!
BRRGH!!
GOURMET 230: BETRAYAL!!
BLRSH
ZSSSH
...
DID THE NEVER-ENDING ELECTRIC SHOCK ...
...FINALLY PUT AN END TO YOUR GOURMET CELLS' REGENERATION?
SO THAT'S THE TRUE FORM YOU'VE HAD ALL THESE 200 YEARS.
YOU WRAPPED YOUR FACE IN BANDAGES TO HIDE IT, DIDN'T YOU?

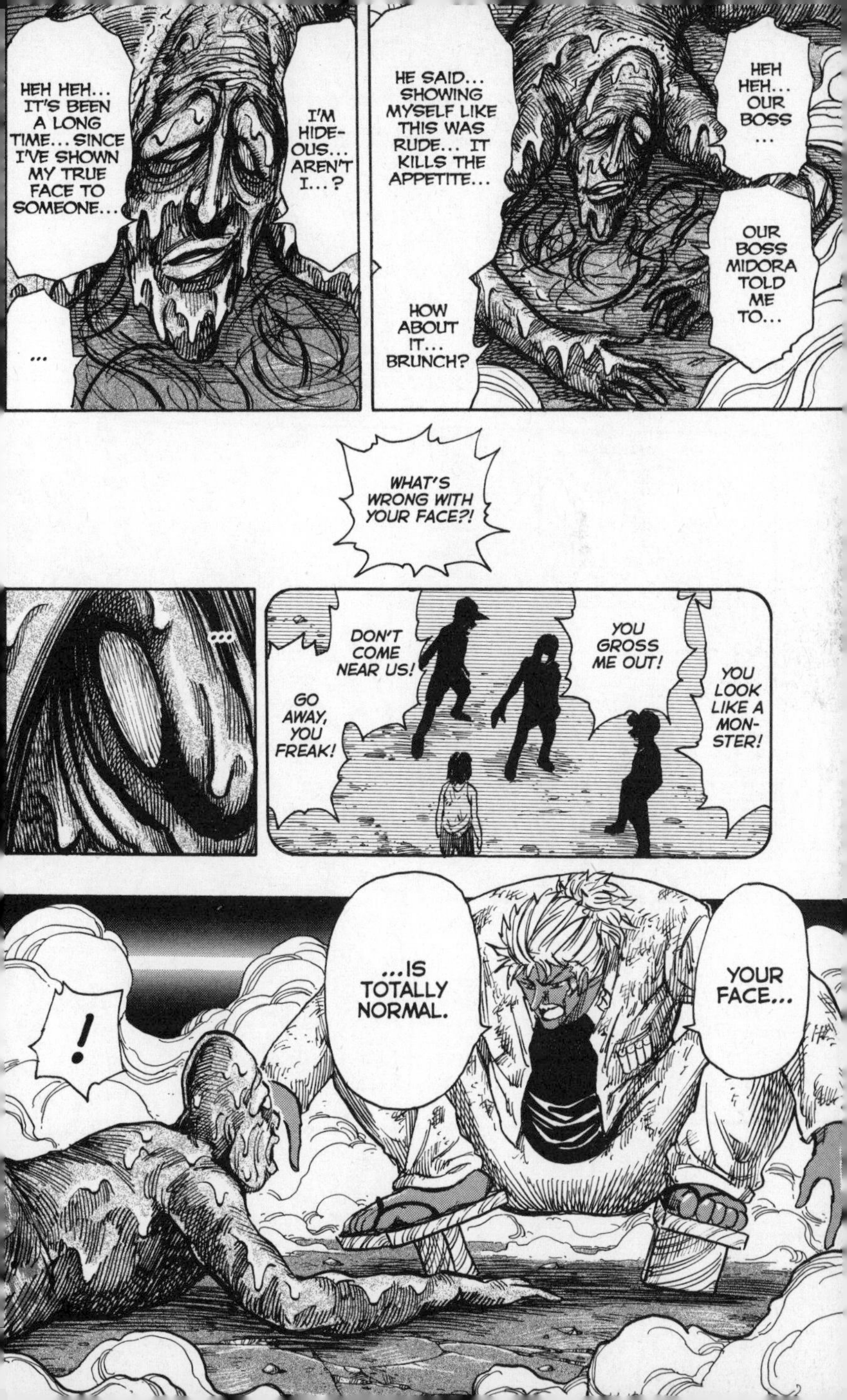
HEH HEH... OUR BOSS...
OUR BOSS MIDORA TOLD ME TO...
HE SAID... SHOWING MYSELF LIKE THIS WAS RUDE... IT KILLS THE APPETITE...
HOW ABOUT IT... BRUNCH?
HEH HEH... IT'S BEEN A LONG TIME... SINCE I'VE SHOWN MY TRUE FACE TO SOMEONE...
I'M HIDEOUS... AREN'T I...?
...
WHAT'S WRONG WITH YOUR FACE?!
YOU GROSS ME OUT!
YOU LOOK LIKE A MONSTER!
DON'T COME NEAR US!
GO AWAY, YOU FREAK!
...
YOUR FACE...
...IS TOTALLY NORMAL.
!

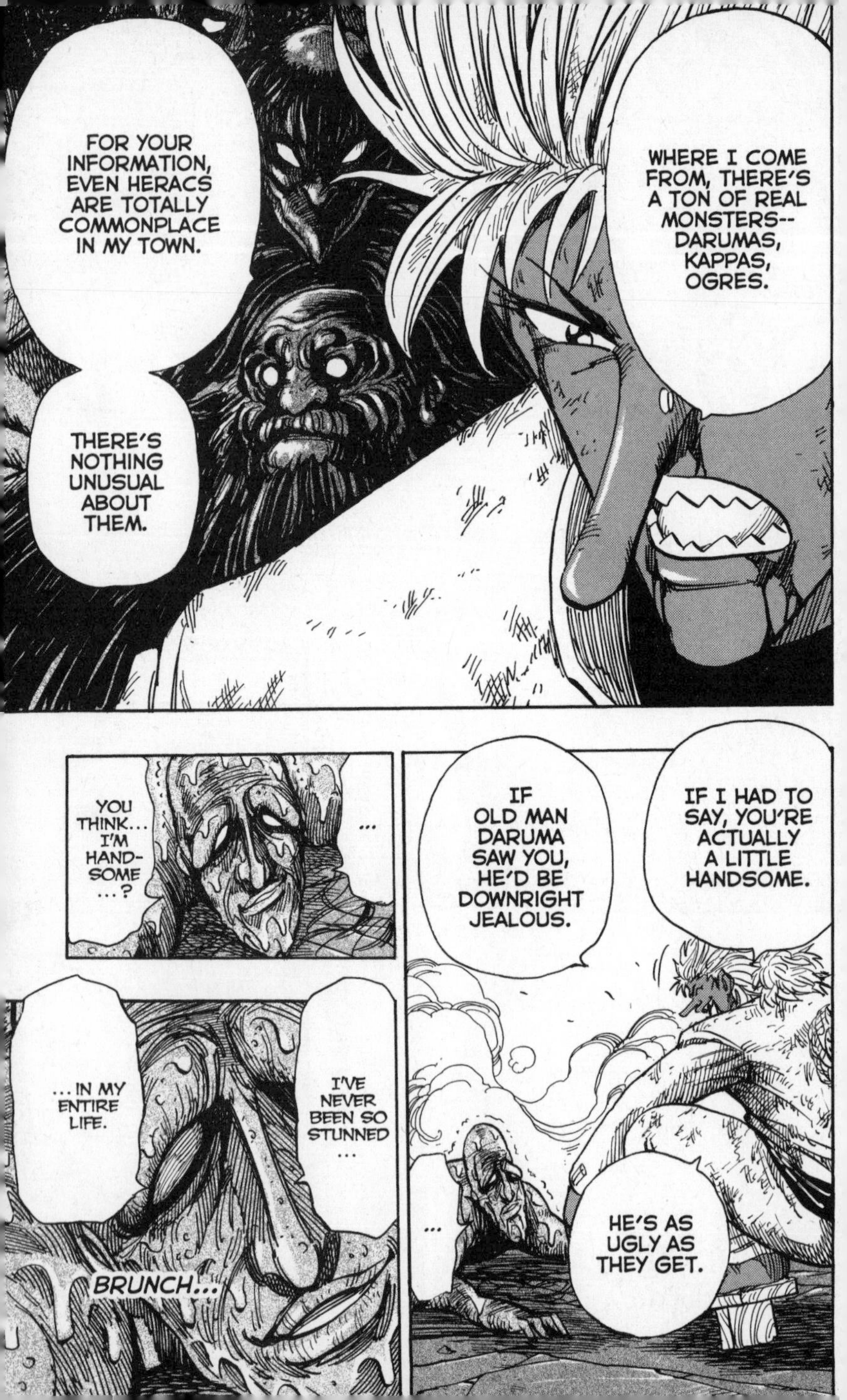
WHERE I COME FROM, THERE'S A TON OF REAL MONSTERS-- DARUMAS, KAPPAS, OGRES.
FOR YOUR INFORMATION, EVEN HERACS ARE TOTALLY COMMONPLACE IN MY TOWN.
THERE'S NOTHING UNUSUAL ABOUT THEM.
IF I HAD TO SAY, YOU'RE ACTUALLY A LITTLE HANDSOME.
IF OLD MAN DARUMA SAW YOU, HE'D BE DOWNRIGHT JEALOUS.
HE'S AS UGLY AS THEY GET.
...
...
YOU THINK... I'M HAND-SOME ...?
I'VE NEVER BEEN SO STUNNED ...
...IN MY ENTIRE LIFE.
BRUNCH...

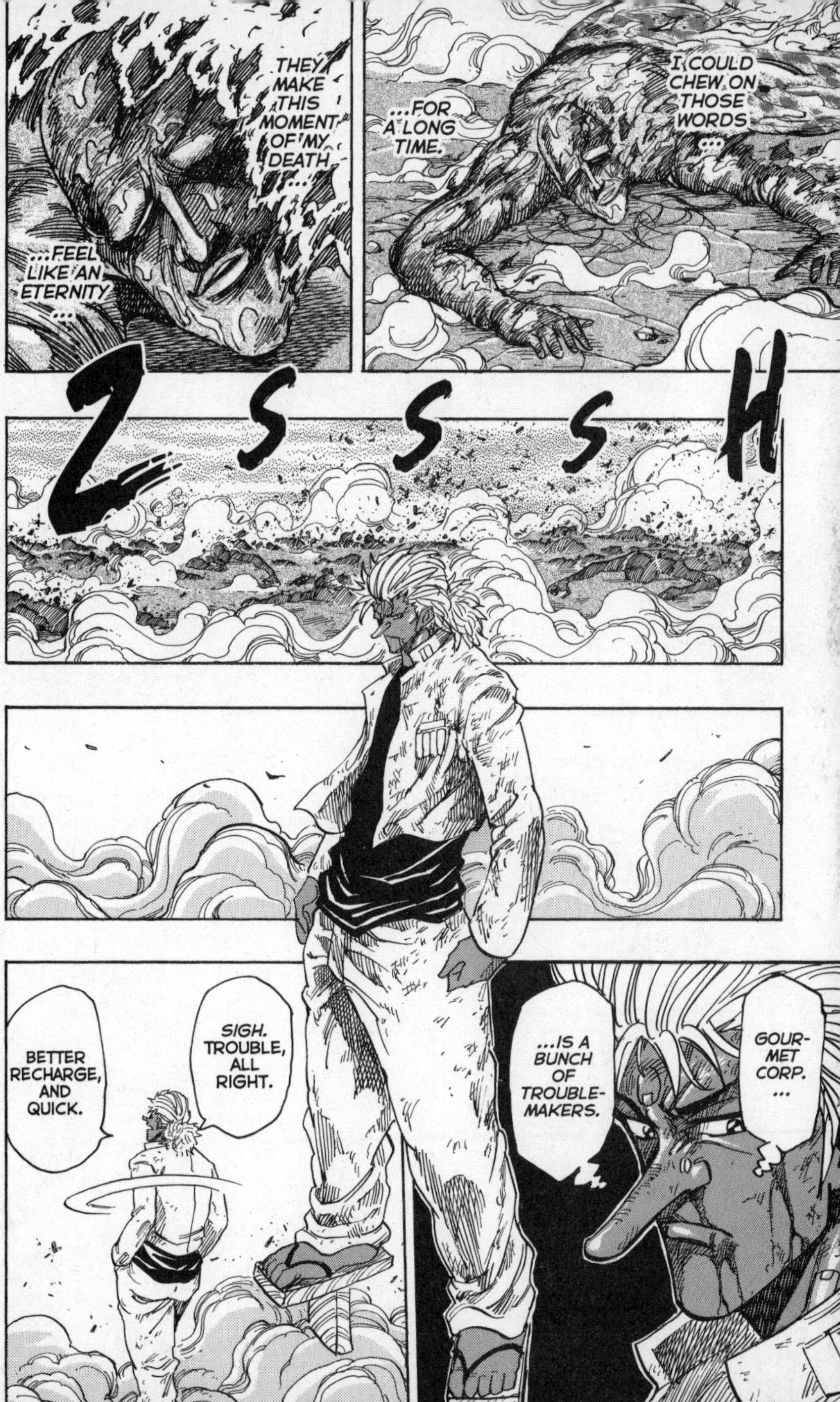
I COULD CHEW ON THOSE WORDS...
...FOR A LONG TIME.
THEY MAKE THIS MOMENT OF MY DEATH...
...FEEL LIKE AN ETERNITY...
ZSSSH
GOURMET CORP. ...
...IS A BUNCH OF TROUBLE-MAKERS.
SIGH. TROUBLE, ALL RIGHT.
BETTER RECHARGE, AND QUICK.

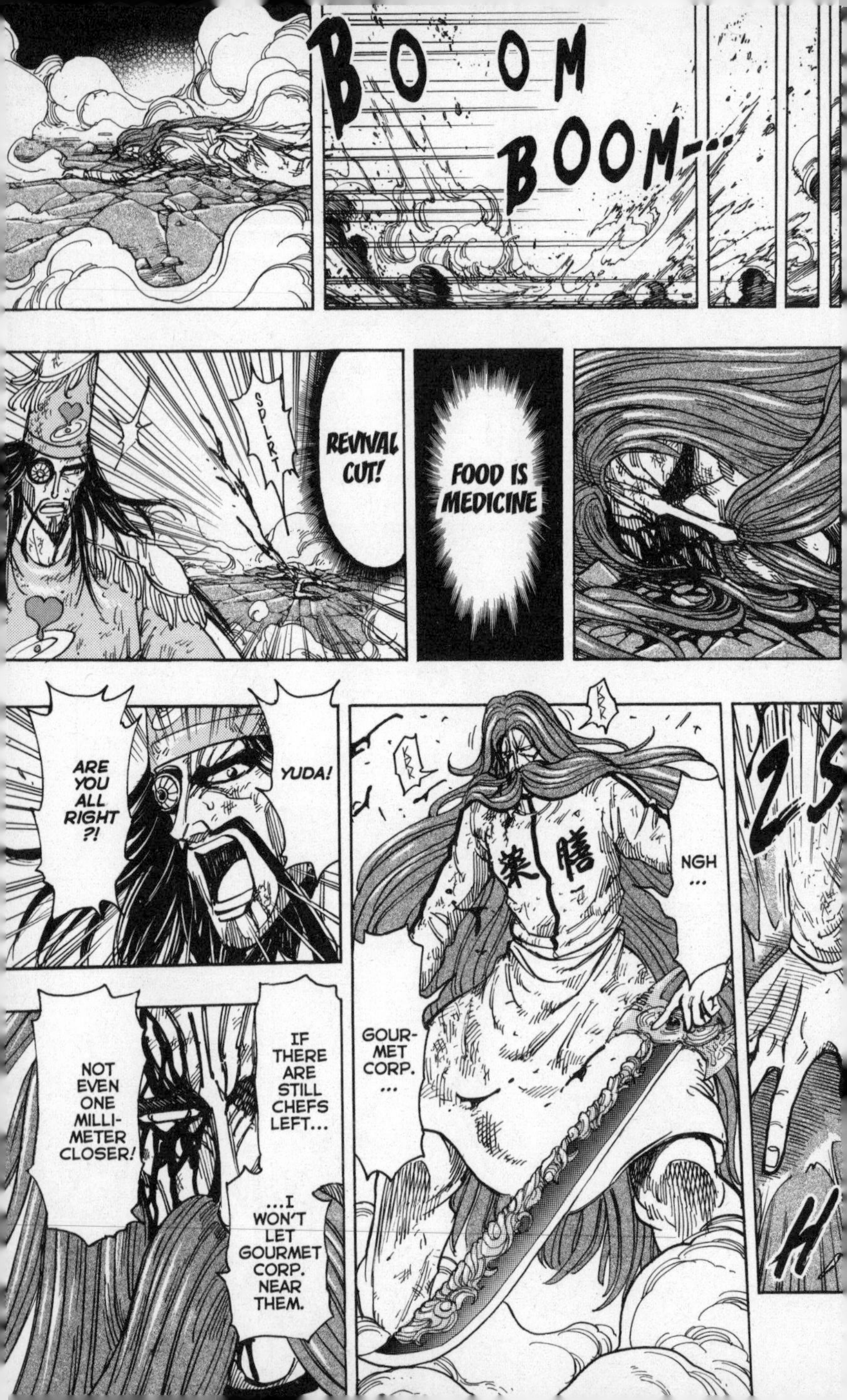
BOOM
BOOM...
FOOD IS MEDICINE
REVIVAL CUT!
SPLRT
KRR
KRR
NGH...
GOURMET CORP....
YUDA!
ARE YOU ALL RIGHT?!
IF THERE ARE STILL CHEFS LEFT...
...I WON'T LET GOURMET CORP. NEAR THEM.
NOT EVEN ONE MILLIMETER CLOSER!

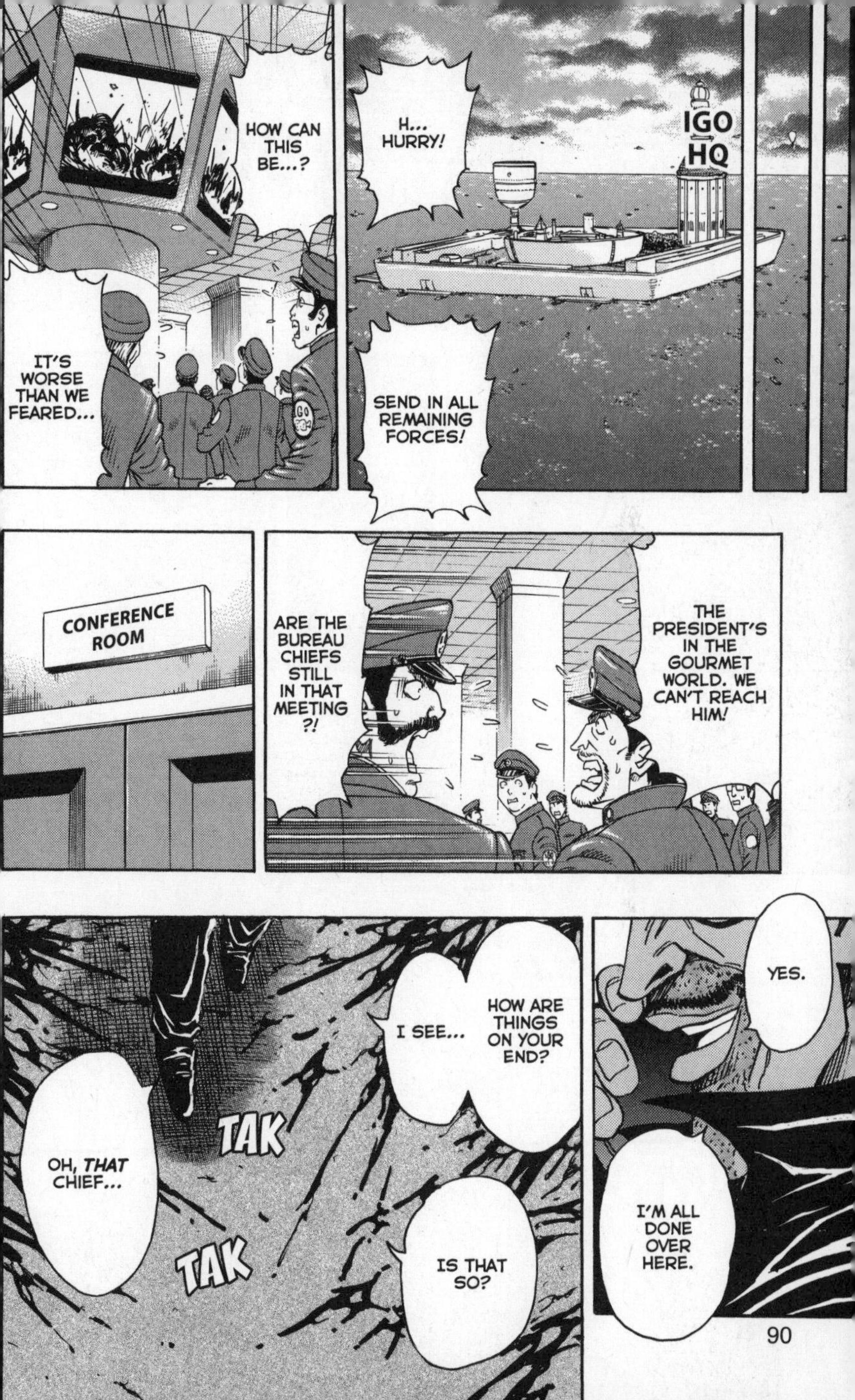
IGO HQ
H... HURRY!
SEND IN ALL REMAINING FORCES!
HOW CAN THIS BE...?
IT'S WORSE THAN WE FEARED...
ARE THE BUREAU CHIEFS STILL IN THAT MEETING?!
THE PRESIDENT'S IN THE GOURMET WORLD. WE CAN'T REACH HIM!
CONFERENCE ROOM
YES.
I'M ALL DONE OVER HERE.
HOW ARE THINGS ON YOUR END?
I SEE...
TAK
IS THAT SO?
TAK
OH, *THAT* CHIEF...

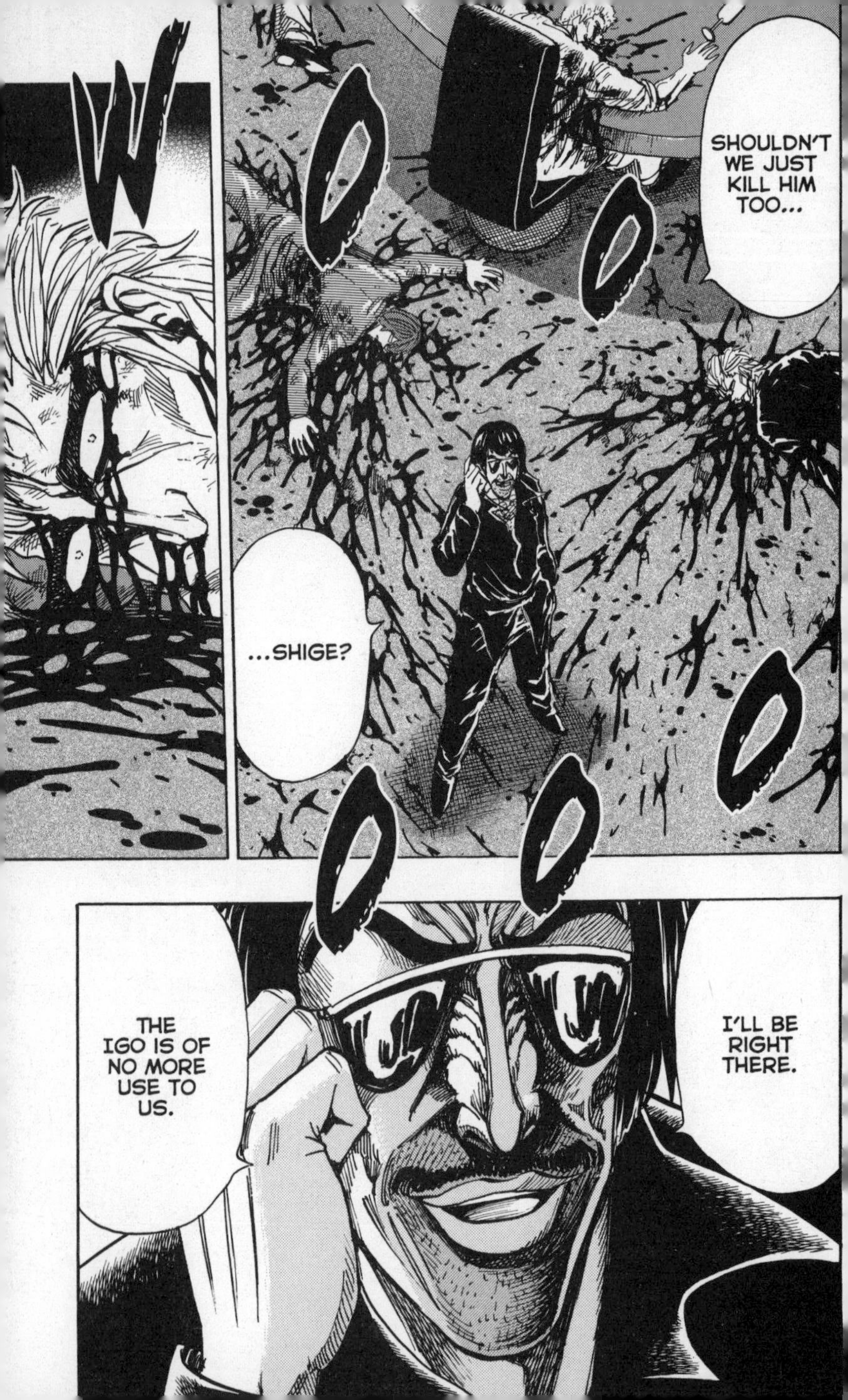
SHOULDN'T WE JUST KILL HIM TOO...
...SHIGE?
W
I'LL BE RIGHT THERE.
THE IGO IS OF NO MORE USE TO US.

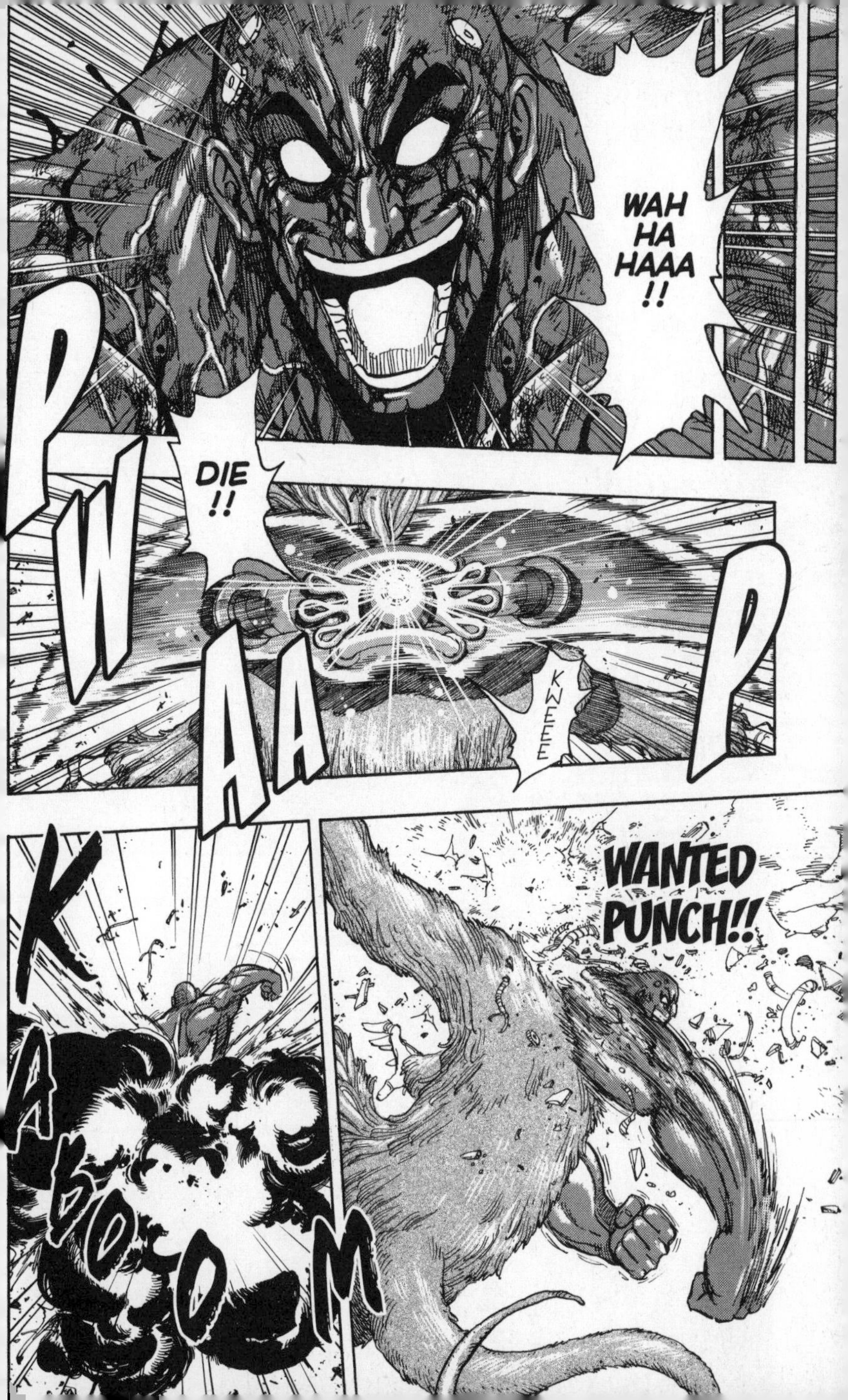
WAH HA HAAA!!
DIE!!
PWAAP
KWEEE
WANTED PUNCH!!
KABOOM

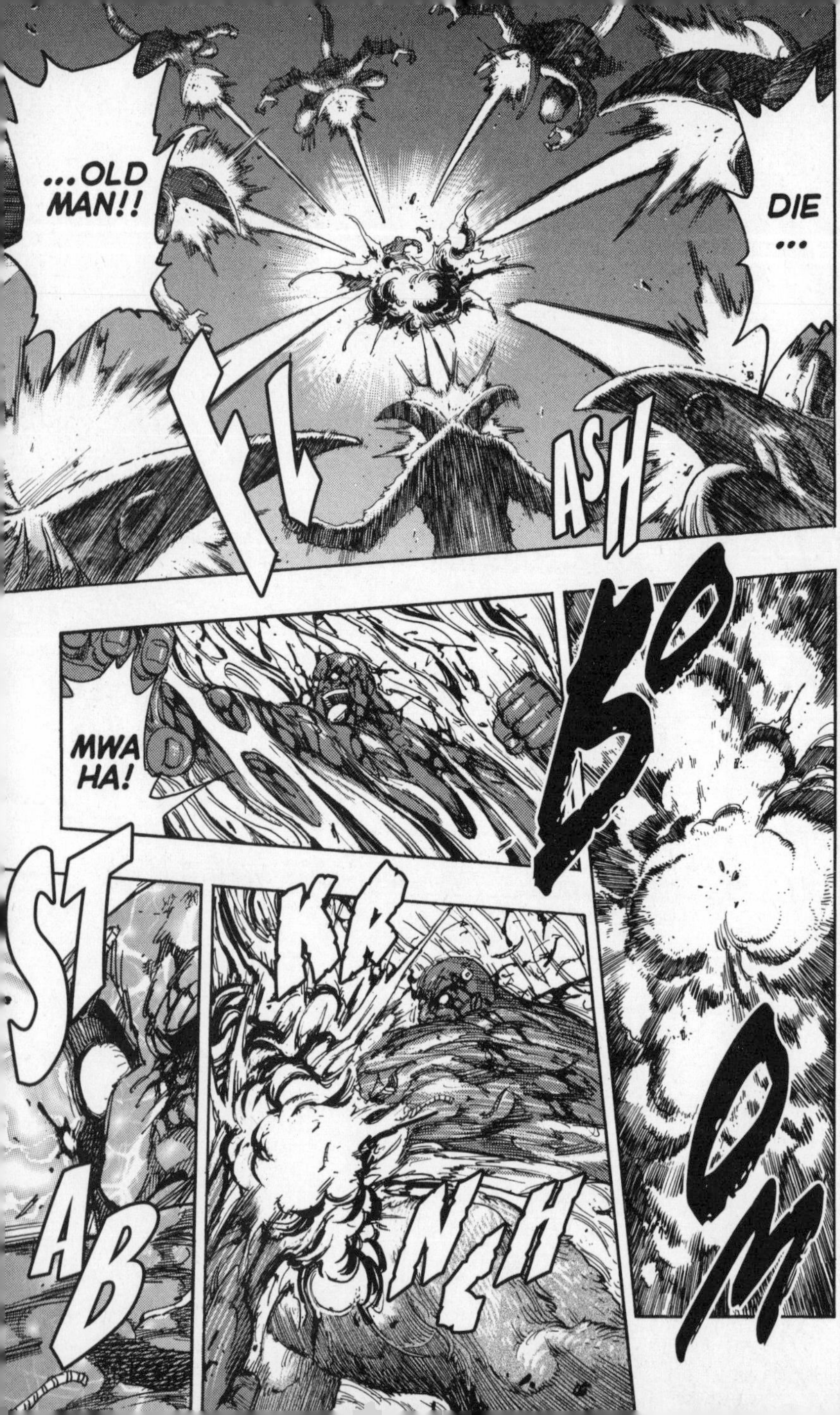
DIE ...
...OLD MAN!!
FLASH
MWA HA!
STAB

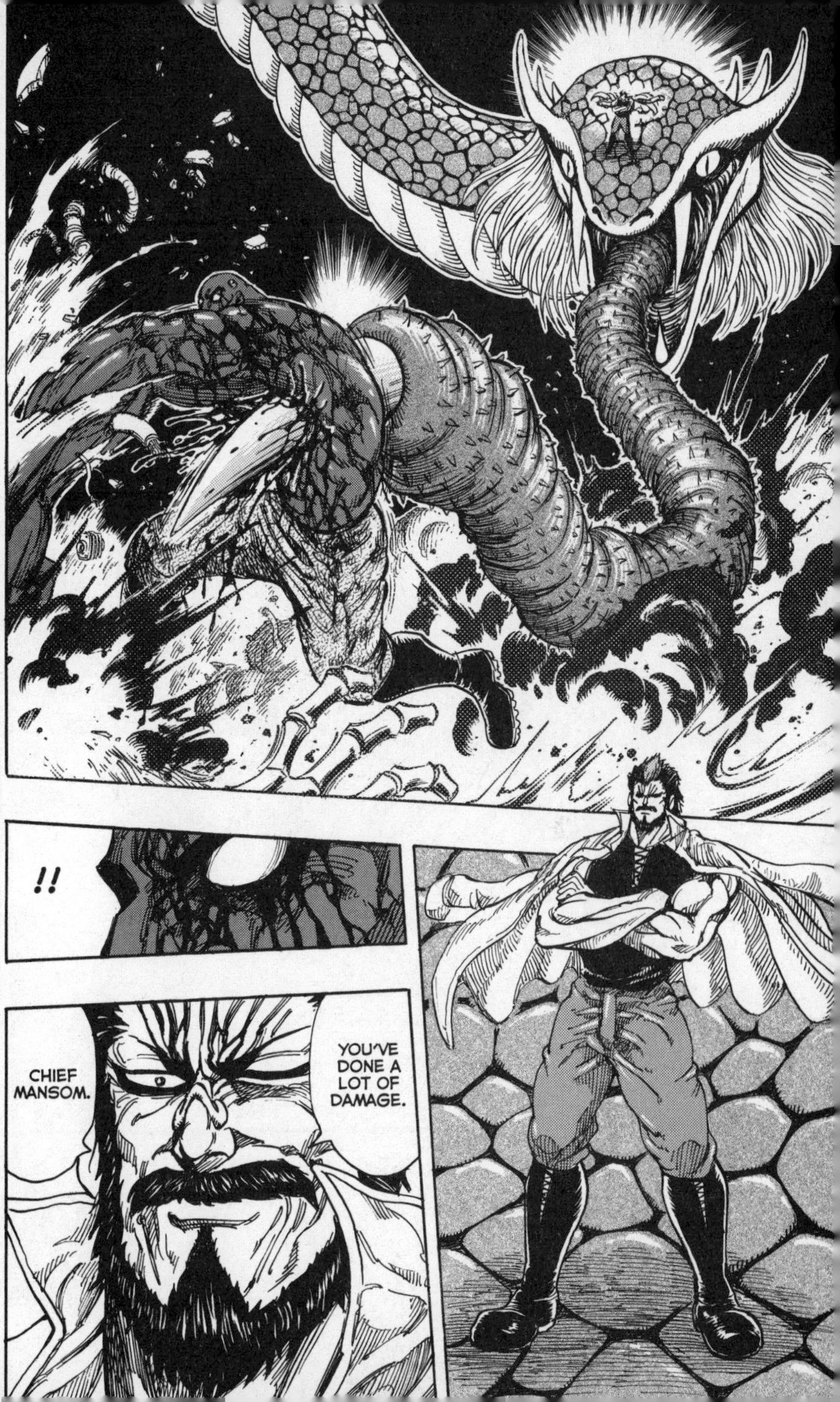
!!
YOU'VE DONE A LOT OF DAMAGE.
CHIEF MANSOM.

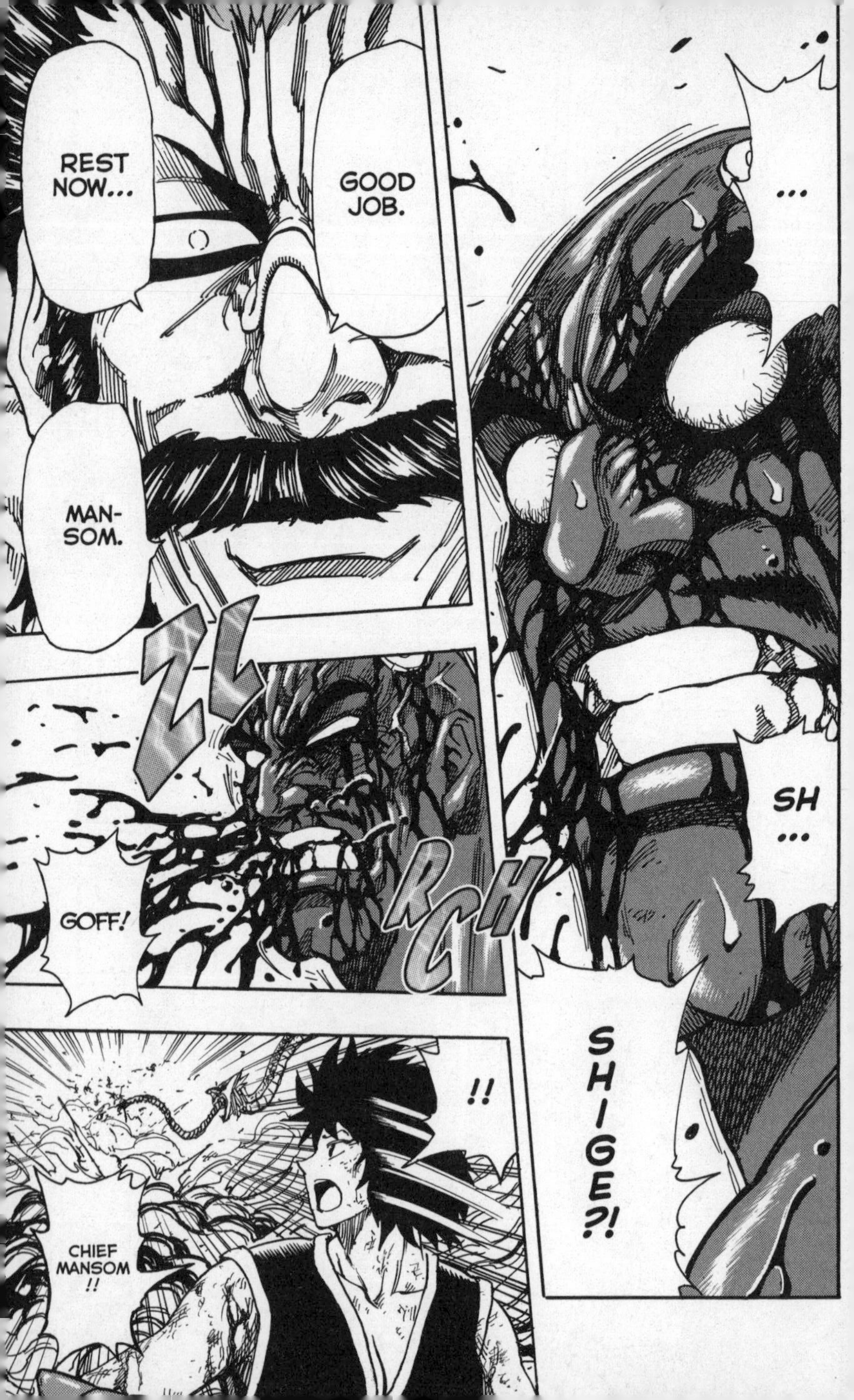
...
SH...
SHIGE?!
GOOD JOB.
REST NOW...
MAN-SOM.
GOFF!
!!
CHIEF MANSOM !!

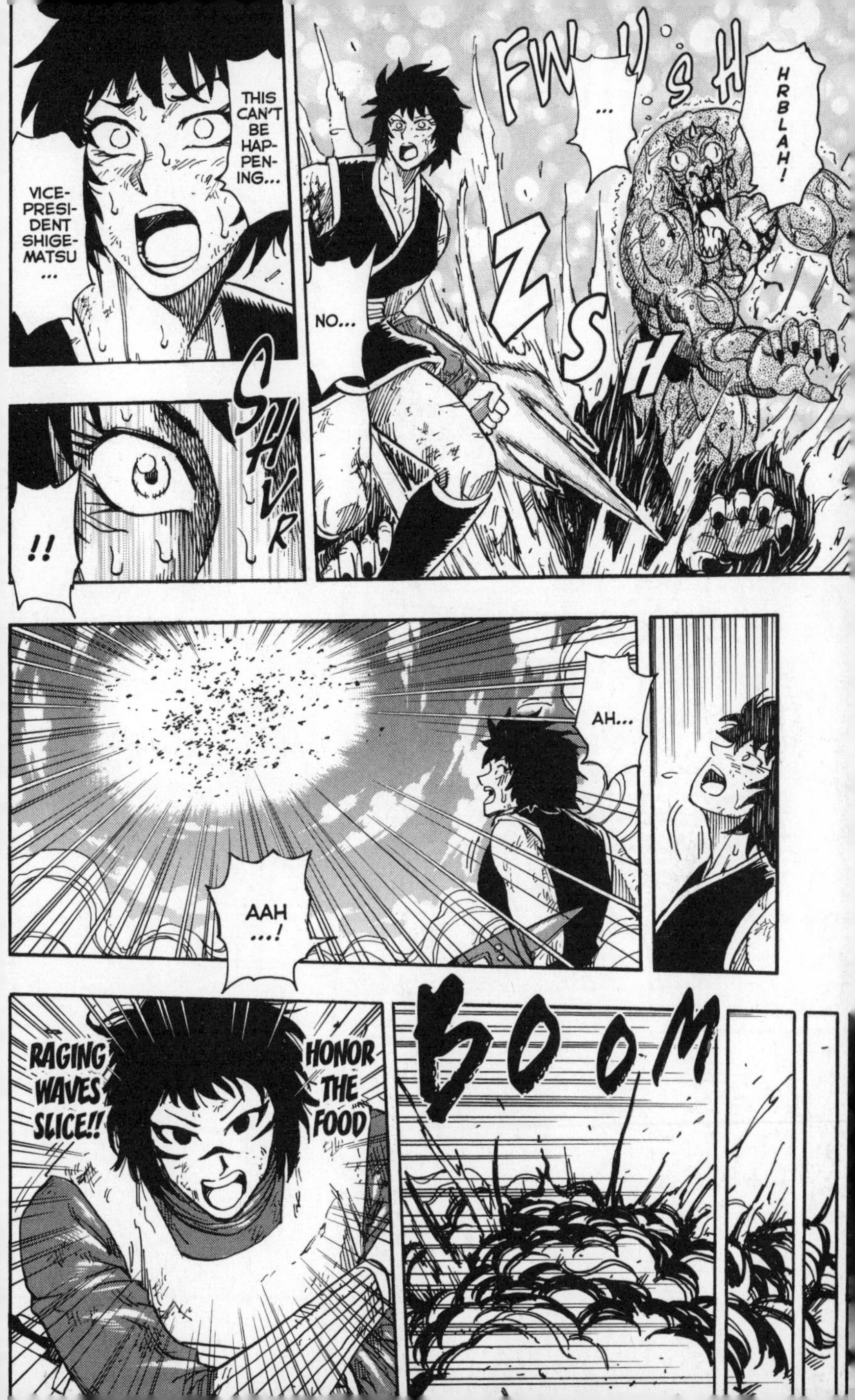
HRBLAH!
...
ZSH
NO...
THIS CAN'T BE HAP-PEN-ING...
VICE-PRESI-DENT SHIGE-MATSU ...
SHVR
!!
AH...
AAH ...!
BOOM
HONOR THE FOOD
RAGING WAVES SLICE!!

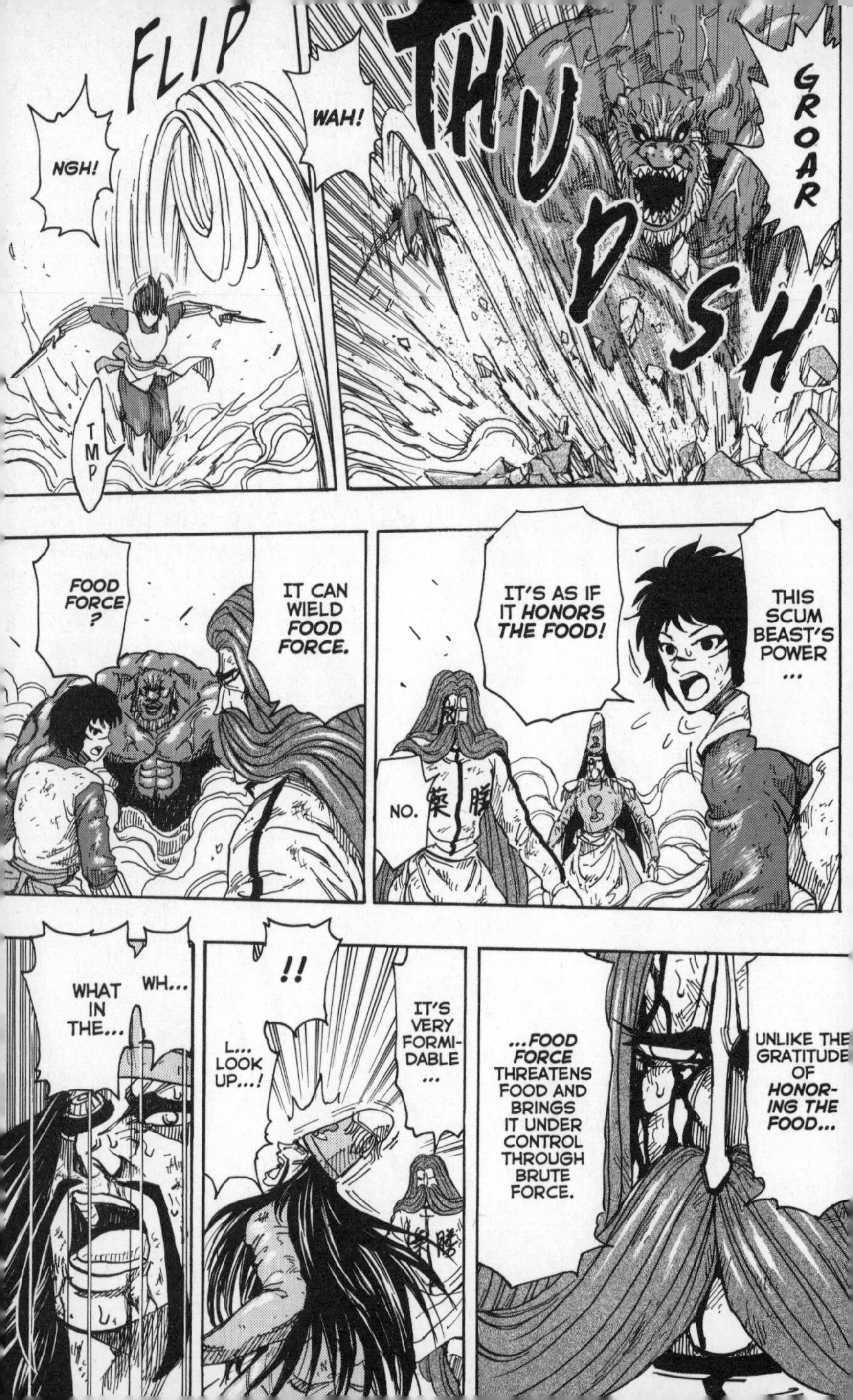
GROAR
THUDSH
WAH!
FLIP
NGH!
TMP
THIS SCUM BEAST'S POWER...
IT'S AS IF IT HONORS THE FOOD!
NO.
IT CAN WIELD FOOD FORCE.
FOOD FORCE?
UNLIKE THE GRATITUDE OF HONORING THE FOOD...
...FOOD FORCE THREATENS FOOD AND BRINGS IT UNDER CONTROL THROUGH BRUTE FORCE.
IT'S VERY FORMIDABLE...
!!
L... LOOK UP...!
WH...
WHAT IN THE...

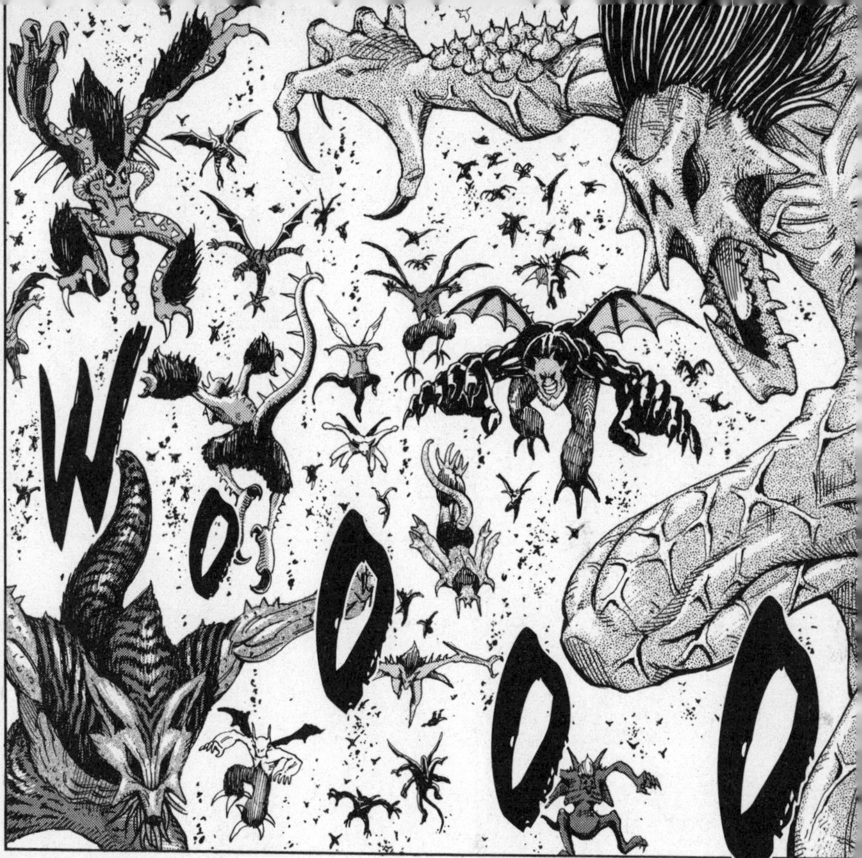
WOOOOO

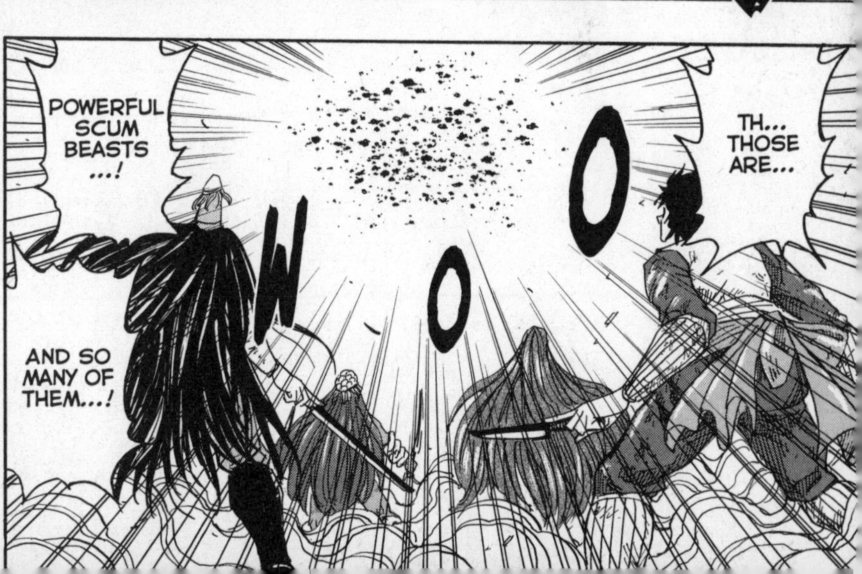
TH... THOSE ARE...
WOOO
POWERFUL SCUM BEASTS ...!
AND SO MANY OF THEM...!

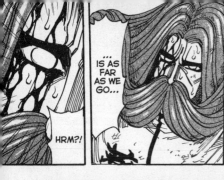

...IS AS FAR AS WE GO...

HRM?!

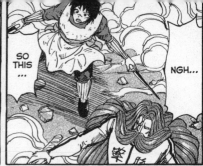

SO THIS...

NGH...

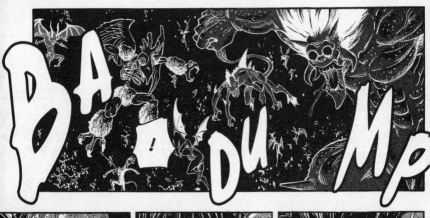

BA DUMP

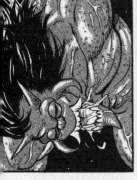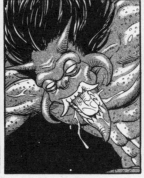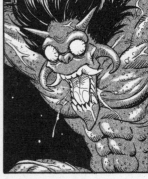

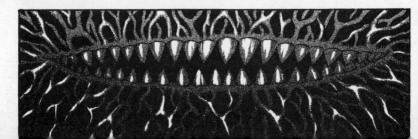

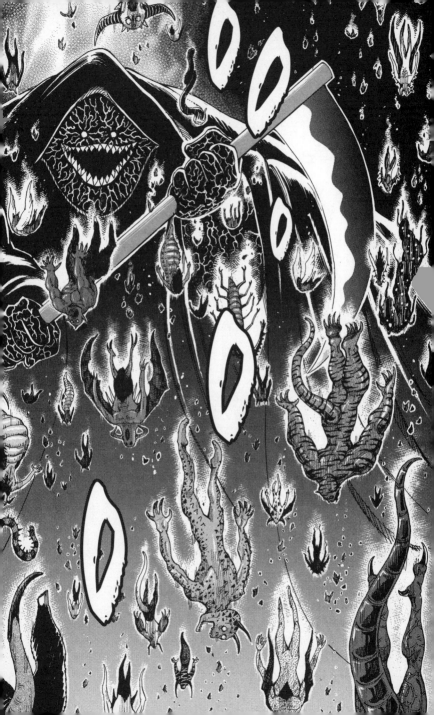

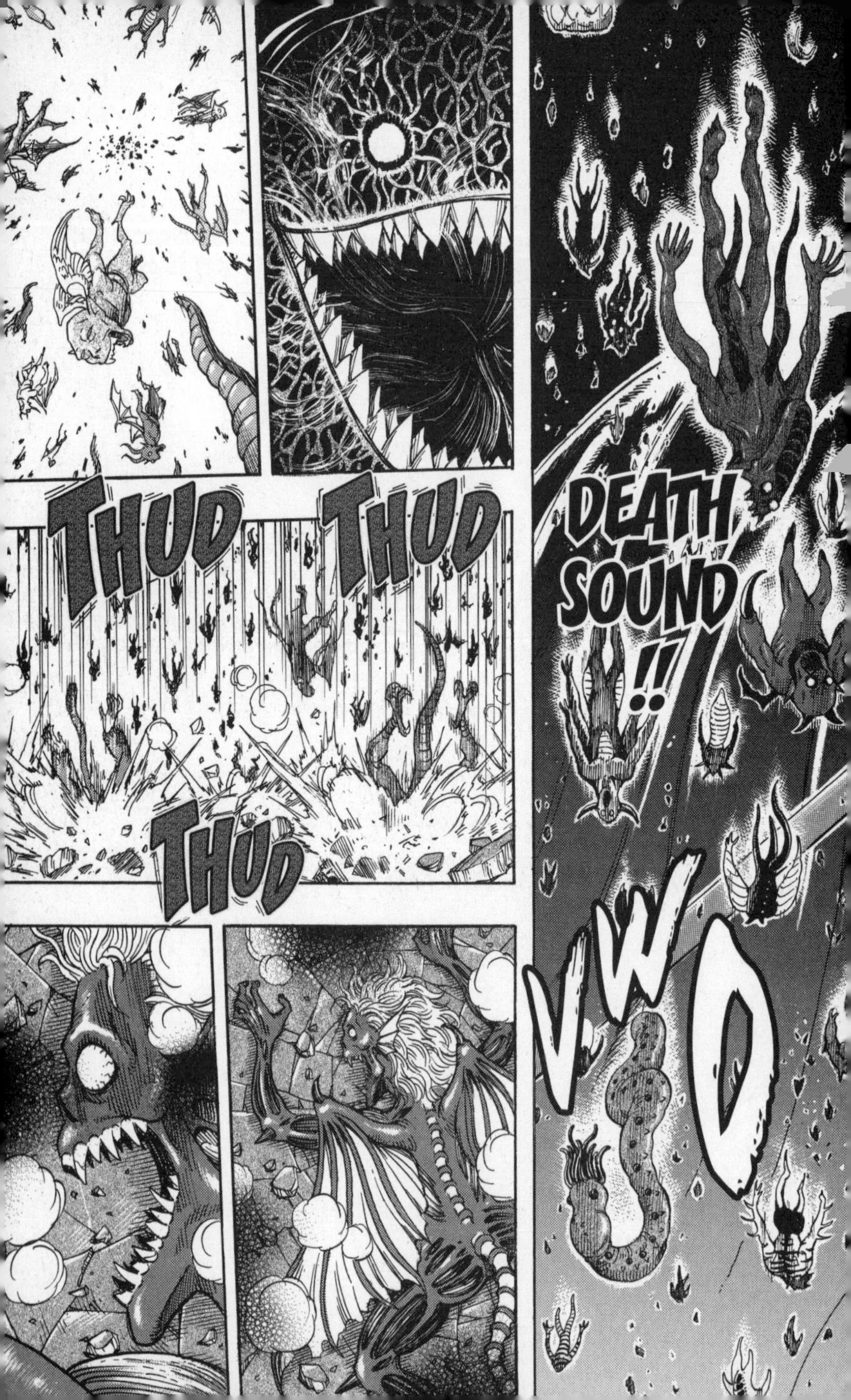
DEATH SOUND!!
VWO
THUD
THUD
THUD

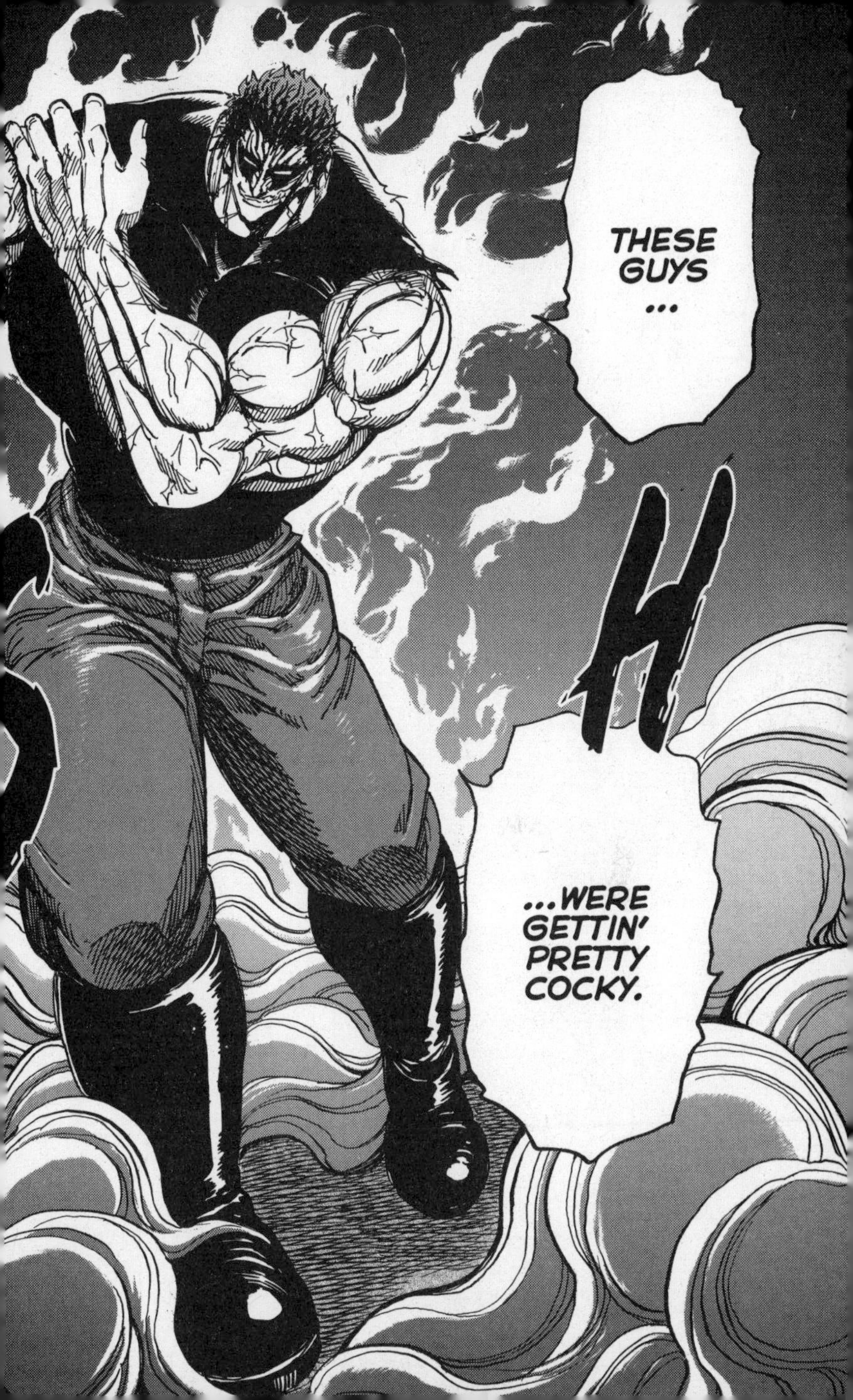
THESE GUYS ...
...WERE GETTIN' PRETTY COCKY.

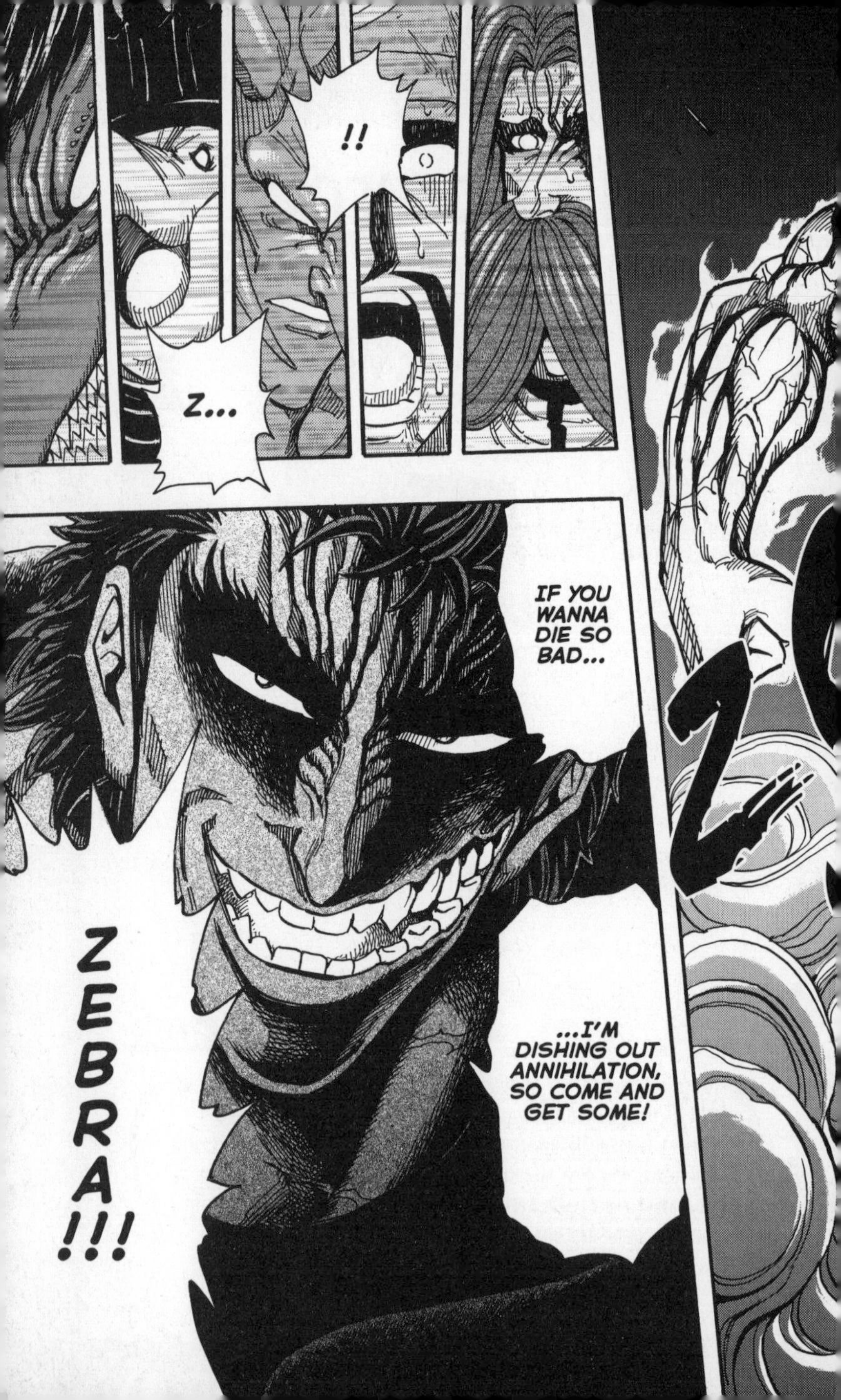
!!
Z...
IF YOU WANNA DIE SO BAD...
...I'M DISHING OUT ANNIHILATION, SO COME AND GET SOME!
ZEBRA!!!

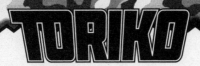

TORIKO

GOURMET CHECKLIST
Vol. 255

 SHOCK LEMON
(FRUIT)

CAPTURE LEVEL: 5
HABITAT: TROPICS
LENGTH: 12 CM
HEIGHT: ---
WEIGHT: 200 G
PRICE: 6,000 YEN PER FRUIT

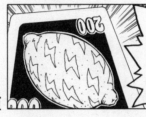

IT'S HAPPENED AGAIN!! IT DOESN'T GET LUCKIER THAN THE SHOCK LEMON* FOR 200 POINTS!!

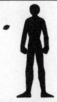

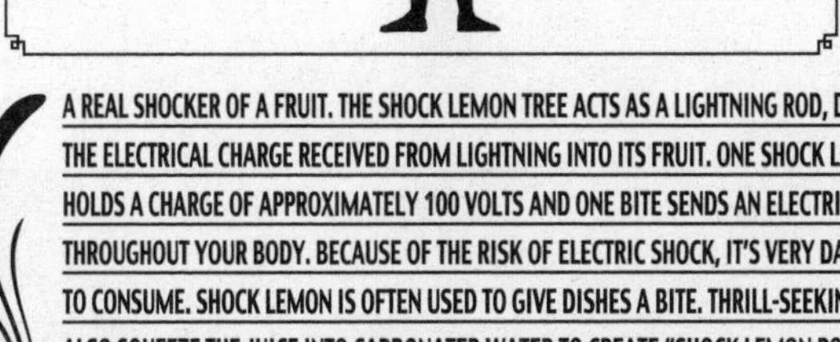

SCALE

A REAL SHOCKER OF A FRUIT. THE SHOCK LEMON TREE ACTS AS A LIGHTNING ROD, DIVERTING THE ELECTRICAL CHARGE RECEIVED FROM LIGHTNING INTO ITS FRUIT. ONE SHOCK LEMON HOLDS A CHARGE OF APPROXIMATELY 100 VOLTS AND ONE BITE SENDS AN ELECTRIC CURRENT THROUGHOUT YOUR BODY. BECAUSE OF THE RISK OF ELECTRIC SHOCK, IT'S VERY DANGEROUS TO CONSUME. SHOCK LEMON IS OFTEN USED TO GIVE DISHES A BITE. THRILL-SEEKING TEENS ALSO SQUEEZE THE JUICE INTO CARBONATED WATER TO CREATE "SHOCK LEMON POP."

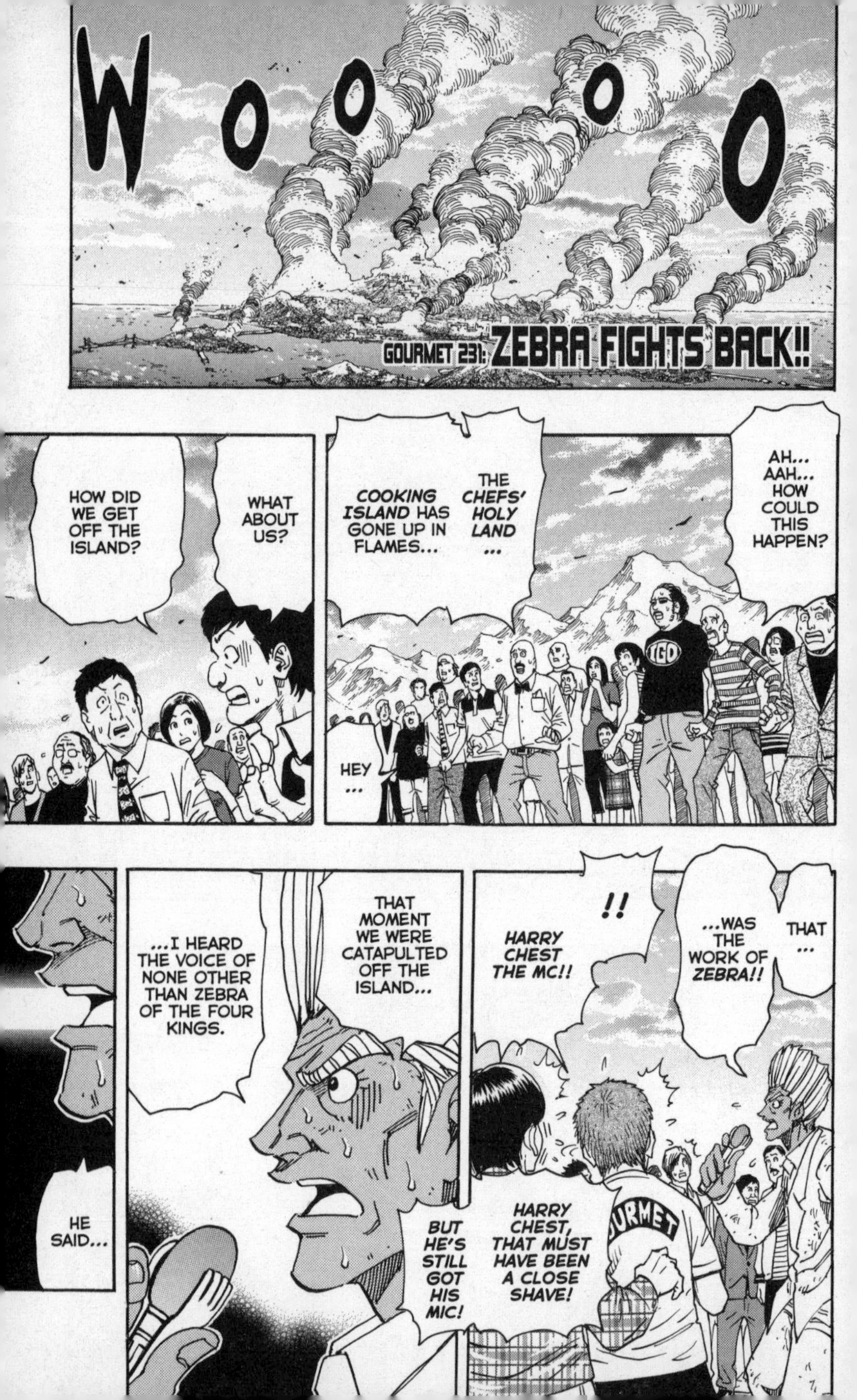
WOOOOO
GOURMET 231: ZEBRA FIGHTS BACK!!
AH... AAH... HOW COULD THIS HAPPEN?
THE CHEFS' HOLY LAND...
COOKING ISLAND HAS GONE UP IN FLAMES...
HEY...
WHAT ABOUT US?
HOW DID WE GET OFF THE ISLAND?
THAT...
...WAS THE WORK OF ZEBRA!!
!!
HARRY CHEST THE MC!!
HARRY CHEST, THAT MUST HAVE BEEN A CLOSE SHAVE!
BUT HE'S STILL GOT HIS MIC!
GOURMET
THAT MOMENT WE WERE CATAPULTED OFF THE ISLAND...
...I HEARD THE VOICE OF NONE OTHER THAN ZEBRA OF THE FOUR KINGS.
HE SAID...

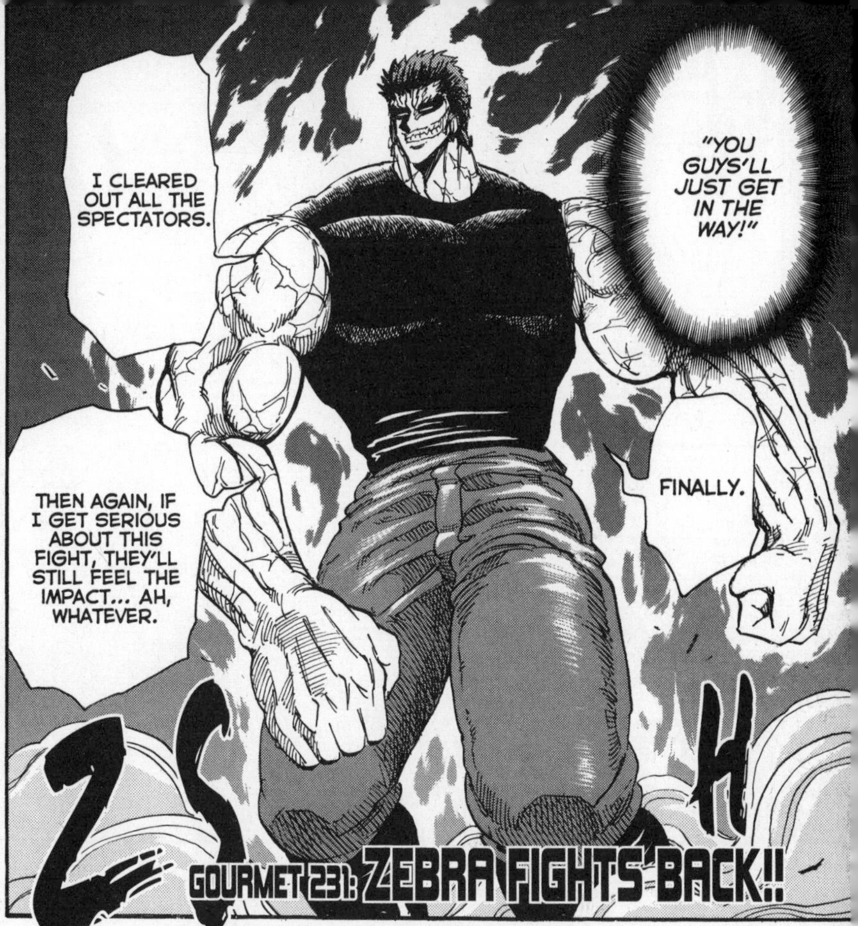
"YOU GUYS'LL JUST GET IN THE WAY!"
I CLEARED OUT ALL THE SPECTATORS.
FINALLY.
THEN AGAIN, IF I GET SERIOUS ABOUT THIS FIGHT, THEY'LL STILL FEEL THE IMPACT... AH, WHATEVER.
ZSH

GOURMET 231: ZEBRA FIGHTS BACK!!

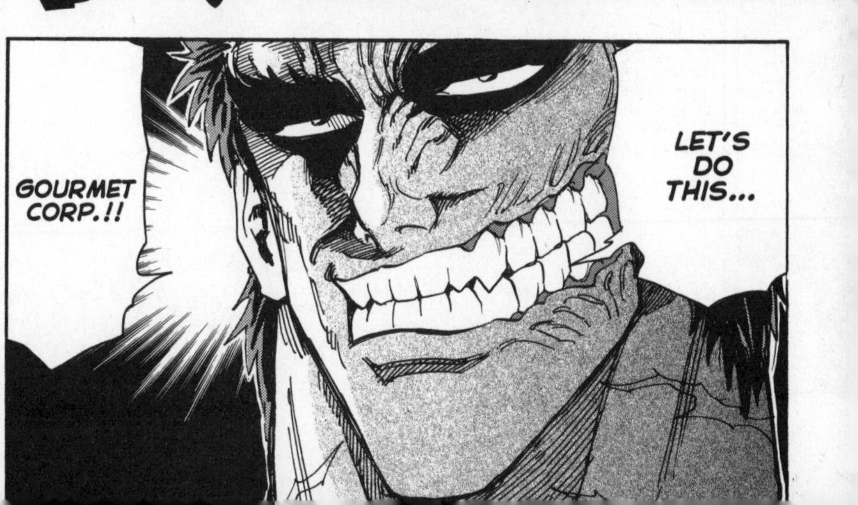
LET'S DO THIS...
GOURMET CORP.!!

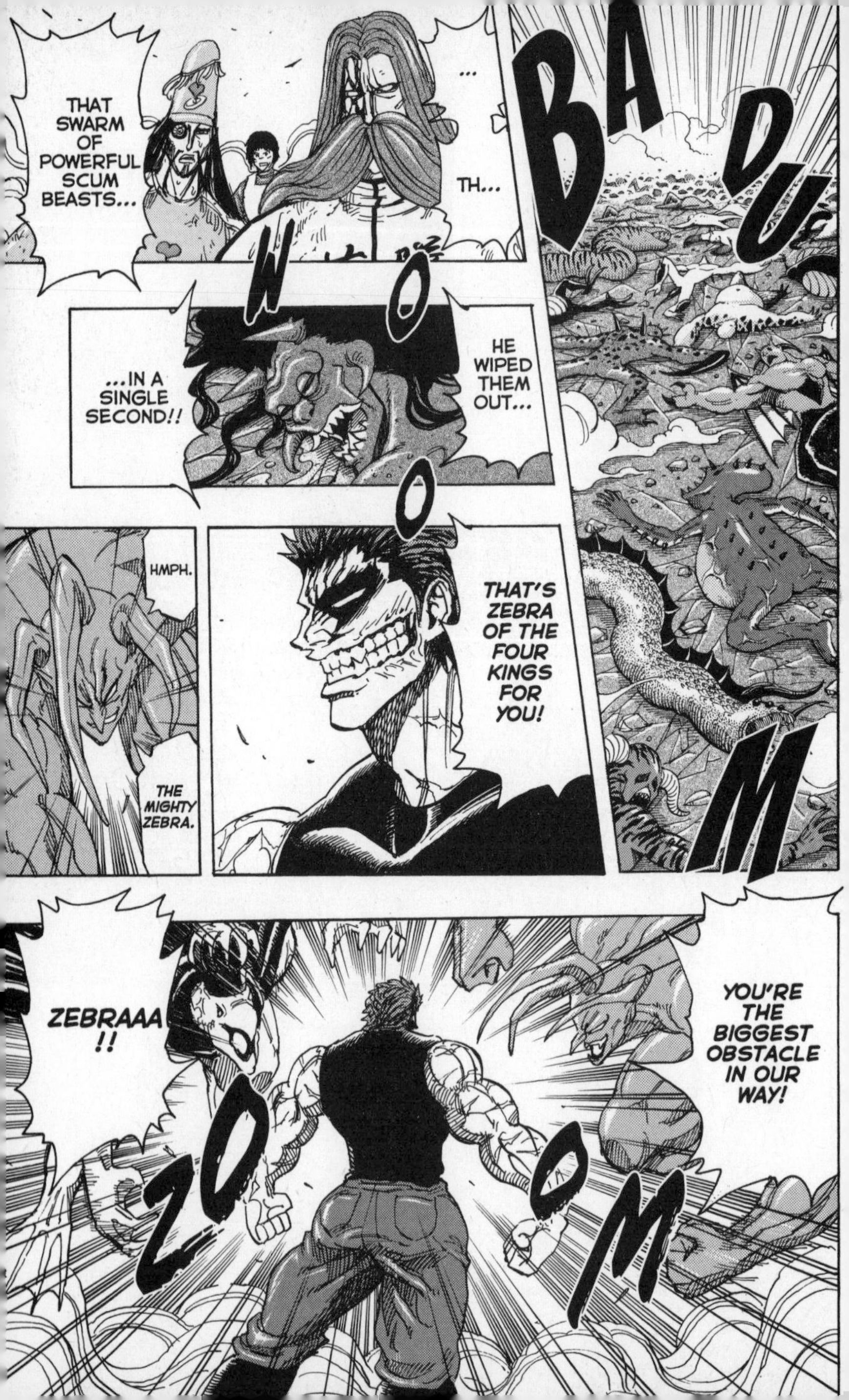
BADUM
...
TH...
THAT SWARM OF POWERFUL SCUM BEASTS...
WOOO
HE WIPED THEM OUT...
...IN A SINGLE SECOND!!
THAT'S ZEBRA OF THE FOUR KINGS FOR YOU!
HMPH.
THE MIGHTY ZEBRA.
YOU'RE THE BIGGEST OBSTACLE IN OUR WAY!
ZEBRAAA !!
ZOOM

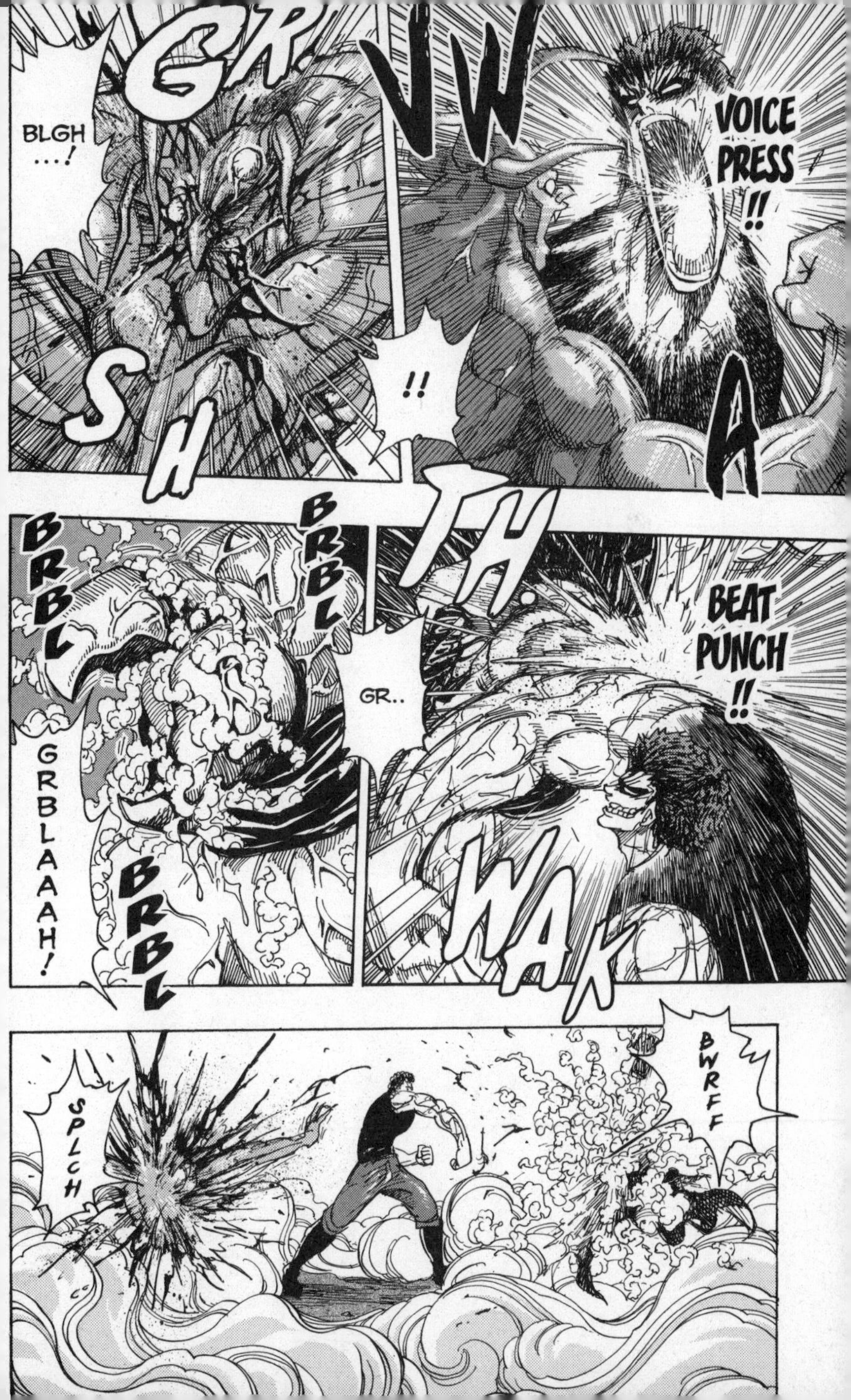
VOICE PRESS!!
GR
NW
!!
BLGH ...!
SH
A
TH
BEAT PUNCH!!
GR..
WAK
BRBL
BRBL
GRBLAAAH!
BRBL
BWRFF
SPLCH

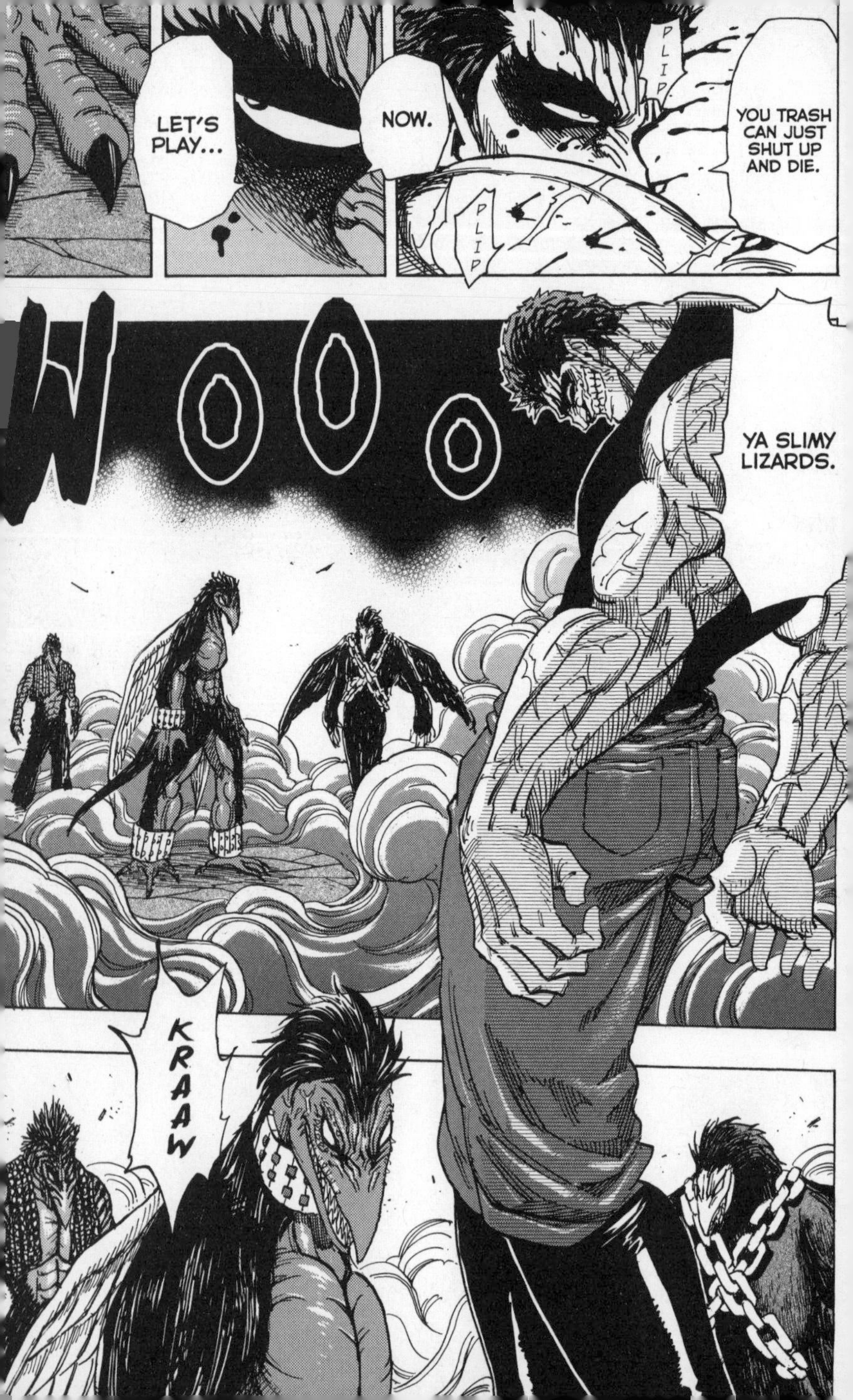
YOU TRASH CAN JUST SHUT UP AND DIE.
PLIP
PLIP
NOW.
LET'S PLAY...
YA SLIMY LIZARDS.
WOOO
KRAAW

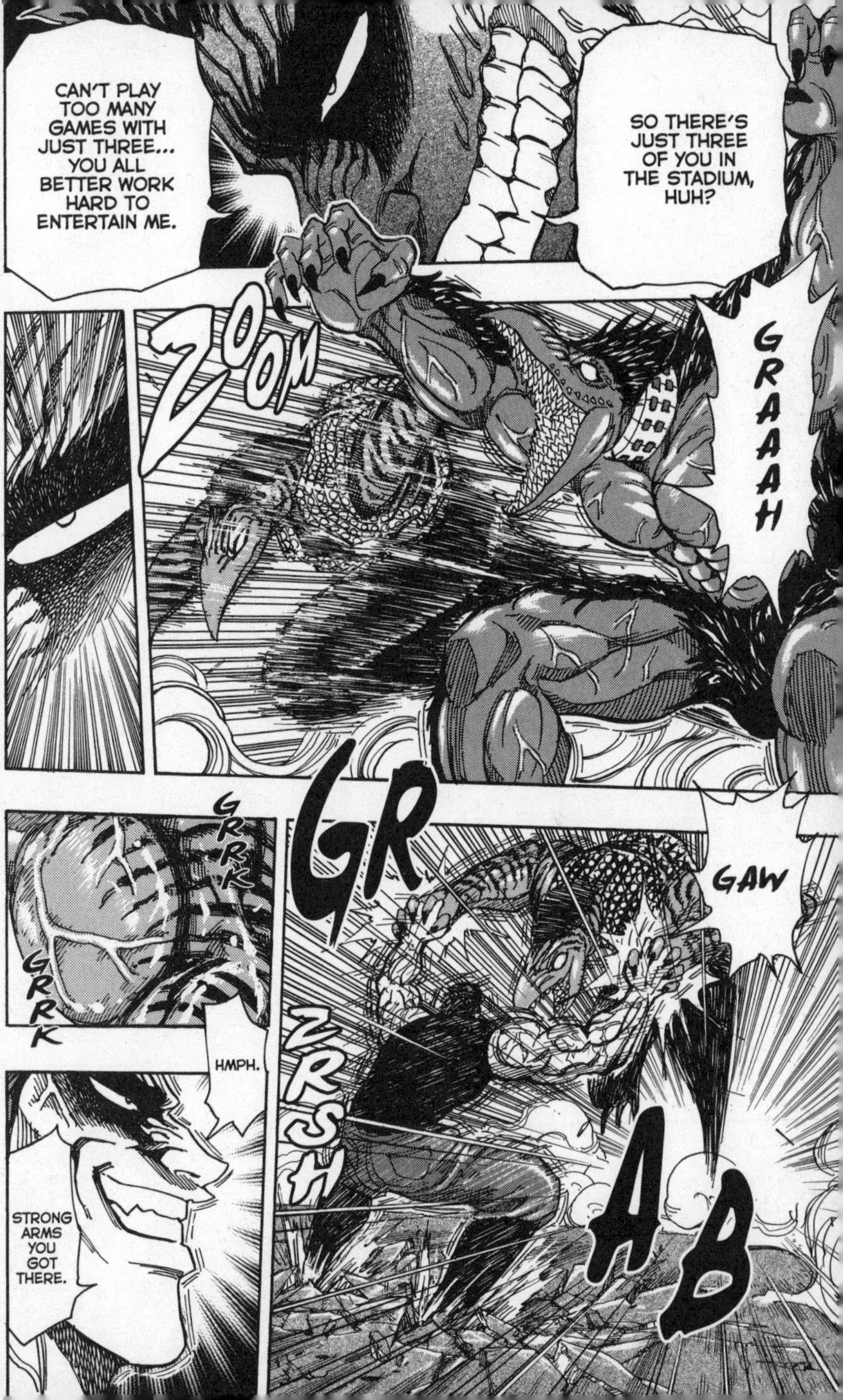
SO THERE'S JUST THREE OF YOU IN THE STADIUM, HUH?
CAN'T PLAY TOO MANY GAMES WITH JUST THREE... YOU ALL BETTER WORK HARD TO ENTERTAIN ME.
GRAAAAH
ZOOM
GAW
GR
ZRSH
AB
GRRK
GRRK
HMPH.
STRONG ARMS YOU GOT THERE.

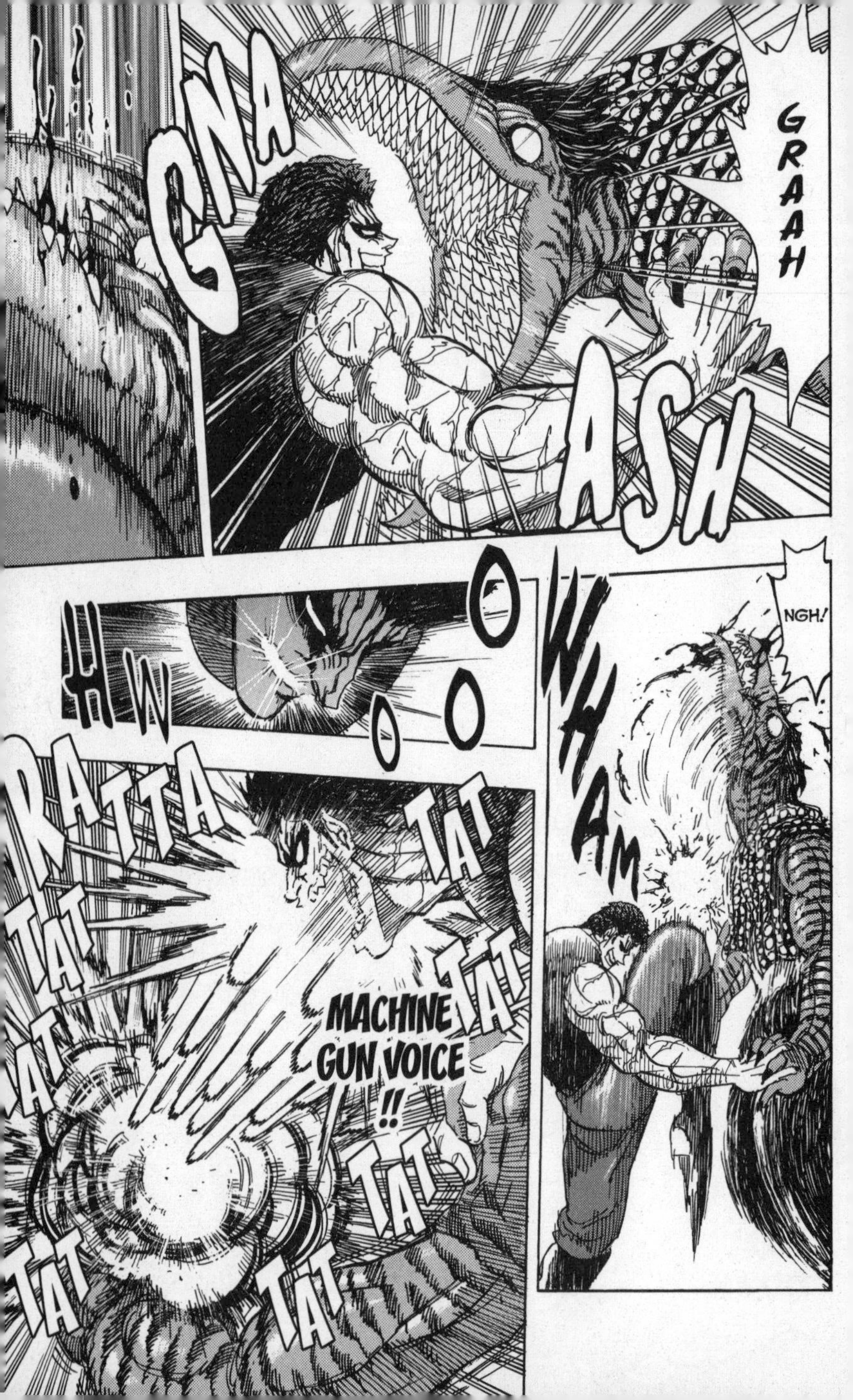
GRAAH
GNASH
NGH!
WHAM
MACHINE GUN VOICE !!
RATTATA TAT TAT TAT TAT TAT TAT TAT TAT

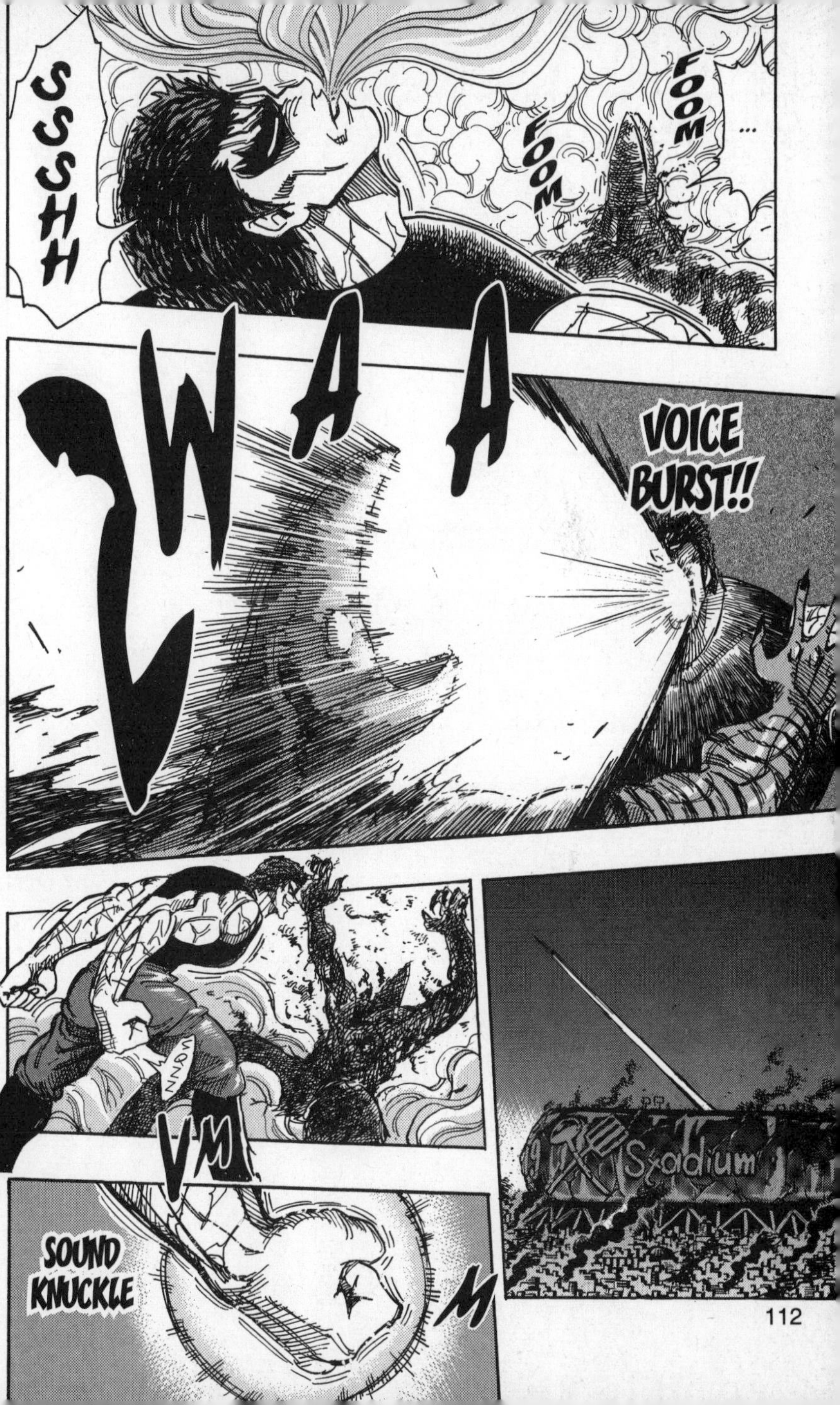
...
FOOM
FOOM
SSSHH
VOICE BURST!!
WAA
Stadium
VMM
SOUND KNUCKLE

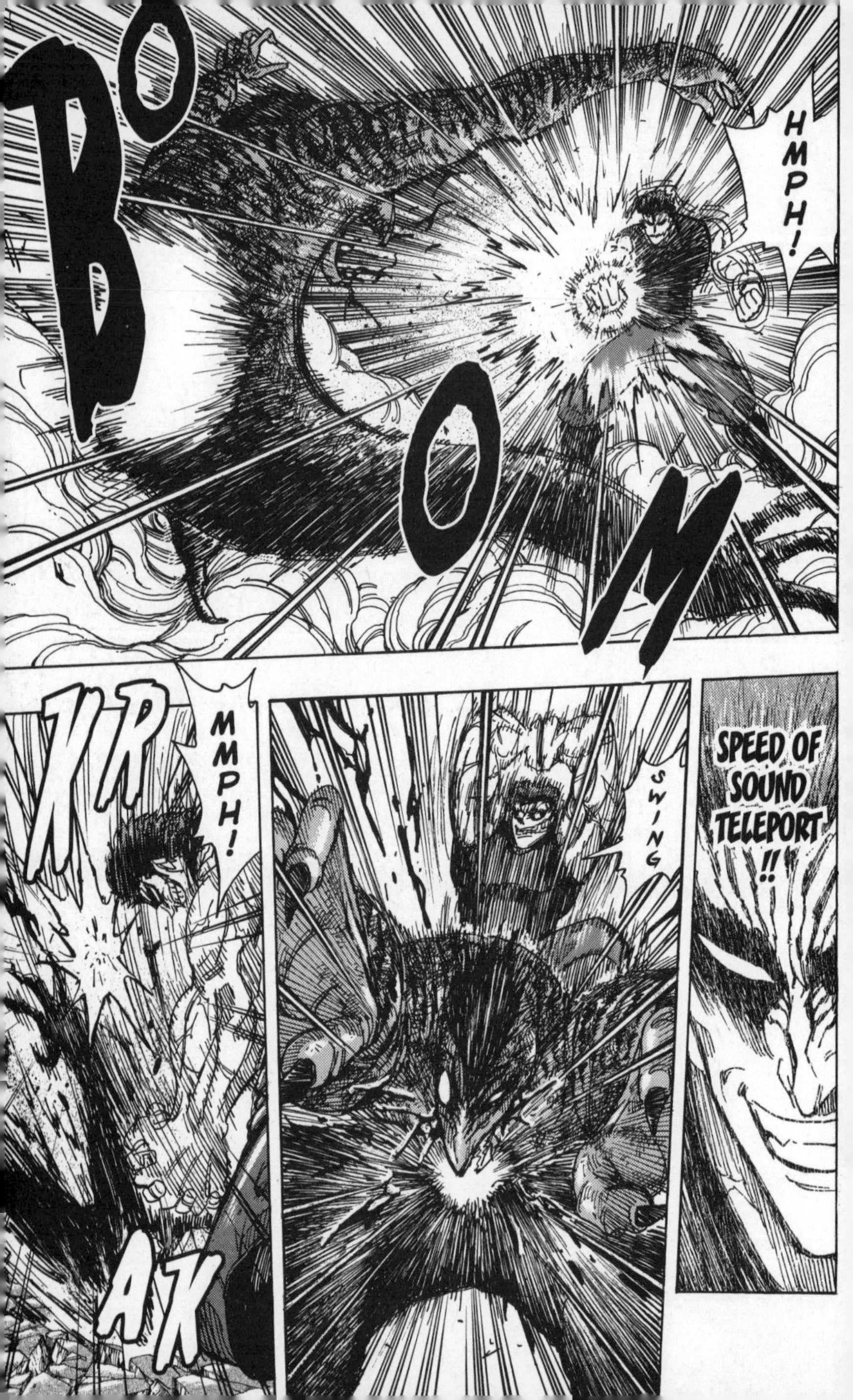
HMPH!
BOOM
SPEED OF SOUND TELEPORT!!
SWING
MMPH!
KR
AK

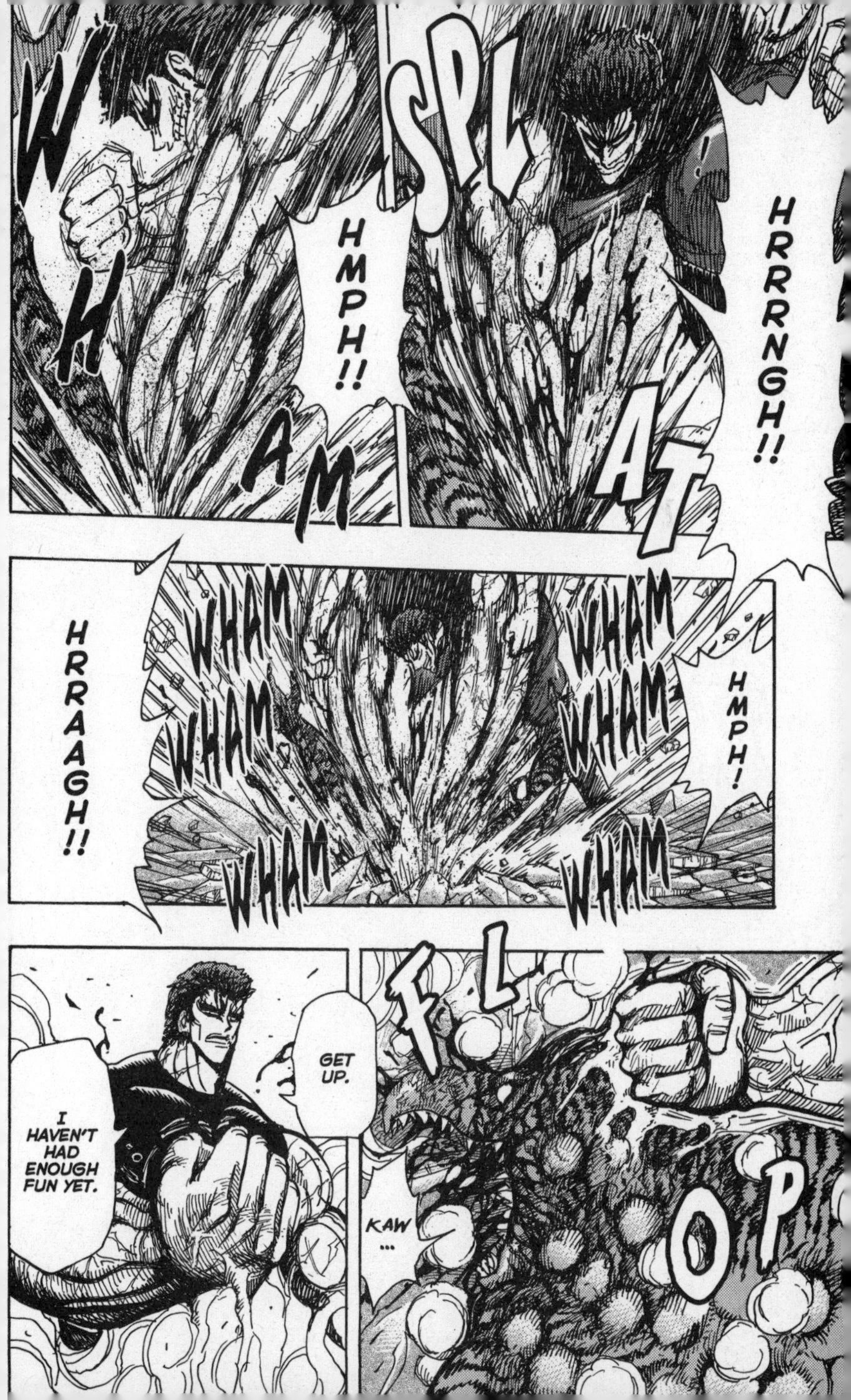
SPLAT
HRRRNGH!!
WHAM
HMPH!!
HMPH!
WHAM WHAM WHAM
WHAM WHAM WHAM
HRRAAGH!!
FLOP
KAW ...
GET UP.
I HAVEN'T HAD ENOUGH FUN YET.

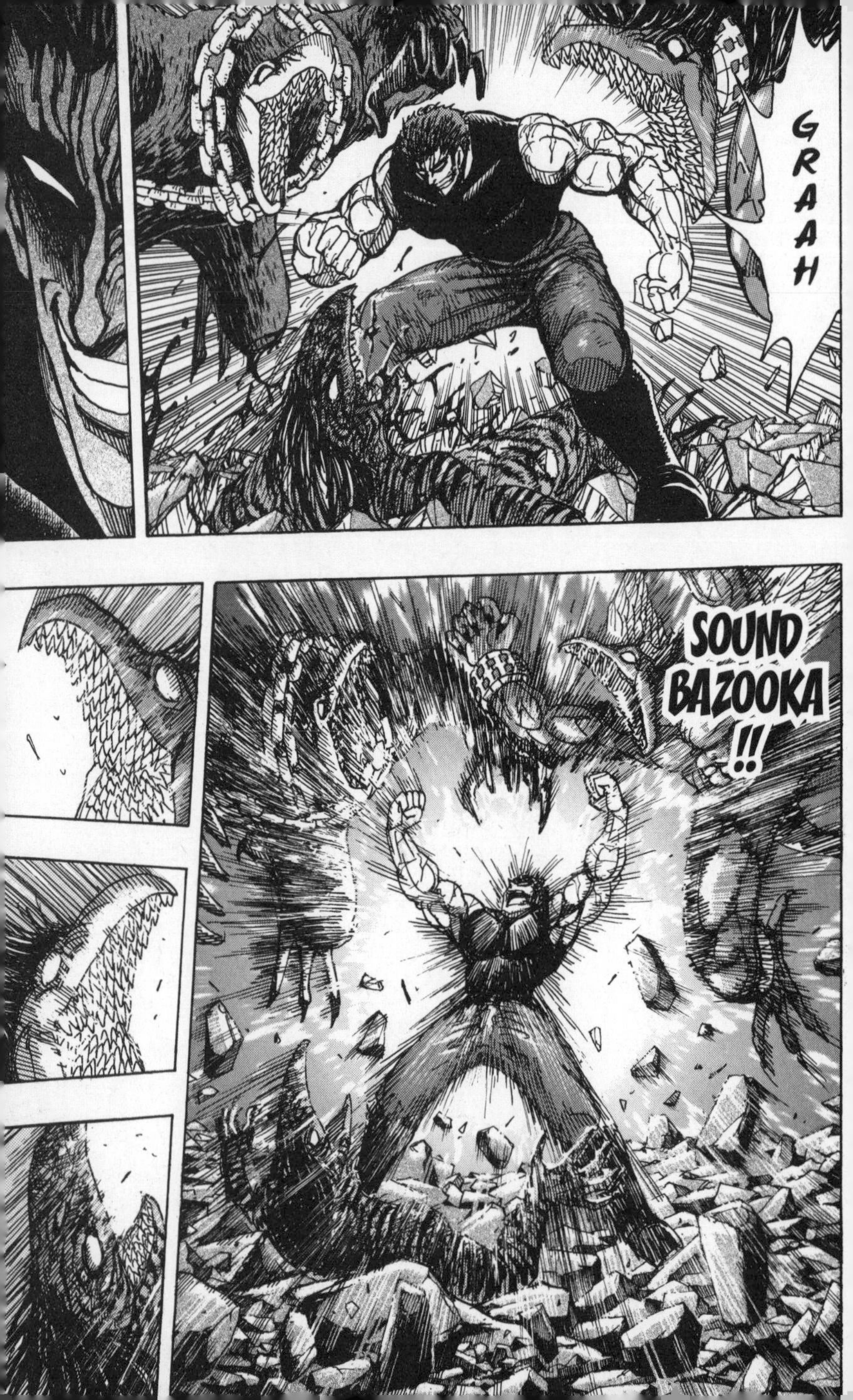
GRAAAH
SOUND BAZOOKA!!

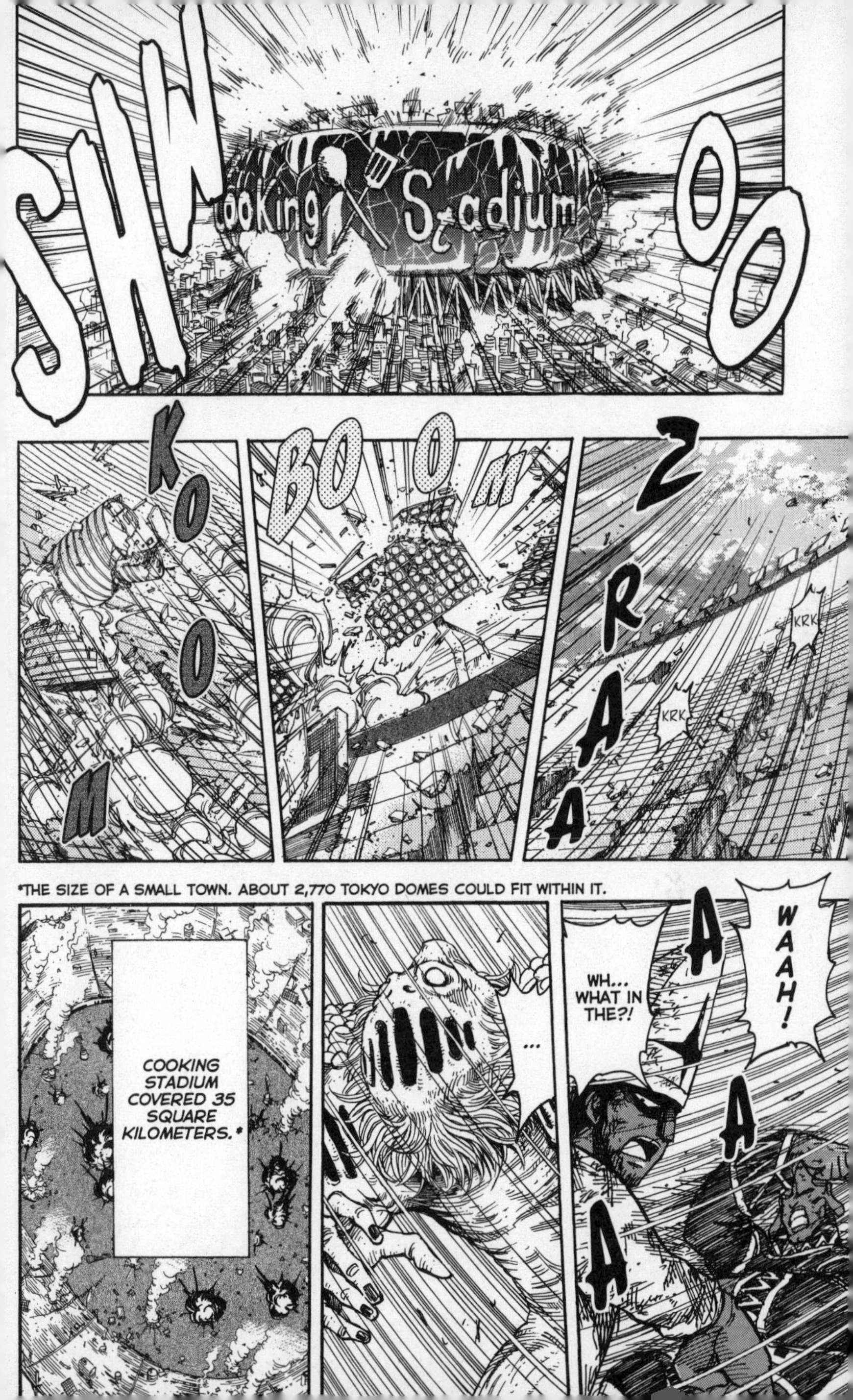
SHWOO
ooking Stadium
ZRAAA
KRK
KRK
BOOOM
KOOOM
WAAH!
AAAA
WH... WHAT IN THE?!
...
COOKING STADIUM COVERED 35 SQUARE KILOMETERS.*

*THE SIZE OF A SMALL TOWN. ABOUT 2,770 TOKYO DOMES COULD FIT WITHIN IT.

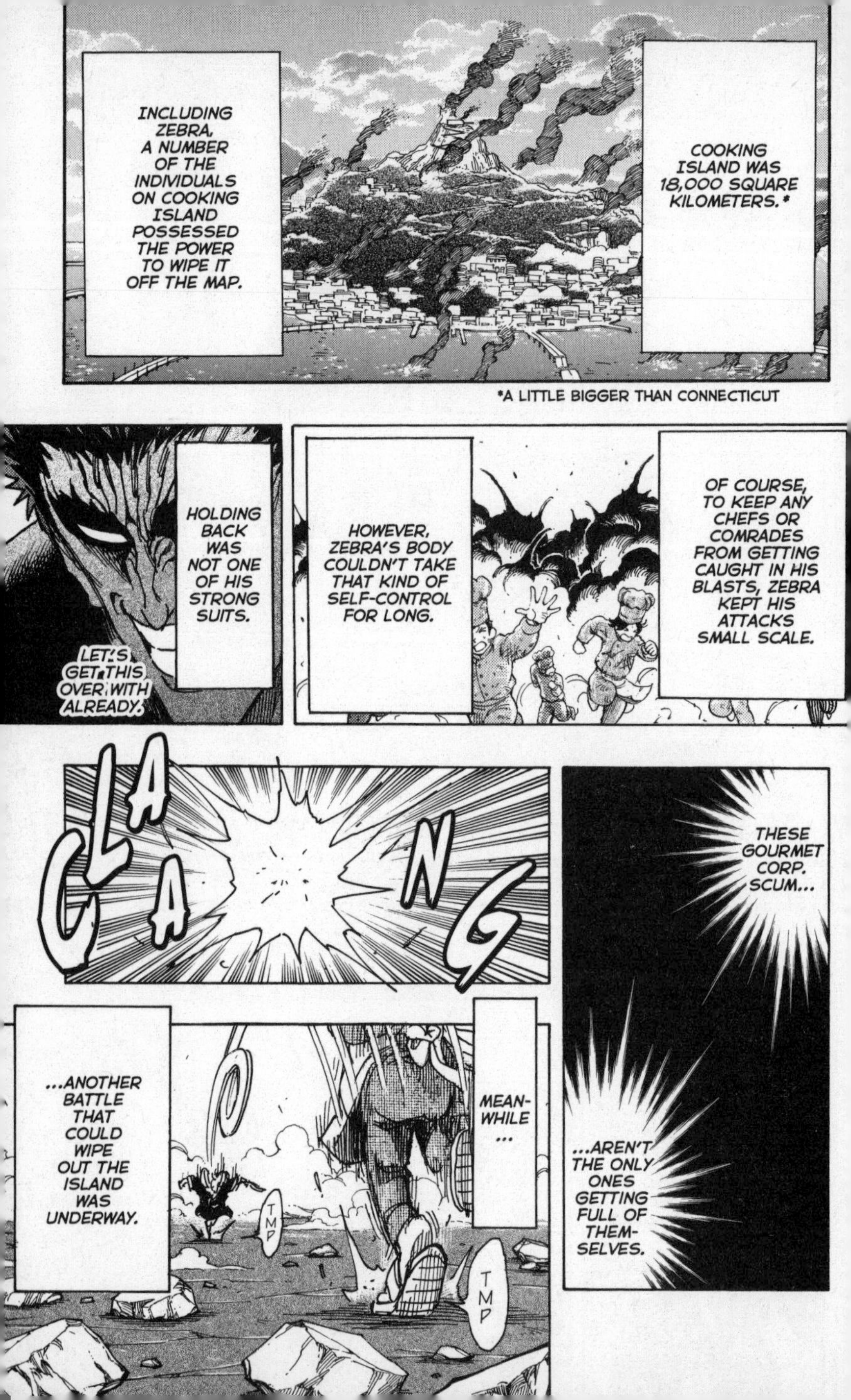
COOKING ISLAND WAS 18,000 SQUARE KILOMETERS.*
INCLUDING ZEBRA, A NUMBER OF THE INDIVIDUALS ON COOKING ISLAND POSSESSED THE POWER TO WIPE IT OFF THE MAP.
OF COURSE, TO KEEP ANY CHEFS OR COMRADES FROM GETTING CAUGHT IN HIS BLASTS, ZEBRA KEPT HIS ATTACKS SMALL SCALE.
HOWEVER, ZEBRA'S BODY COULDN'T TAKE THAT KIND OF SELF-CONTROL FOR LONG.
HOLDING BACK WAS NOT ONE OF HIS STRONG SUITS.
LET'S GET THIS OVER WITH ALREADY.
THESE GOURMET CORP. SCUM...
...AREN'T THE ONLY ONES GETTING FULL OF THEM-SELVES.
CLANG
MEAN-WHILE...
...ANOTHER BATTLE THAT COULD WIPE OUT THE ISLAND WAS UNDERWAY.
TMP
TMP

*A LITTLE BIGGER THAN CONNECTICUT

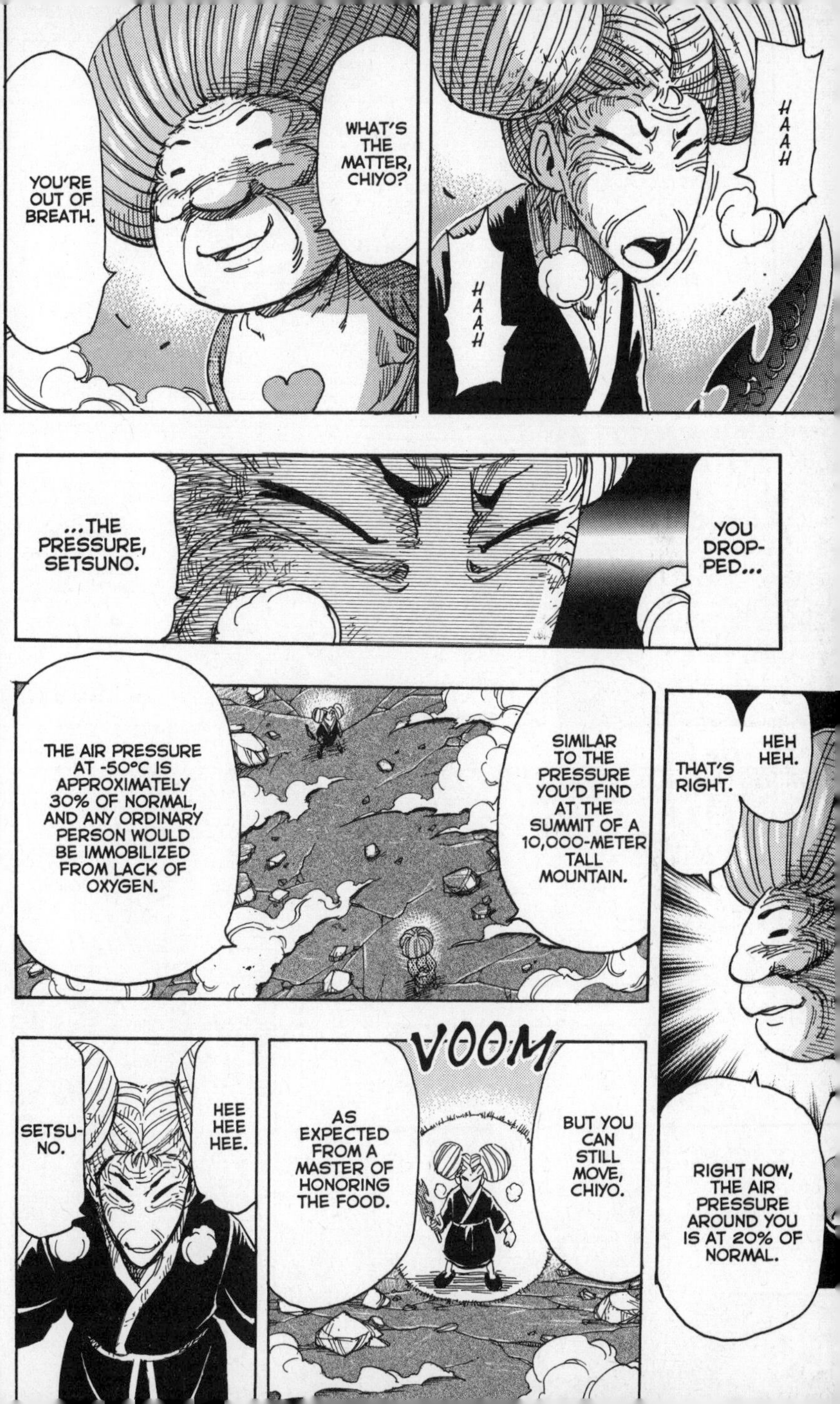
HAAAH
HAAAH
WHAT'S THE MATTER, CHIYO?
YOU'RE OUT OF BREATH.
YOU DROPPED...
...THE PRESSURE, SETSUNO.
HEH HEH.
THAT'S RIGHT.
RIGHT NOW, THE AIR PRESSURE AROUND YOU IS AT 20% OF NORMAL.
SIMILAR TO THE PRESSURE YOU'D FIND AT THE SUMMIT OF A 10,000-METER TALL MOUNTAIN.
THE AIR PRESSURE AT -50°C IS APPROXIMATELY 30% OF NORMAL, AND ANY ORDINARY PERSON WOULD BE IMMOBILIZED FROM LACK OF OXYGEN.
VOOM
BUT YOU CAN STILL MOVE, CHIYO.
AS EXPECTED FROM A MASTER OF HONORING THE FOOD.
HEE HEE HEE.
SETSUNO.

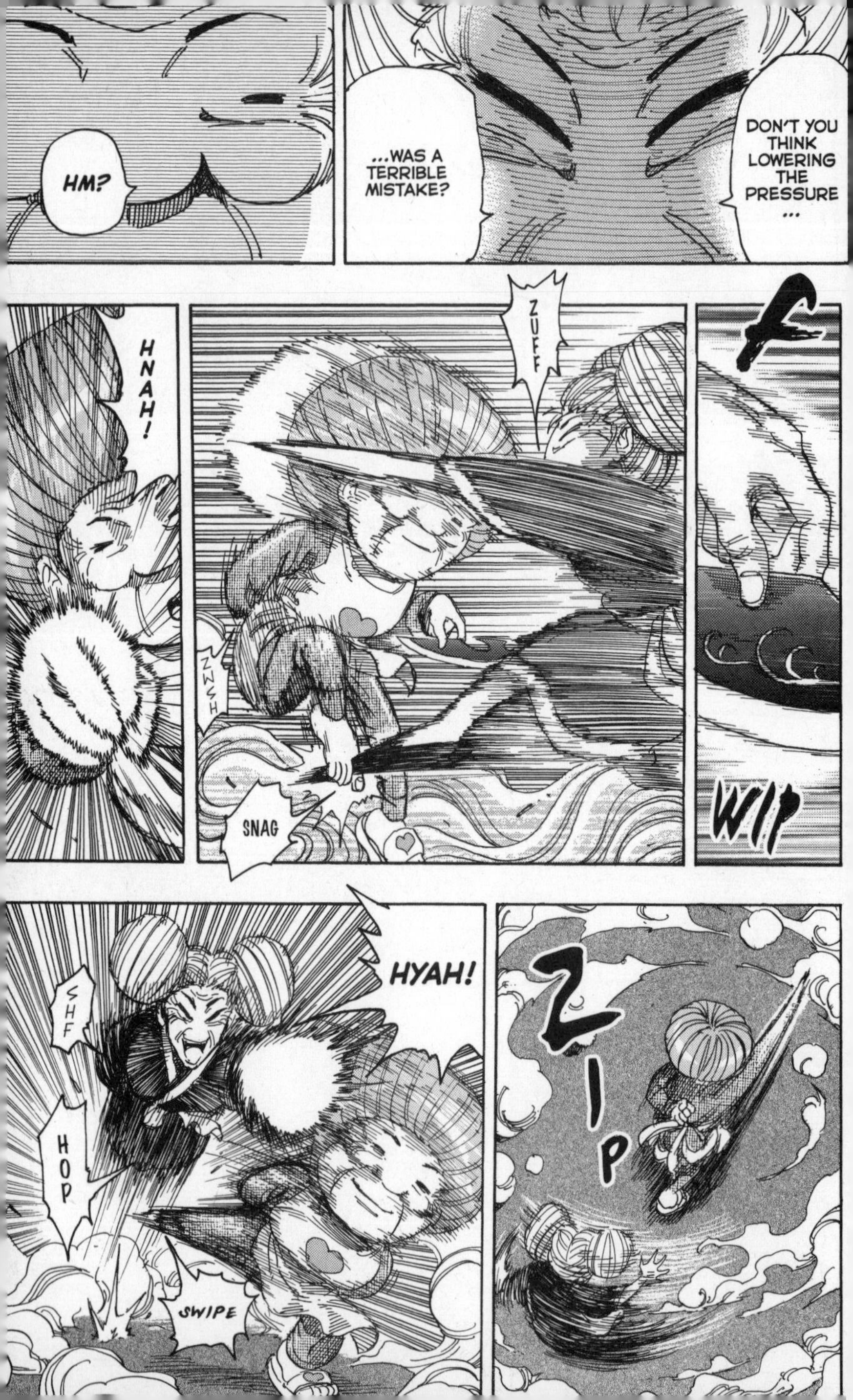
DON'T YOU THINK LOWERING THE PRESSURE ...
...WAS A TERRIBLE MISTAKE?
HM?
WIP
ZUFF
ZWSH
SNAG
HNAH!
ZIP
HYAH!
SHF
HOP
SWIPE

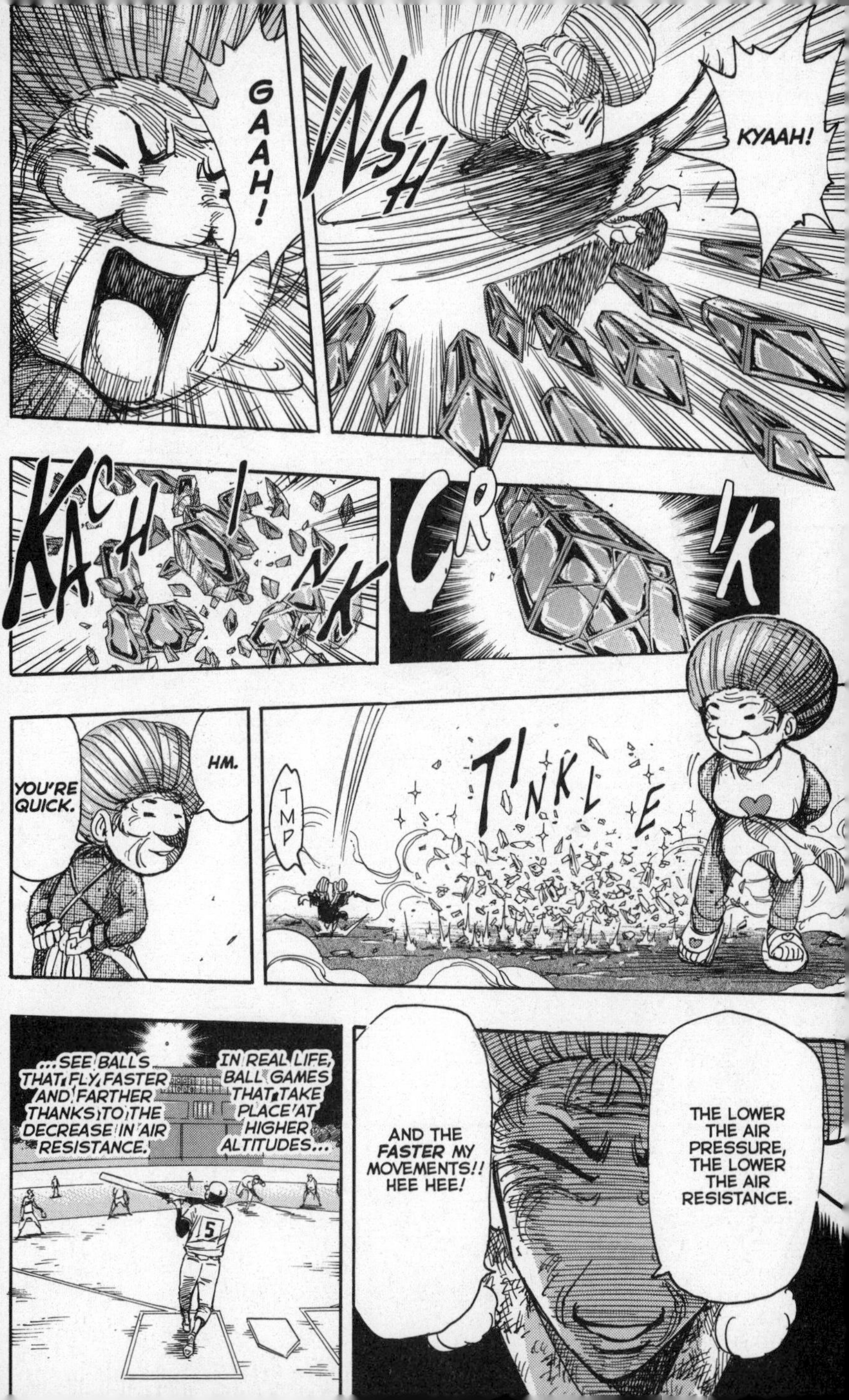
KYAAH!
WSH
GAAH!
CRIK
KACHINK
TMP
TINKLE
HM.
YOU'RE QUICK.
THE LOWER THE AIR PRESSURE, THE LOWER THE AIR RESISTANCE.
AND THE FASTER MY MOVEMENTS!! HEE HEE!
IN REAL LIFE, BALL GAMES THAT TAKE PLACE AT HIGHER ALTITUDES...
...SEE BALLS THAT FLY FASTER AND FARTHER THANKS TO THE DECREASE IN AIR RESISTANCE.
5

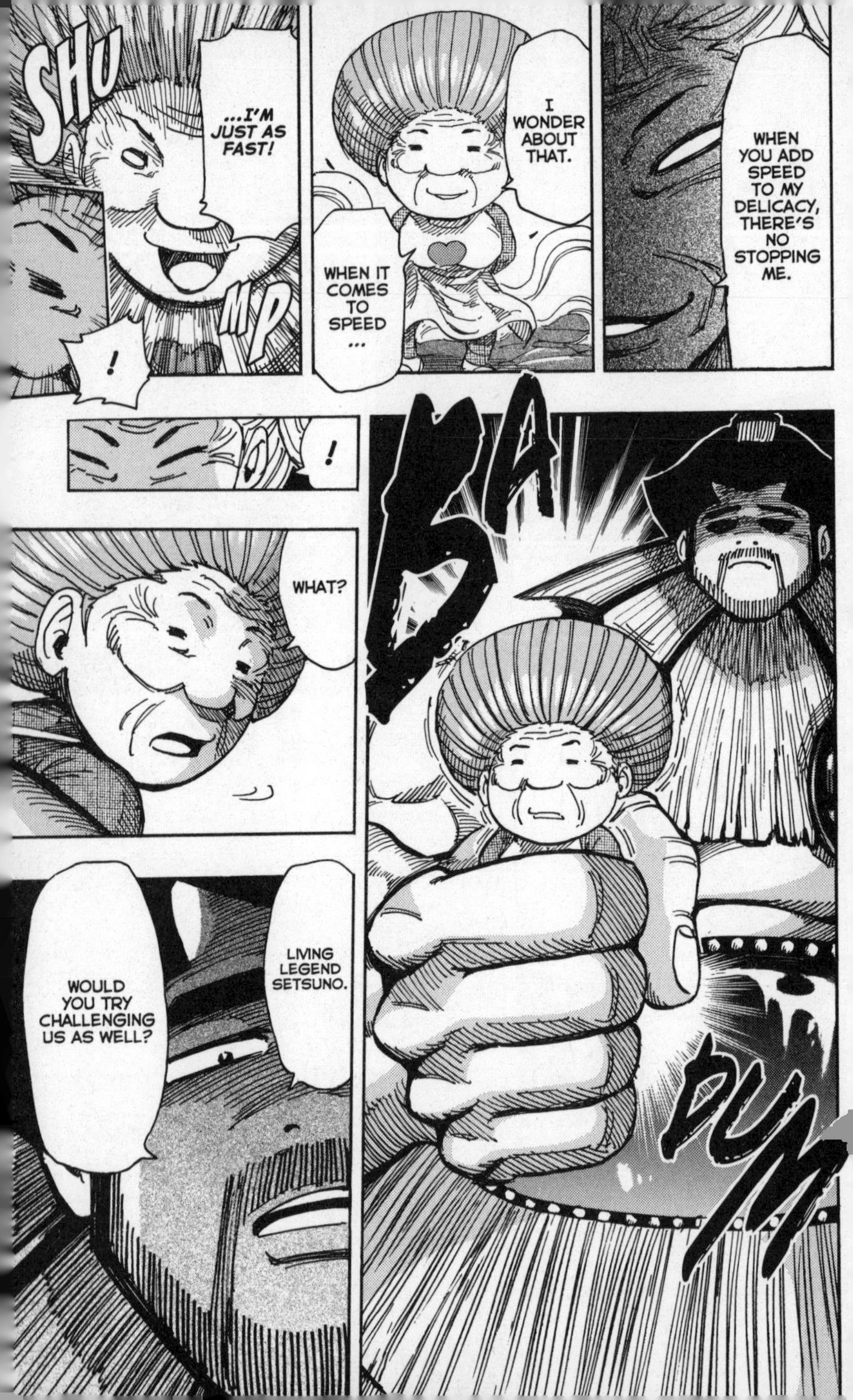
WHEN YOU ADD SPEED TO MY DELICACY, THERE'S NO STOPPING ME.
I WONDER ABOUT THAT.
WHEN IT COMES TO SPEED ...
...I'M JUST AS FAST!
SHU
MP
!
KA
DUN
!
WHAT?
LIVING LEGEND SETSUNO.
WOULD YOU TRY CHALLENGING US AS WELL?

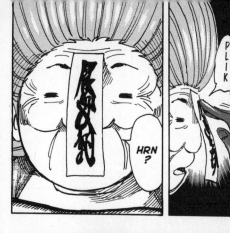

HRN ?

PLIK

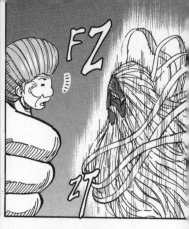

FZ

ZT

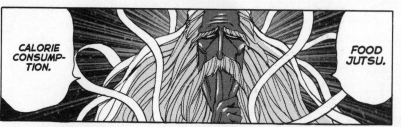

CALORIE CONSUMP- TION.

FOOD JUTSU.

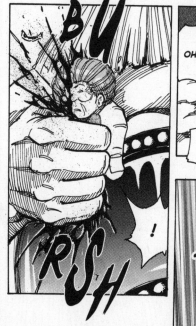

BU

RSH

!

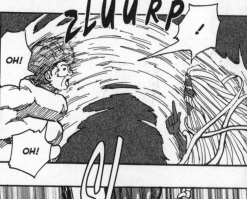

ZLUURP !

OH!

OH!

SL

SINGLE SLICE...

...SAMSARA SEVER!!

ASH

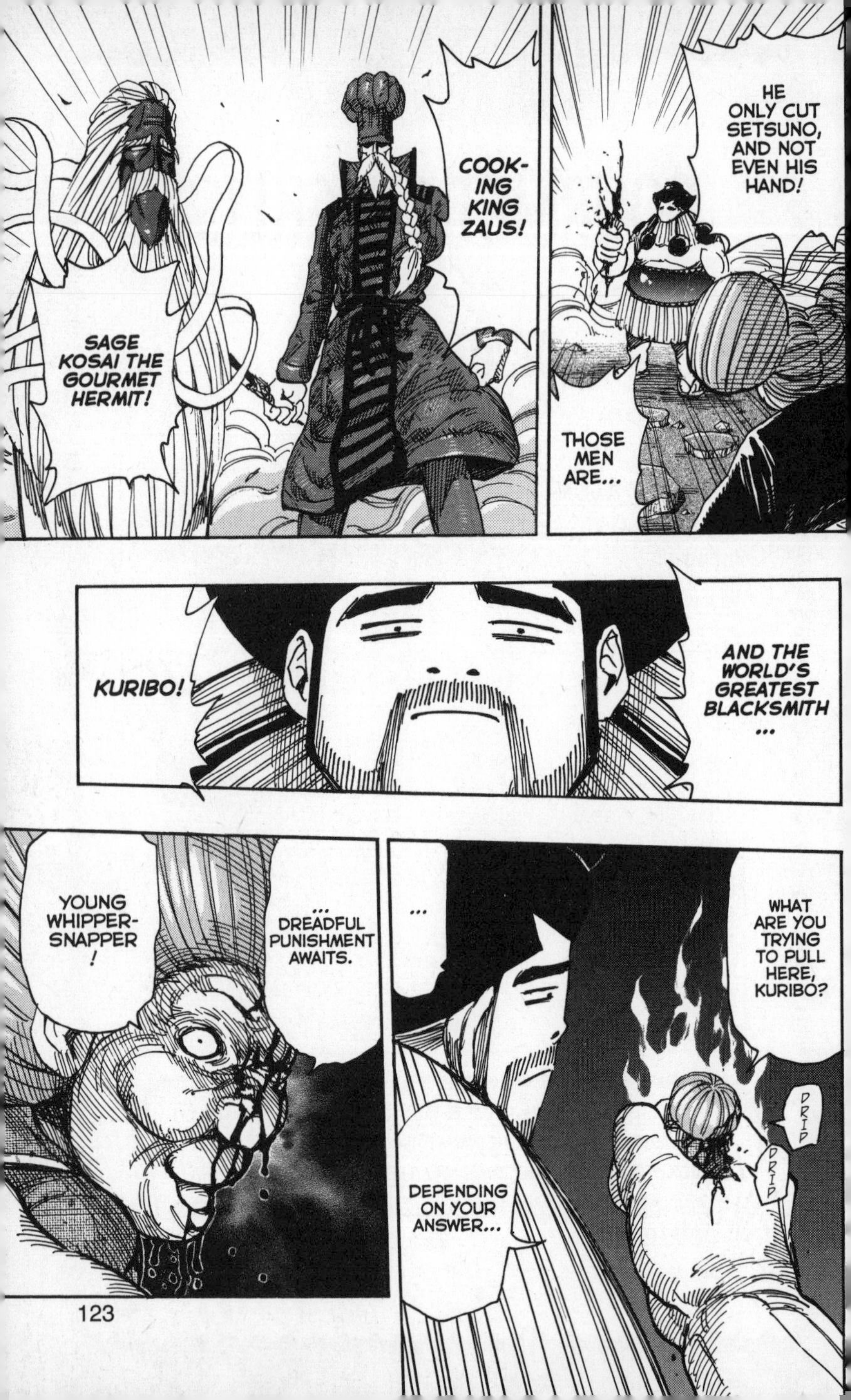
HE ONLY CUT SETSUNO, AND NOT EVEN HIS HAND!
THOSE MEN ARE...
COOK-ING KING ZAUS!
SAGE KOSAI THE GOURMET HERMIT!
AND THE WORLD'S GREATEST BLACKSMITH...
KURIBO!
WHAT ARE YOU TRYING TO PULL HERE, KURIBO?
DRIP
DRIP
...
DEPENDING ON YOUR ANSWER...
...DREADFUL PUNISHMENT AWAITS.
YOUNG WHIPPER-SNAPPER!

TORIKO

GOURMET CHECKLIST

Vol. 256

DRAGONFIRE
(INSECT)

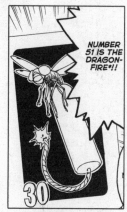

NUMBER 51 IS THE DRAGON-FIRE*!!
30

CAPTURE LEVEL: 15

HABITAT: COLD REGIONS

LENGTH: 25 CM

HEIGHT: ---

WEIGHT: 1.5 KG

PRICE: 80,000 YEN PER BUG

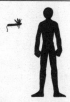

SCALE

THIS DEADLY DRAGONFLY'S THORAX IS A STICK OF TNT! IT IS GOOD-NATURED AND WON'T DETONATE ITS DYNAMITE UNLESS IT FEELS THREATENED. BUT IF IT DOES, IT ATTACKS BY SEVERING ITS DYNAMITE-THORAX. THE DYNAMITE-THORAX IS COMPOSED OF RICH MEAT AND NITROGLYCERIN, WHICH MIX AND EXPLODE WHEN IT DETACHES. THIS INGREDIENT REQUIRES SPECIAL PREPARATION, AS YOU MUST CAPTURE IT WITH THORAX ATTACHED SO THAT YOU CAN EXTRACT JUST THE MEAT.

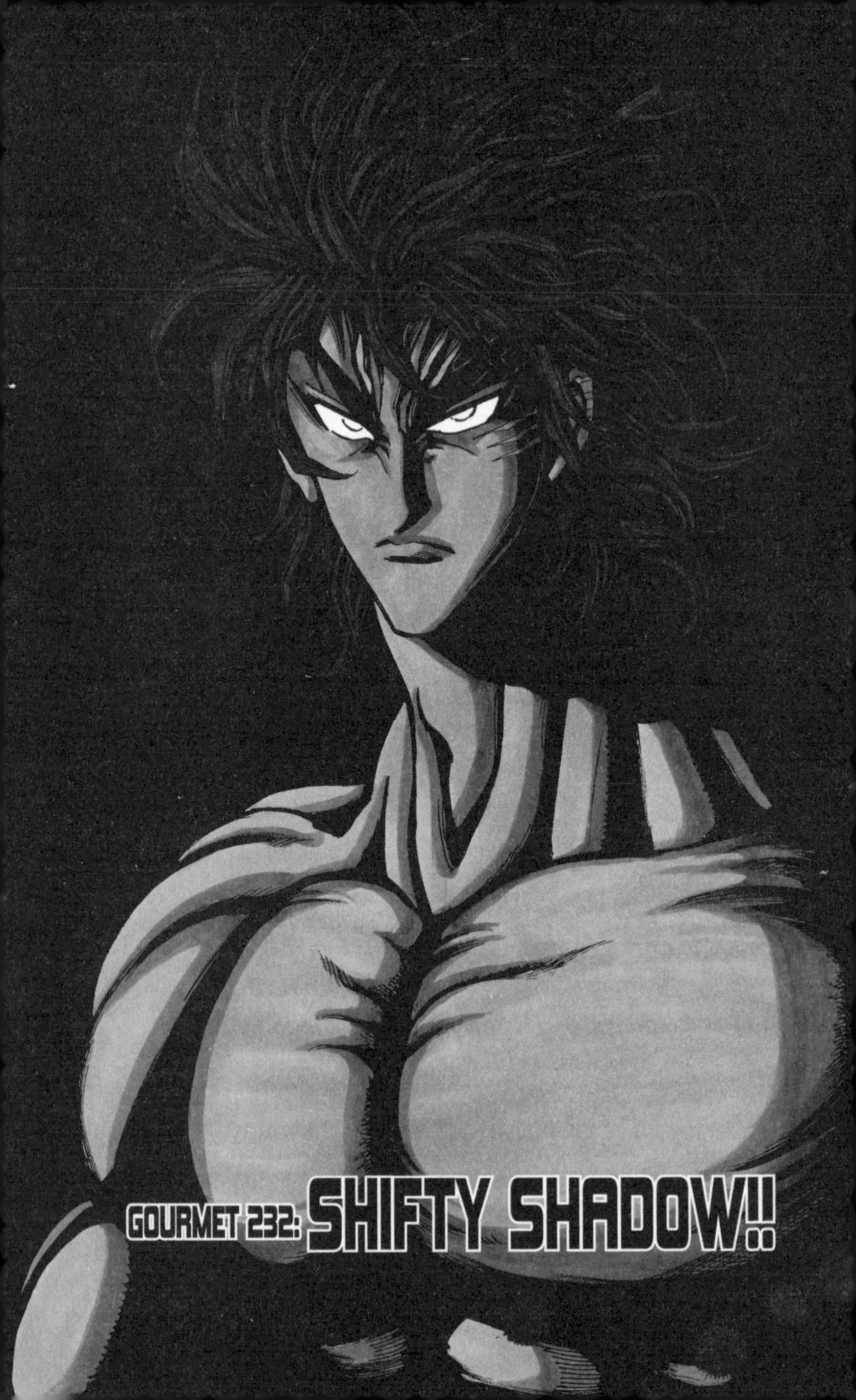
GOURMET 232: SHIFTY SHADOW!!

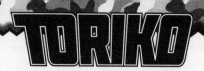

GOURMET CHECKLIST
Vol. 257

ROCK LIZARD
(SHELLED MAMMAL)

CAPTURE LEVEL: 39
HABITAT: VOLCANOES
LENGTH: 3 METERS
HEIGHT: ---
WEIGHT: 400 KG
PRICE: 100 G / 2,500 YEN (MEAT);
1 KG / 100,000 YEN (STONE)

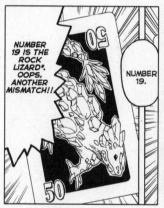

NUMBER 19 IS THE ROCK LIZARD*. OOPS, ANOTHER MISMATCH!!

NUMBER 19.

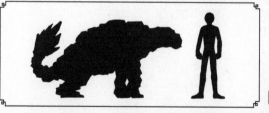

SCALE

A GIANT LIZARD THAT LIVES DEEP WITHIN VOLCANOES, CLOSE TO THE MANTLE. ITS BODY IS COVERED IN A COAT OF ROCK. IT CAN LAUNCH THOSE ROCKS TO ATTACK, AND IT REGENERATES QUICKLY—FIFTEEN STONES WILL REGROW WITHIN THIRTY SECONDS. THE ROCKS ARE HIGH QUALITY, AND CAN BE USED FOR MANY PURPOSES INCLUDING STONE COOKWARE. ROCK LIZARD IS MOSTLY VALUED FOR ITS ROCKS, BUT THE MEAT INSIDE THAT PROTECTIVE COAT IS ACTUALLY QUITE TENDER.

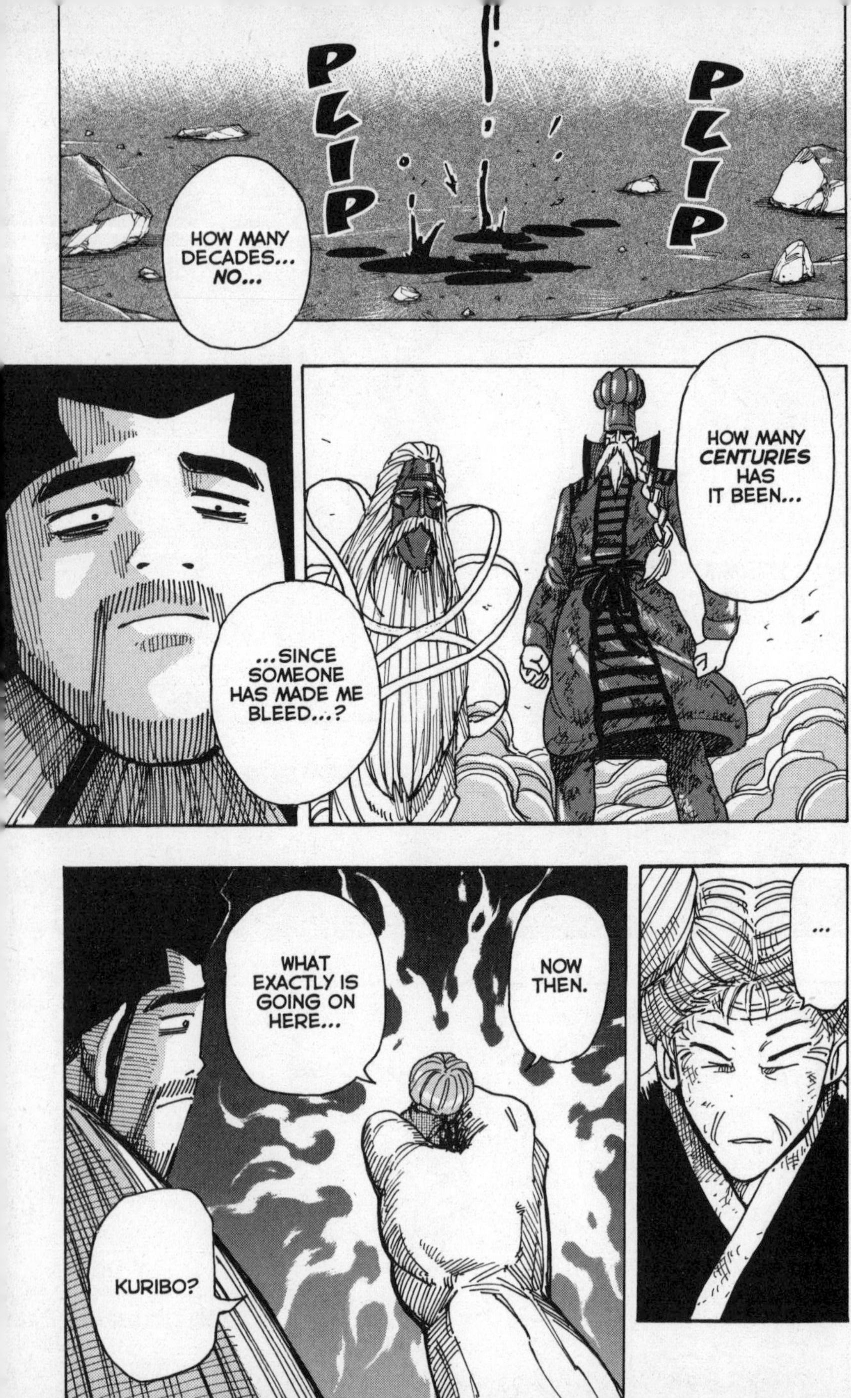
PLIP
PLIP
HOW MANY DECADES... NO...
HOW MANY CENTURIES HAS IT BEEN...
...SINCE SOMEONE HAS MADE ME BLEED...?
...
NOW THEN.
WHAT EXACTLY IS GOING ON HERE...
KURIBO?

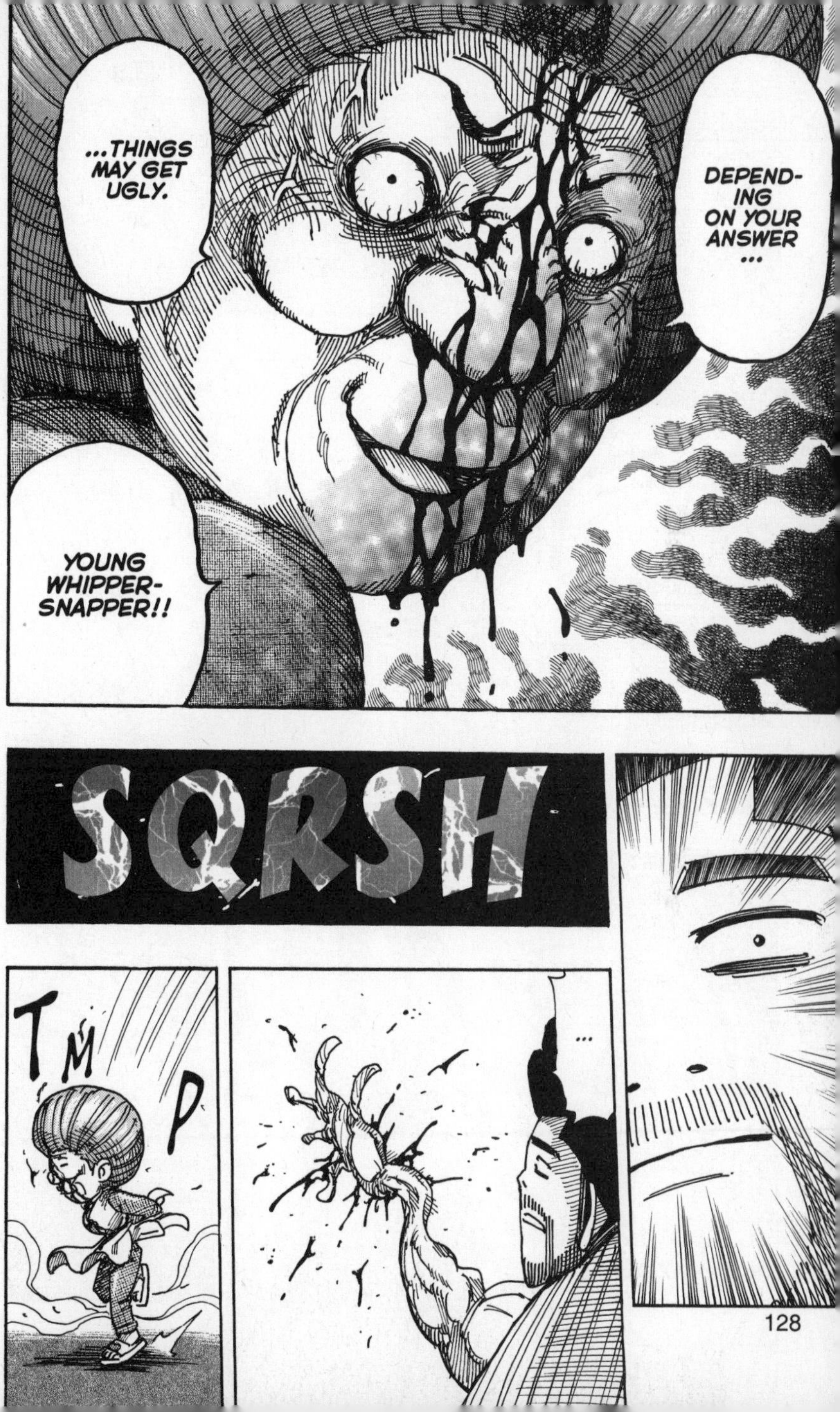
DEPEND-ING ON YOUR ANSWER ...
...THINGS MAY GET UGLY.
YOUNG WHIPPER-SNAPPER!!
SQRSH
...
TMP

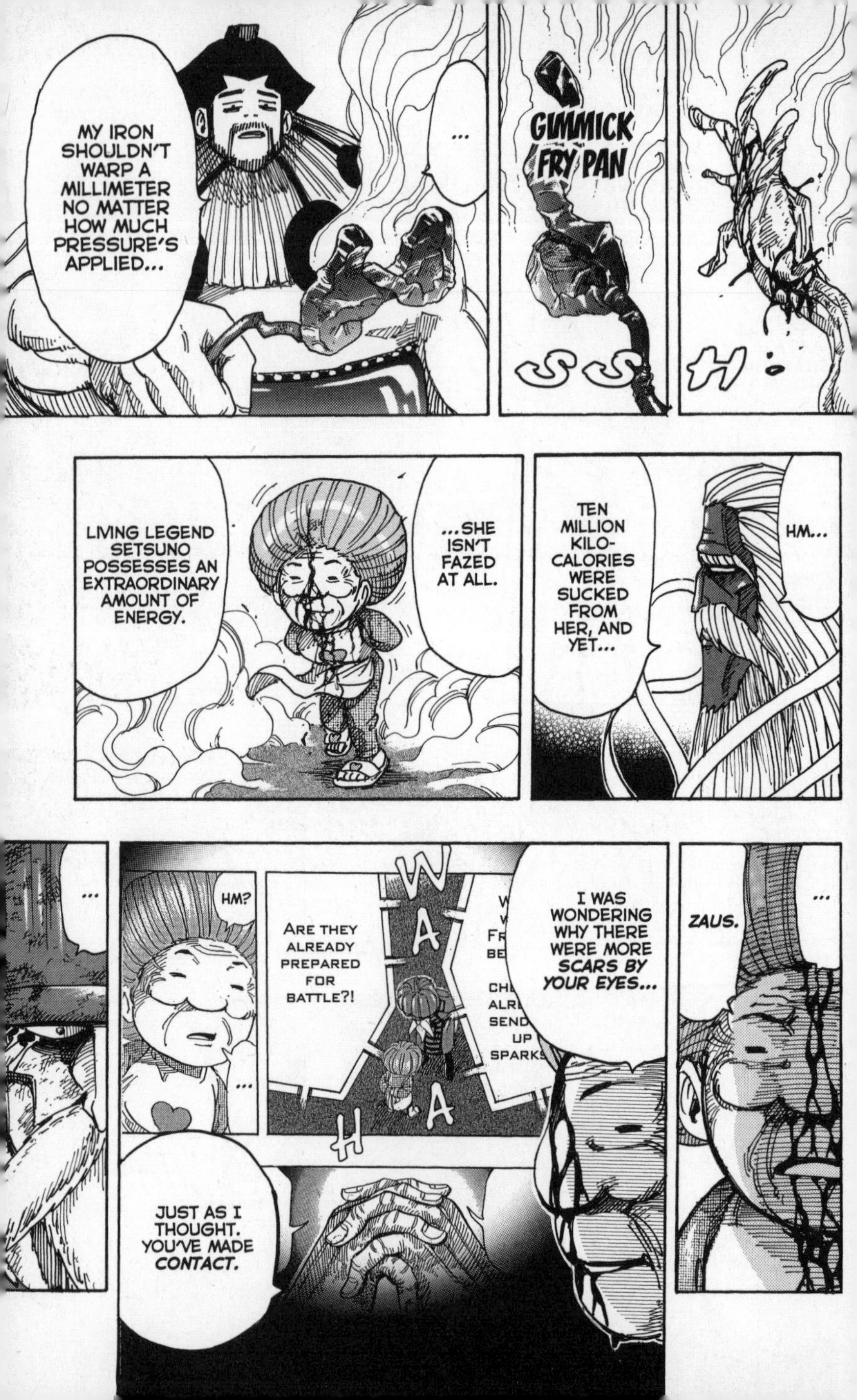
H
GIMMICK FRY PAN
SS
...
MY IRON SHOULDN'T WARP A MILLIMETER NO MATTER HOW MUCH PRESSURE'S APPLIED...
HM...
TEN MILLION KILO-CALORIES WERE SUCKED FROM HER, AND YET...
...SHE ISN'T FAZED AT ALL.
LIVING LEGEND SETSUNO POSSESSES AN EXTRAORDINARY AMOUNT OF ENERGY.
...
ZAUS.
I WAS WONDERING WHY THERE WERE MORE SCARS BY YOUR EYES...
WA
HA
ARE THEY ALREADY PREPARED FOR BATTLE?!
HM?
...
...
JUST AS I THOUGHT. YOU'VE MADE CONTACT.

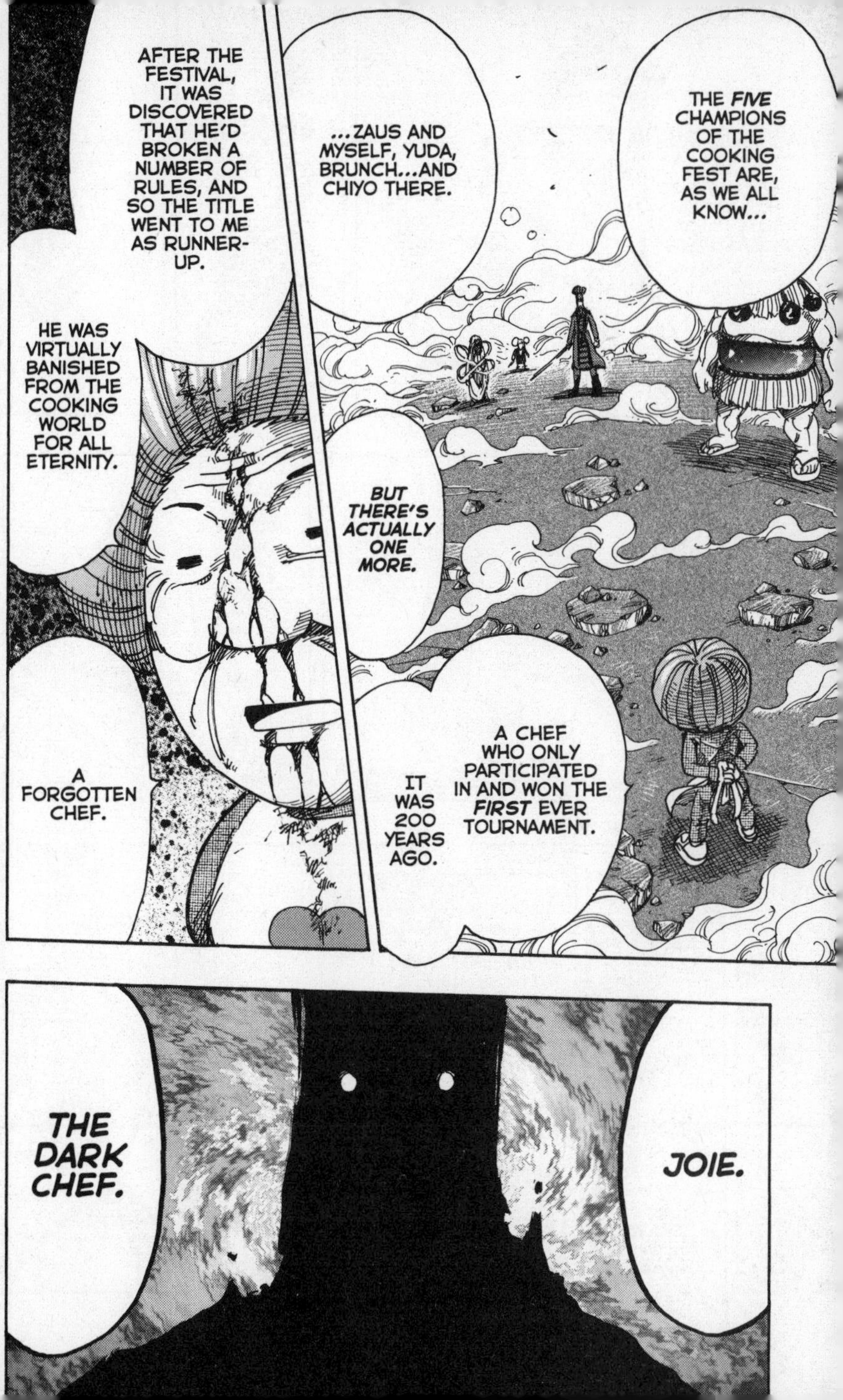
THE *FIVE* CHAMPIONS OF THE COOKING FEST ARE, AS WE ALL KNOW...
...ZAUS AND MYSELF, YUDA, BRUNCH...AND CHIYO THERE.
BUT THERE'S ACTUALLY ONE MORE.
A CHEF WHO ONLY PARTICIPATED IN AND WON THE *FIRST* EVER TOURNAMENT.
IT WAS 200 YEARS AGO.
AFTER THE FESTIVAL, IT WAS DISCOVERED THAT HE'D BROKEN A NUMBER OF RULES, AND SO THE TITLE WENT TO ME AS RUNNER-UP.
HE WAS VIRTUALLY BANISHED FROM THE COOKING WORLD FOR ALL ETERNITY.
A FORGOTTEN CHEF.
JOIE.
THE DARK CHEF.

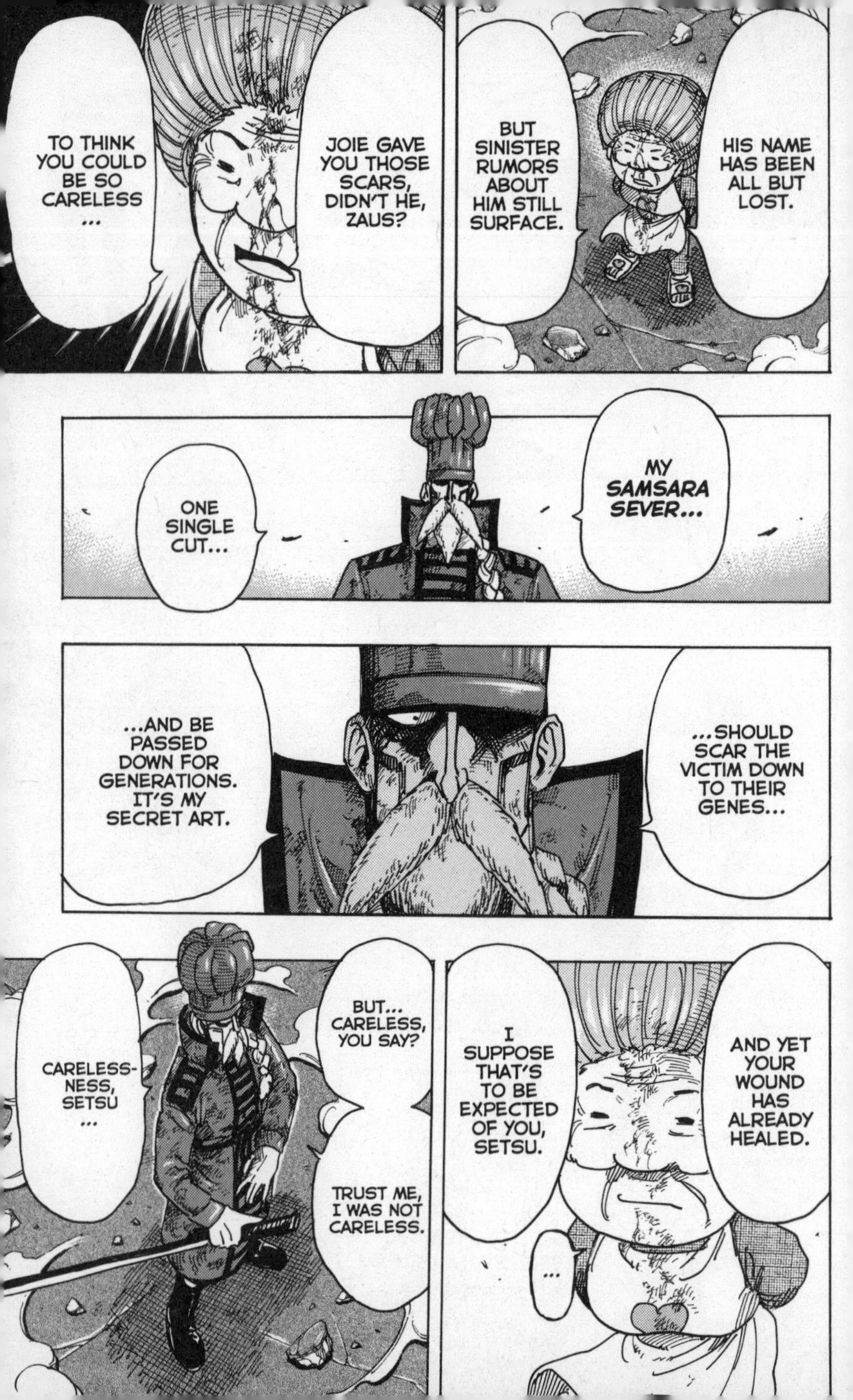
HIS NAME HAS BEEN ALL BUT LOST.
BUT SINISTER RUMORS ABOUT HIM STILL SURFACE.
JOIE GAVE YOU THOSE SCARS, DIDN'T HE, ZAUS?
TO THINK YOU COULD BE SO CARELESS ...
MY SAMSARA SEVER...
ONE SINGLE CUT...
...SHOULD SCAR THE VICTIM DOWN TO THEIR GENES...
...AND BE PASSED DOWN FOR GENERATIONS. IT'S MY SECRET ART.
AND YET YOUR WOUND HAS ALREADY HEALED.
I SUPPOSE THAT'S TO BE EXPECTED OF YOU, SETSU.
...
CARELESS-NESS, SETSU ...
BUT... CARELESS, YOU SAY?
TRUST ME, I WAS NOT CARELESS.

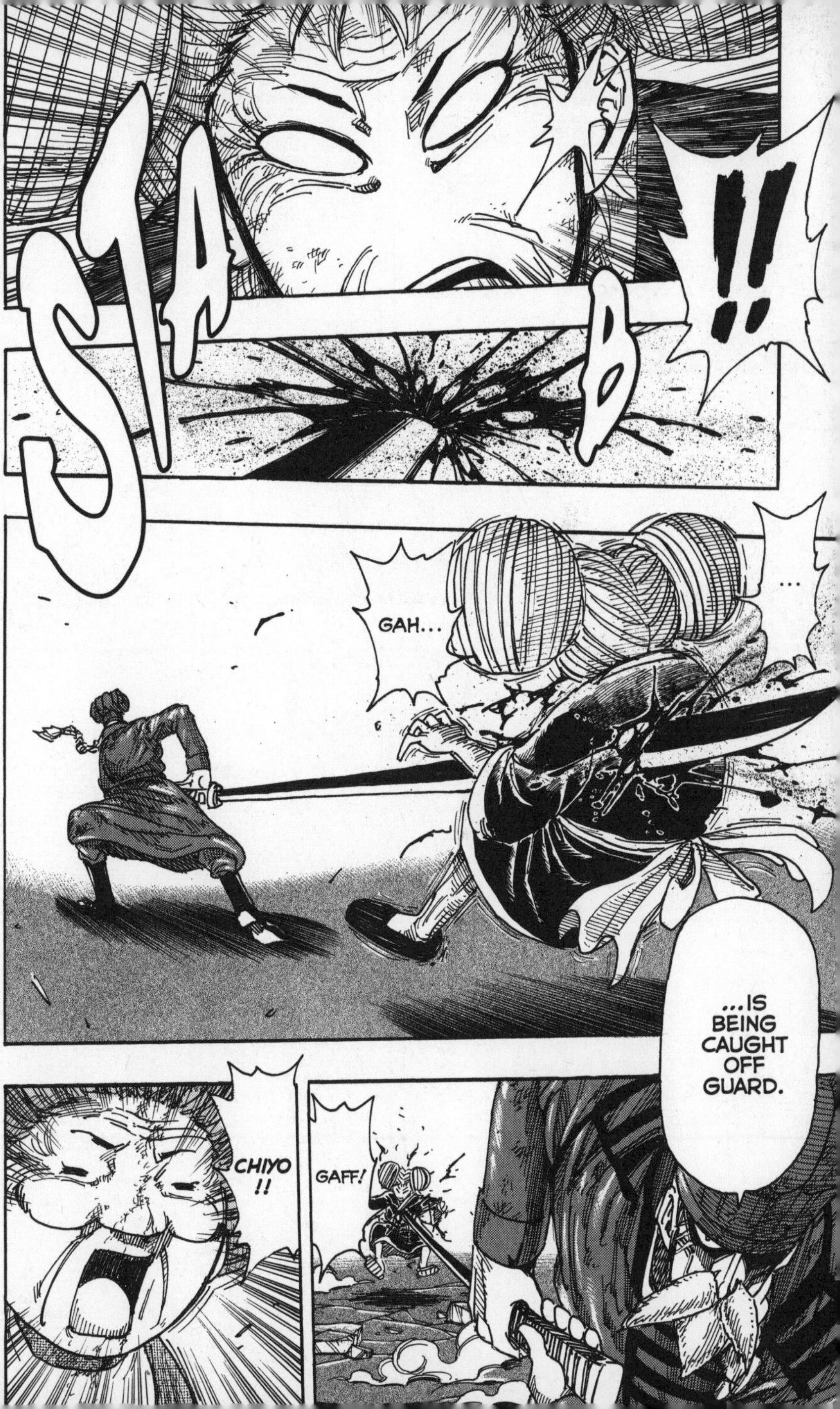
!!
STAB
...
GAH...
...IS BEING CAUGHT OFF GUARD.
GAFF!
CHIYO !!

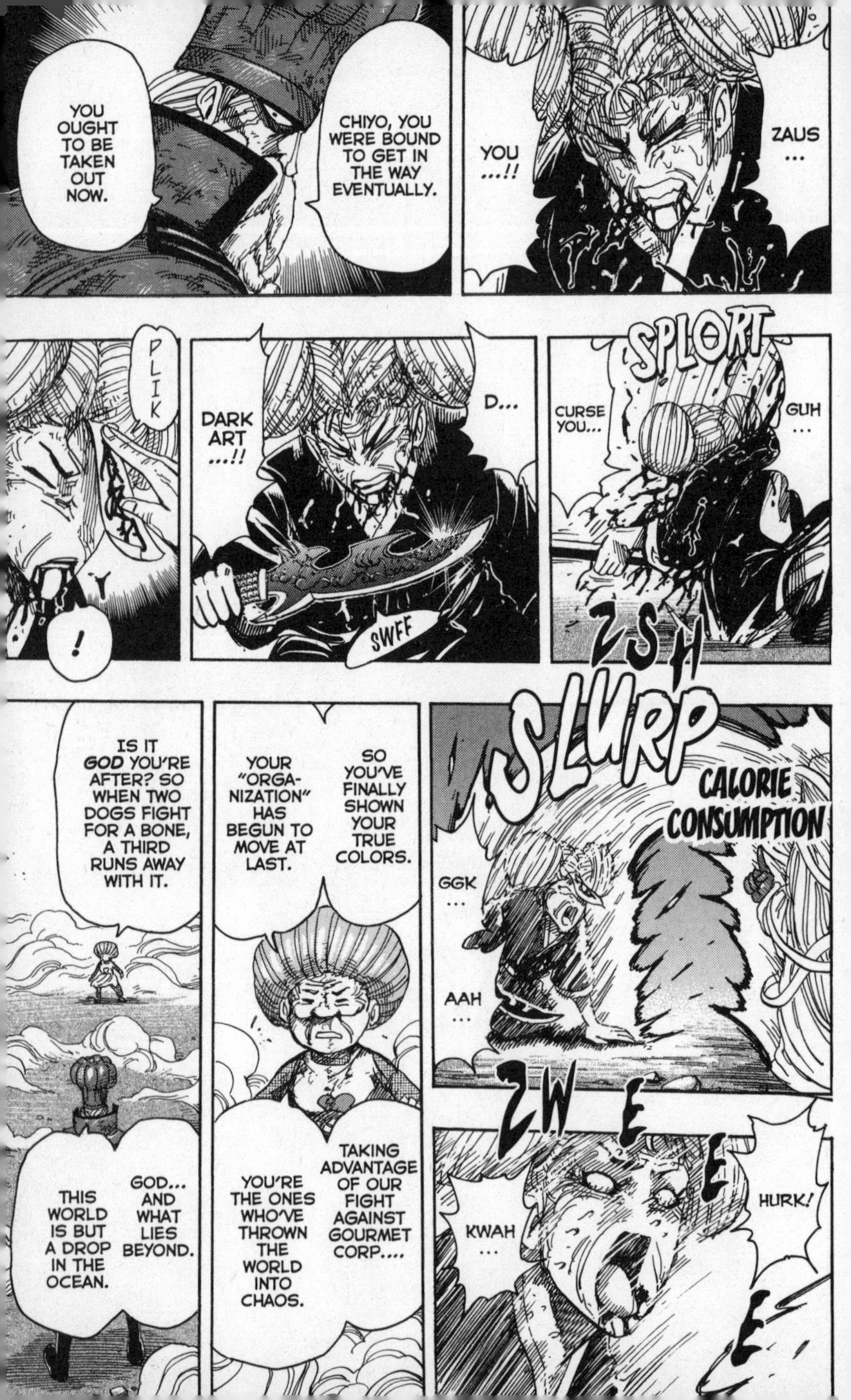
ZAUS...
YOU...!!
CHIYO, YOU WERE BOUND TO GET IN THE WAY EVENTUALLY.
YOU OUGHT TO BE TAKEN OUT NOW.
SPLORT
GUH...
CURSE YOU...
ZSH
D...
DARK ART...!!
SWFF
PLIK
!
SLURP
CALORIE CONSUMPTION
GGK...
AAH...
ZWEEE
HURK!
KWAH...
SO YOU'VE FINALLY SHOWN YOUR TRUE COLORS.
YOUR "ORGA-NIZATION" HAS BEGUN TO MOVE AT LAST.
TAKING ADVANTAGE OF OUR FIGHT AGAINST GOURMET CORP....
YOU'RE THE ONES WHO'VE THROWN THE WORLD INTO CHAOS.
IS IT *GOD* YOU'RE AFTER? SO WHEN TWO DOGS FIGHT FOR A BONE, A THIRD RUNS AWAY WITH IT.
GOD... AND WHAT LIES BEYOND.
THIS WORLD IS BUT A DROP IN THE OCEAN.

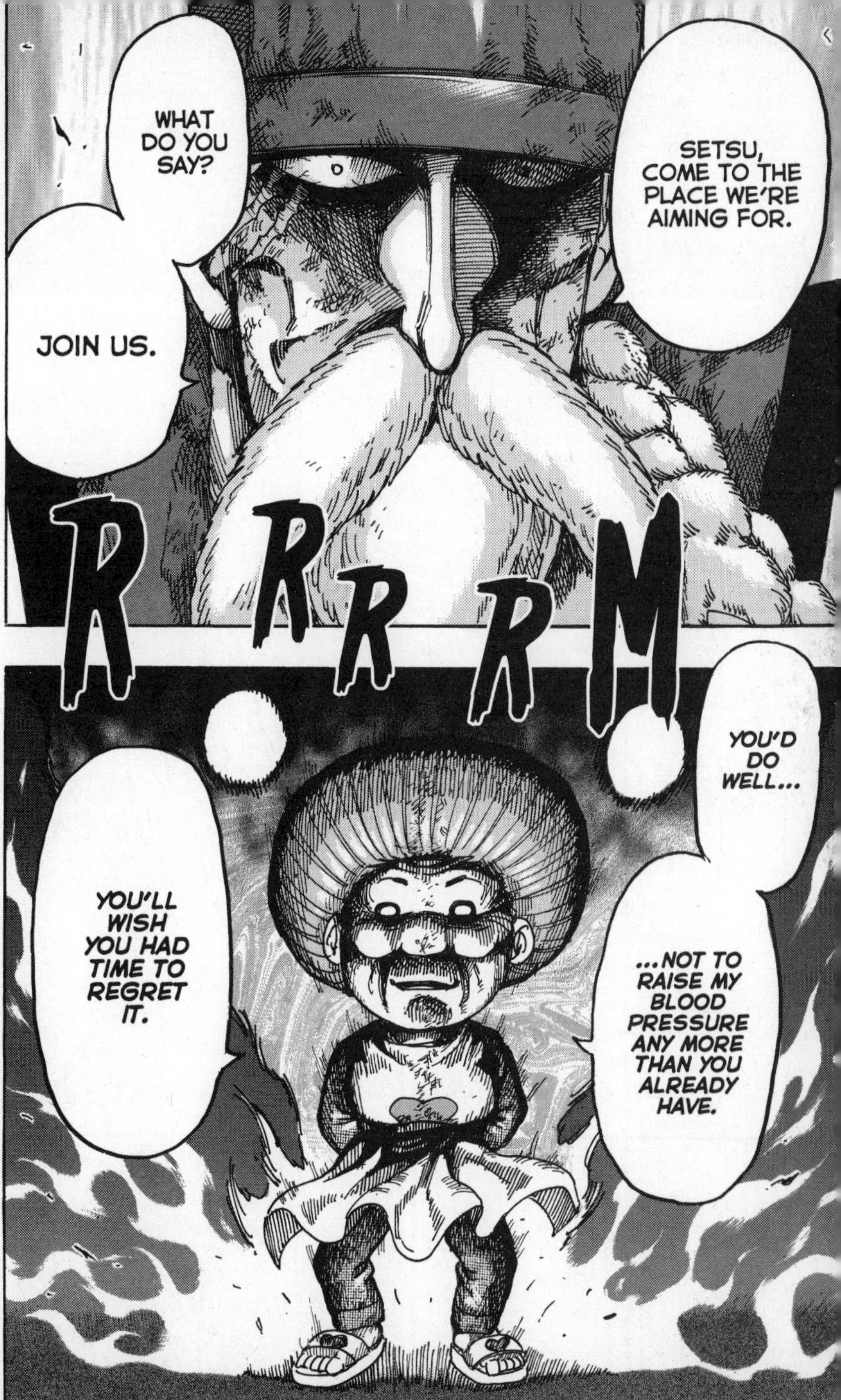
SETSU, COME TO THE PLACE WE'RE AIMING FOR.
WHAT DO YOU SAY?
JOIN US.
RRRRM
YOU'D DO WELL...
...NOT TO RAISE MY BLOOD PRESSURE ANY MORE THAN YOU ALREADY HAVE.
YOU'LL WISH YOU HAD TIME TO REGRET IT.

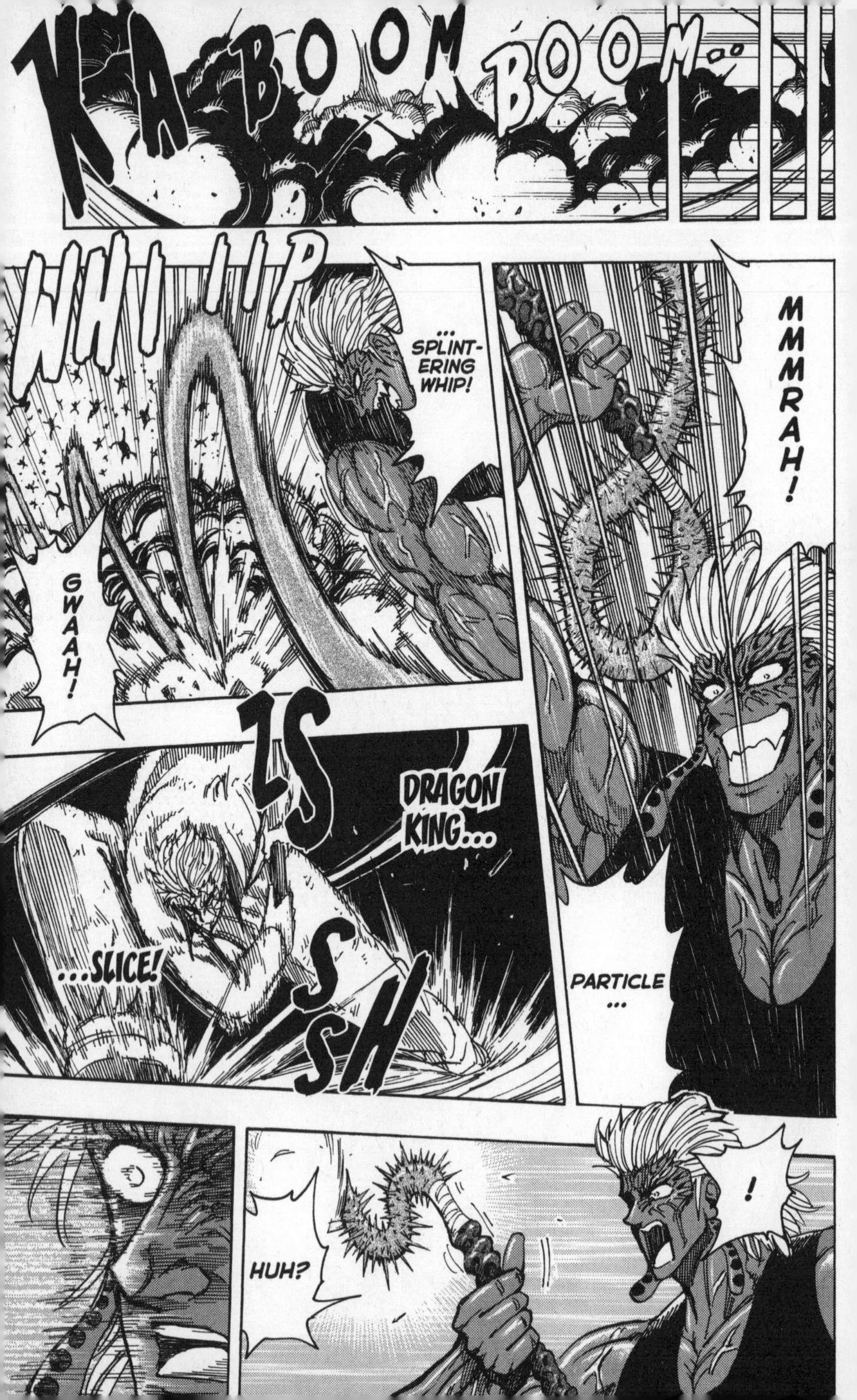
KA-BOOM
BOOM...
MMMRAH!
PARTICLE...
...SPLINTERING WHIP!
WHIIIP
GWAAH!
DRAGON KING...
ZSSSH
...SLICE!
!
HUH?

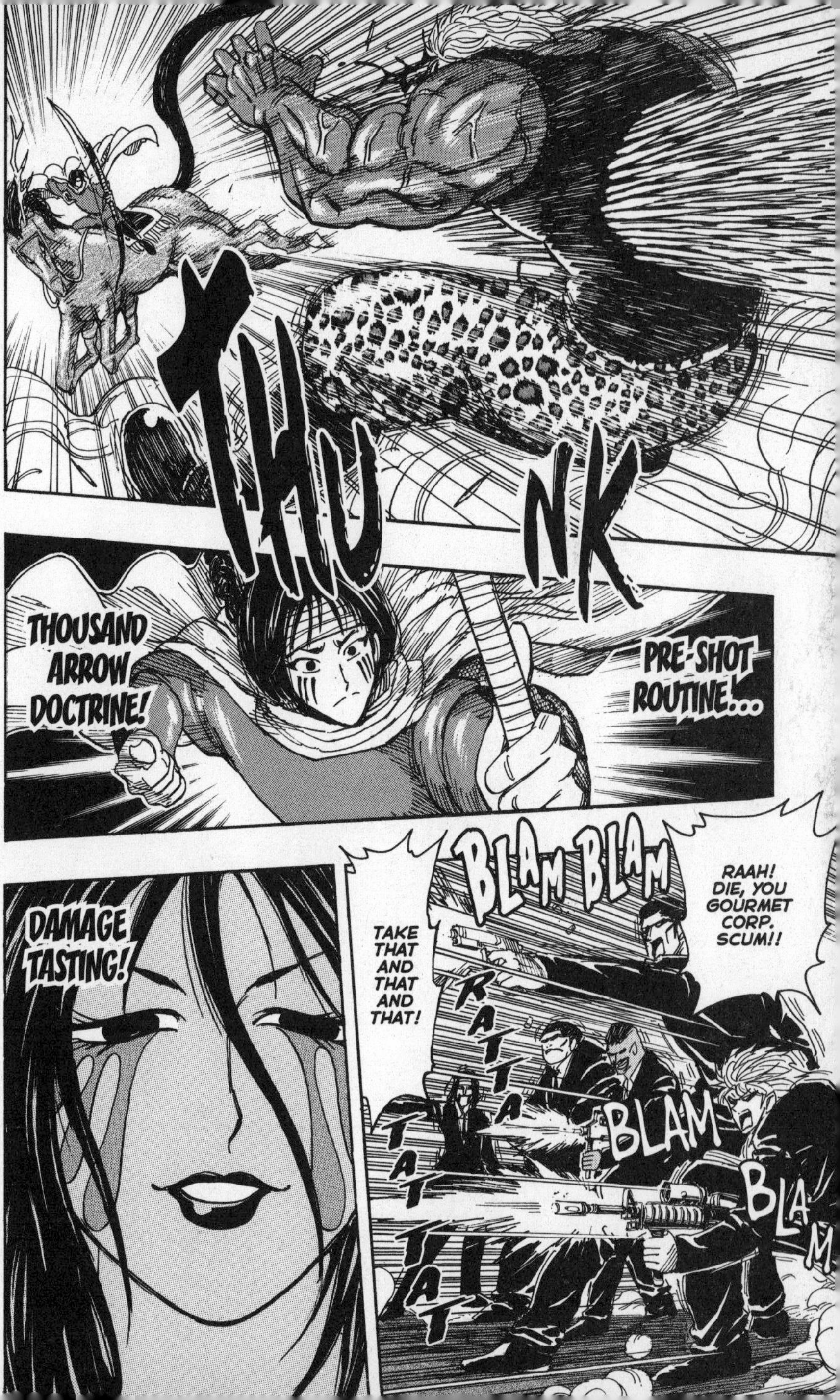
THUNK
PRE-SHOT ROUTINE!...
THOUSAND ARROW DOCTRINE!
BLAM BLAM
RAAH! DIE, YOU GOURMET CORP. SCUM!!
TAKE THAT AND THAT AND THAT!
RATTA
BLAM
BLAM
TAT
TAT
DAMAGE TASTING!

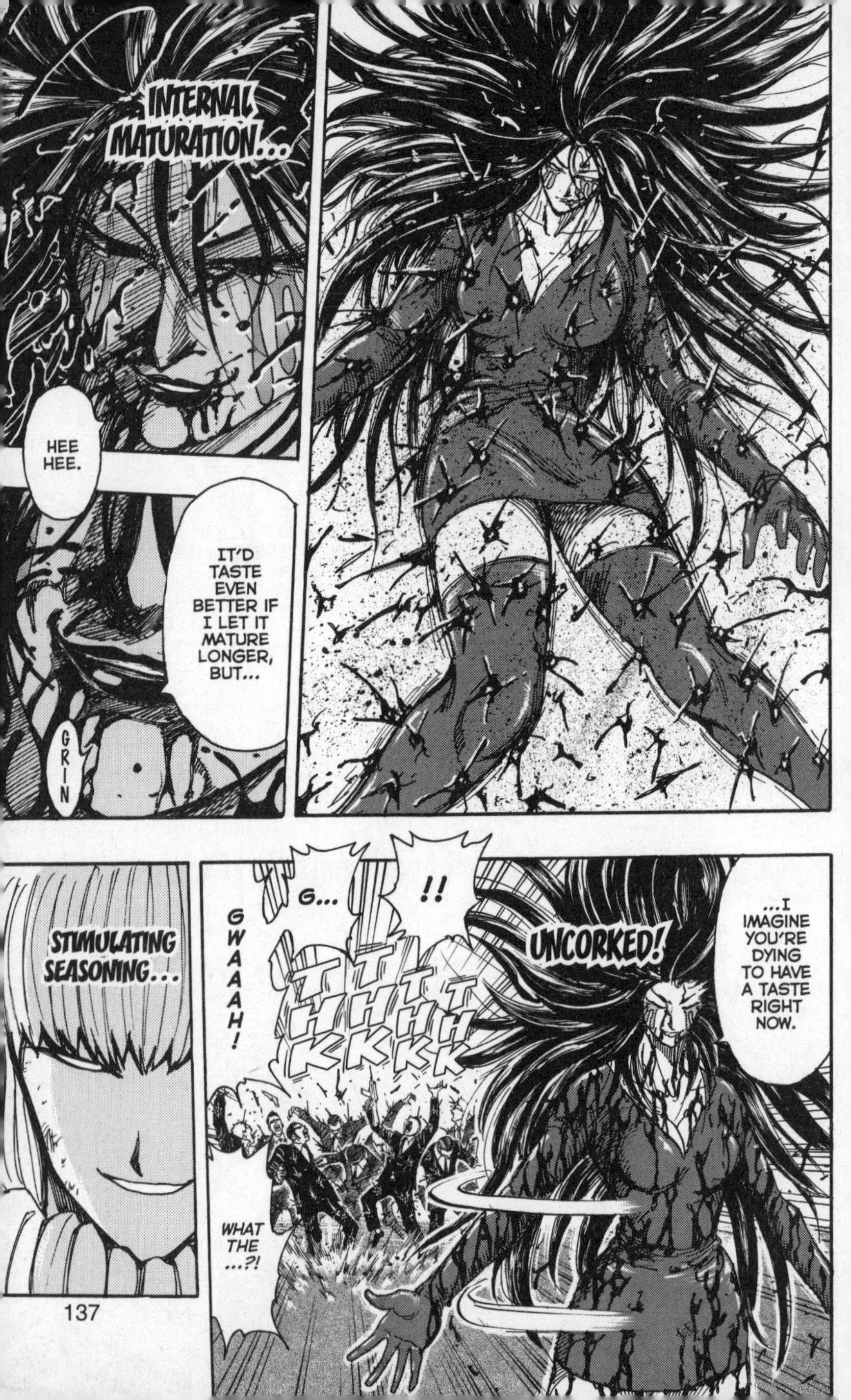
INTERNAL MATURATION...
HEE HEE.
IT'D TASTE EVEN BETTER IF I LET IT MATURE LONGER, BUT...
GRIN
...I IMAGINE YOU'RE DYING TO HAVE A TASTE RIGHT NOW.
UNCORKED!
!!
G...
TTTT HHHH KKKK
GWAAAAH!
WHAT THE ...?!
STIMULATING SEASONING...

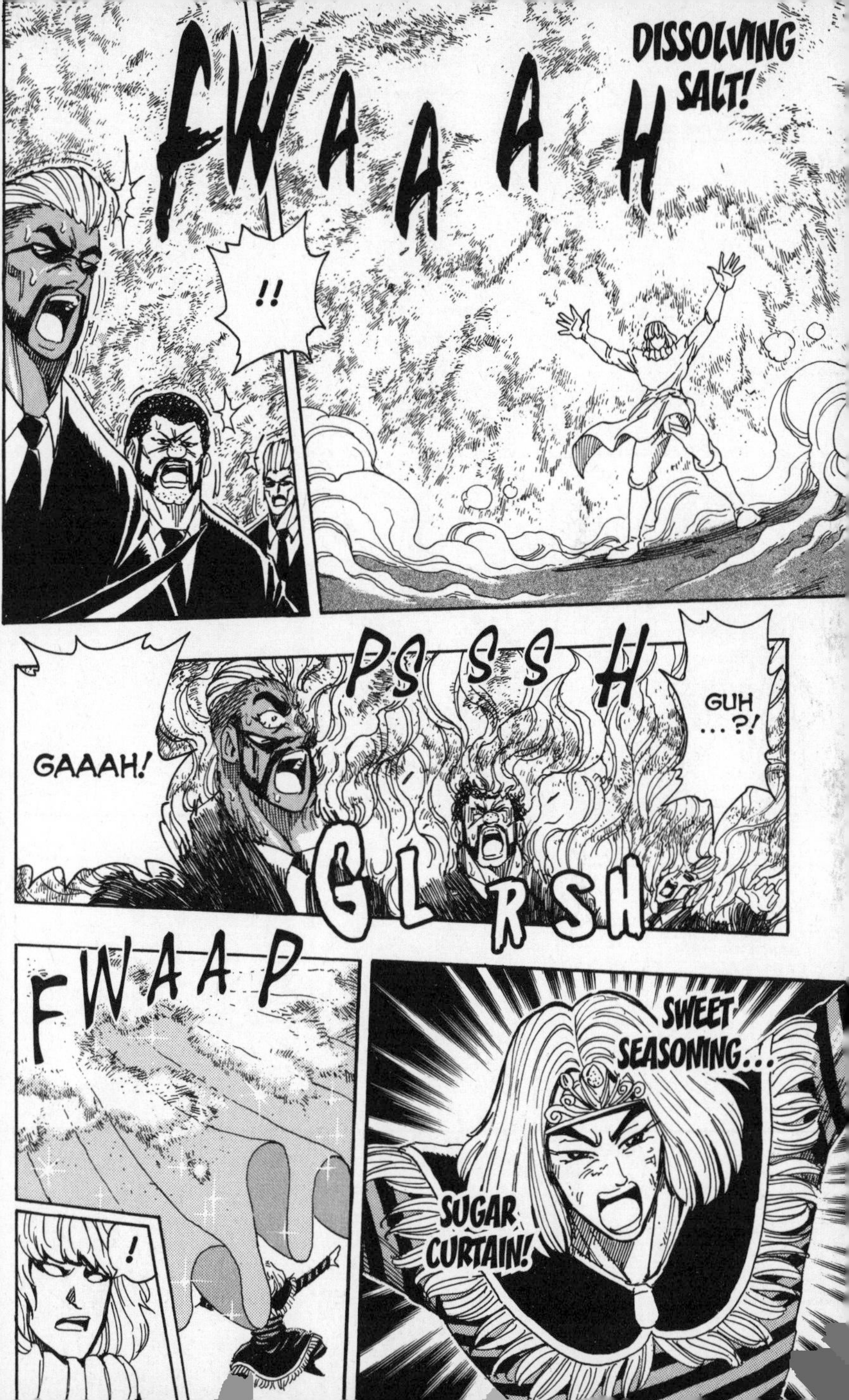
DISSOLVING SALT!
FWAAAH
!!
GUH ...?!
PSSSH
GAAAH!
GLRSH
SWEET SEASONING...
SUGAR CURTAIN!
FWAAP
!

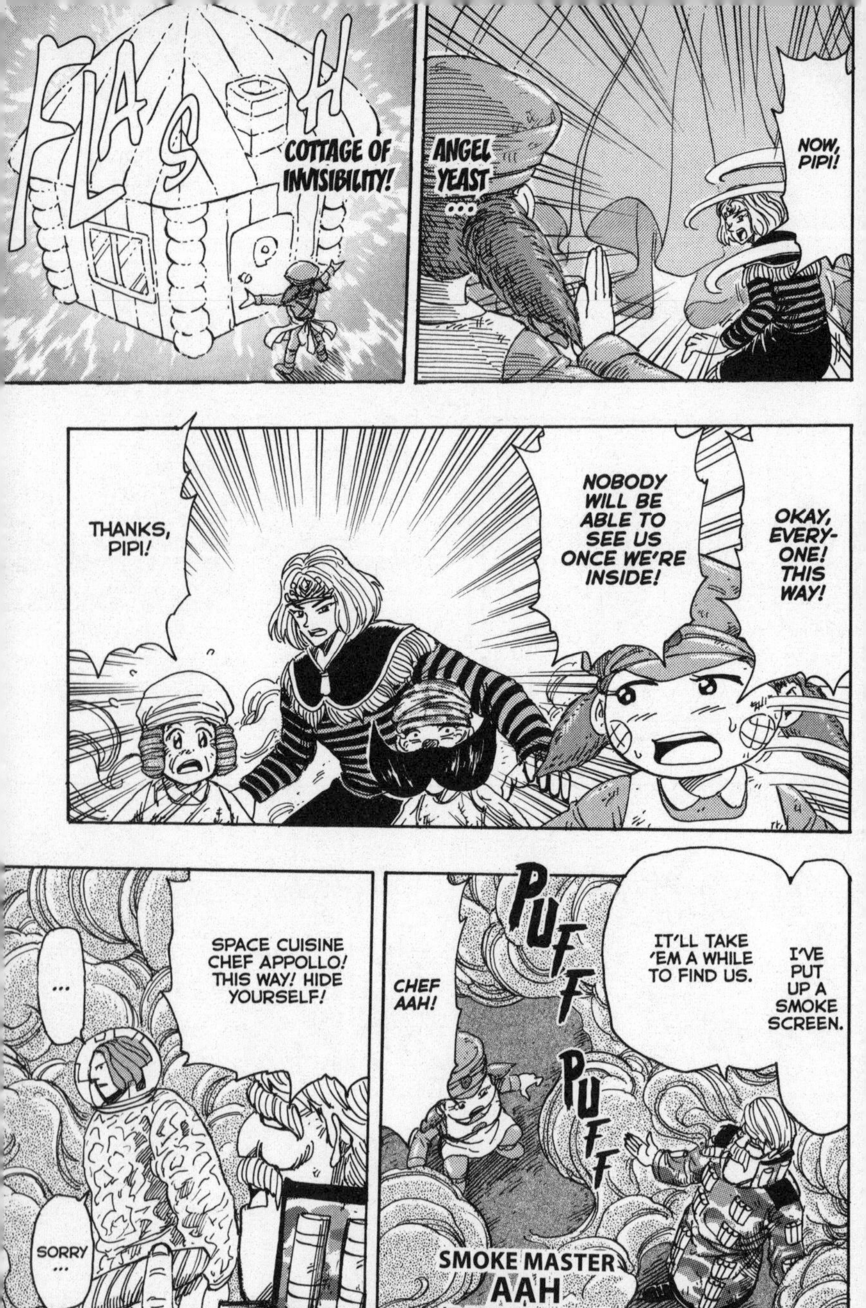
NOW, PIPI!
ANGEL YEAST...
FLASH
COTTAGE OF INVISIBILITY!
OKAY, EVERYONE! THIS WAY!
NOBODY WILL BE ABLE TO SEE US ONCE WE'RE INSIDE!
THANKS, PIPI!
I'VE PUT UP A SMOKE SCREEN.
IT'LL TAKE 'EM A WHILE TO FIND US.
PUFF PUFF PUFF
CHEF AAH!
SMOKE MASTER AAH (RANKED 73RD)
SPACE CUISINE CHEF APPOLLO! THIS WAY! HIDE YOURSELF!
...
SORRY...

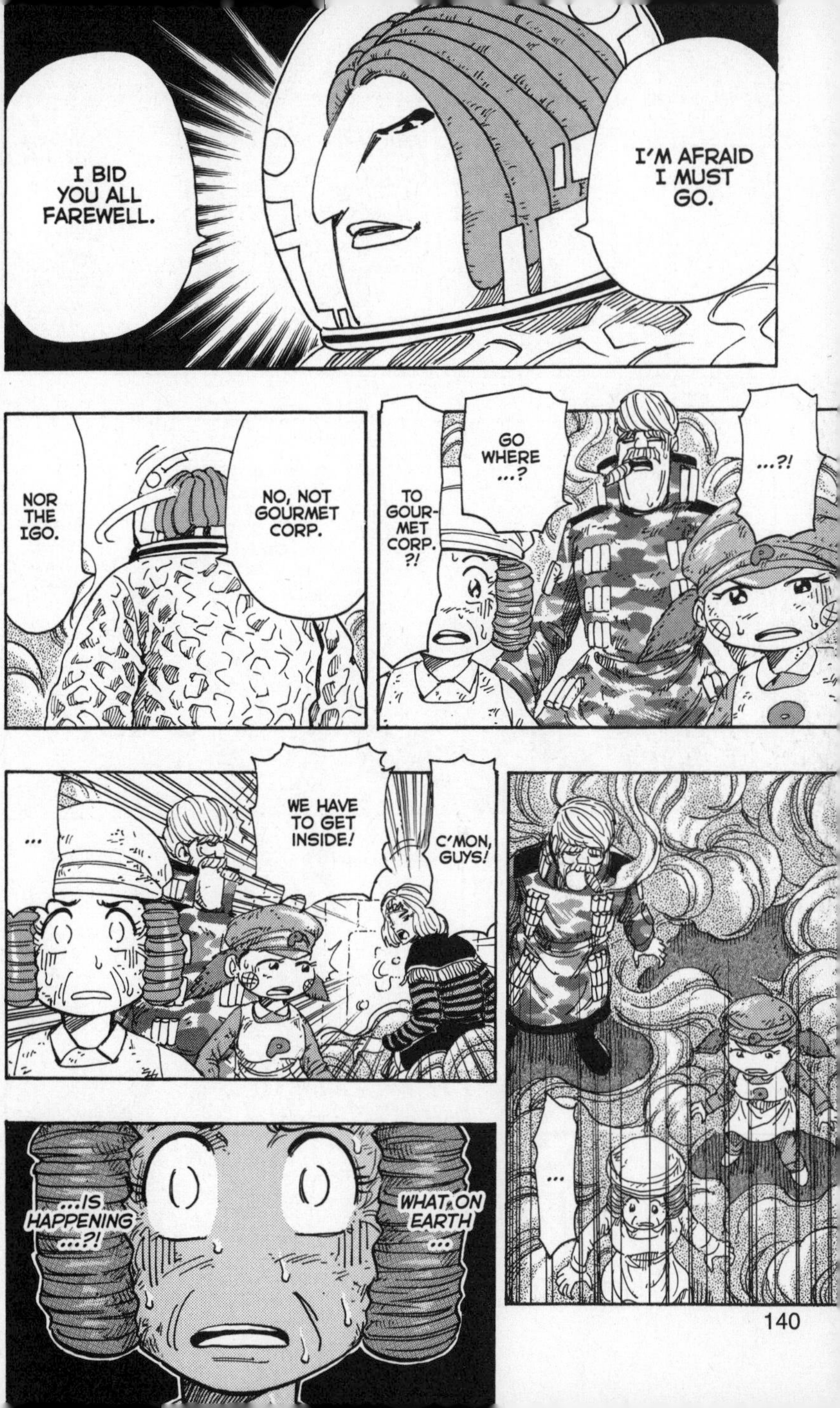
I'M AFRAID I MUST GO.
I BID YOU ALL FAREWELL.
...?!
GO WHERE ...?
TO GOURMET CORP. ?!
NO, NOT GOURMET CORP.
NOR THE IGO.
...
C'MON, GUYS!
WE HAVE TO GET INSIDE!
...
WHAT ON EARTH ...
...IS HAPPENING ...?!

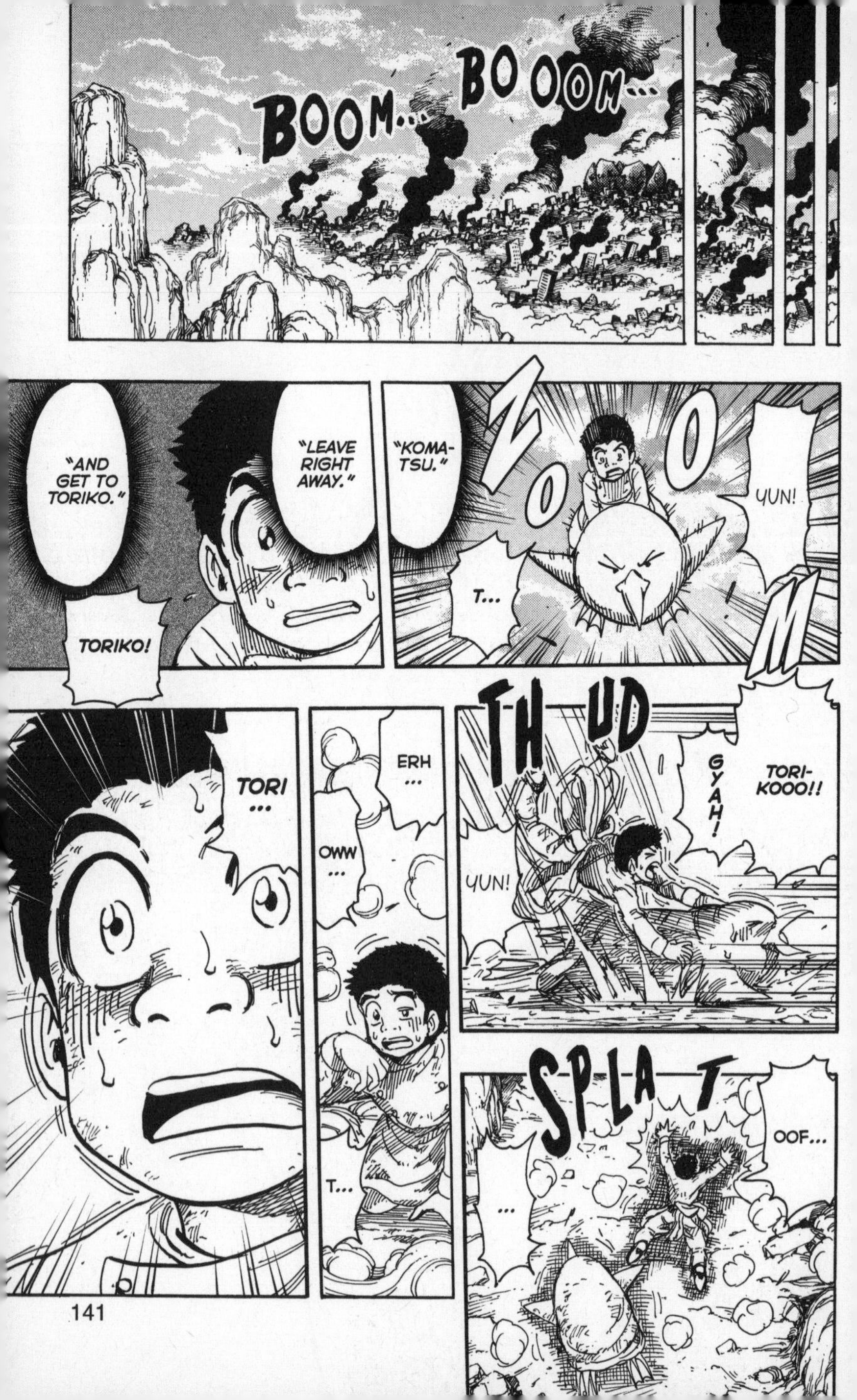
BOOM...
BOOOM...
NOOOM
YUN!
T...
"KOMA-TSU."
"LEAVE RIGHT AWAY."
"AND GET TO TORIKO."
TORIKO!
THUD
TORI-KOOO!!
GYAH!
YUN!
SPLAT
OOF...
...
ERH...
OWW...
T...
TORI...

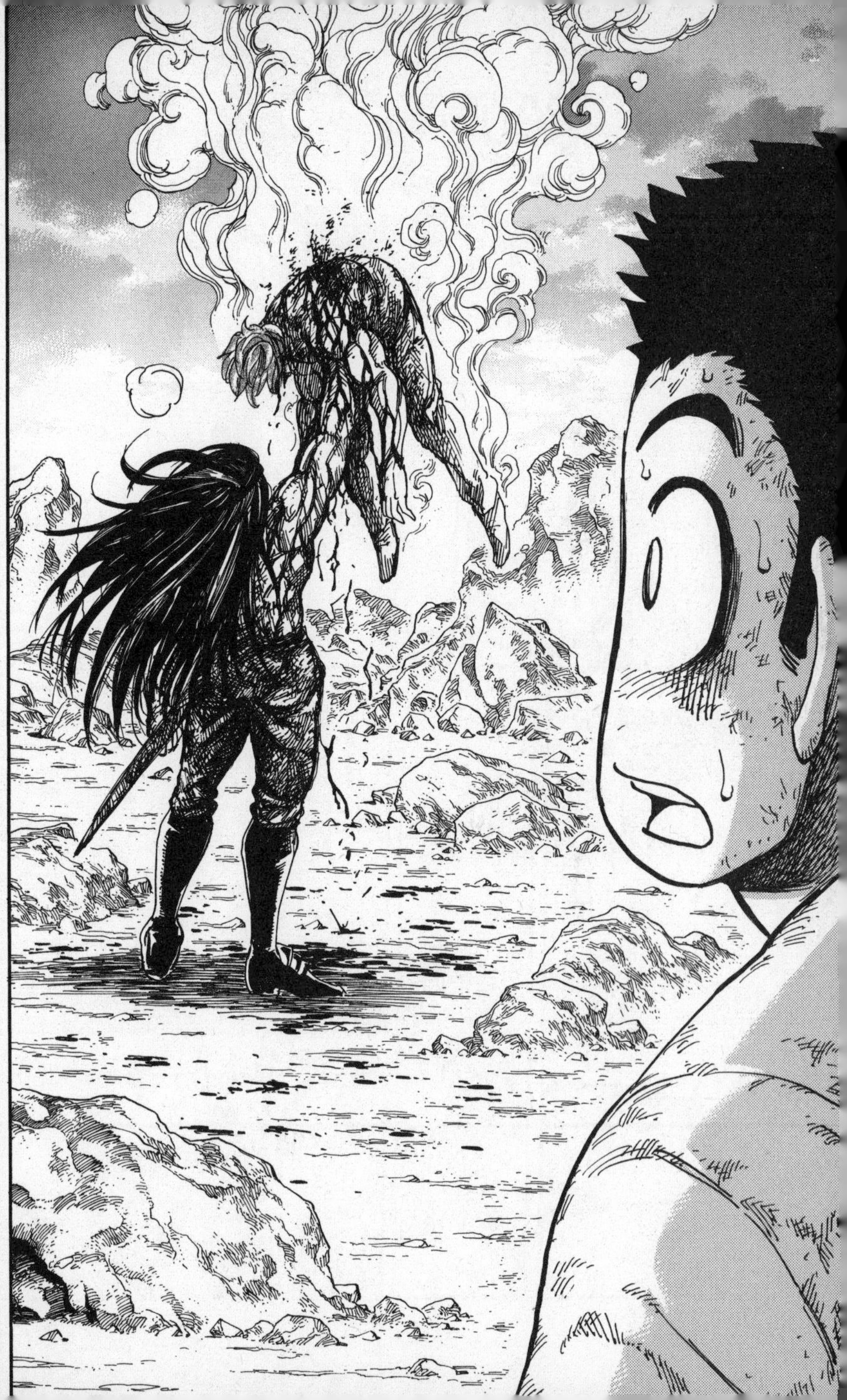

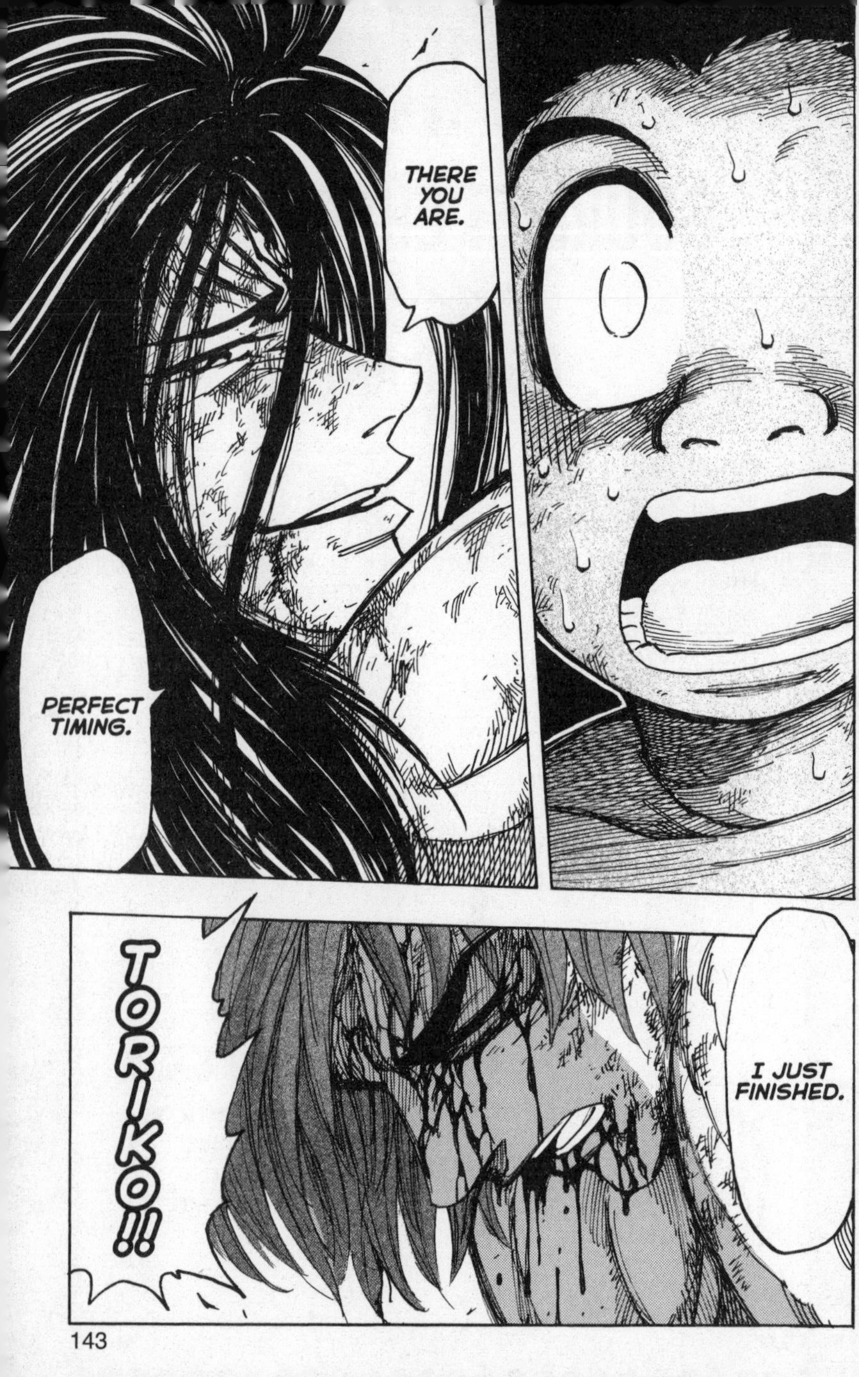
THERE YOU ARE.
PERFECT TIMING.
I JUST FINISHED.
TORIKO!!

TORIKO

GOURMET CHECKLIST

Vol. 258

FLAVOR ANT
(INSECT)

CAPTURE LEVEL: 5

HABITAT: WIDESPREAD

LENGTH: 1.5 CM

HEIGHT: ---

WEIGHT: 5 G

PRICE: 10 YEN PER ANT

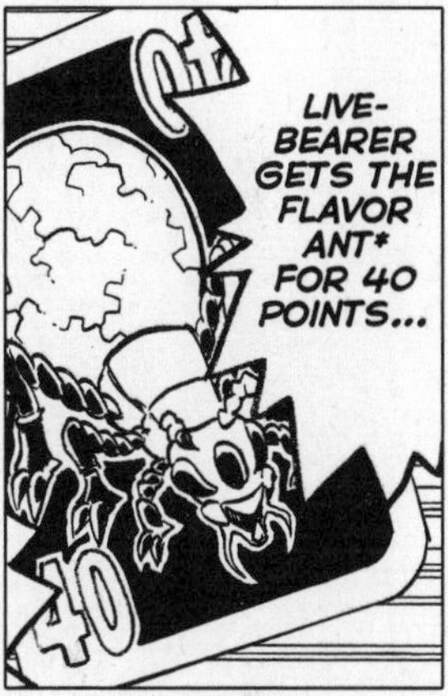
LIVE-BEARER GETS THE FLAVOR ANT* FOR 40 POINTS...
40

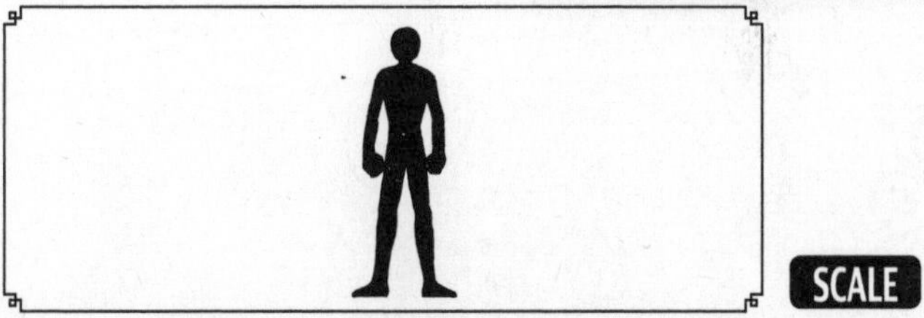
SCALE

THE FLAVOR OF THIS ANT DEPENDS ON WHERE IT LIVES. IT CAN TASTE SHOCKINGLY SPICY OR MELLOW AND SWEET LIKE HONEY, AND SO ON. DIFFERENT FLAVORS ARE LOCAL SPECIALTIES. IT IS THIS WIDE VARIETY OF FLAVORS THAT EARNED IT ITS NAME, AND IT CAN BE TURNED INTO A NUMBER OF DIFFERENT SEASONINGS. YOU CAN TELL THE FLAVOR OF THE ANT BY THE COLOR OF ITS BULBOUS ABDOMEN.

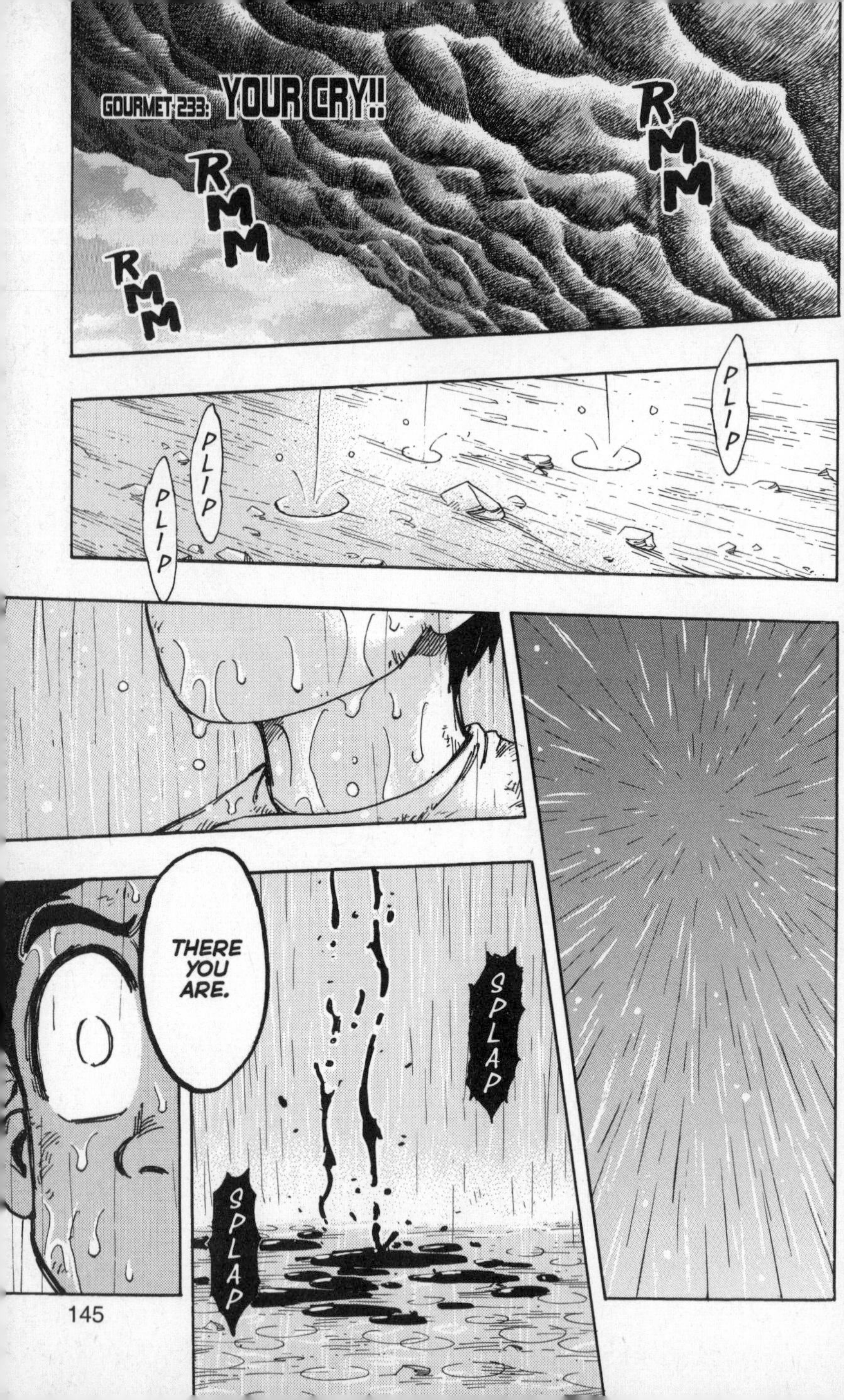
GOURMET 233: YOUR CRY!!
RMM
RMM
RMM
PLIP
PLIP
PLIP
THERE YOU ARE.
SPLAP
SPLAP

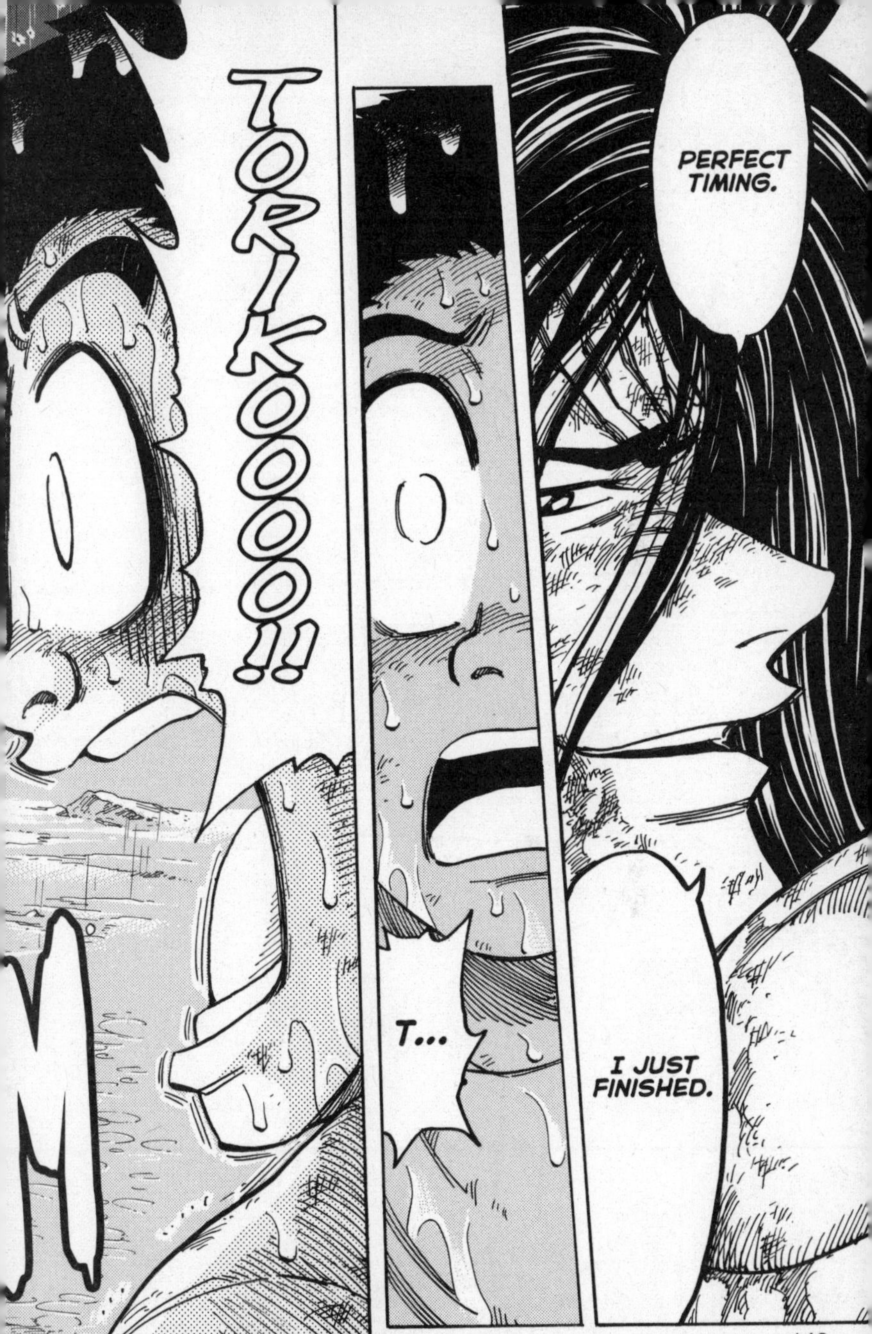
PERFECT TIMING.
I JUST FINISHED.
T...
TORIKOOOOO!!

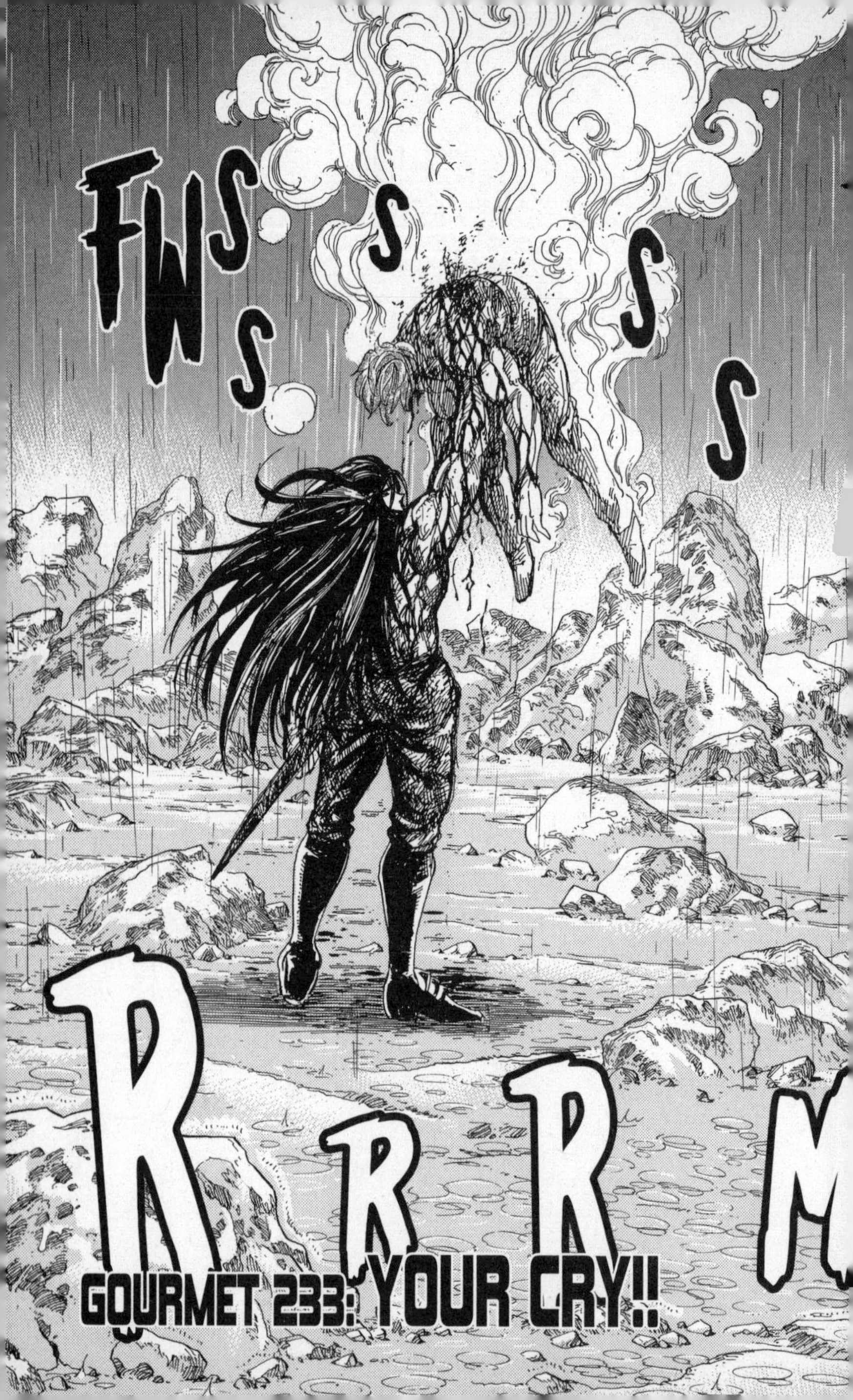
FWSSSSSS
RRRM
GOURMET 233: YOUR CRY!!

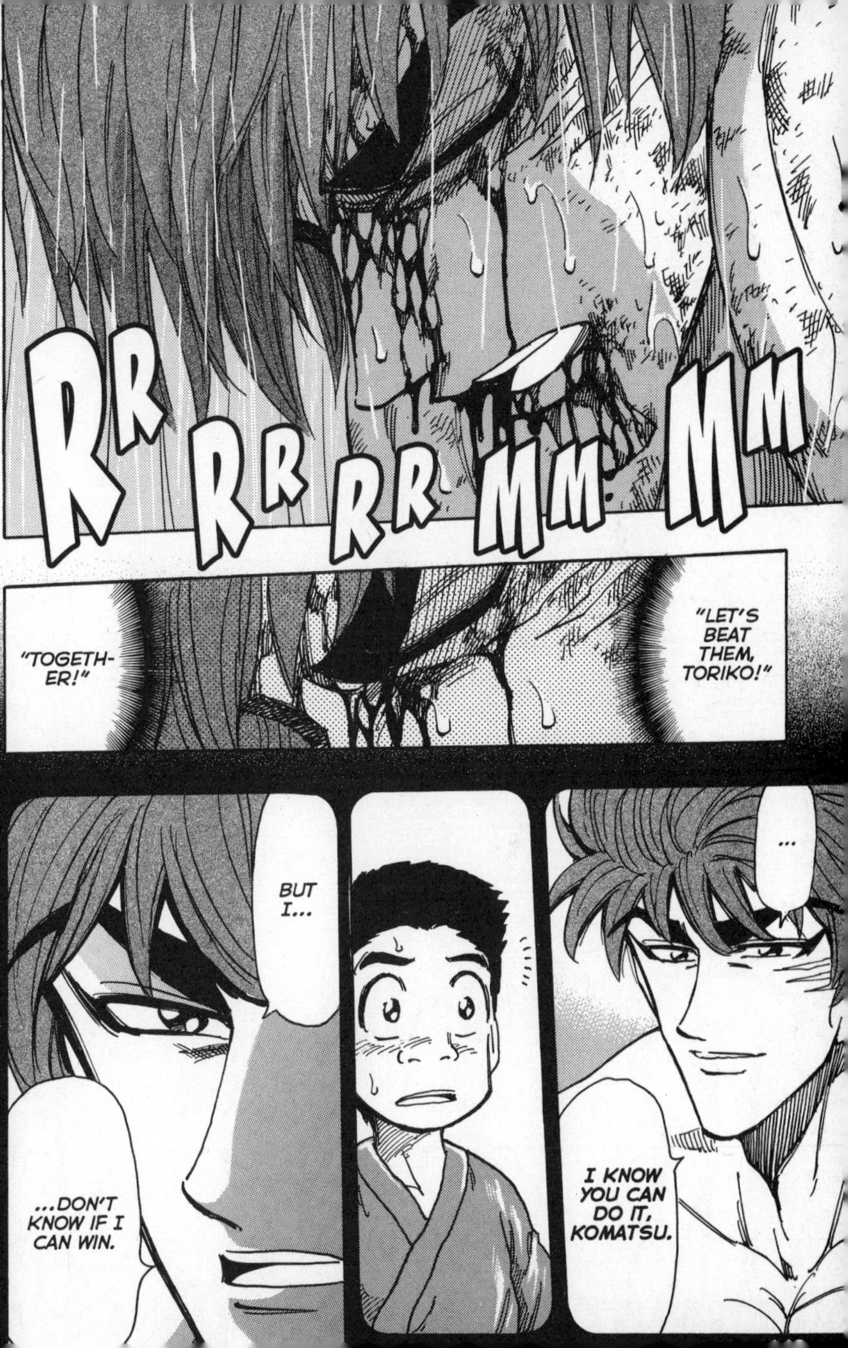
RRRRRRMMMM
"LET'S BEAT THEM, TORIKO!"
"TOGETH-ER!"
...
I KNOW YOU CAN DO IT, KOMATSU.
BUT I...
...DON'T KNOW IF I CAN WIN.

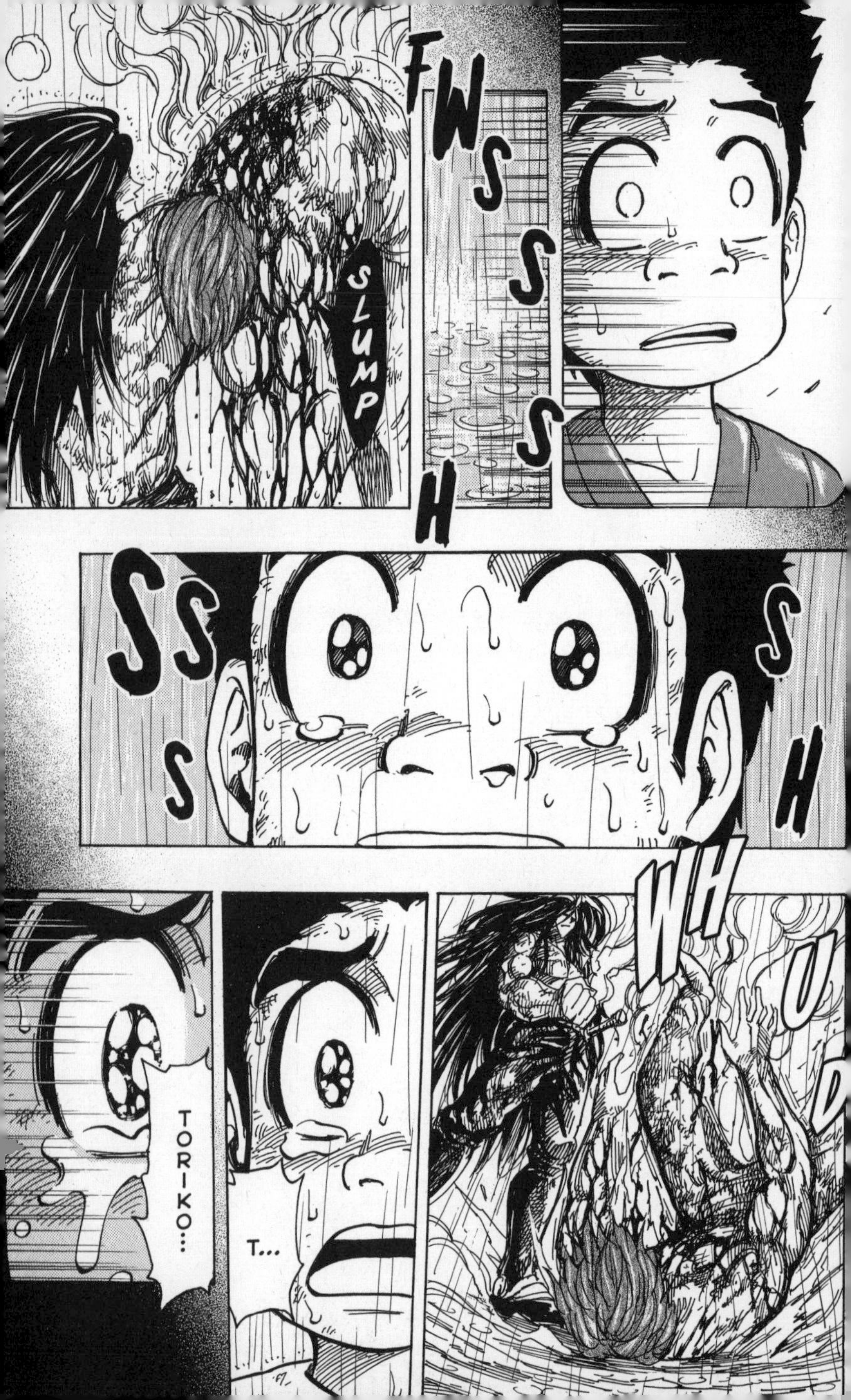
FWSSSH
SLUMP
SSSSH
WHUD
T...
TORIKO...

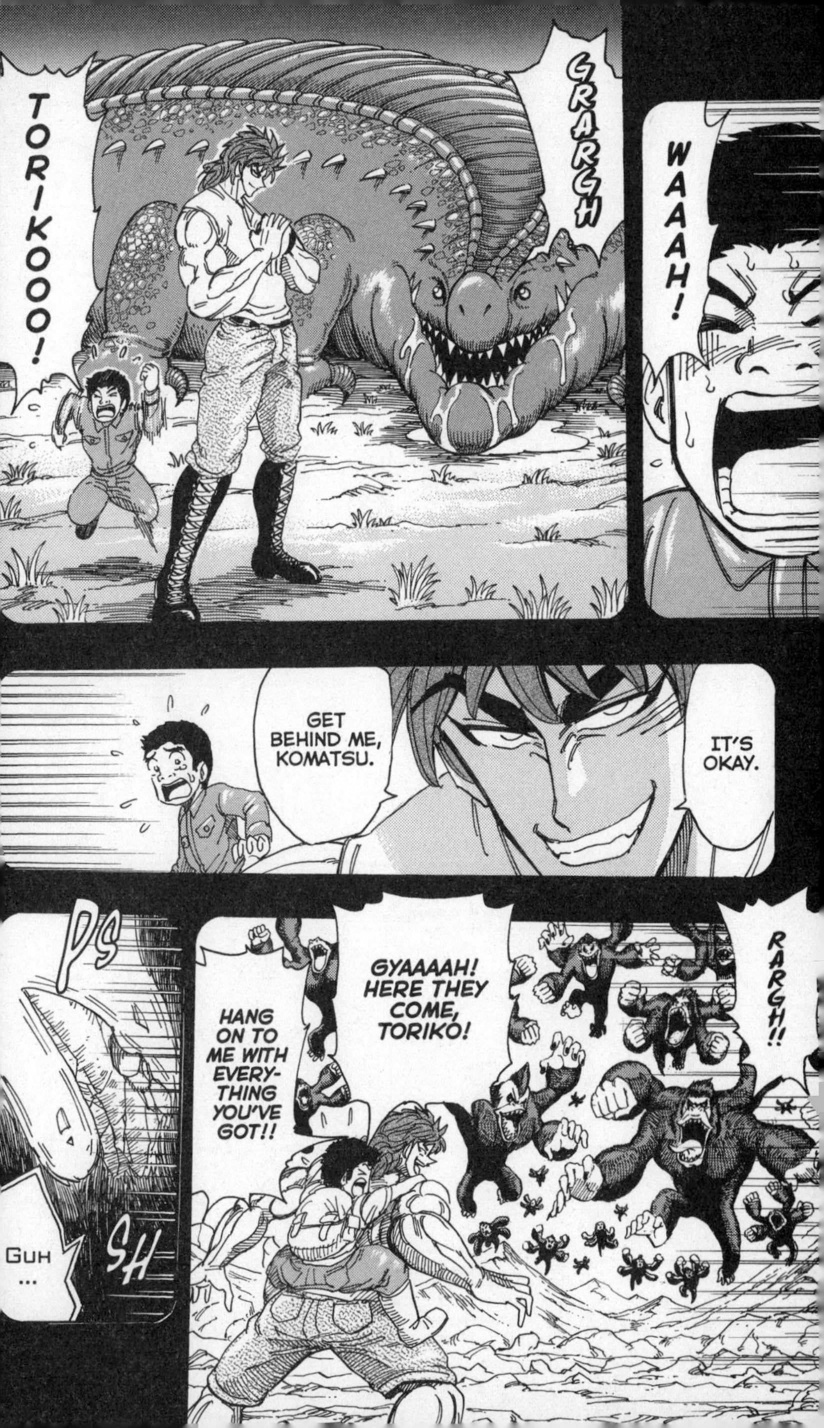
WAAAAH!
GRARGH
TORIKOOOO!
IT'S OKAY.
GET BEHIND ME, KOMATSU.
RARGH!!
GYAAAAH! HERE THEY COME, TORIKO!
HANG ON TO ME WITH EVERY-THING YOU'VE GOT!!
PS
SH
Guh ...

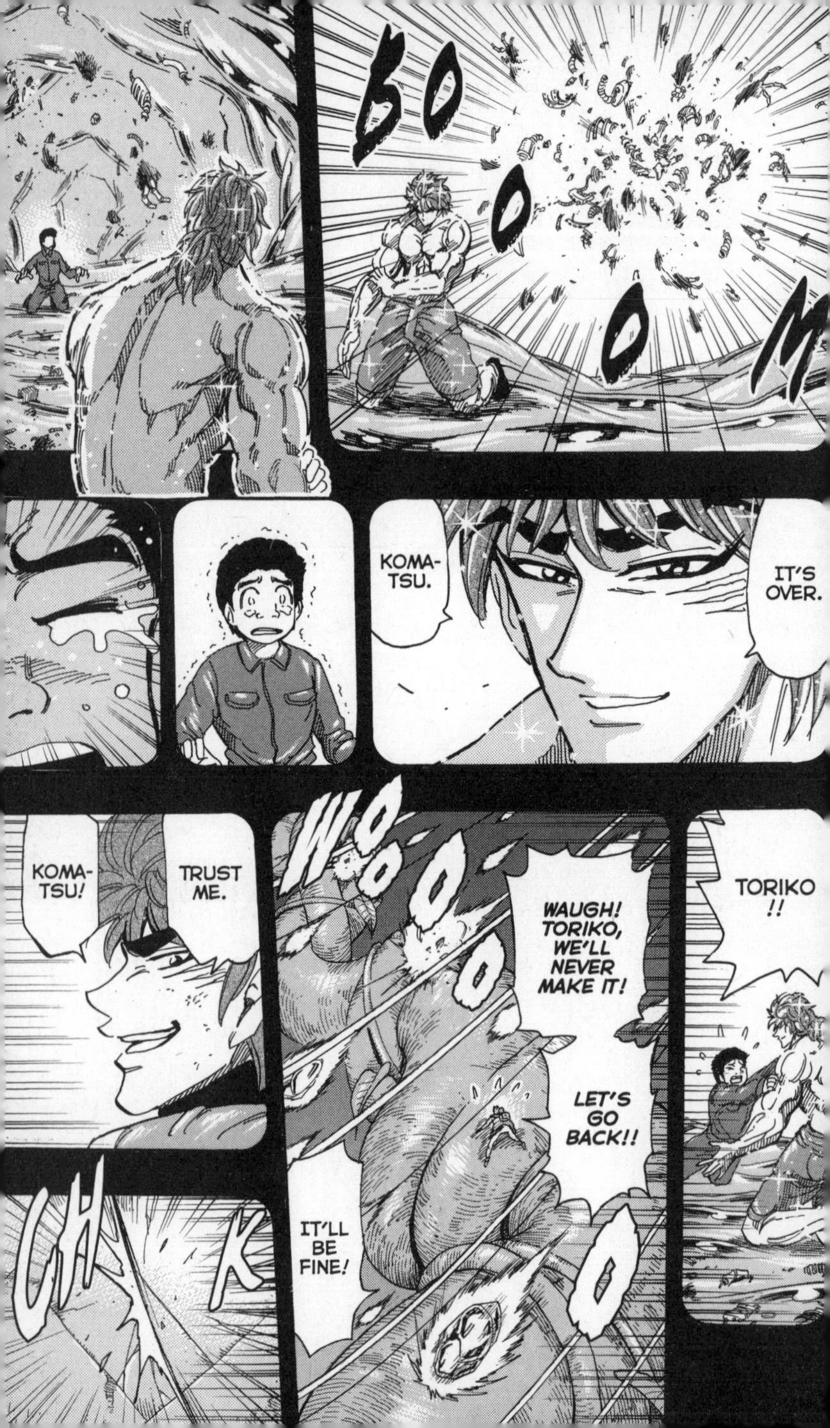
BOOOOM
KOMA-TSU.
IT'S OVER.
TORIKO !!
WAUGH! TORIKO, WE'LL NEVER MAKE IT!
LET'S GO BACK!!
IT'LL BE FINE!
WOOOOOO
KOMA-TSU!
TRUST ME.
CH K

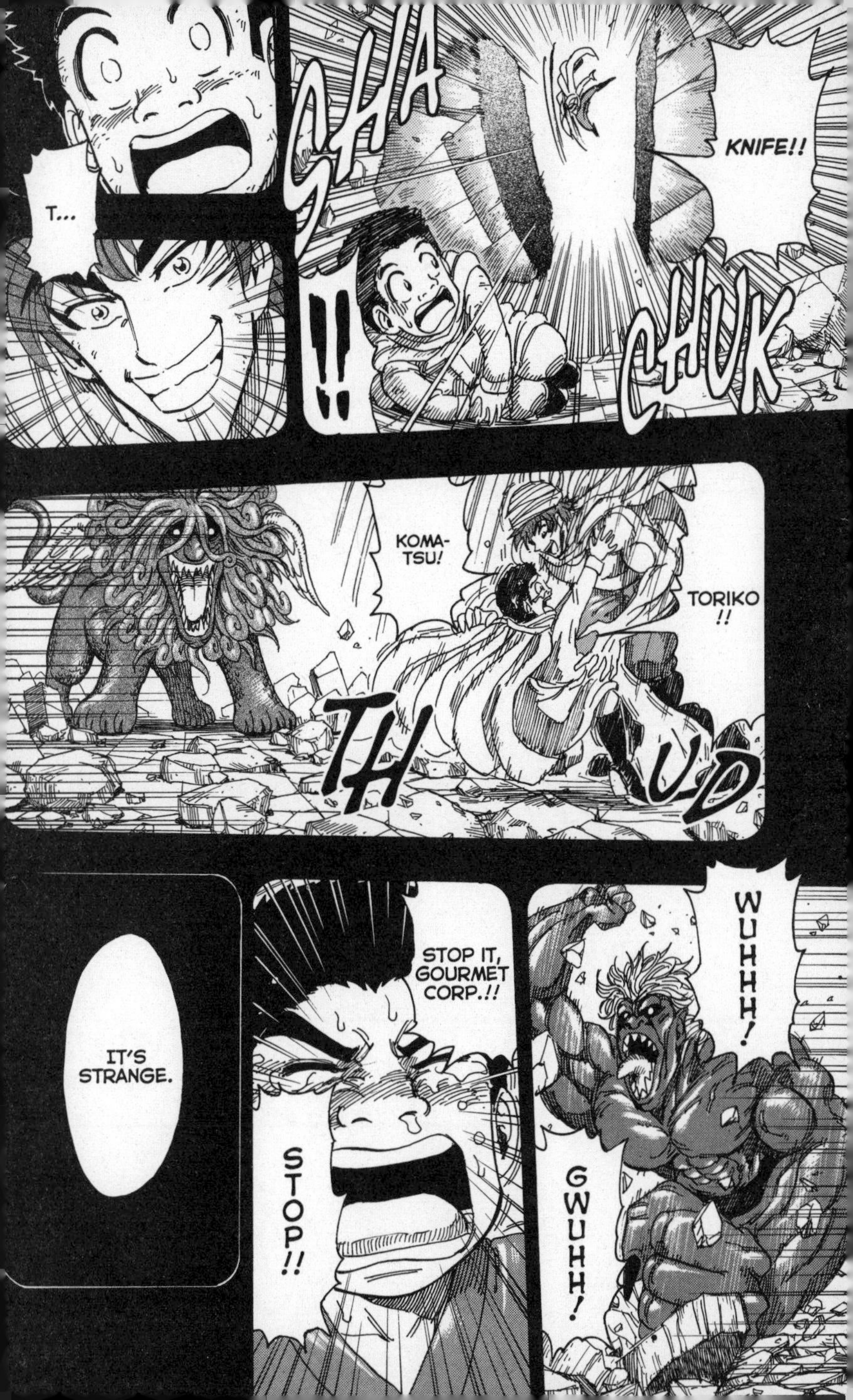
KNIFE!!
SHA
CHUK
!!
T...
TORIKO!!
KOMA-TSU!
TH
UD
WUHHH!
GWUHH!
STOP IT, GOURMET CORP.!!
STOP!!
IT'S STRANGE.

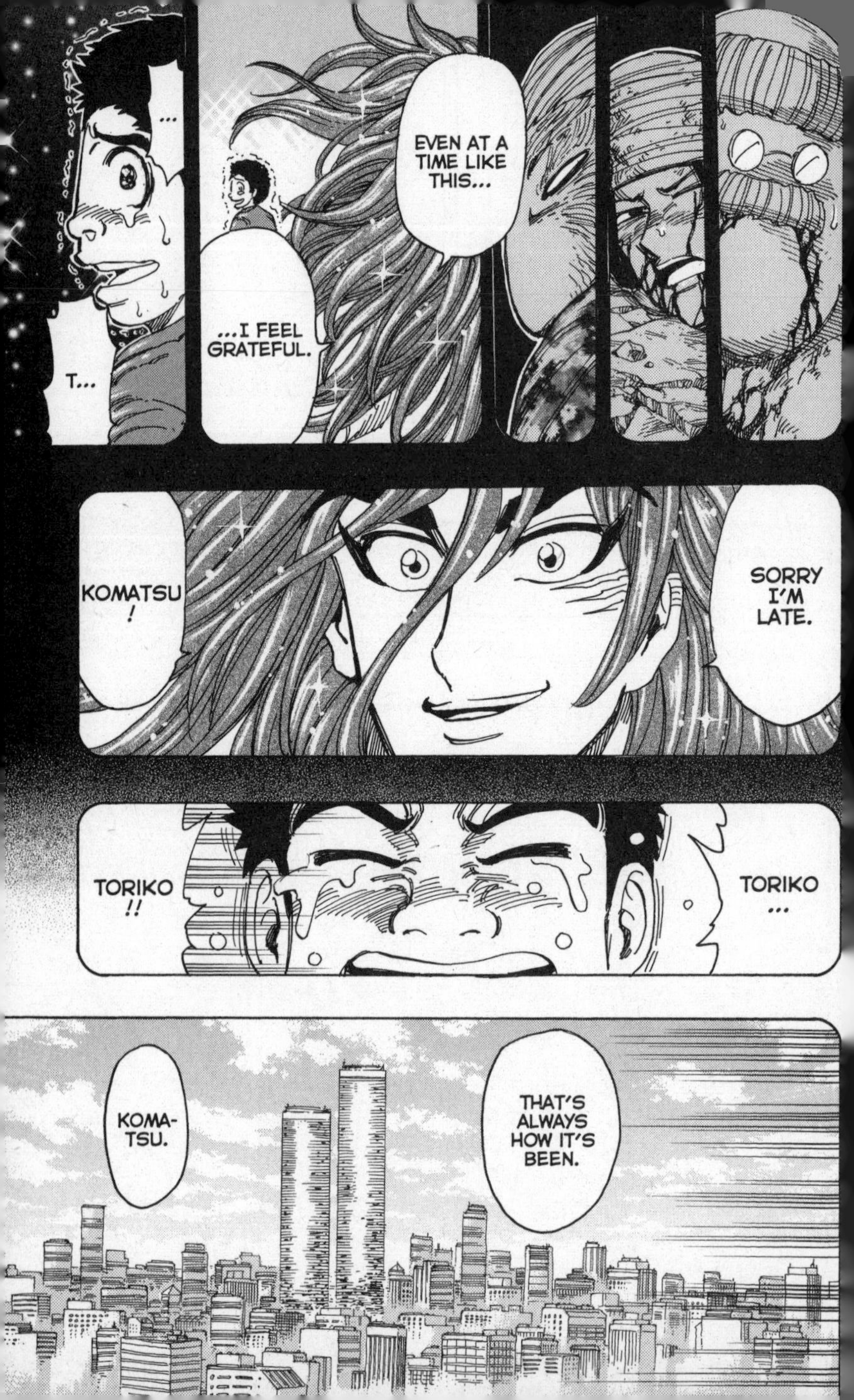
EVEN AT A TIME LIKE THIS...
...I FEEL GRATEFUL.
...
T...
SORRY I'M LATE.
KOMATSU!
TORIKO...
TORIKO!!
THAT'S ALWAYS HOW IT'S BEEN.
KOMATSU.

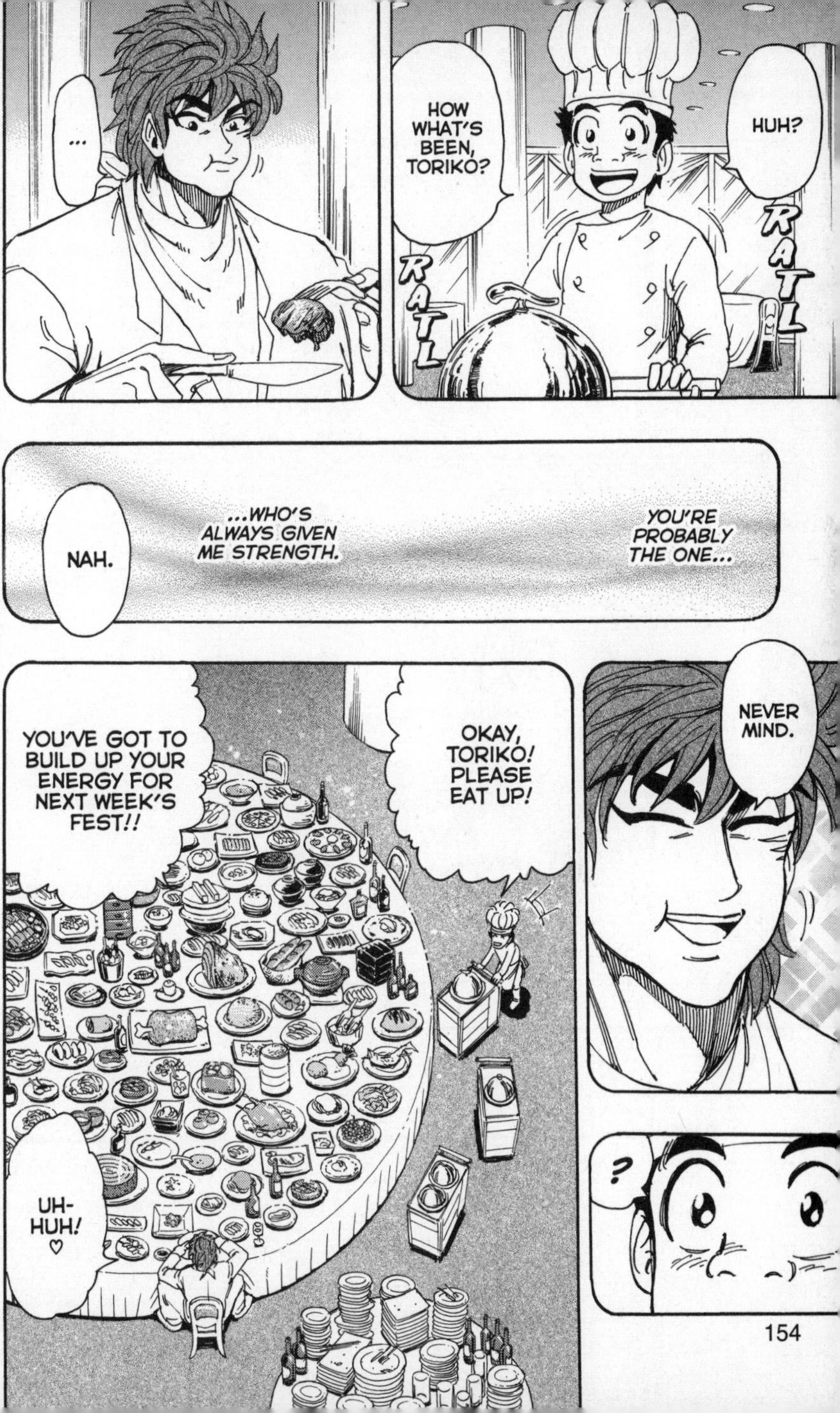
HUH?
RATTL
HOW WHAT'S BEEN, TORIKO?
RATTL
...
YOU'RE PROBABLY THE ONE...
...WHO'S ALWAYS GIVEN ME STRENGTH.
NAH.
NEVER MIND.
?
OKAY, TORIKO! PLEASE EAT UP!
YOU'VE GOT TO BUILD UP YOUR ENERGY FOR NEXT WEEK'S FEST!!
UH-HUH! ♡

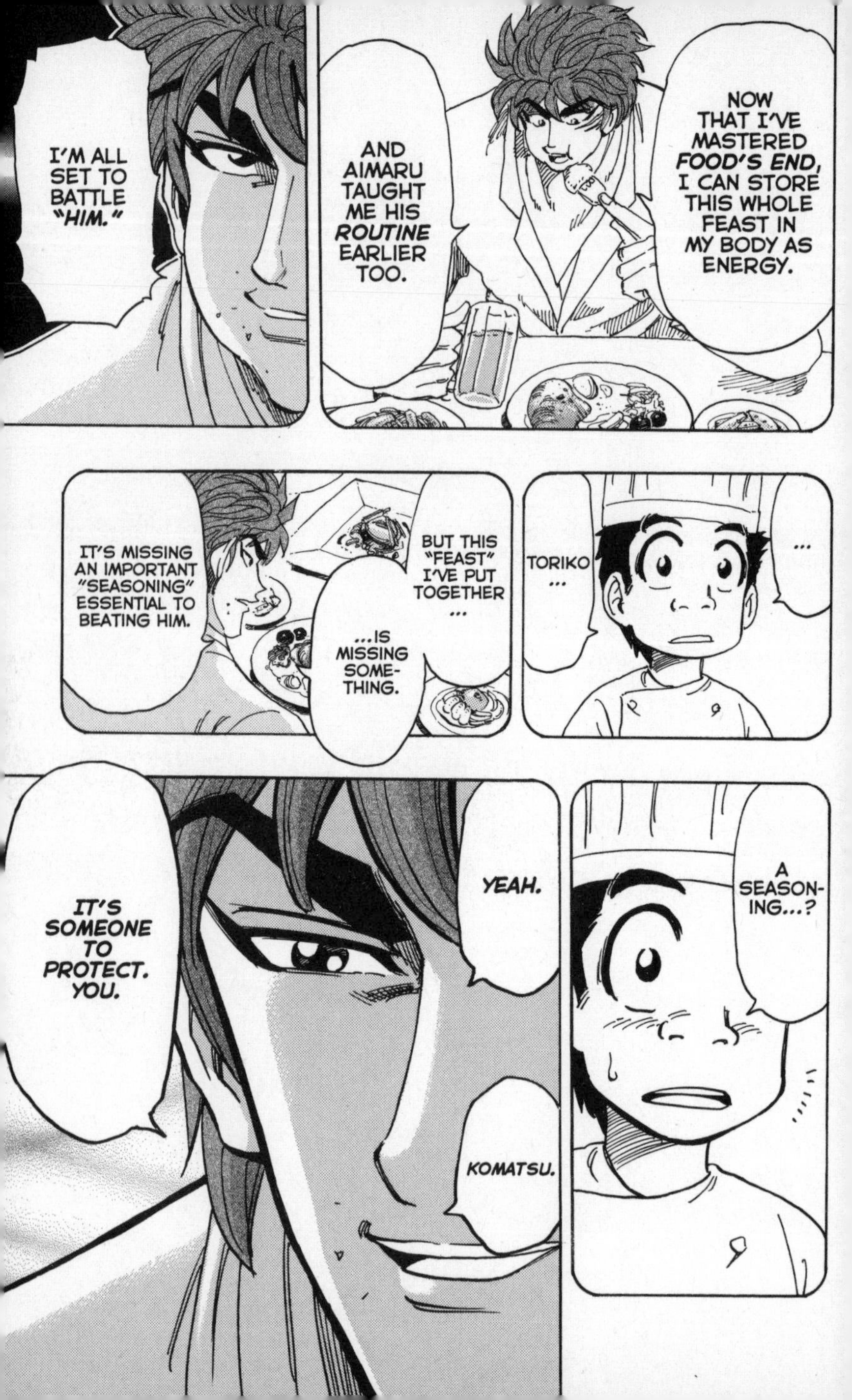
NOW THAT I'VE MASTERED FOOD'S END, I CAN STORE THIS WHOLE FEAST IN MY BODY AS ENERGY.
AND AIMARU TAUGHT ME HIS ROUTINE EARLIER TOO.
I'M ALL SET TO BATTLE "HIM."
...
TORIKO ...
BUT THIS "FEAST" I'VE PUT TOGETHER ...
...IS MISSING SOMETHING.
IT'S MISSING AN IMPORTANT "SEASONING" ESSENTIAL TO BEATING HIM.
A SEASON-ING...?
YEAH.
IT'S SOMEONE TO PROTECT. YOU.
KOMATSU.

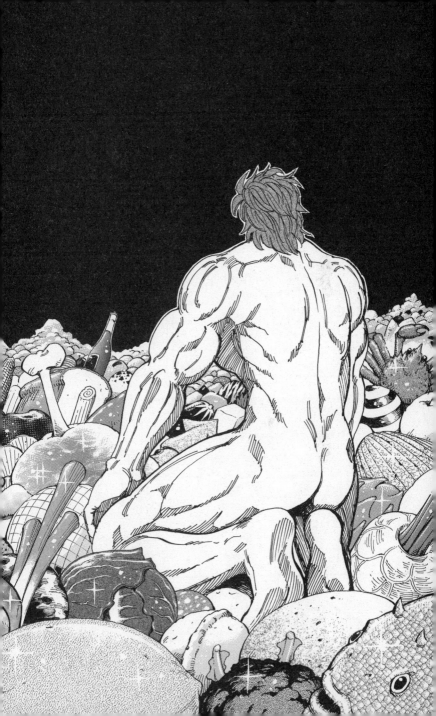

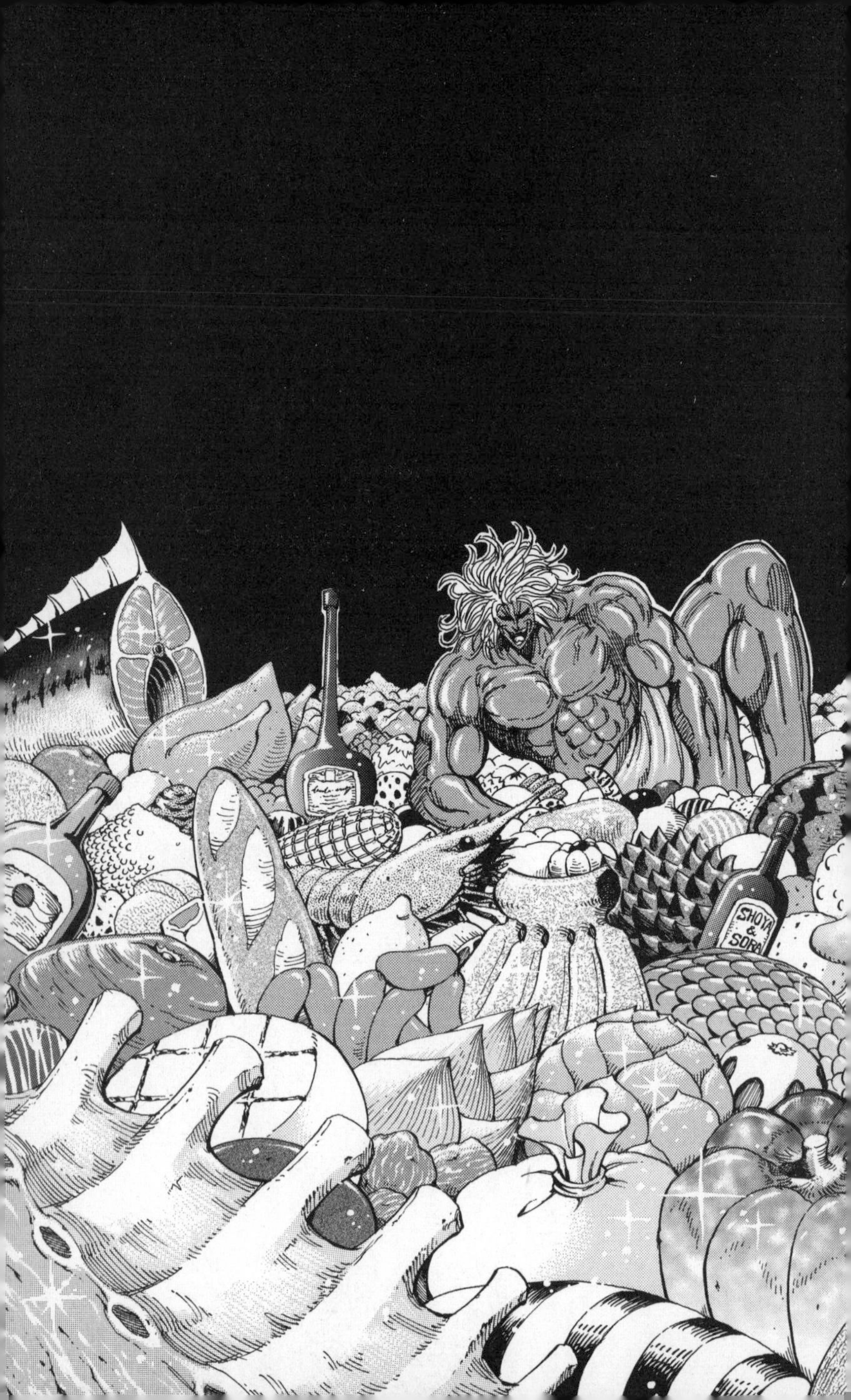
SHOYA & SORA

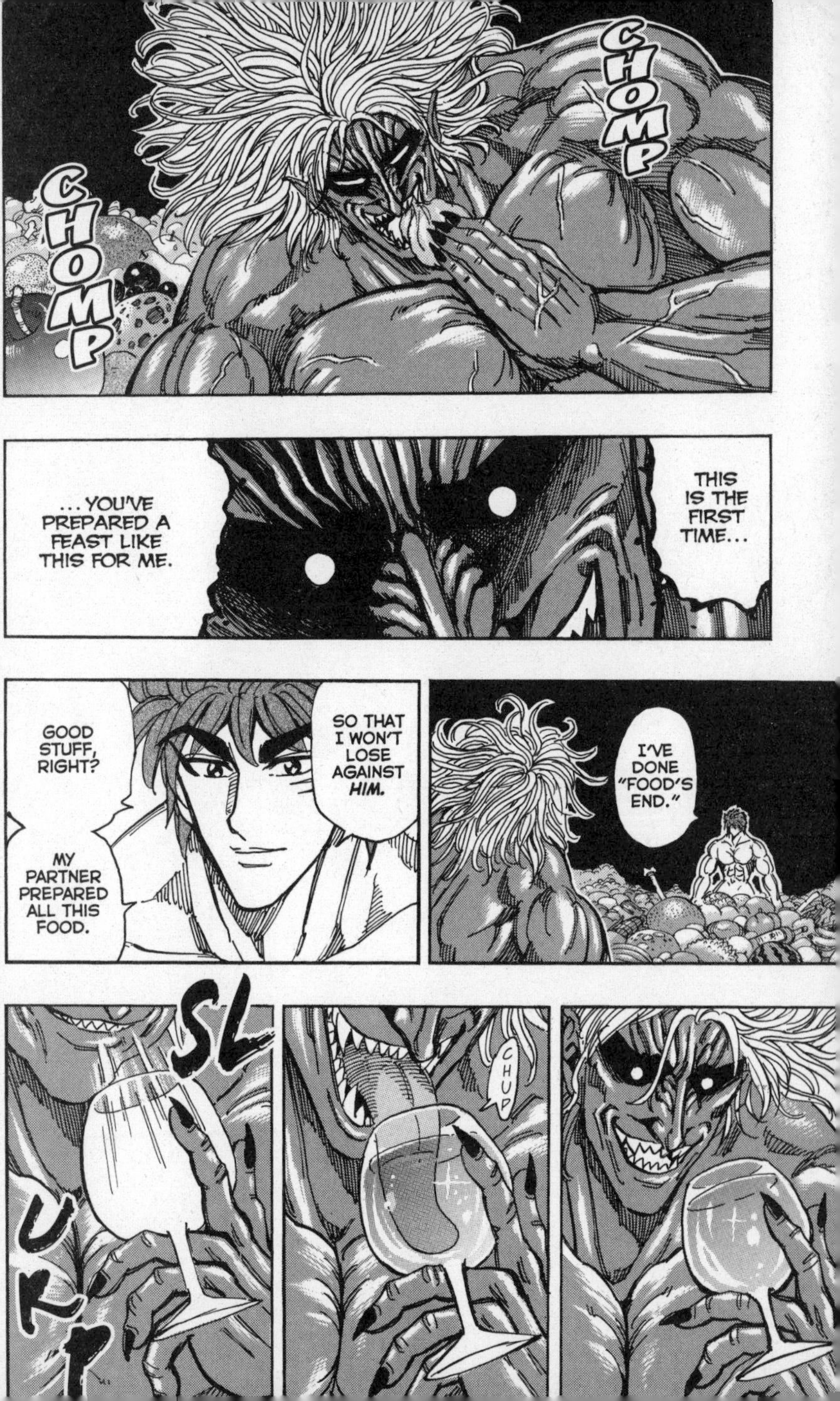
CHOMP
CHOMP
THIS IS THE FIRST TIME...
...YOU'VE PREPARED A FEAST LIKE THIS FOR ME.
I'VE DONE "FOOD'S END."
SO THAT I WON'T LOSE AGAINST *HIM.*
GOOD STUFF, RIGHT?
MY PARTNER PREPARED ALL THIS FOOD.
CHUP
SL
URP

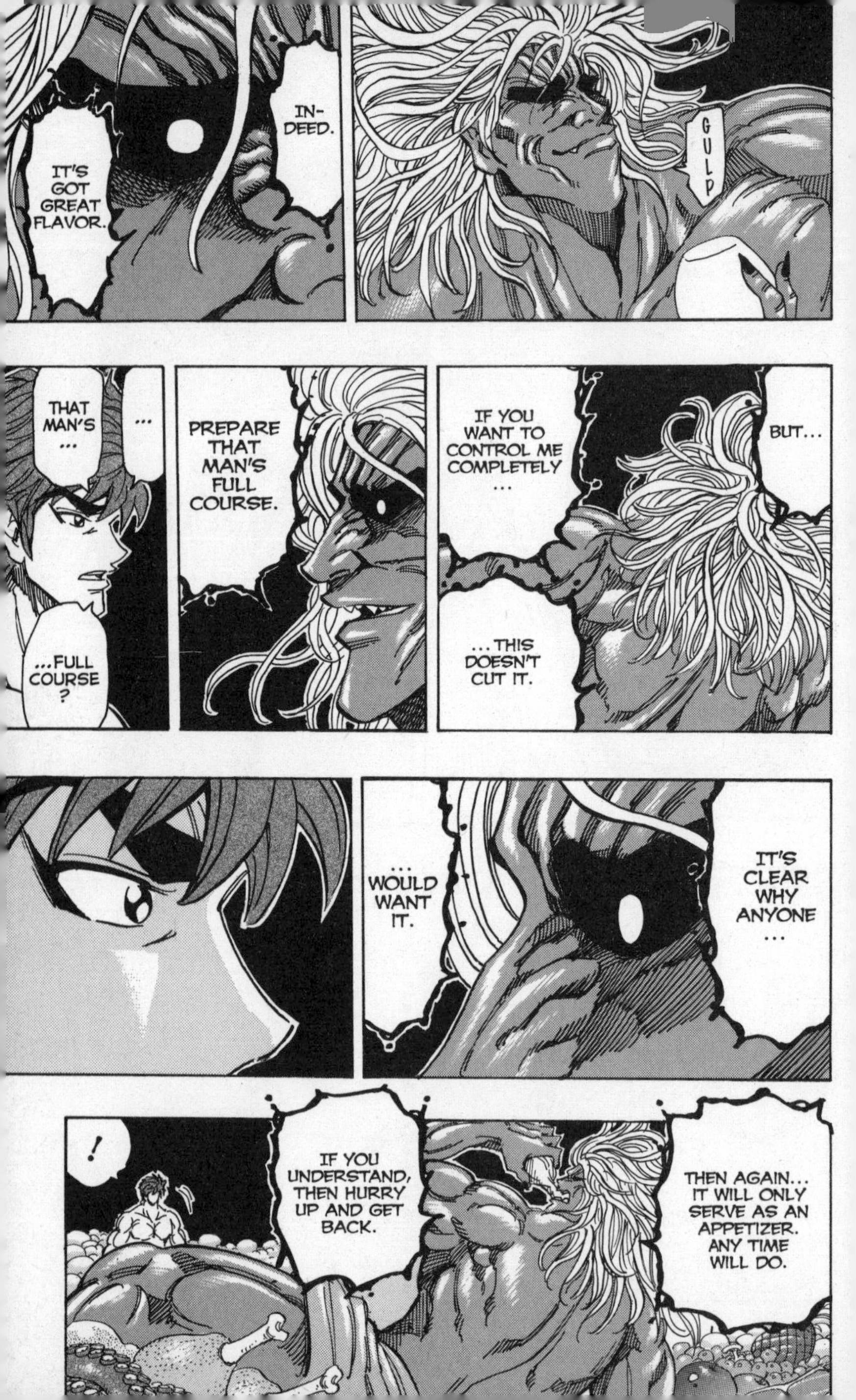
GULP
IN-DEED.
IT'S GOT GREAT FLAVOR.
BUT...
IF YOU WANT TO CONTROL ME COMPLETELY...
...THIS DOESN'T CUT IT.
PREPARE THAT MAN'S FULL COURSE.
...
THAT MAN'S...
...FULL COURSE?
IT'S CLEAR WHY ANYONE...
...WOULD WANT IT.
THEN AGAIN... IT WILL ONLY SERVE AS AN APPETIZER. ANY TIME WILL DO.
IF YOU UNDERSTAND, THEN HURRY UP AND GET BACK.
!

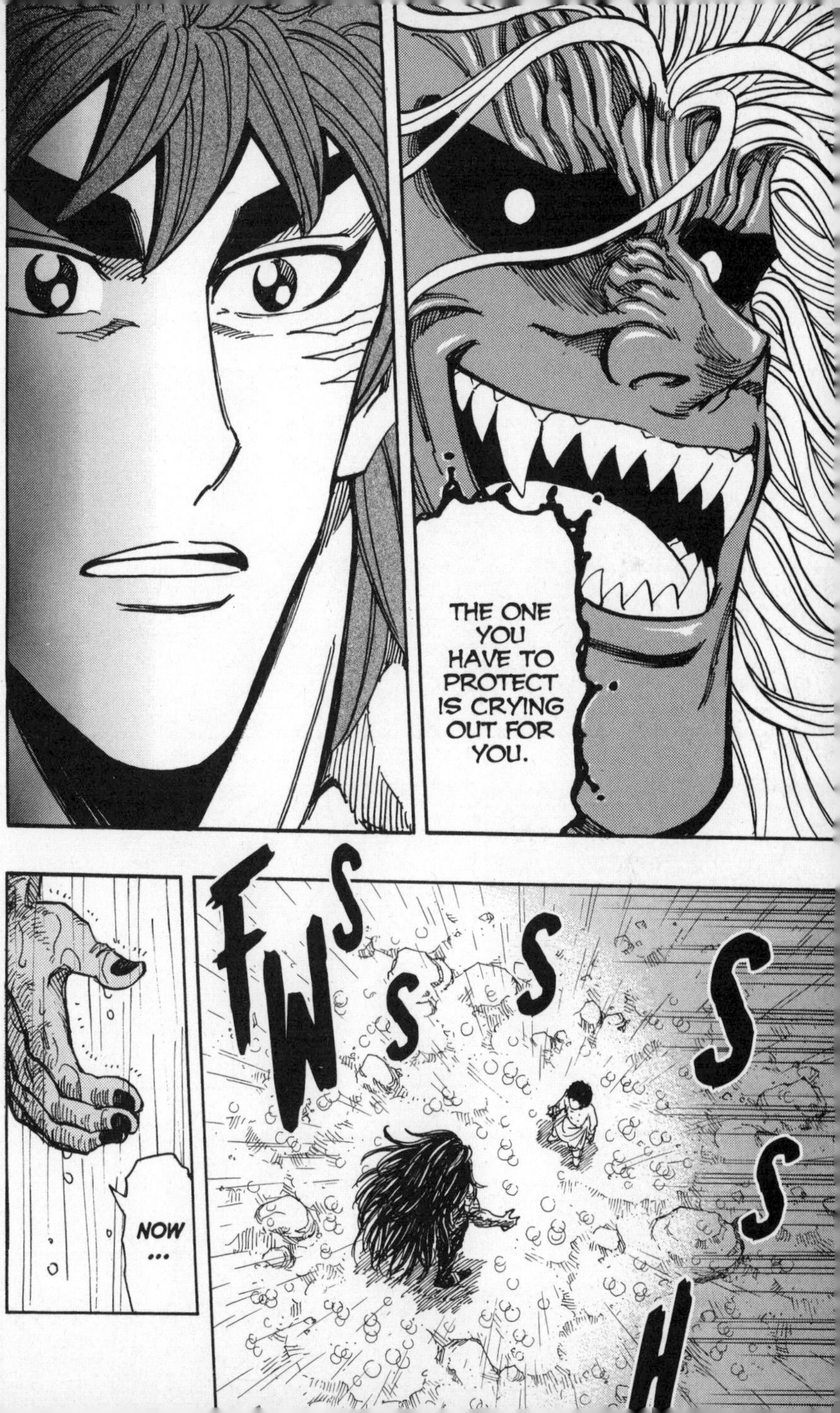
THE ONE YOU HAVE TO PROTECT IS CRYING OUT FOR YOU.
FWSSSSSSSH
NOW ...

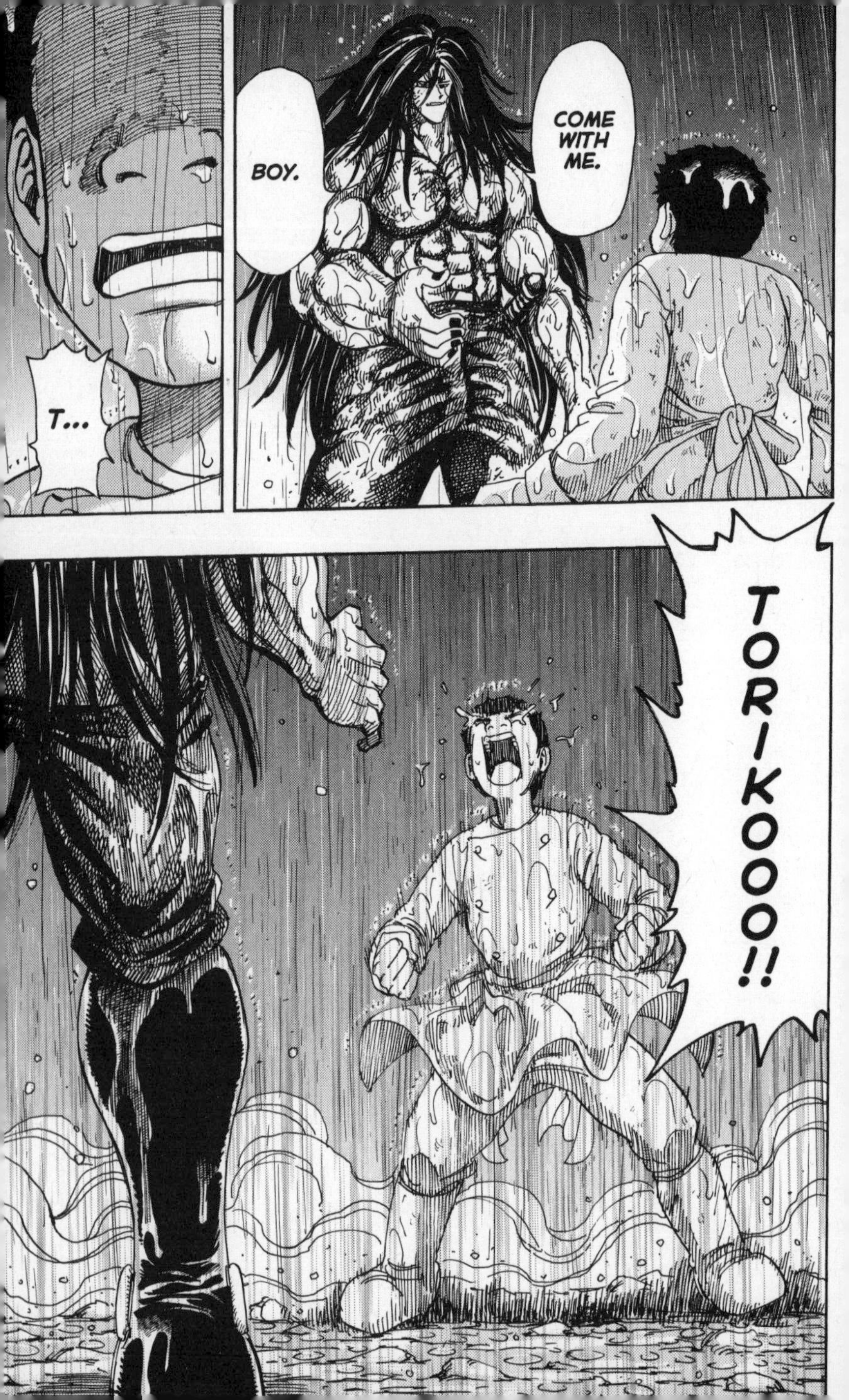
COME WITH ME.
BOY.
T...
TORIKOOOO!!

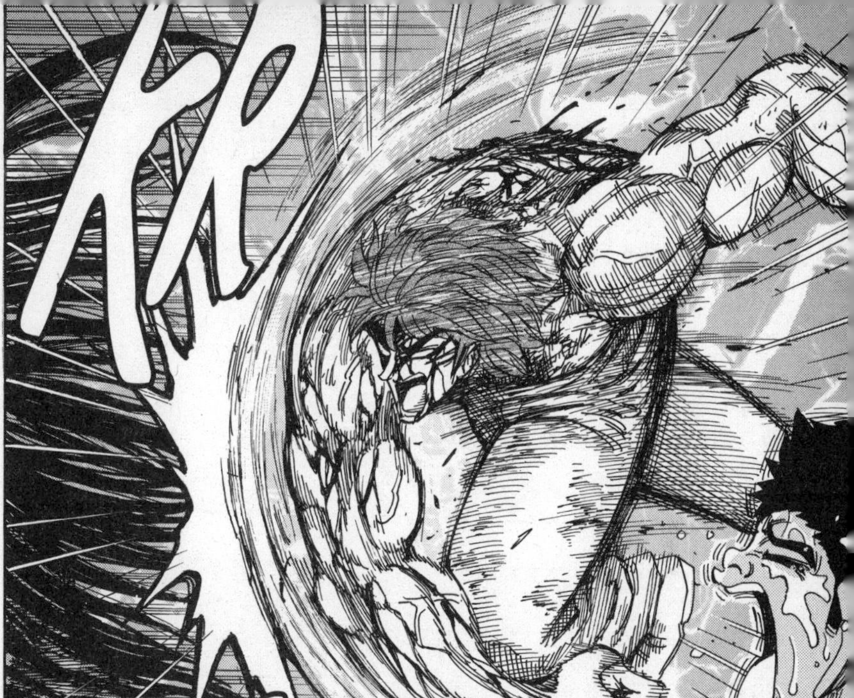
KRAAK
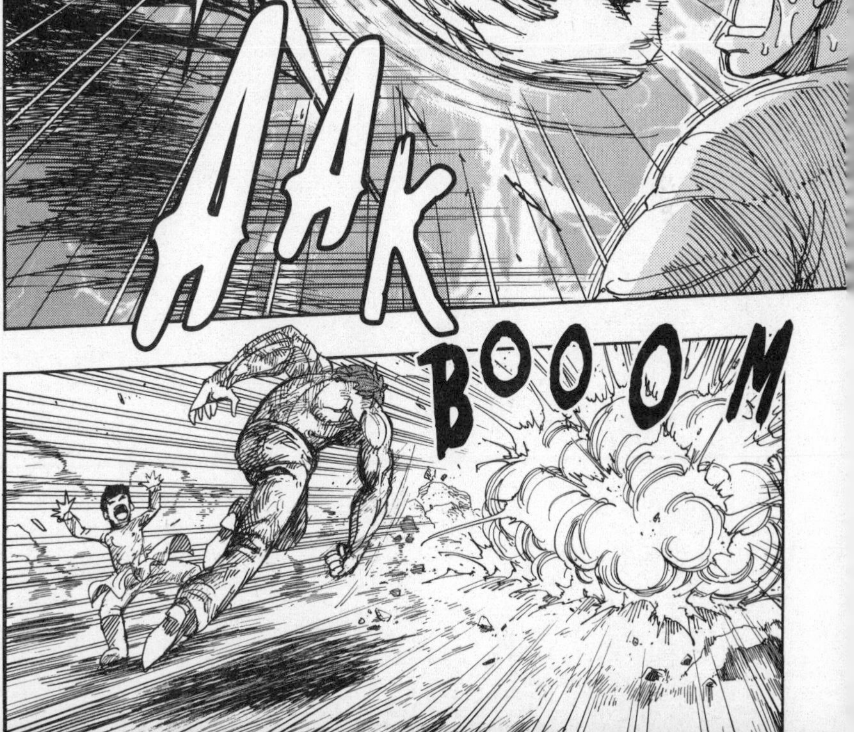
BOOOM

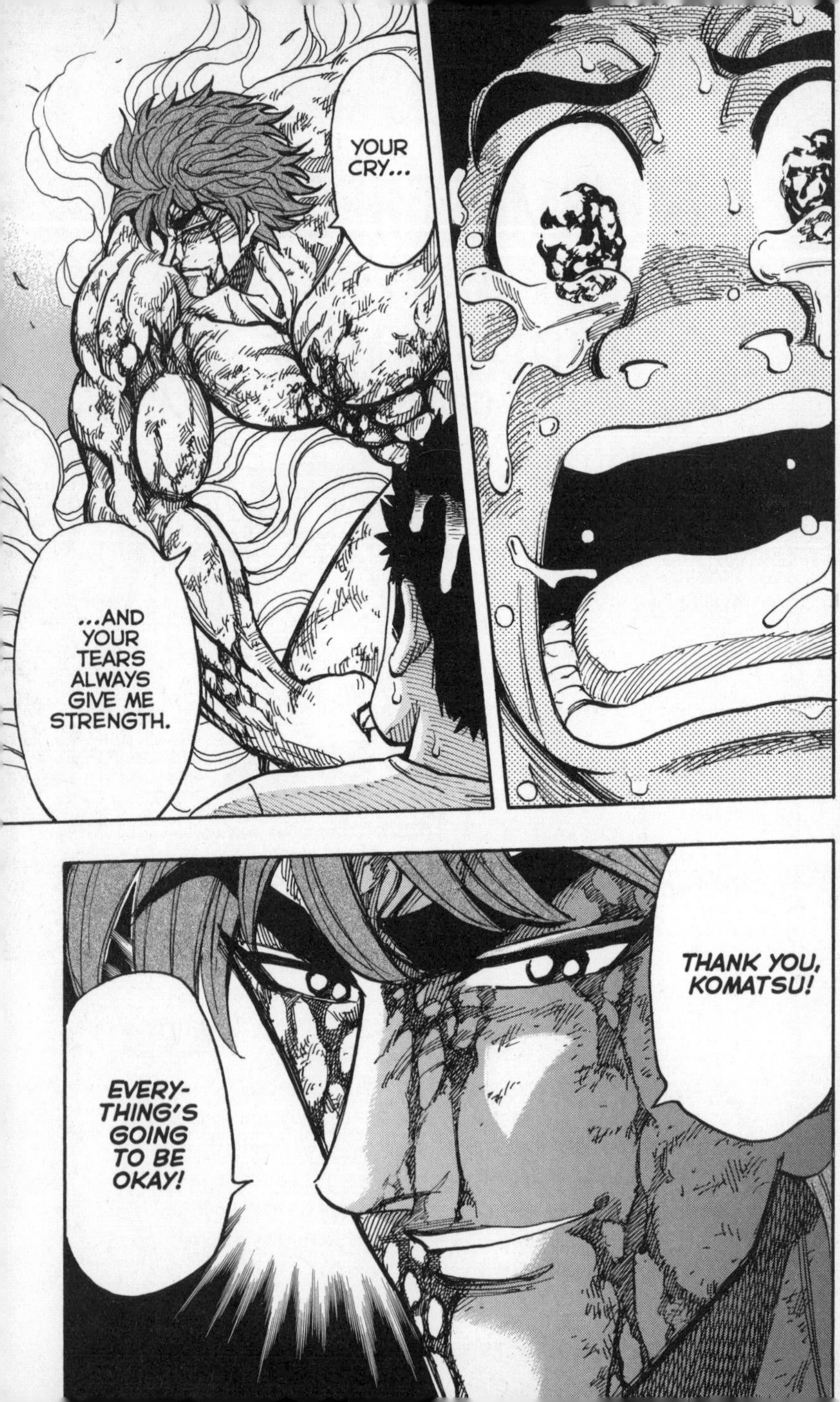
YOUR CRY...
...AND YOUR TEARS ALWAYS GIVE ME STRENGTH.
THANK YOU, KOMATSU!
EVERY-THING'S GOING TO BE OKAY!

TORIKO

GOURMET CHECKLIST

Vol. 259

BUBBLE ABALONE
(SHELLFISH)

CAPTURE LEVEL: 5
HABITAT: CLEAR OCEANS
LENGTH: 10 CM
HEIGHT: ---
WEIGHT: 250 G
PRICE: 200,000 YEN PER ABALONE

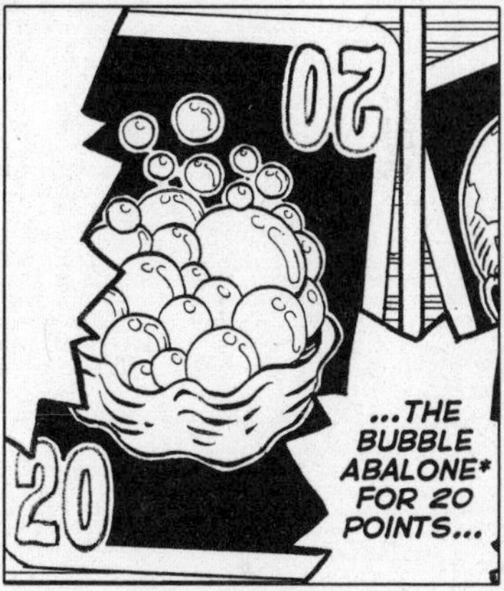
20
20
...THE BUBBLE ABALONE* FOR 20 POINTS...

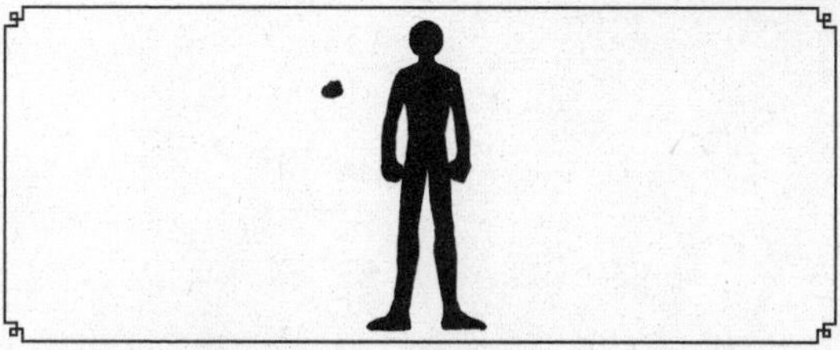

SCALE

A SHELL ENVELOPED IN BEAUTIFUL BUBBLES FORMED FROM MYRIAD MINERALS. THE BUBBLES POSSESS A PEARLY SHEEN AND ARE COMPOSED OF THE HIGH-QUALITY AMINO ACIDS FOUND IN PEARLS AND THE HIGHEST QUALITY COLLAGEN. THE ESSENCE EXTRACTED FROM BUBBLE ABALONE PLAYS A LARGE ROLE IN THE ACTIVATION OF CELLS AND IS RESPONSIBLE FOR SMOOTH SKIN. BECAUSE OF THAT, BUBBLE ABALONE IS USED AS AN INGREDIENT IN SKIN CARE PRODUCTS. BEAUTIFUL EMPRESSES OF THE ORIENT AND DESERT QUEENS OF ANTIQUITY ARE FAMOUS FOR THEIR LOVE OF BUBBLE ABALONE.

GOURMET 234: BEYOND THE LIMIT!!

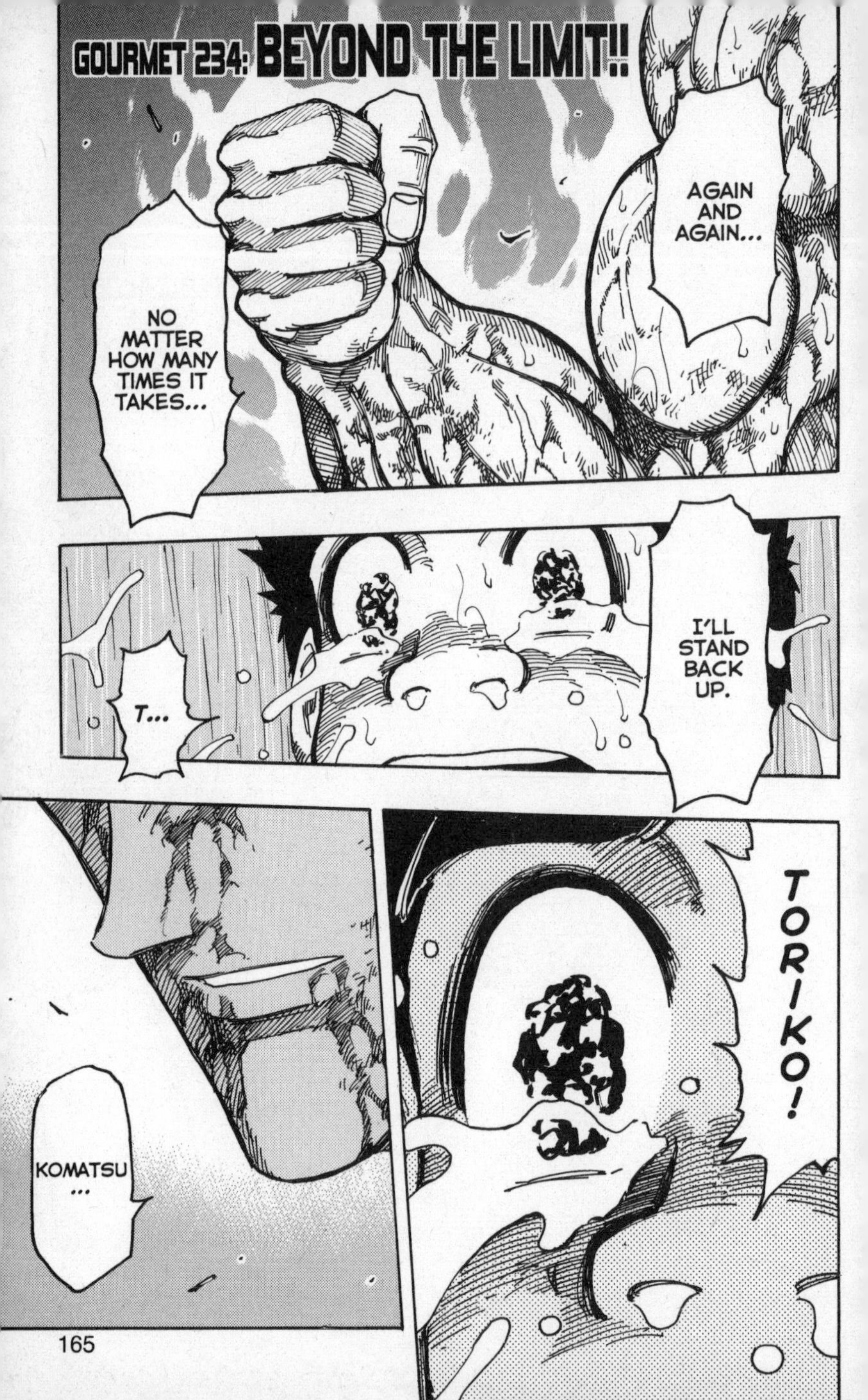
AGAIN AND AGAIN...
NO MATTER HOW MANY TIMES IT TAKES...
I'LL STAND BACK UP.
T...
TORIKO!
KOMATSU ...

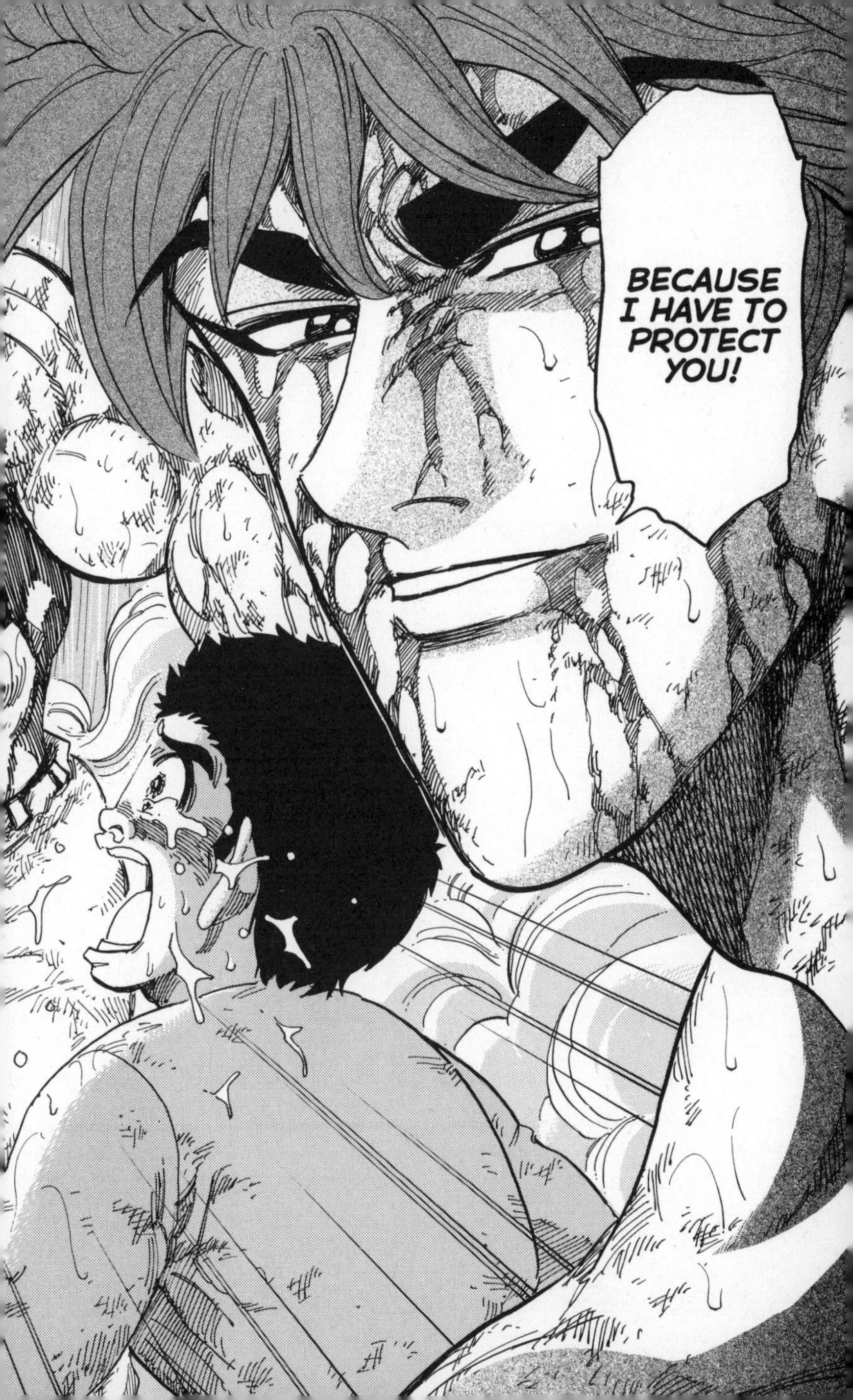
BECAUSE I HAVE TO PROTECT YOU!

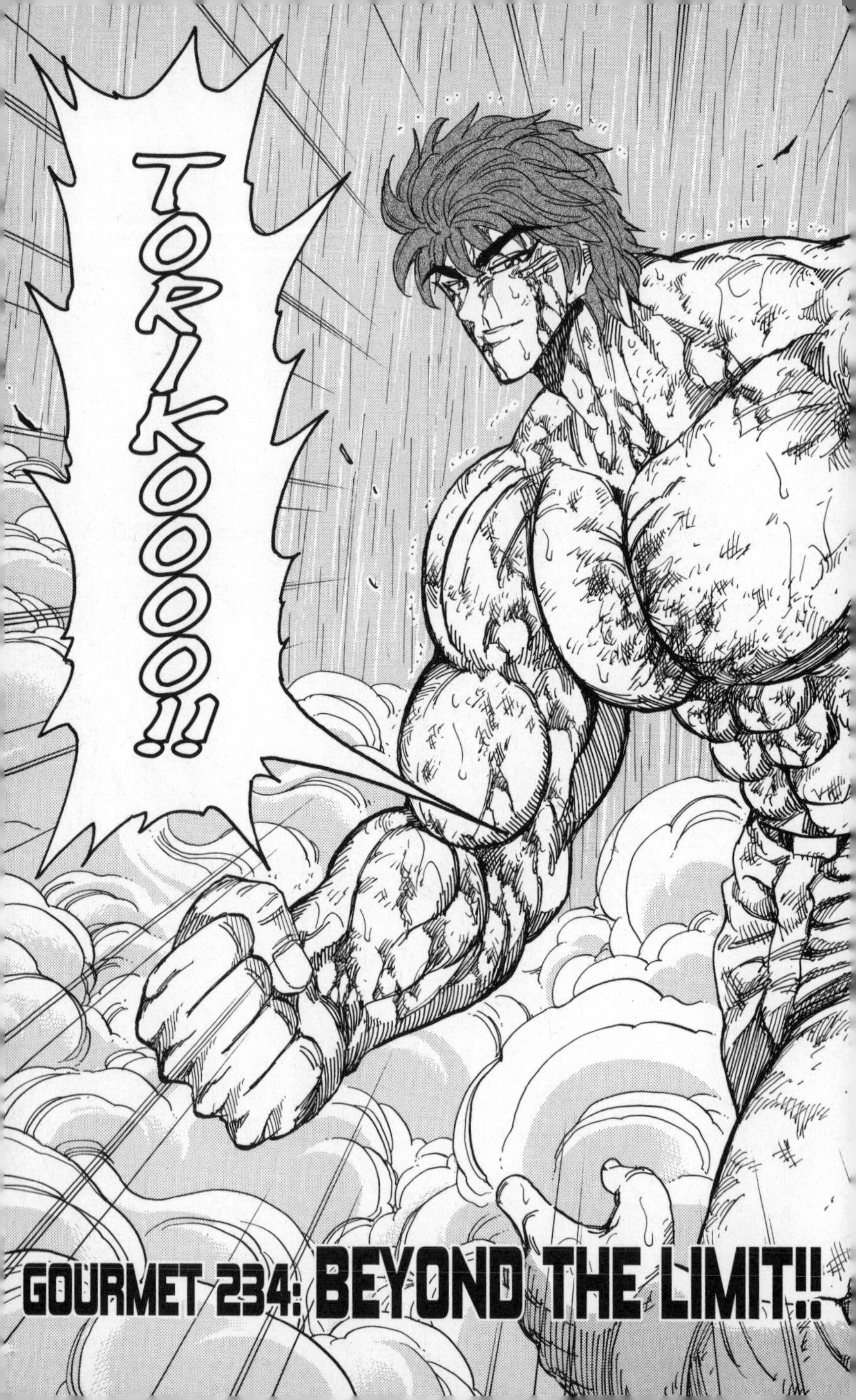
TORIKOOOOO!!
GOURMET 234: BEYOND THE LIMIT!!

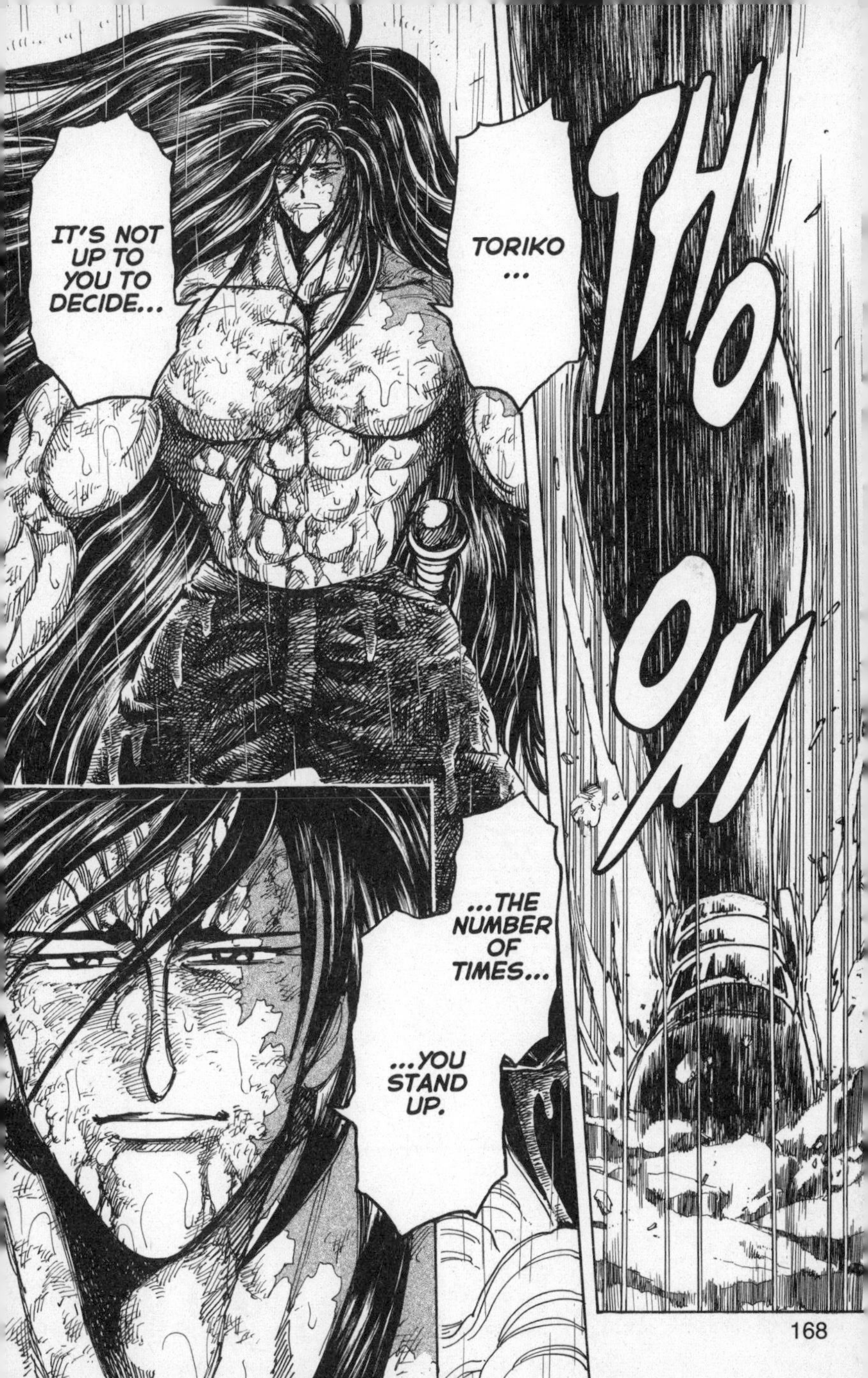
THOOM
TORIKO...
IT'S NOT UP TO YOU TO DECIDE...
...THE NUMBER OF TIMES...
...YOU STAND UP.

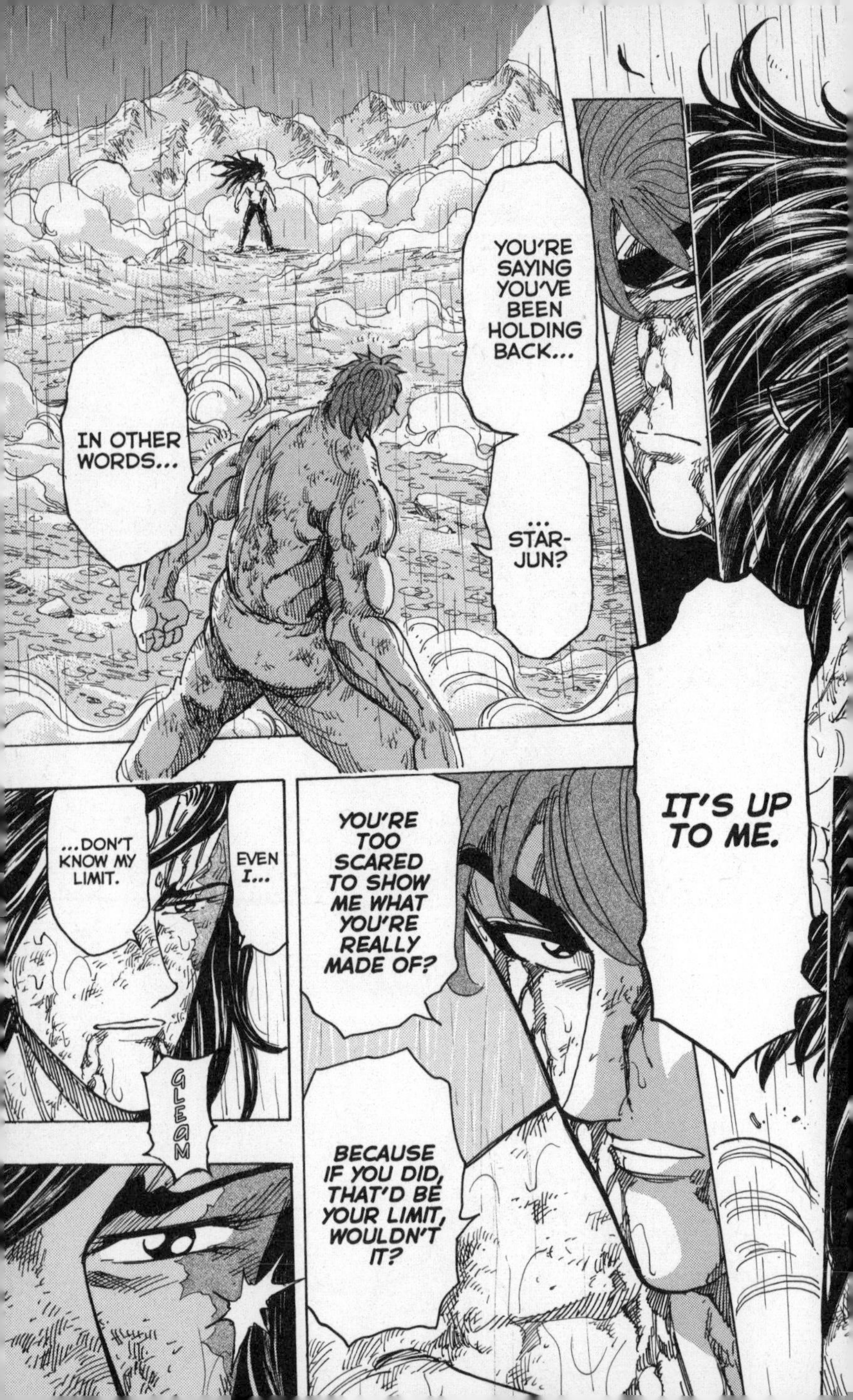
YOU'RE SAYING YOU'VE BEEN HOLDING BACK...
... STAR-JUN?
IN OTHER WORDS...
YOU'RE TOO SCARED TO SHOW ME WHAT YOU'RE REALLY MADE OF?
BECAUSE IF YOU DID, THAT'D BE YOUR LIMIT, WOULDN'T IT?
IT'S UP TO ME.
EVEN I...
...DON'T KNOW MY LIMIT.
GLEAM

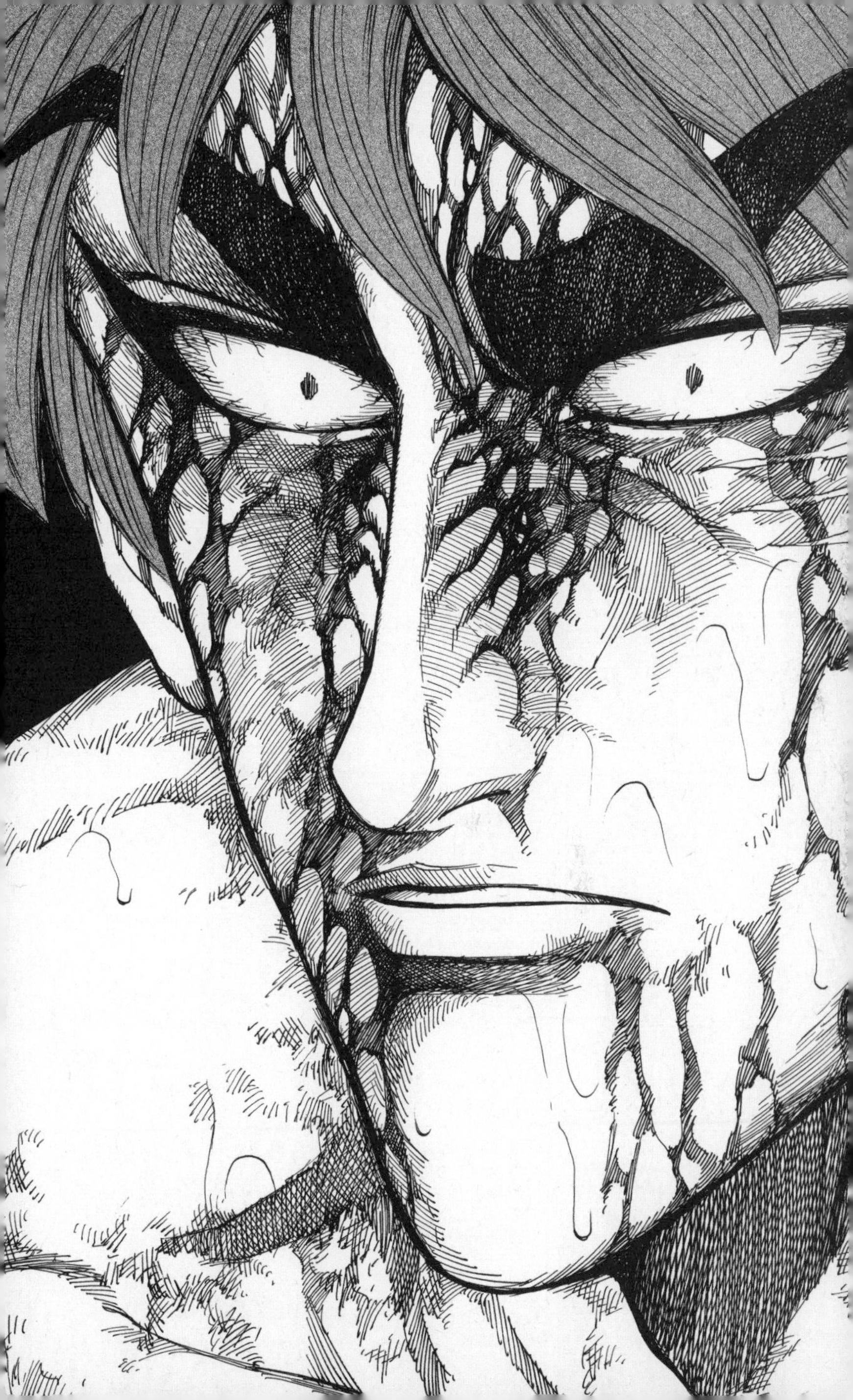

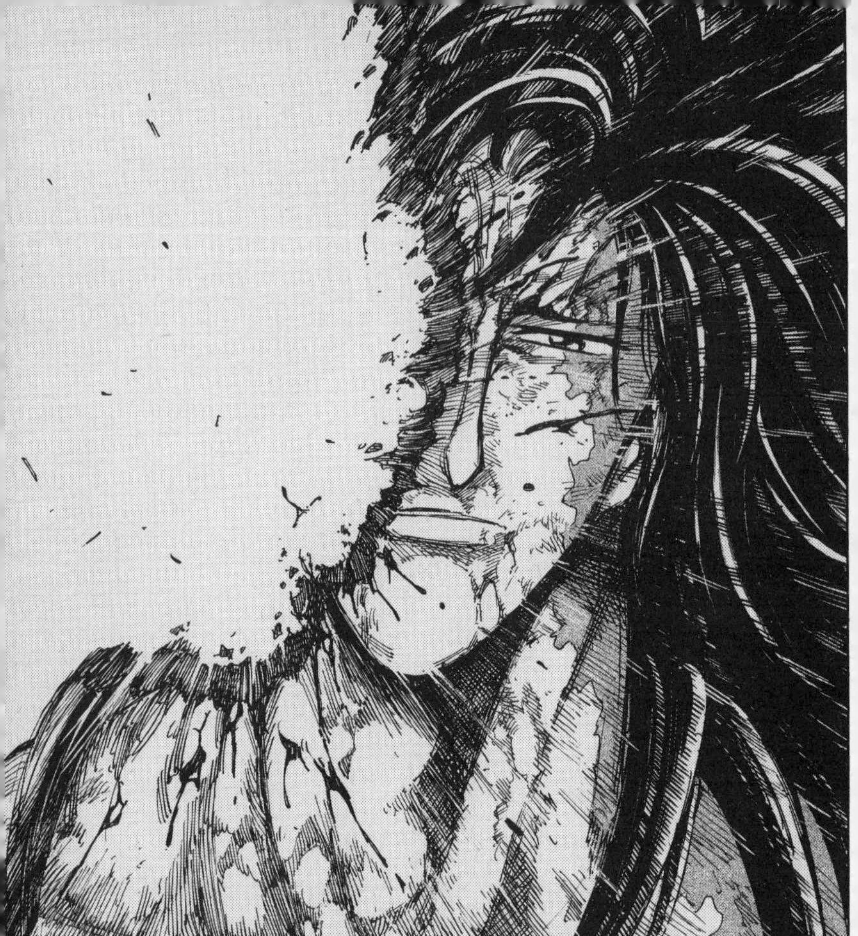
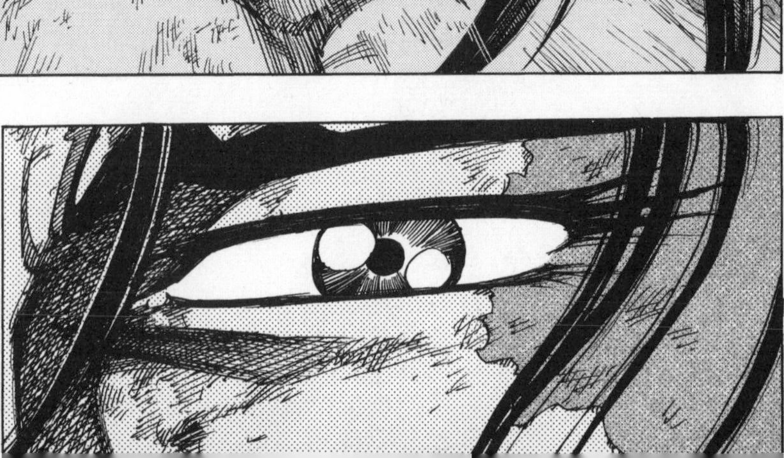

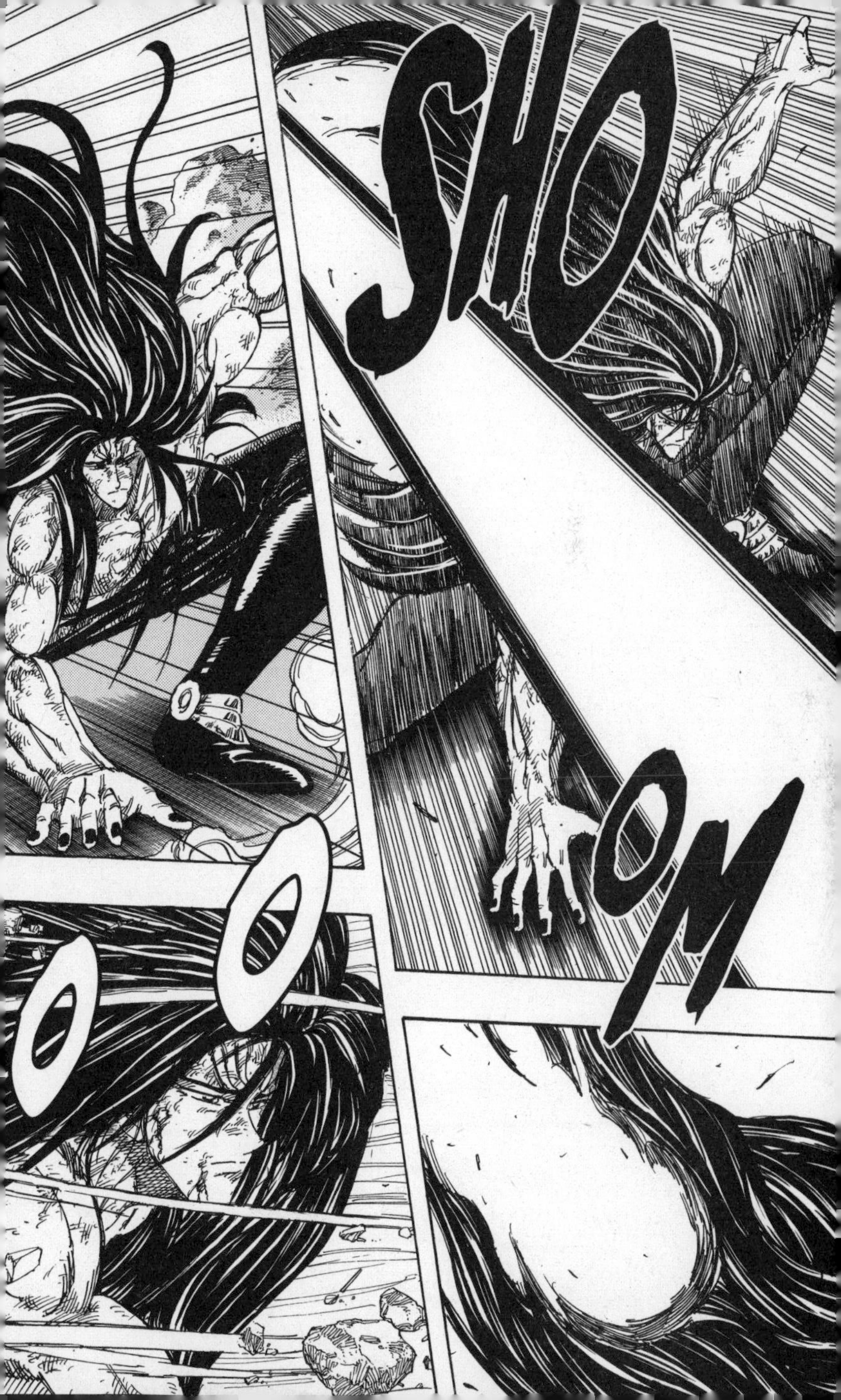
SHO
OM
OO

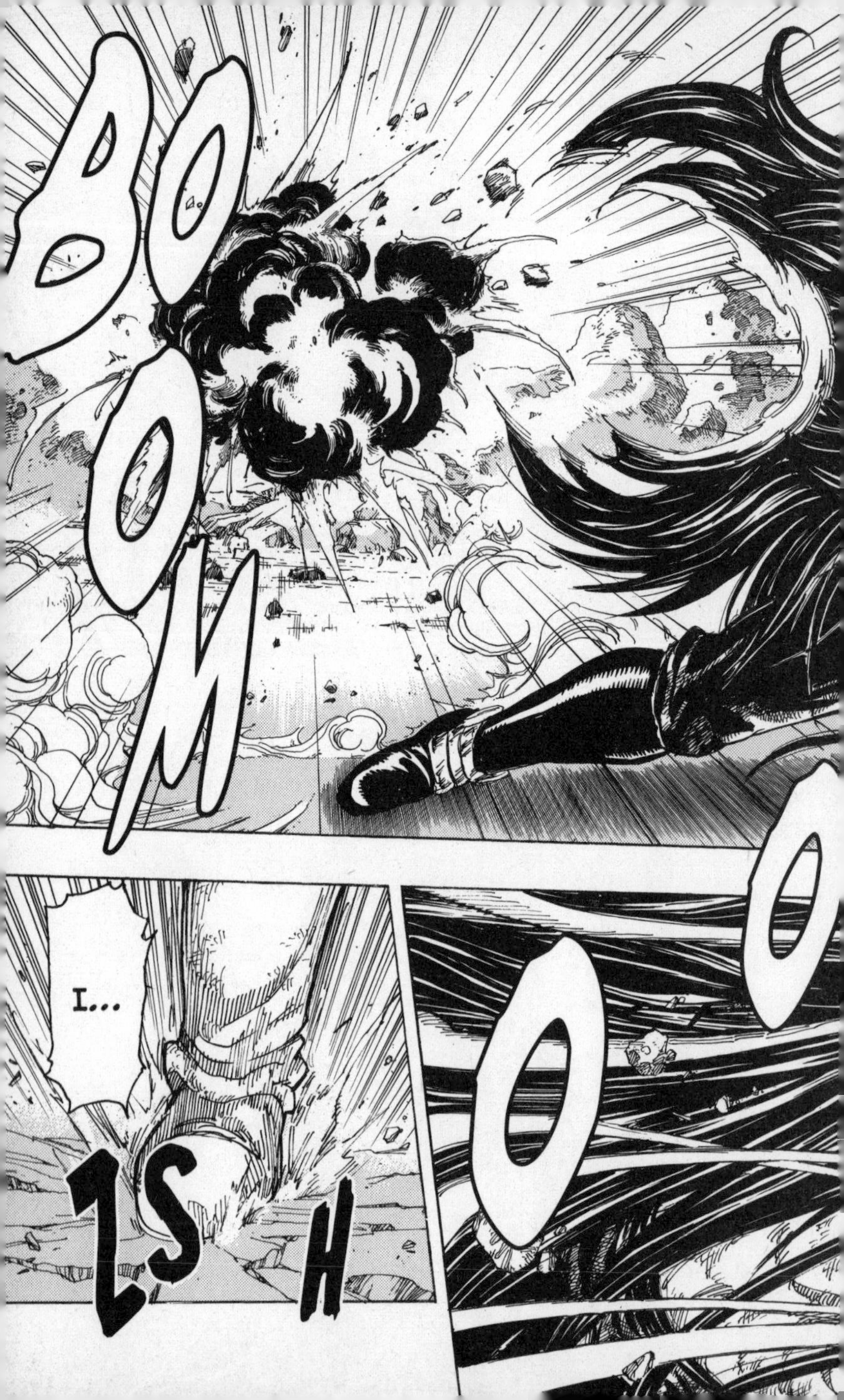
BOOM
I...
ZSH

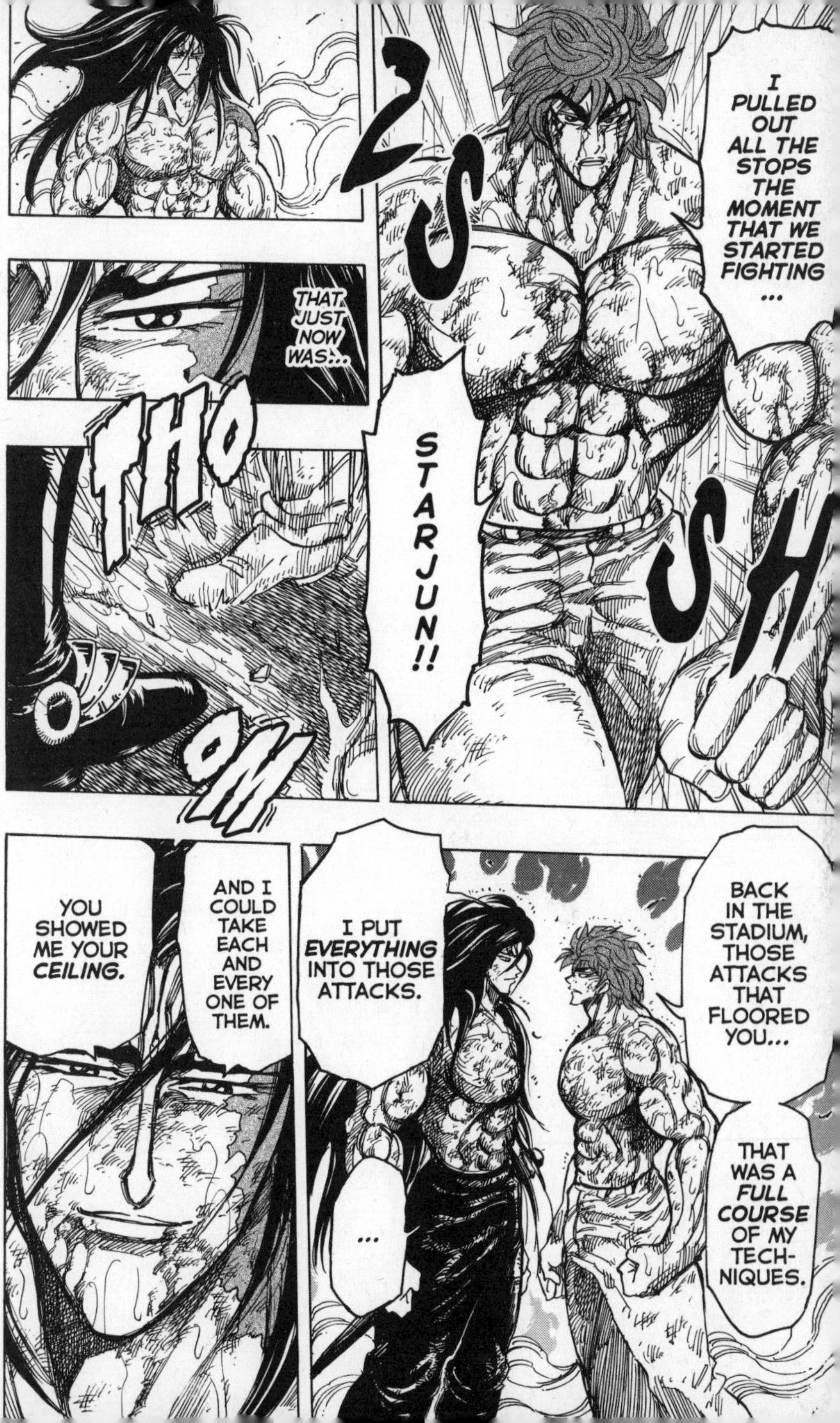
ZS
I PULLED OUT ALL THE STOPS THE MOMENT THAT WE STARTED FIGHTING...
STARJUN!!
SH
THAT JUST NOW WAS...
THOOOM
BACK IN THE STADIUM, THOSE ATTACKS THAT FLOORED YOU...
THAT WAS A *FULL COURSE* OF MY TECH-NIQUES.
I PUT *EVERYTHING* INTO THOSE ATTACKS.
...
AND I COULD TAKE EACH AND EVERY ONE OF THEM.
YOU SHOWED ME YOUR *CEILING.*

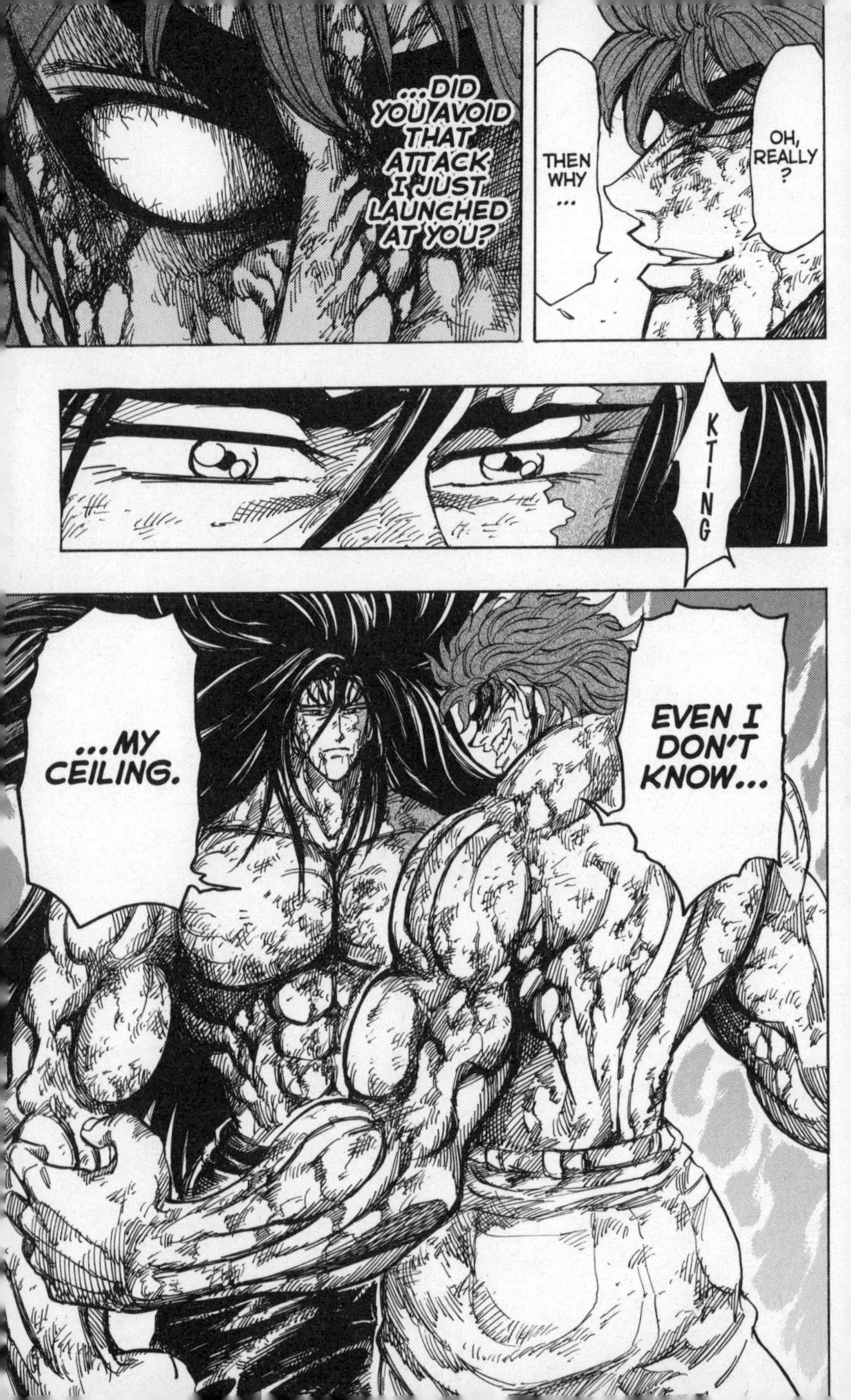
OH, REALLY ?
THEN WHY ...
...DID YOU AVOID THAT ATTACK I JUST LAUNCHED AT YOU?
KTING
EVEN I DON'T KNOW...
...MY CEILING.

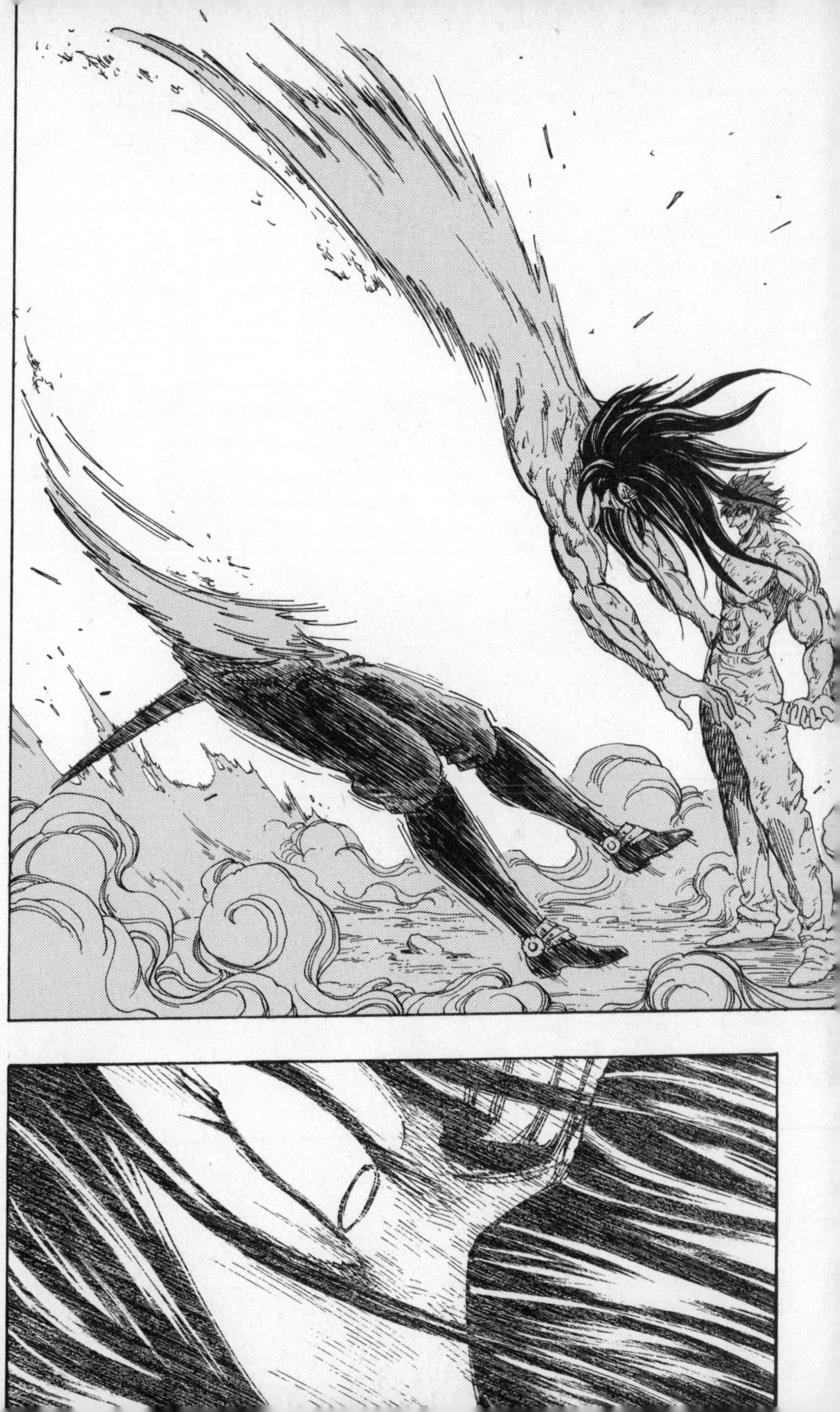

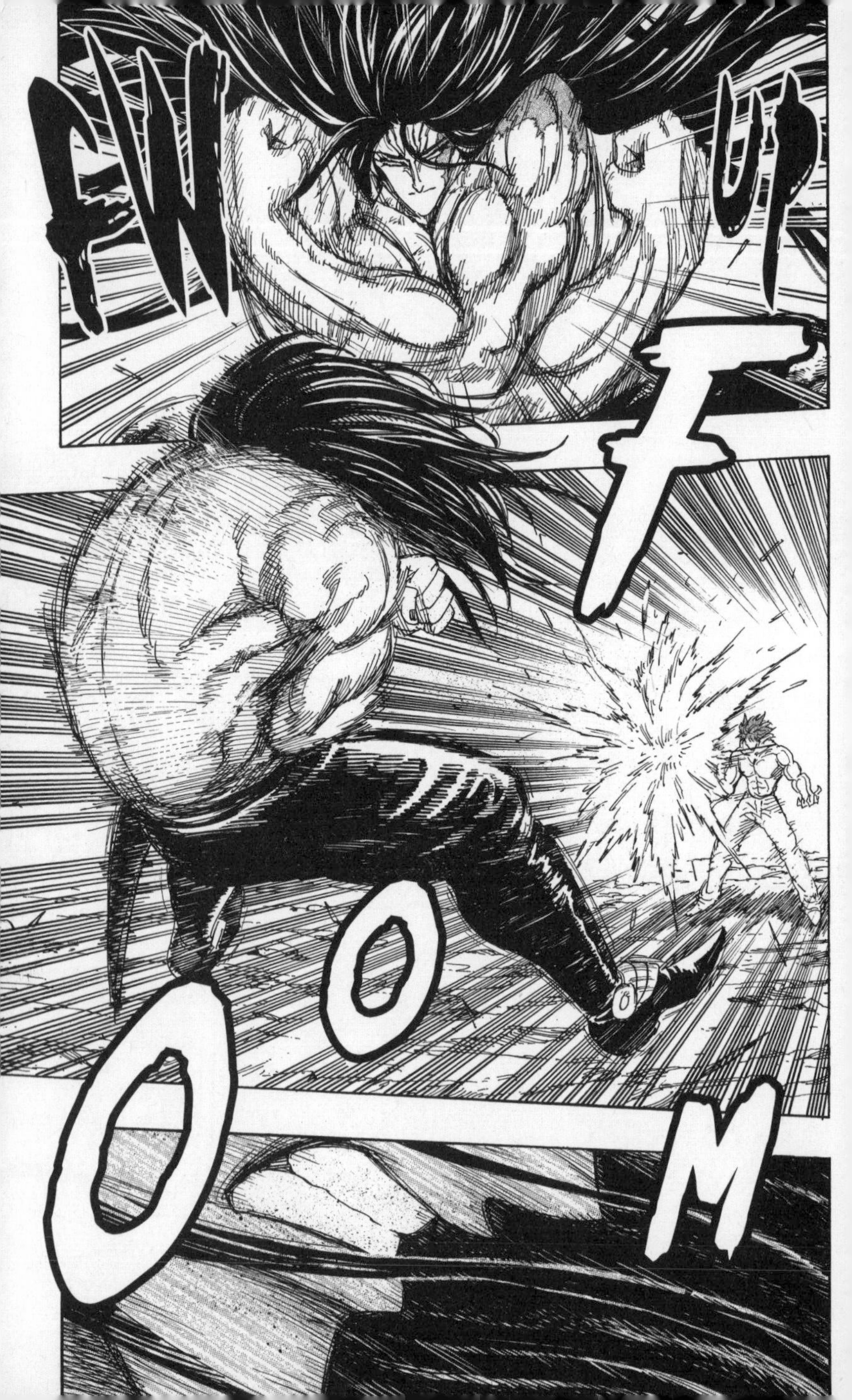
FWUP
FOOM

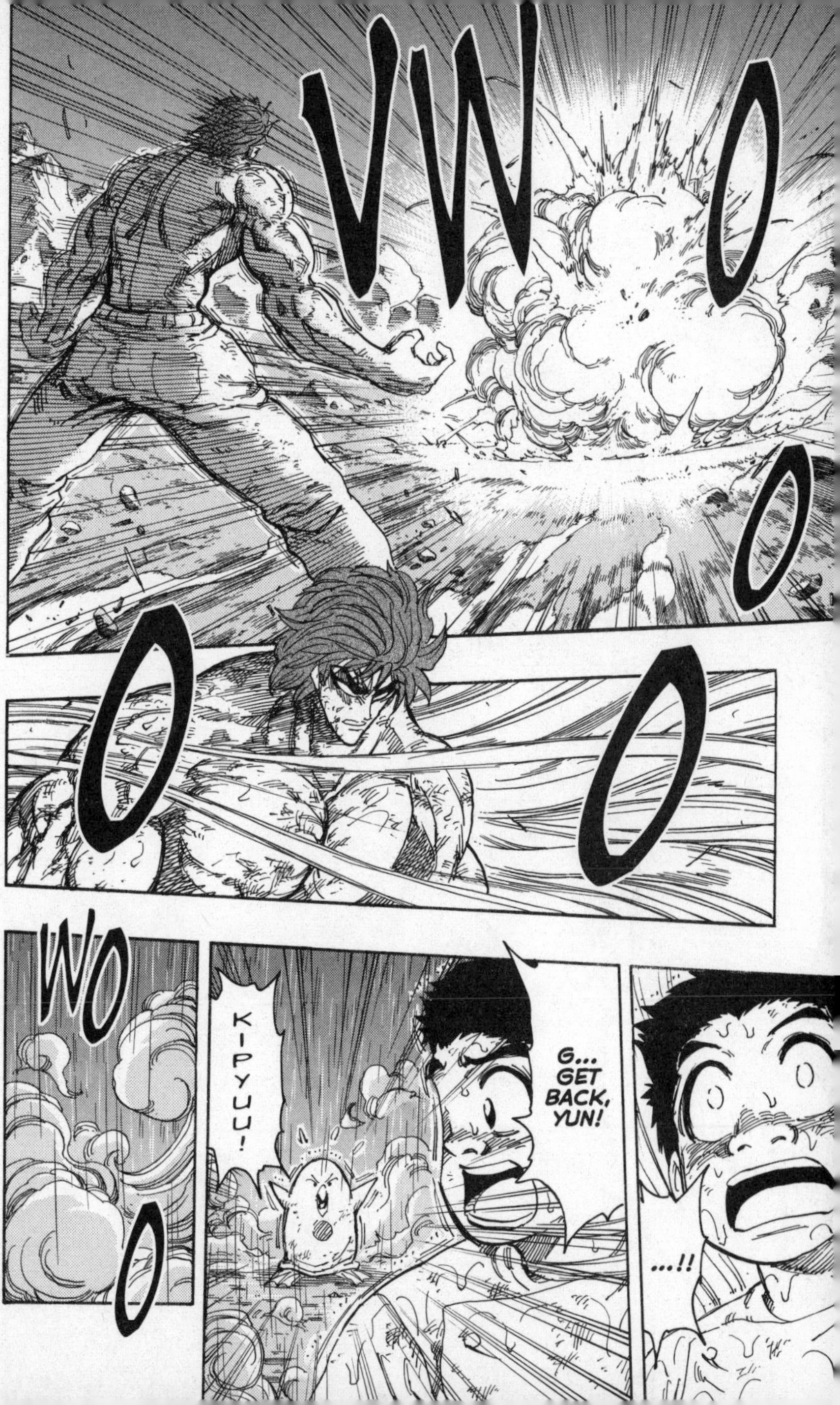
VWOOOO
...!!
G... GET BACK, YUN!
KIPYUU!
WOO

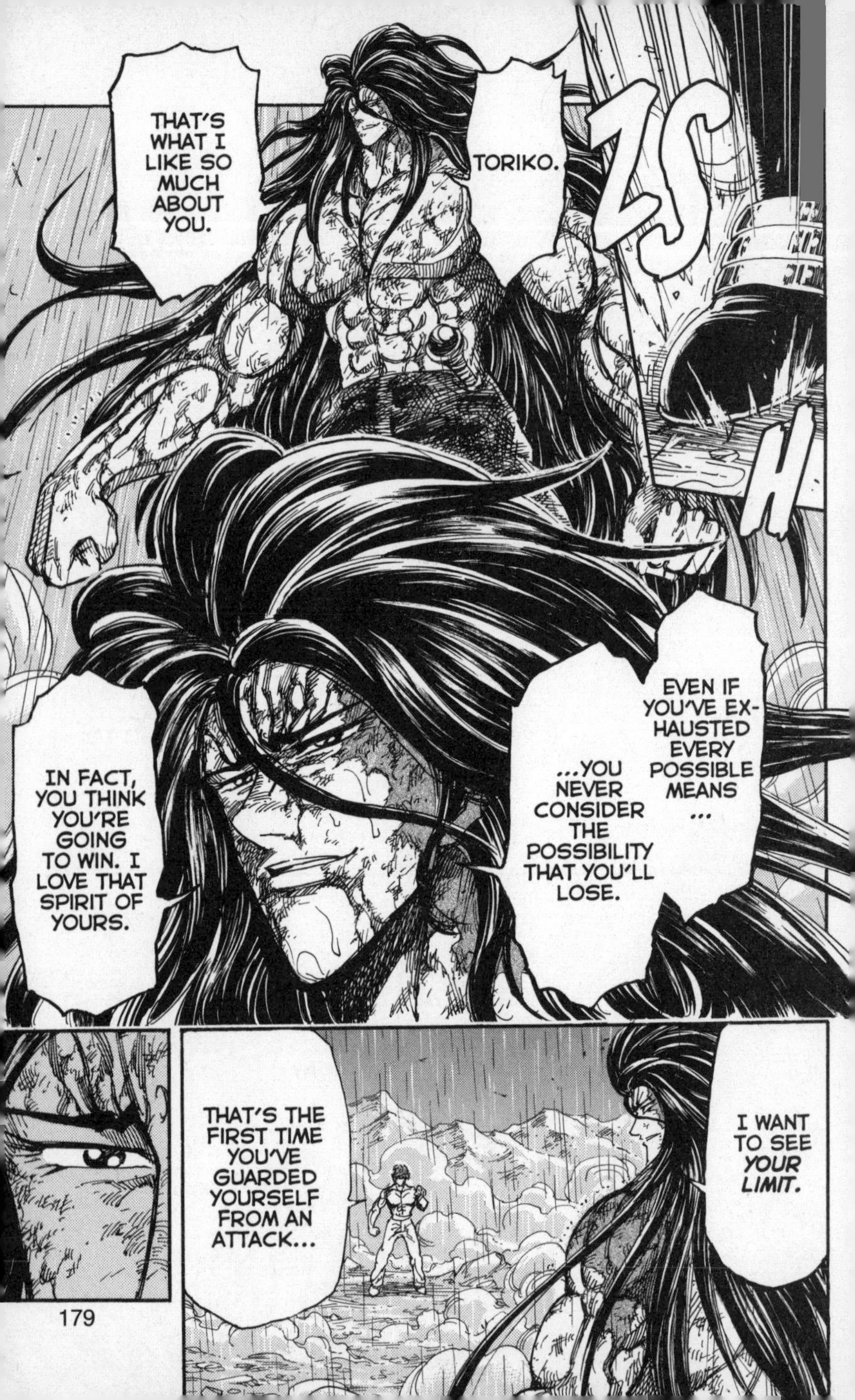
ZS
H
TORIKO.
THAT'S WHAT I LIKE SO MUCH ABOUT YOU.
EVEN IF YOU'VE EXHAUSTED EVERY POSSIBLE MEANS...
...YOU NEVER CONSIDER THE POSSIBILITY THAT YOU'LL LOSE.
IN FACT, YOU THINK YOU'RE GOING TO WIN. I LOVE THAT SPIRIT OF YOURS.
I WANT TO SEE *YOUR LIMIT.*
THAT'S THE FIRST TIME YOU'VE GUARDED YOURSELF FROM AN ATTACK...

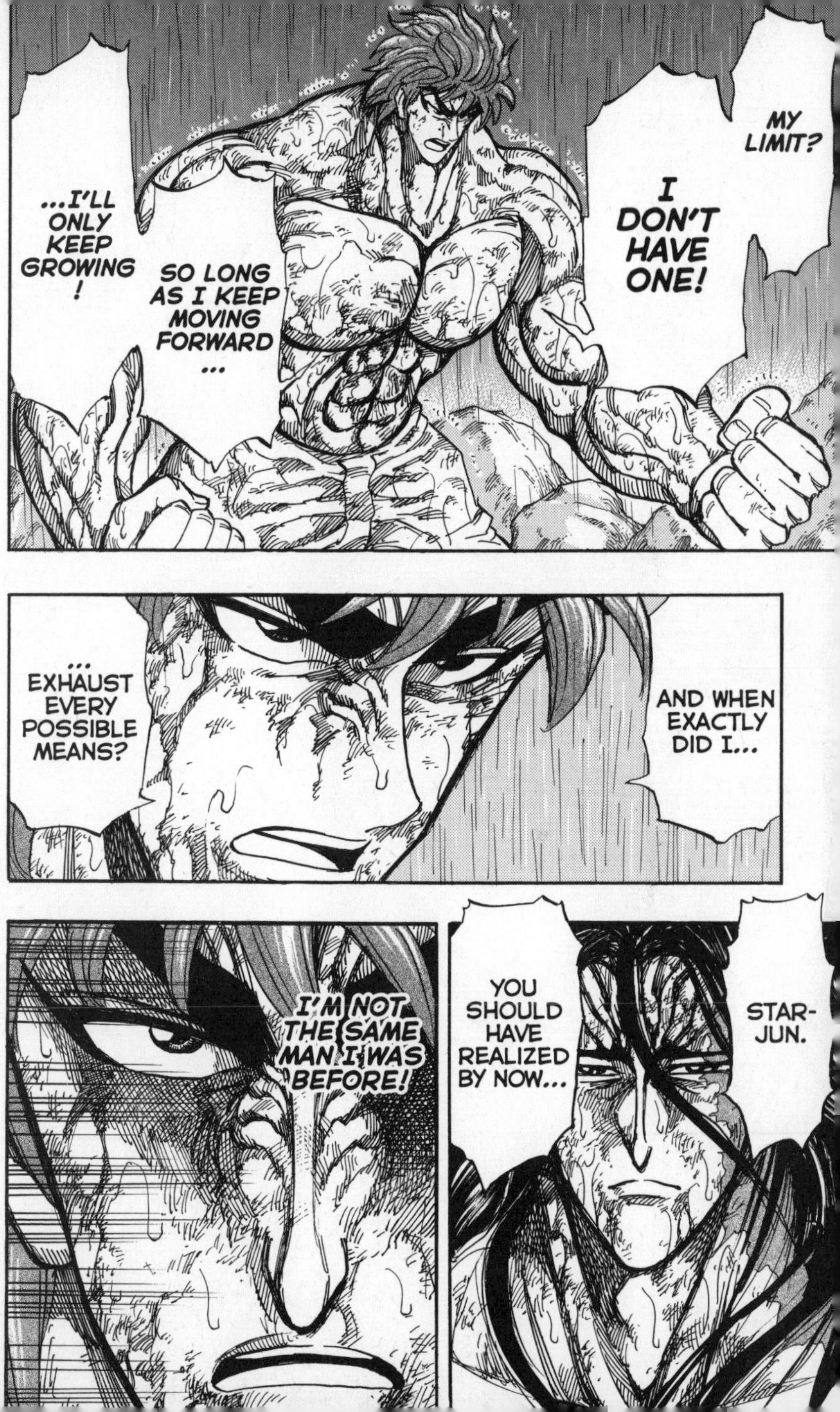
MY LIMIT?
I DON'T HAVE ONE!
SO LONG AS I KEEP MOVING FORWARD...
...I'LL ONLY KEEP GROWING!
AND WHEN EXACTLY DID I...
...EXHAUST EVERY POSSIBLE MEANS?
STAR-JUN.
YOU SHOULD HAVE REALIZED BY NOW...
I'M NOT THE SAME MAN I WAS BEFORE!

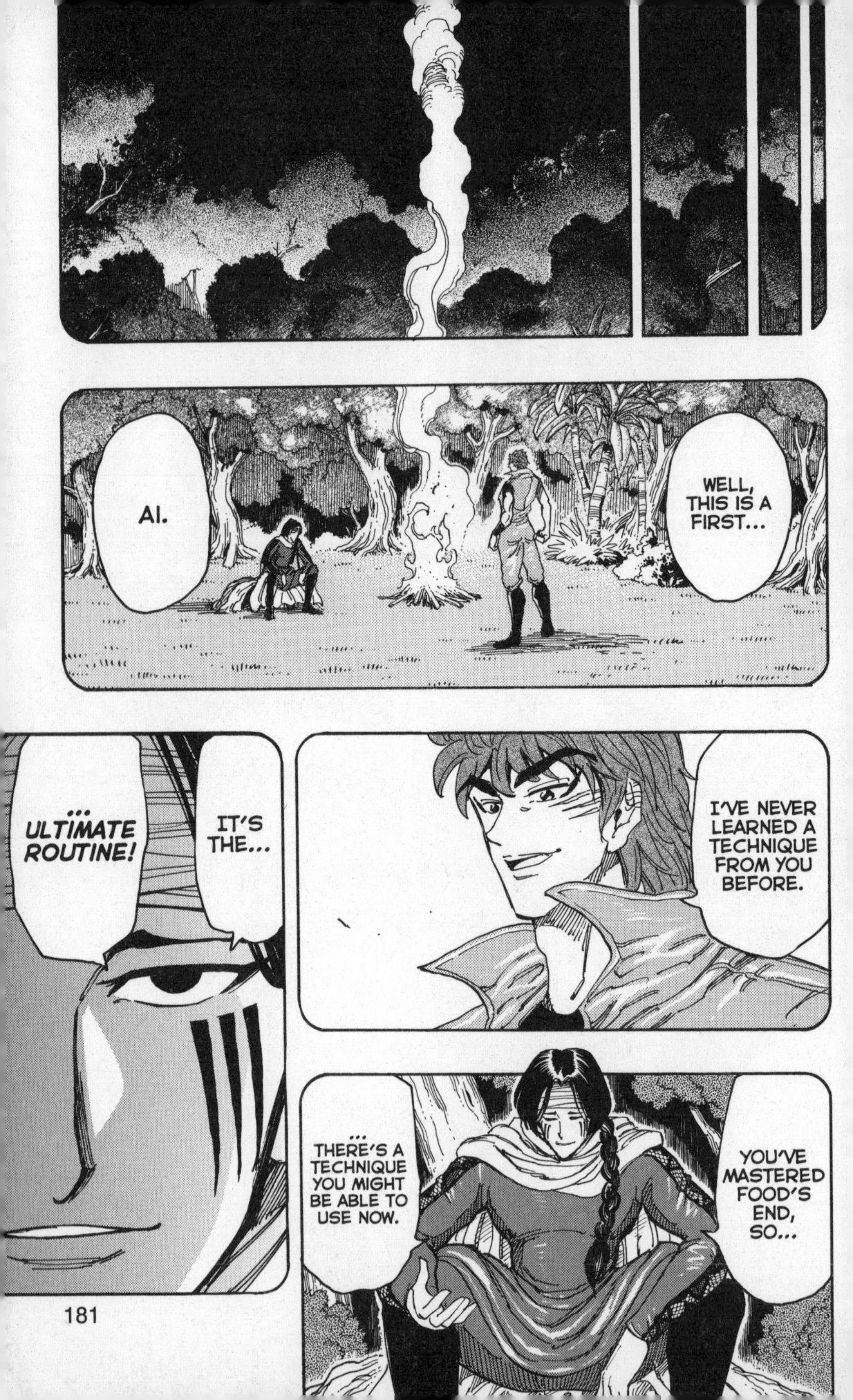
WELL, THIS IS A FIRST...
AI.
I'VE NEVER LEARNED A TECHNIQUE FROM YOU BEFORE.
YOU'VE MASTERED FOOD'S END, SO...
...THERE'S A TECHNIQUE YOU MIGHT BE ABLE TO USE NOW.
IT'S THE...
...ULTIMATE ROUTINE!

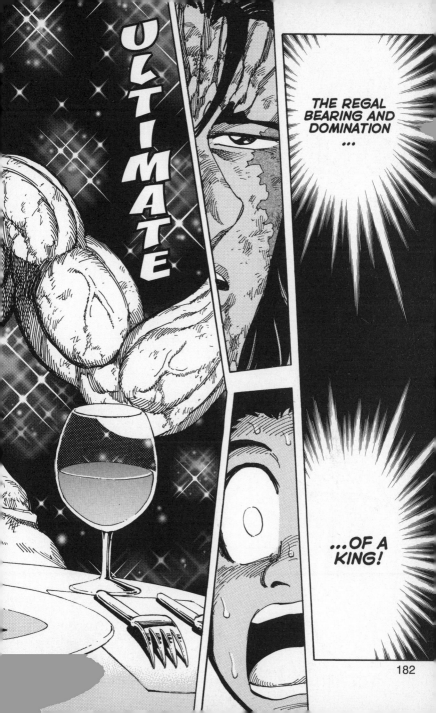

ULTIMATE

THE REGAL BEARING AND DOMINATION...

...OF A KING!

182

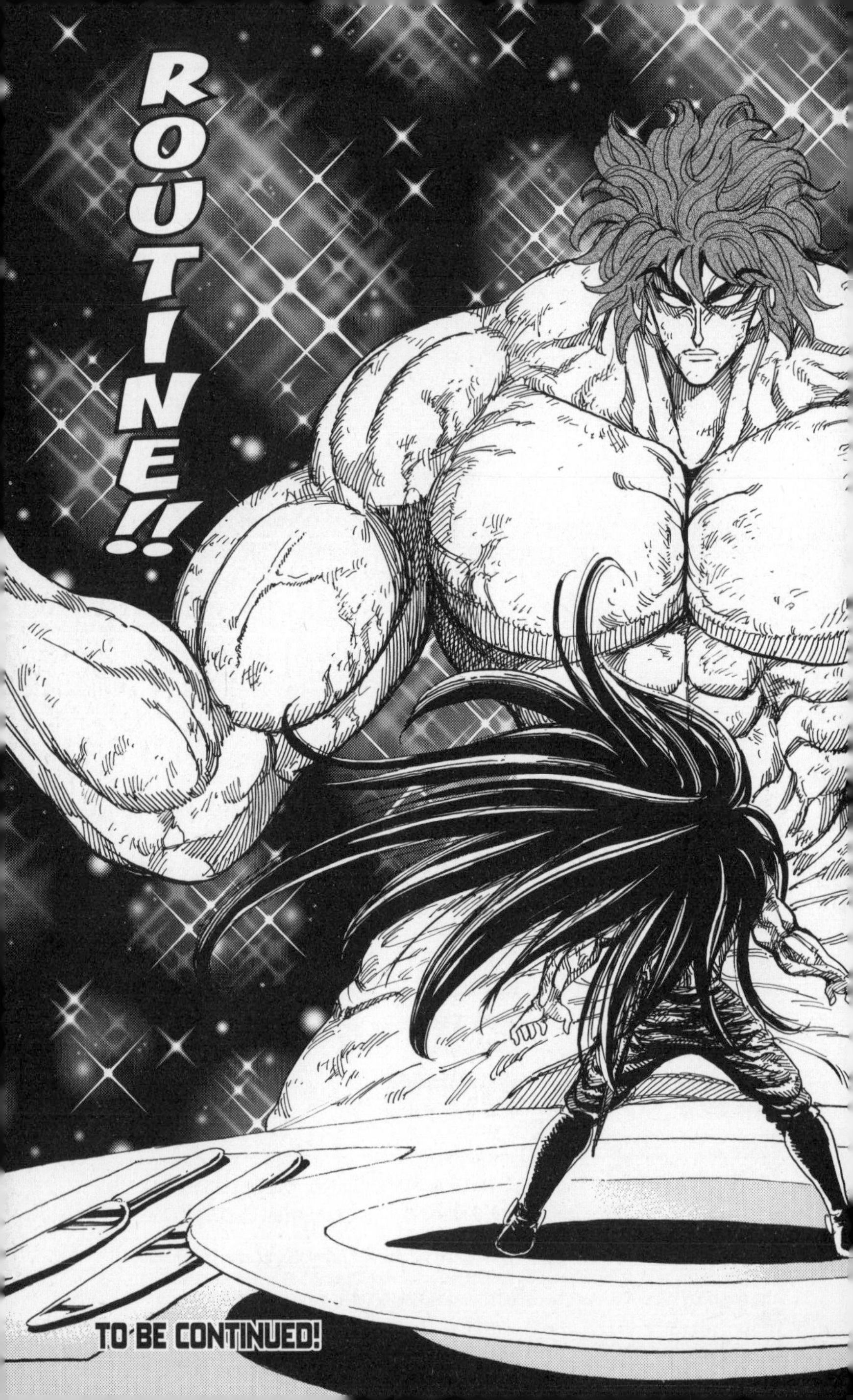
ROUTINE!!
TO BE CONTINUED!

CHARACTER PROFILE

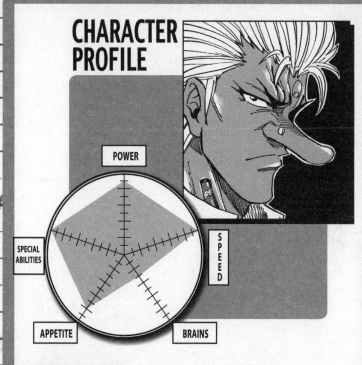

POWER

SPECIAL ABILITIES

SPEED

APPETITE

BRAINS

BRUNCH

AGE:	24	**BIRTHDAY:**	APRIL 4
BLOOD TYPE:	B	**SIGN:**	ARIES
HEIGHT:	227 CM	**WEIGHT:**	195 KG
EYESIGHT:	20/4	**SHOE SIZE:**	42 CM

SPECIAL MOVES/ABILITIES:
- Electric Punch, Electric Chop, Lightning Knife, Vortex Thunderstorm Dicer, Electric Cutter, Howling Lightning Kama-Itachi, Wide-Range Cascade Circuit Electric Strike

Ranked third in the World Chef Ranking, he's the head chef of the grotesque eatery "Tengu Castle." Though he's always top-ranked, he's only ever attended the Cooking Fest once before. That one time he reigned supreme as the genius chef that he is. However, his conduct is so abysmal that he's called the poster child of delinquent chefs.

COMING NEXT VOLUME

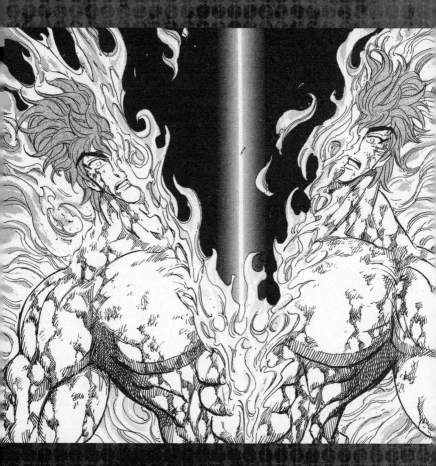

HIDDEN STRENGTH

It's fork vs. flame as Toriko and longtime rival Starjun duel for dominance. At first the two seem evenly matched—for every new combination of Fork, Knife and Spiked Punch Toriko conjures with the Ultimate Routine, Starjun has a fire burst or blade to counter. But while their battle rages on, NEO continues to viciously decimate *both* the IGO and Gourmet Corp. Who will survive to help their side win?

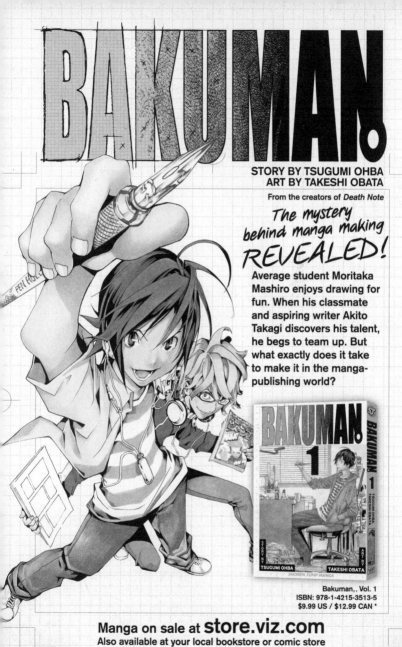

BAKUMAN

STORY BY TSUGUMI OHBA
ART BY TAKESHI OBATA

From the creators of *Death Note*

The mystery behind manga making REVEALED!

Average student Moritaka Mashiro enjoys drawing for fun. When his classmate and aspiring writer Akito Takagi discovers his talent, he begs to team up. But what exactly does it take to make it in the manga-publishing world?

Bakuman, Vol. 1
ISBN: 978-1-4215-3513-5
$9.99 US / $12.99 CAN *

Manga on sale at store.viz.com

Also available at your local bookstore or comic store

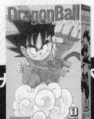

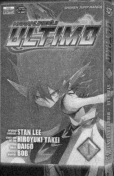
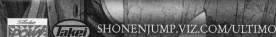

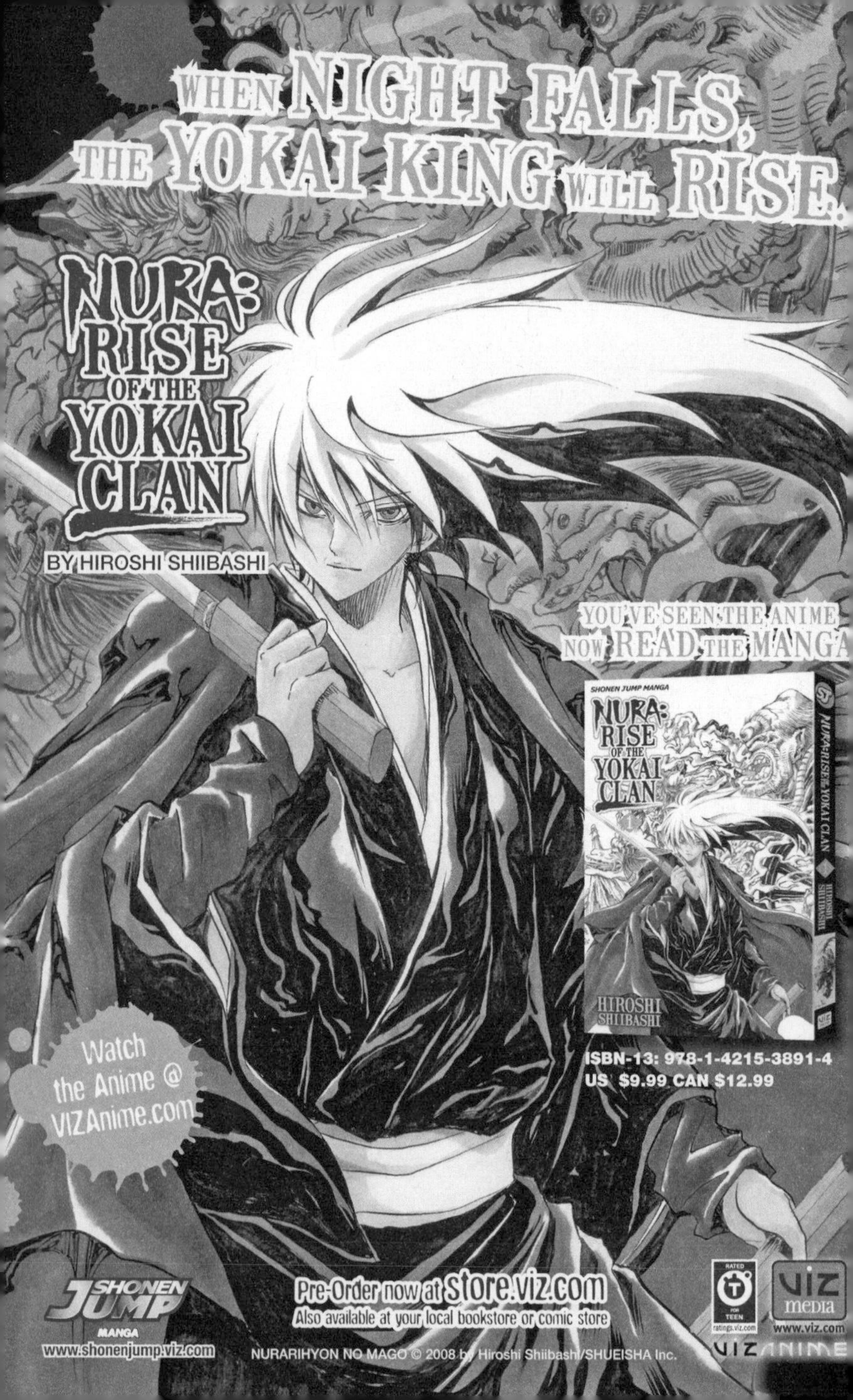
WHEN NIGHT FALLS, THE YOKAI KING WILL RISE.
NURA: RISE OF THE YOKAI CLAN
BY HIROSHI SHIIBASHI
YOU'VE SEEN THE ANIME NOW READ THE MANGA
SHONEN JUMP MANGA
NURA: RISE OF THE YOKAI CLAN
1
HIROSHI SHIIBASHI
ISBN-13: 978-1-4215-3891-4
US $9.99 CAN $12.99
Watch the Anime @ VIZAnime.com
SHONEN JUMP MANGA
www.shonenjump.viz.com
Pre-Order now at store.viz.com
Also available at your local bookstore or comic store
RATED T FOR TEEN
ratings.viz.com
VIZ media
www.viz.com
VIZ ANIME
NURARIHYON NO MAGO © 2008 by Hiroshi Shiibashi/SHUEISHA Inc.

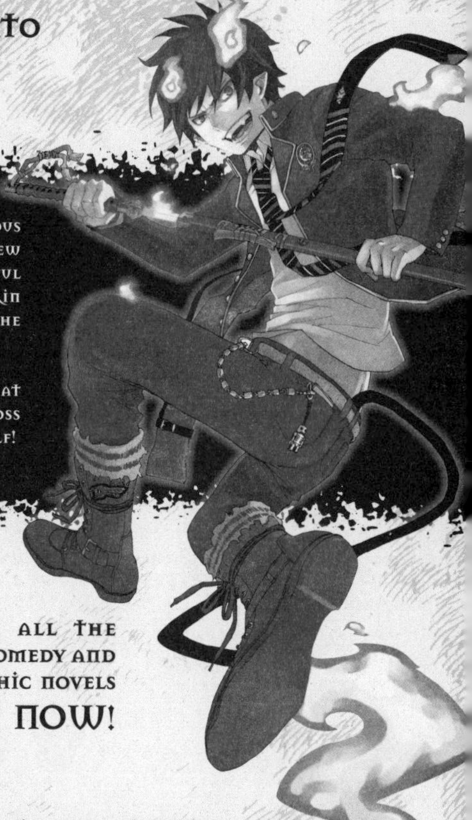

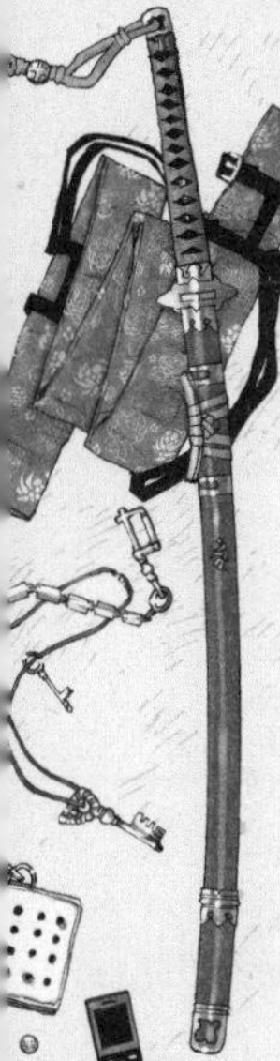

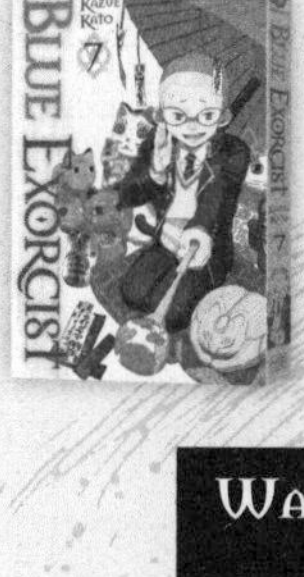

Kazue Kato
BLUE EXORCIST
7

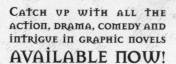

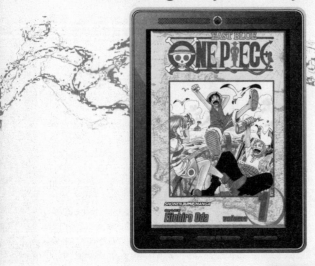
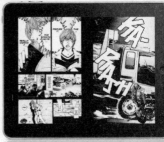
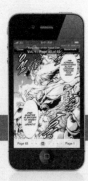

You're Reading in the Wrong Direction!!

1
3
2
2
1
3
5
6
4

Whoops! Guess what? You're starting at the wrong end of the comic!

...It's true! In keeping with the original Japanese format, **Toriko** is meant to be read from right to left, starting in the upper-right corner.

Unlike English, which is read from left to right, Japanese is read from right to left, meaning that action, sound effects and word-balloon order are completely reversed... something which can make readers unfamiliar with Japanese feel pretty backwards themselves. For this reason, manga or Japanese comics published in the U.S. in English have sometimes been published "flopped"—that is, printed in exact reverse order, as though seen from the other side of a mirror.

By flopping pages, U.S. publishers can avoid confusing readers, but the compromise is not without its downside. For one thing, a character in a flopped manga series who once wore in the original Japanese version a T-shirt emblazoned with "M A Y" (as in "the merry month of") now wears one which reads "Y A M"! Additionally, many manga creators in Japan are themselves unhappy with the process, as some feel the mirror-imaging of their art skews their original intentions.

We are proud to bring you Mitsutoshi Shimabukuro's **Toriko** in the original unflopped format. For now, though, turn to the other side of the book and let the adventure begin...!

—Editor

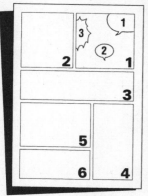

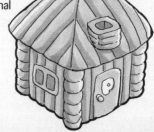

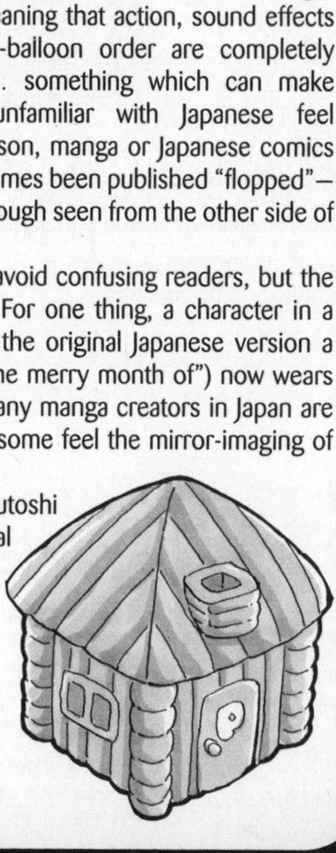